MW01622976

MULTI-TIERED SYSTEMS OF SUPPORT

A Practical Guide to Implementing Preventative Practice

Gary E. Schaffer
Niagara University

Los Angeles | London | New Delhi
Singapore | Washington DC | Melbourne

FOR INFORMATION:

SAGE Publications, Inc.
2455 Teller Road
Thousand Oaks, California 91320
E-mail: order@sagepub.com

SAGE Publications Ltd.
1 Oliver's Yard
55 City Road
London, EC1Y 1SP
United Kingdom

SAGE Publications India Pvt. Ltd.
B 1/I 1 Mohan Cooperative Industrial Area
Mathura Road, New Delhi 110 044
India

SAGE Publications Asia-Pacific Pte. Ltd.
18 Cross Street #10-10/11/12
China Square Central
Singapore 048423

Copyright © 2023 by SAGE Publications, Inc.

All rights reserved. Except as permitted by U.S. copyright law, no part of this work may be reproduced or distributed in any form or by any means, or stored in a database or retrieval system, without permission in writing from the publisher.

All third-party trademarks referenced or depicted herein are included solely for the purpose of illustration and are the property of their respective owners. Reference to these trademarks in no way indicates any relationship with, or endorsement by, the trademark owner.

Printed in Canada

Library of Congress Cataloging-in-Publication Data

Names: Schaffer, Gary, author.

Title: Multi-tiered systems of support: a practical guide to preventative practice / Gary Schaffer.

Identifiers: LCCN 2022008988 | ISBN 9781071831144 (paperback) | ISBN 9781071831113 (adobe pdf) | ISBN 9781071831137 (epub) | ISBN 9781071831120 (epub)

Subjects: LCSH: Multi-tiered systems of support (Education) | Response to intervention (Learning disabled children) | Behavior modification.

Classification: LCC LB3430.5 .S34 2023 | DDC 303.3/24–dc23/eng/20220511

LC record available at https://lccn.loc.gov/2022008988

This book is printed on acid-free paper.

Acquisitions Editor: Leah Fargotstein
Product Associate: Paloma Phelps
Production Editor: Vijayakumar
Copy Editor: Christobel Colleen Hopman
Typesetter: TNQ Technologies
Proofreader: Benny Willy Stephen
Indexer: TNQ Technologies
Cover Designer: Lysa Becker
Marketing Manager: Monica Velasquez

22 23 24 25 26 10 9 8 7 6 5 4 3 2 1

• Brief Contents •

• Detailed Contents •

• List of Figures and Tables •

List of Figures

List of Tables

• Preface •

Although implementing preventative practice models that comprise Multi-Tiered Systems of Support (MTSS) is often viewed as a daunting and challenging endeavor for educators, it does not have to be this way! In fact, it can be very simple and straightforward once educators learn that the intervention service delivery models that comprise MTSS, such as Response to Intervention and School-Wide Positive Behavior of Support, all share a set of common elements that can be adopted into any school. Therefore, this book seeks to break down and simplify preventative practice models by being your "go-to" step-by-step guide for everything MTSS!

Covering MTSS from a "whole child" perspective, *Multi-Tiered Systems of Support: A Practical Guide to Preventative Practice* seeks to empower current and future educators in setting up learners for the greatest success in the academic, behavioral, social, and emotional domains. Consequently, the text explores and breaks down each tier of Response to Intervention, School-Wide Positive Behavior Support, Social-Emotional RTI, and Suicide Prevention and Intervention.

To simplify the often overwhelming task of understanding MTSS, an easily relatable analogy is used in that constructing an effective MTSS model follows the same four basic steps to building a house. These four basic steps include: laying the foundation, raising a framework, putting up the walls, and covering the house with a roof. Therefore, this book makes the analogy that the history of MTSS represents the foundation of the house, the four common components to all intervention service delivery models represent the framework of the house, the four intervention service delivery models that comprise MTSS represent the walls of the house, and the roof that covers the house represents MTSS as a whole.

In addition to the analogy of building the MTSS "house," diagrams, checklists, flowcharts, case examples, summaries, and discussion questions accompany each chapter and provide readers both critical guidance along with a "blueprint" for constructing the model. To provide readers an overview of supports they can use to maximize student success and remediate areas in which learners may struggle, descriptions of cutting-edge interventions, programs, universal screeners, and progress monitoring measures are provided. Additional guidance is offered to readers in the areas of data-based decision-making and infusing culturally responsive practices into RTI, SWPBS, Social-Emotional RTI, and Suicide Prevention and Intervention.

Finally, each chapter of the book concludes with a summary and provides vital discussion questions to further advance understanding of the text. A glossary is also provided at the end of the book to define key terms used throughout the text. Overall, *Multi-Tiered Systems of Support: A Practical Guide to Preventative Practice* offers a unique perspective on MTSS and one that is easy to understand, compelling, and simple to implement. By reading this text, readers will obtain significant insight into the following:

1. The historical context in which MTSS arose and early concepts that are related to MTSS.
2. A detailed overview of the four common components that link all intervention service delivery models together under MTSS including varying levels of

interventions and supports, universal screening, progress monitoring, and data-based decision-making.

3. The four main intervention service delivery models that comprise MTSS, including Response to Intervention, School-Wide Positive Behavior Support, Social-Emotional Response to Intervention, and Suicide Prevention and Intervention.
4. The interventions, universal screening, and progress monitoring measures that are unique to each intervention service delivery model.
5. Data-based decision-making within MTSS.
6. Infusing culturally responsive practices into MTSS.
7. Overcoming barriers to MTSS implementation.
8. The roles and responsibilities of educators within MTSS.
9. Considerations for implementing MTSS in alternative practice settings.

Book Structure

Multi-Tiered Systems of Support opens by reviewing the historical context under which MTSS arose and the commonalities and differences between MTSS and the intervention service delivery models that comprise it. Subsequently, the book describes the four critical components that link all intervention service delivery models under MTSS of which include varying levels of evidence-based interventions and supports, universal screening, progress monitoring, and data-based decision-making. After describing these critical components, the book provides descriptions of the four major intervention service delivery models that comprise MTSS, namely, Response to Intervention, School-Wide Positive Behavior Support, social-emotional response to intervention, and suicide prevention and intervention. Suggestions are then made for infusing culturally responsive practices into each intervention service delivery model described.

Along with suggestions for infusing culturally responsive practices into each intervention service delivery model, checklists and case studies take readers through each tier of RTI, SWPBS, Social-Emotional RTI, and Suicide Prevention and Intervention. Following the chapters describing each intervention service delivery model, the book explores challenges to implementing MTSS and guides in overcoming each challenge. The book concludes by exploring the implementation of MTSS in alternative settings, such as juvenile justice facilities and day habilitation programs for the developmentally disabled. Each chapter of the book concludes with a summary and provides vital discussion questions to further advance understanding of the text. At the end of the book, a glossary is provided to define key terms used throughout the text and detailed flowcharts provide a visual for taking readers through Response to Intervention, School-Wide Positive Behavior Support, social-emotional response to intervention, and suicide prevention and intervention.

The overall goal of the book is to systematically take readers through setting up MTSS in simple and easily relatable terms in regards to the four basic steps to building a house. These four basic steps include laying the foundation, raising a framework, putting up the walls, and covering the house with a roof. The book uses each of these four steps as an analogy in constructing MTSS. To elaborate, the book makes the analogy that the history of MTSS represents the foundation of the house, the four critical components to MTSS represent the framework of the house, the four intervention service delivery models that comprise MTSS represent the walls of the house, and the roof that covers the house represents MTSS as a whole. Through this analogy, readers obtain a unique perspective on implementing MTSS. Additionally, readers will have a convenient resource that will save them time in locating information on interventions and measures of universal screening and progress monitoring that are unique to each intervention service delivery model.

Unique Features of the Text

- This book utilizes diagrams, checklists, flowcharts, case studies, summaries, and discussion questions to facilitate understanding for each intervention service delivery model outlined in the text, namely, Response to Intervention, School-Wide Positive Behavior Support, Social-Emotional RTI, and Suicide Prevention and Intervention.
- This book provides readers with interventions, universal screening, and progress monitoring measures that are unique to each intervention service delivery model.
- This book provides detailed guidance on data-based decision-making within Response to Intervention, School-Wide Positive Behavior Support, Social-Emotional RTI, and Suicide Prevention and Intervention.
- This book seamlessly integrates social-emotional learning (SEL) into the intervention service delivery model of social-emotional RTI.
- This book provides an extensive historical overview of the origins of MTSS and intervention service delivery models.
- This book explores how MTSS, the Every Student Succeeds Act, and implementation science share common components and complement one another.
- This book defines key terms commonly used throughout it in a glossary.

Course Market

Many different instructors will find what they have been looking for in this book. Common courses include Tiered Instruction and Intervention, Consultation and Intervention, Counseling and Behavior Therapy, Interventions to Develop Academic and Behavioral Skills, and many others, as well as more general courses in instruction and educational psychology where instructors want to cover MTSS in more depth. The widest variety of courses that could use this book are found at the graduate level in teaching, school psychology, school counseling, and school administration.

Why I Wrote This Book

Growing up as a struggling learner, I now often look back at my grade school years, and education as a whole, as a frustrating time filled with lost opportunities to remediate some of my learning deficits and to optimize my success as a student. I am sure that for many former struggling learners turned educators, I am not alone in my sentiments. However, I am also sure that if my teachers were aware of best evidence-based practices and MTSS in the late 1980s, they would have excitedly implemented them to provide the best opportunities for all students to learn, grow, and succeed both in and out of school.

You see, MTSS is not just a simple framework to provide the best opportunities for all students to succeed nor is it just a boring way to remediate academic, behavioral, social, and emotional deficits. It is an exciting reform movement and opportunity for each educator, school, district, and organization to provide the best equitable instruction and services to every child. Despite MTSS providing fertile ground for equitable and best-evidence-based practices to flourish and grow, scholarly articles and legislative guidance on what the framework is and is not have often been vague, convoluted, and time-consuming for current and future educators to digest. Therefore, despite great efforts, there remains confusion among educators regarding MTSS that has resulted in poorly implemented models of Response to Intervention, School-Wide Positive Behavior Support, Social-Emotional RTI, and Suicide Prevention and Intervention.

However, the great news is that MTSS does not have to be hard to understand nor does it have to be so complicated. In fact, it can be fun to learn about the rich history of where MTSS came from and how to implement it effectively. This text seeks to make learning about MTSS fun and easy by relating the setting up of MTSS to a task that is familiar to most people—the four basic steps of building a house. Yes, you, or should I say we, are going to build the house of MTSS together using the four steps of laying the foundation, raising a framework, putting up walls, and covering the house with a roof. This book makes the analogy that the history of MTSS represents the foundation of the house, the four common components to all intervention service delivery models represent the framework of the house, the four intervention service delivery models that comprise MTSS represent the walls of the house, and the roof that covers the house represents MTSS as a whole. Therefore, after understanding how to construct the house of MTSS, you are well on your way to creating a welcoming home, or should I say school, for all learners to succeed and thrive in!

• Acknowledgments •

I have been extremely fortunate in my life to have wonderful family, friends, colleagues, and graduate students. Without each, this book would not have been possible. To my wife, Anna, your patience and love for me as I engage in endless research, writing, and forgetting where I put my glasses or car keys knows no bounds. To my parents, Sue and Gary Schaffer Sr. and brother, Corey, thank you for always supporting me throughout my life and never giving up on me.

Thank you to my friends for always pulling me away from my work when I need it the most. There are too many of you to list, but I would be remiss if I did not mention some by name. In particular, thank you to Alex and Tera Domaradzki, Paul and Julia Brunskole, Brian and Jen Brunskole, Peter Miller, Rick and Ashley Greenland, John and Costenah Greenland, John and Elise Pogorzelski, Phil and Danielle Puccia, Rich and Amanda Budnik, Justin and Ronnie Daugherty, Rich and Tina Schulz, Eric and Dallas Heim, Mike and Ashley Rosky, Robert Smith, Brett Tokarczyk, and Joseph Chille.

A huge part of my life and success is owed to Niagara University and to my professors-turned-work colleagues who have always believed in me. Thank you to Dr. Lisa Kilanowski, Dr. Kristine Augustyniak, Dr. Shannon Hodges, Dr. Jennifer Beebe and Dr. Chandra Foote. Every postsecondary educational institution and instructor should strive to be as inclusive, accepting, and caring as Niagara University and the professors and staff that comprise it.

Aside from those at Niagara University, I would like to thank my research and professional colleagues who I have met along the way and supported many of my research and professional efforts. Thank you to Christopher Van Houten, Dr. Stacy Bender, Dr. Elizabeth Power, Dr. Amy Fisk, Dr. Andrew Shanock, Dr. Mitch Samet, Dr. Peter Faustino, Dr. John Kelly, Dr. Andrew Livanis, and Kelly Caci. Finally, to my past, present, and future graduate students, each of you inspires me, and I certainly thank you for it!

SAGE and the author are grateful for feedback from the following reviewers in the development of this text:

Zoee Bartholomew, Dominican University of California

Julie Brandon, California State University, Dominguez Hills

Kristine A. Camacho, Worcester State University

Anna Fritts, Gonzaga University and the Washington Education Association

Keri Giordano, Kean University

Janet Grier, Brenau University

Sarah Harry, Ball State University

Kathee Hennigan Bautista, Azusa Pacific University

Kelli Henson, Nicholls State University

Tammy J. Ladwig, University of Wisconsin Oshkosh

Marcel Lebrun, Plymouth State University

Maria L. Manning, Eastern Kentucky University

Cecilia Mendoza, California State University, Fresno

Kim Sherman, Tulane University

Marge Terhaar, Meredith College

• About the Author •

Growing up as a struggling student with Attention-Deficit Hyperactivity Disorder and a learning disability, Gary Schaffer has dedicated his professional practices and life to helping all learners succeed. Gary received a Bachelor's Degree in Special Education and English and subsequently went on to become a school psychologist and clinical mental health counselor. As a school psychologist, Gary has practiced across school, hospital, and state agency settings where he primarily worked with diverse learners and individuals with developmental disabilities. Currently, Gary is employed full-time at Niagara University where he teaches graduate students in school psychology and counseling. Additionally, Gary provides consultation and assessment services for Erie County Medical Center (ECMC).

Outside of working for Niagara University and ECMC, Gary served on the New York State Association of School Psychologists board and has met with both state and national legislators in regards to the Every Student Succeeds Act, Multi-Tiered Systems of Support, and increasing the availability of mental health services for children. Additionally, Gary has authored numerous scholarly articles, books, book chapters, and programs in the areas of MTSS, school psychology leadership, autism, and suicide prevention and intervention. He has presented on and offers consultation in Multi-Tiered Systems of Support and best preventative practices under three-tiered frameworks, such as RTI and SWPBS. He can be reached through his email at geschaffer@gmail.com or followed on Twitter at @GE_Schaffer.

Understanding the History and Formation of MTSS

Learning Objectives

After reading this chapter, you should be able to:

- Explain the need for Multi-Tiered Systems of Support (MTSS).
- Compare the similarities and differences between MTSS and intervention service delivery models.
- Describe the steps to building the MTSS house.
- Discuss the foundations of MTSS how the framework was initially influenced by teaching and school psychology practice.
- State how Response to Intervention (RTI) and school-wide positive behavior support (SWPBS) integrate under MTSS.

The Need for MTSS

Throughout the history of the United States' education system, a long-standing battle has been waged in bringing lower-performing students with achievement gaps up to proficiency and improving teaching practices to do so. However, despite these ongoing efforts to remediate achievement gaps and place American children in the best position to become productive citizens, the United States continues to underperform compared to other developed nations (National Center for Education Statistics, 2018). In 2018, the United States Department of Education reported that fourth graders across the country were performing lower than 12 education systems in other developed nations in average reading literacy scores (National Center for Education Statistics, 2018). Similarly, at the eighth-grade level, seven education systems in developed countries had higher science scores than the United States, and eight education systems had higher average mathematics scores (National Center for Education Statistics, 2018).

In an increasingly globally competitive world, it is crucial for all children, regardless of race, ethnicity, disability, or learning status, to receive a sound education based on best evidence-based practice and teaching pedagogy. Therefore, under bipartisan support on December 10, 2015, the **Every Student Succeeds Act (ESSA)** was signed into law by President Obama renewing the United States' commitment to providing equal education to all learners (National Association of School Psychologists, 2016). The ESSA Act replaced its predecessor, the **No Child Left Behind (NCLB) Act** as the federal education law governing the United States' K-12 public education policy (National Association of School Psychologists, 2016). Going into effect at the beginning of the 2017–2018 school year, ESSA included a number of structural changes, most important being that it became the first bill since 1980 to narrow the federal government's role in education (National Association of School Psychologists, 2016). Therefore, state and local jurisdictions regained substantial control in designing their own program and accountability systems to determine the standards students are held to (National Association of School Psychologists, 2016). To improve outcomes for all learners, especially those who have been underserved, ESSA (2015) suggested that schools and districts implement **MTSS**.

Introduction to MTSS and Intervention Service Delivery Models

MTSS is a term used by schools to define their process of delivering evidence-based interventions to students to improve their learning, behavior, and social-emotional outcomes (Wexler, 2017). Two primary goals of MTSS are to improve teacher instruction through the utilization of evidence-based pedagogy and increase students' chances of succeeding socially, emotionally, behaviorally, and academically. MTSS is composed of two or more intervention service delivery models (Averill & Rinaldi, 2011; Schaffer, 2017). **Intervention service delivery models** are triangular three-tiered frameworks utilized to provide evidence-based interventions, programs, and supports to children in general education. As the child does not respond to the interventions or supports provided within an intervention service delivery model, they advance to the next tier and receive more intense interventions. To determine whether the child is responding to the interventions provided, data are frequently collected on their progress and analyzed (Gresham, 2005; Shapiro, 2013; Wexler, 2017).

Each intervention service delivery model focuses on an area to promote learning and remediate deficits. For example, RTI is a three-tiered intervention service delivery model that focuses on providing evidence-based and sound instruction to students to best assist them in meeting academic goals (Preston, Wood, & Stecker, 2016). Similarly, SWPBS is a three-tiered intervention service delivery model that focuses on supporting students in meeting behavioral expectations by creating a warm, caring, and welcoming school environment (Preston et al., 2016). Therefore, intervention service delivery models are designed to promote optimal learning, behavior, and social-emotional development for children in general education. For students presenting with academic, behavior, or social-emotional concerns, intervention service delivery models seek to remediate these deficits early on before they lead to disability placement or significant learning, behavior, or social-emotional problems. Intervention service delivery models have become to be viewed as "systems" under MTSS because they provide educators a "systemic" format for implementing interventions and evaluating student progress.

The main difference between MTSS and intervention service delivery models is that MTSS "houses," integrates, and aligns commonalities across triangular, multi-tiered intervention service delivery models (Wexler, 2017). Although RTI and SWPBS are the most common intervention service delivery models that fall under the MTSS, deviations from these original two models have been developed by districts to address social-emotional concerns (social-emotional RTI) and suicide (suicide prevention and intervention). Each of these intervention service delivery models helps to promote uniformity across schools, provides early intervention to students, abides by state guidelines, and recognizes that academic, behavioral, and social-emotional difficulties tend to be interconnected and often do not operate independently of one another (Eagle, Dowd-Eagle, Snyder, & Holtzman, 2015; Harn, Basaraba, Chard, & Fritz, 2015; Schaffer, 2017). As can be inferred from this discussion, both MTSS and the intervention service delivery models that comprise it, like RTI, are not part of a special education referral process (Preston et al., 2016). Rather MTSS and intervention service delivery models are general education initiatives to prevent future learning delays and behavioral difficulties.

To prevent future learning delays and behavioral difficulties, MTSS is built on six foundational principles. First, MTSS purports that all children have the capability of meeting grade-level expectations, regardless of individual factors, such as disability or socioeconomic status (Wexler, 2017). Second, MTSS employs a preventative model to proactively determine which children need increasing supports based on their academic, behavioral, or social-emotional needs (National Association of School Psychologists, 2016; Wexler, 2017). Third, MTSS places emphasis on implementing empirically validated instruction and interventions (Wexler, 2017; Sugai & Horner, 2009). Fourth, MTSS utilizes data to make decisions about instruction, intervention planning, allocation of resources, and the overall effectiveness of school practices (Shapiro, 2013; Wexler, 2017). Fifth, under MTSS, instruction must meet the child's unique needs (Wexler, 2017). Finally, along with promoting learning for all students, MTSS is an opportunity for districts to adopt reform efforts to their school culture (Sugai & Horner, 2009; Wexler, 2017).

Although ESSA does not require districts and schools to utilize MTSS to help bring students to proficiency, it does offer substantial access to funding streams for states and districts who wish to implement the framework (Grant et al., 2017; National Association of School Psychologists, 2016). Part of the reason ESSA provides access to funding streams for schools and districts implementing MTSS is that the framework is increasingly being found effective in reforming curricula to meet student needs, turning around underperforming schools, and improving outcomes for all learners (National Association of School Psychologists, 2016).

Despite ESSA prioritizing the need for expanded access to comprehensive and integrated intervention service delivery models under MTSS, many school districts experience considerable difficulty conceptualizing, outlining, and executing the framework. This difficulty in implementing MTSS could be due to educators being resistant to change, not receiving adequate training in MTSS, or lacking appropriate guidance from policymakers (Arden & Pentimonti, 2017). Either way, it has become clear that educators trying to implement MTSS often find it challenging, confusing to navigate, and even frustrating.

Steps to Building the MTSS House

To truly understand what MTSS is and make it less daunting, educators need to relate implementing MTSS to a task that is familiar to them, such as building a house. Therefore, this book seeks to take educators through building the "house of multi-tiered systems of support." As everyone knows, building a house contains four basic steps of which include: (1) laying the foundation, (2) raising the framework, (3) putting up walls, and (4) covering the house with a roof.

The remainder of this chapter focuses on the first step to building a house and involves laying the foundation for the house to sit on. To lay the foundation of MTSS, educators must understand the history of it. After developing a sound understanding of the history of MTSS, the next step involves raising a framework for the house walls to rest on. Four pillars create the framework for MTSS and link all intervention service delivery models under the model. These four pillars are varying levels of evidence-based interventions and supports, universal screening, progress monitoring, and data-based decision-making. After raising a solid framework, the next step in constructing the MTSS "house" involves putting up the four walls. The four walls that make up the MTSS house include the intervention service delivery models of RTI, SWPBS, social-emotional RTI, and suicide prevention and intervention. The final step to building the MTSS house involves putting a roof over all the components that comprise it. MTSS, as a whole, acts as the roof to the house as it covers all the aforementioned components that comprise the model.

Notice that there is a rule of four in developing and implementing MTSS. To elaborate, there are four basic steps to building a house. Additionally, there are four "pillars" that create the framework to MTSS and link all intervention service delivery models under it. Finally, there are four intervention service delivery models that make up the "walls" to the house. By remembering the construction of the MTSS house as consisting of a rule of four, educators can easily recall the essential components of building the model. Figure 1.1 provides a diagram of how to conceptualize MTSS and the intervention service delivery models of RTI, SWPBS, social-emotional RTI, and suicide prevention and intervention.

FIGURE 1.1 ● Multi-Tiered Systems of Support and Intervention Services Delivery Models Within an MTSS Framework

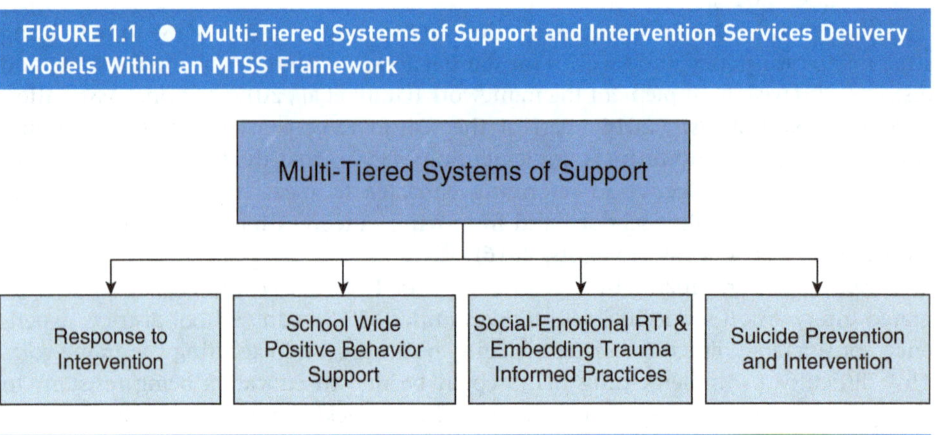

Foundations of MTSS

The building blocks that form the foundations of MTSS and intervention service delivery models are not new. Educators may be surprised to learn that several features of intervention service delivery models that integrate well under MTSS are over a century old. For educators to truly understand and appreciate the future of MTSS, they must understand how faulty reactionary past practices came to be and why such methods have fallen out of favor. Central to this understanding is the birth of **psycho-educational testing** and the origins of school psychology practice. Understanding the history of MTSS and how it came to be forming a solid foundation to implement the model.

School psychology is a branch of professional psychology that focuses on helping children, families, and learners of all ages succeed academically, socially, behaviorally, and emotionally (American Psychological Association, n.d.; National Association of School Psychologists, 2014). The "school" in school psychology represents the type psychology these professionals engage in as opposed to the place in which they practice. Therefore, although many school psychologists practice inside the four walls of the school, many others are self-employed or work in agency, hospital, or university settings (National Association of School Psychologists, 2014). To improve school and agency-wide practices, school psychologists often consult with teachers, families, and other professionals, such as school counselors (National Association of School Psychologists, 2014). Compared to other practices of psychology, school psychologists are uniquely trained in the areas of data collection and analysis, collaboration, counseling, research and program evaluation, prevention and intervention services, and crisis response (National Association of School Psychologists, 2014). Arguably, the most traditional role for school psychologists to engage in is that of psycho-educational testing. In brief, psycho-educational testing or psycho-educational assessment entails the evaluation of a child to determine if there is the presence or absence of a disability that may interfere with learning, behavior, or social-emotional functioning (American Psychological Association, n.d.; National Association of School Psychologists, 2014).

Psycho-educational testing has been both the hallmark and Achilles' heel of school psychology practice for well over a century. Despite changes in education under ESSA, both teachers and administrators have continued to view the school psychologist's primary role as one that involves using IQ and achievement tests to determine special education eligibility (McGill, Dombrowski, & Canivez, 2018; Farrell, 2010). The anticipation, practice, and re-emerging role of school psychologists being limited to a testing-based profession is steeped in both educational history and legislation (Fagan & Wise, 2007; Farrell, 2010). However, without psycho-educational testing, the field of school psychology may be a practice that never obtained the prominence that it has reached in the twenty-first century. In a sense, the psycho-educational testing "key" that let school psychology out of the cage and into a highly valued profession also shackled the occupation to a wall of endless assessments. Perhaps no other profession has struggled more than school psychology to evolve past only one of the many duties that the occupation could entail.

Connection Between School Psychology, Teaching, and MTSS

School psychology's link to psycho-educational testing dates back to 1905 when Alfred Binet was asked by the Ministry of Public Instruction in France to assess problems exhibited by children who were unable to follow the general school curriculum (Farrell, 2010; Routh, 2019). Binet went on to develop the Binet-Simon Intelligence Test which was utilized to detect intellectually disabled children who were viewed as incapable of learning in a mainstream school and who should be placed in separate classes or special schools (Farrell, 2010; Routh, 2019). However, the essential components of school psychology practice were delineated nearly a decade earlier by Lightner Witmer who, as an English and history teacher at Rugby Academy in Philadelphia, was intrigued that although some of his students appeared capable and motivated remained unable to learn course content (D'Amato et al., 2011; Routh, 2019; Thomas, 2009). In 1896, Witmer outlined a plan for a role within applied psychology entitled "The Clinical

Method in Psychology and the Diagnostic Method of Teaching" (D'Amato et al., 2011; Fagan, 1996; Fagan & Wise, 2007; Routh, 2019).

Witmer's plan involved investigating mental development in children by statistical and clinical methods, developing a hospital training school for the treatment of children with defects interfering in their school progress, and the training of students for a new profession known as "the expert" who would work with the school in treating intellectually disabled children (D'Amato et al., 2011; Routh, 2019; Thomas, 2009). Taken altogether, Witmer's experience as a teacher and his proposal of having an "expert" in the schools delineated the specialty of school psychology. In addition, Witmer stressed both clinical and empirical methods for the understanding and treatment of children who exhibited psychological and developmental deficits along with focusing on a multidisciplinary problem-solving team approach (D'Amato et al., 2011; Witmer, 1996).

Ultimately, Witmer proposed a **problem-solving process** that involved evidence-based interventions to effectively teach children with learning deficits (D'Amato et al., 2011). These evidence-based interventions would consist of treatments or supports that demonstrated empirical support for effectiveness in remediating learning and behavioral deficits (D'Amato et al., 2011; King & Coughlin, 2016). Ultimately, Witmer's problem-solving process called for the assessment of the disorder, development of hypotheses concerning appropriate intervention, and the provision and evaluation of the intervention (D'Amato et al., 2011; Fagan & Wise, 2007; Routh, 2019). In essence, Witmer's problem-solving process involved the careful monitoring of a student's response to intervention. Such a proposal introduced two early cornerstones that link intervention service delivery models, such as RTI and PBS, under MTSS: utilization of evidence-based interventions and progress monitoring.

Emphasis on Psycho-Educational Testing

Despite Witmer stressing the importance of formulating and utilizing evidence-based interventions and progress monitoring, his ideas were not viewed as groundbreaking when he presented them at the annual American Psychological Association meeting (D'Amato et al., 2011). Moreover, as time progressed, school psychology's emphasis on testing remained a central component of the field. In fact, in the 1920s, Cyril Burt, the UK's first school psychologist believed that the occupation's primary focus was that of "testing children to see if they needed to be educated in a special school" (Farrell, 2010, p. 583). Equal emphasis was not placed on the school psychologist's role as both assessor and proposer of evidence-based intervention but rather one of assessor. Instead, the profession of school psychology took on the role of the "judge, jury, and executer" of sorting children into educational placements and determining whether a child with significant learning deficits could attend education (Farrell, 2010; Maliphant, Frederickson, & Cline, 2013).

Farrell (2010) argues that IQ tests played a critical and definitive role in the rise of school psychology in that if these assessments determined a child's educational placement, there was "a need to employ professionals to use them" (p. 583). Oakland (2000) bolsters Farrell's claims by noting that the rise in the number of school psychologists worldwide was closely linked to the extent that countries have viewed IQ tests as an indispensable tool for the identification of children with special needs. Ultimately, school psychologist's rise to prominence is largely based on the concept that IQ testing was a distinctive task that no other professional could perform (Fagan & Wise, 2007; Farrell, 2010). Despite intelligence testing continuing to grow in popularity in the 1920s, Witmer remained skeptical of utilizing them as the sole assessment of an individual's ability going as far to write a letter to the Editor of the *New York Times* encouraging more holistic methods for determining an individual's competency (Thomas, 2009; Witmer, 1922). For example, in deciding whether children had an intellectual disability, Witmer encouraged the use of lengthy observations and attempts to determine whether the condition was responsive to remedial efforts before making an official diagnosis (Routh, 2019; Thomas, 2009). Therefore, even with IQ tests rising in popularity, Witmer's approach to diagnosing intellectual disability and learning deficits was in line with the methods he initially proposed of attempting an intervention and determining whether a child is responsive to the intervention proposed. Such practices, as mentioned earlier, were the foundations for the intervention service delivery models that comprise MTSS. To understand the contextual timeframe in which two basic components of MTSS arose in and the year school psychology was founded, see Figure 1.2.

Introduction to the Severe Discrepancy Model

By the 1940s and into the 1970s, there was a growing emphasis in education to provide quality instruction to all children (D'Amato et al., 2011; Fagan & Wise, 2007). The concept that all children should be provided quality instruction combined with the advent of the civil rights movement and increased advocacy from parents lead to attention being placed on the idea that children with disabilities should be educated with their nondisabled peers (Heward, Alber-Morgan, & Konrad, 2017; Spaulding & Pratt, 2015). Still, before 1975, few districts provided education for students with disabilities or segregated them into residential schools in the United States (Katsiyannis, Yell, & Bradley, 2001). Although many students with disabilities were denied educational services before 1975, there continued to be an increased need for psychological services in the school setting that focused both on psycho-educational assessment along with the delivery of mental health services (D'Amato et al., 2011). Consequently, the number of school psychologists increased from about 500 in 1940 to about 5,000 in 1970 (D'Amato et al., 2011; Fagan & Wise, 2007).

As advocacy efforts for children with disabilities continued, high profile court cases like Hobson versus Hanson (1967), Mills versus The Board of Education of the District of Columbia (1972), and the Pennsylvania Association for Retarded Citizens versus the Commonwealth of Pennsylvania (1972) eventually led to the passage of the **Education for All Handicapped Children Act (EHCA)** (Heward et al., 2017). EHCA required that all schools that received federal funding provide children with disabilities equal access to education and mandated educating these students in the least restrictive educational environment possible (Heward et al., 2017). As a consequence of ECHA, children suspected of having a disability or who had a disability were entitled to a nondiscriminatory evaluation completed by the school district (Heward et al., 2017). Moreover, the act required IQ testing to determine special education eligibility for the identification of both learning disabilities and intellectual disability. One of the most controversial disability categories under EHCA was that of Specific Learning Disability (SLD), which was defined as:

> *(a) A disorder in one or more of the basic psychological processes involved in understanding or in using language, spoken or written, which may manifest itself in an imperfect ability to listen, think, speak, read, write, spell or do mathematical calculations. (b) Includes such conditions as perceptual disabilities, minimal brain dysfunction, dyslexia and aphasia. (c) Does not include learning problems which are primarily the result of visual hearing, motor or emotional disabilities, or mental retardation, or of environmental, cultural or economic disadvantage. (Individuals with Disabilities Act, 2004)*

Due to EHCA defining a SLD in vague terms, critics and teachers at the time, and even today, have touted the definition as "too vague," citing that it delineates what a SLD isn't rather than what it is (Alfonso & Flanagan, 2018; Beaujean, Benson, McGill, & Dombrowski, 2018; Fletcher et al., 2002; Maki, Floyd, & Roberson, 2015). Therefore, the definition of SLD was, and continues to be, frequently discredited for being exclusionary and convoluted rather than inclusionary and specific (Fletcher et al., 2002). However, despite criticisms, the definition of SLD has remained unchanged since 1975 (Fletcher et al., 2002). Not surprisingly, after the passage of the EHCA, states needed assistance with identifying SLD as there were no agreed-upon diagnostic criteria for determining the presence or absence of the disorder (Alfonso & Flanagan, 2018; Beaujean et al., 2018; Maki et al., 2015).

As a result, the Federal Register published the Procedures for Evaluating Specific Learning Disabilities in 1977 which defined SLD as a severe discrepancy between achievement and intellectual ability in one or more of the following seven areas: oral expression, listening comprehension, written expression, basic reading, reading comprehension, mathematics calculation, or mathematics reasoning (U. S. Office of Education, 1977). Moreover, an individual could not meet eligibility criteria for a SLD if the discrepancy between ability and achievement was not primarily the result of a visual, hearing, or motor handicap, mental retardation, emotional disturbance, or environmental, cultural, or economic disadvantage (U. S. Office of Education, 1977). The inclusion of a **severe discrepancy** between a youth's ability and achievement, as recommended in the Federal Register, propelled school psychology and psycho-educational testing to new heights and helped to solidify school psychologist's role as "gatekeeper" of special education. As a result, school psychologists continued to be in demand profession throughout the 1970s and 1980s that was tasked with endlessly administering intelligence and achievement tests and subsequently determining if a severe discrepancy between the two measures was significant enough to determine the presence of a SLD (see Table 1.1) (Alfonso & Flanagan, 2018; Beaujean et al., 2018). Such a process further de-emphasized the problem-solving process and preventative practices that Witmer originally proposed.

TABLE 1.1 ● Example of Severe Discrepancy Model

Student	IQ Test Score	Achievement Test Score	Qualifies as Learning Disabled
Danny	90	96	No
Stephanie	120	97	Yes
Kristen	77	69	No

Note. District A: Severe discrepancy criteria: 22 point discrepancy = Severe Discrepancy.
Average IQ/Achievement Score = 90–109.

Controversy Surrounding the Severe Discrepancy Model

Ironically, when Samuel Kirk coined the term of learning disability (LD) in 1962, he did not incorporate a "severe discrepancy between achievement and intellectual ability" into his definition (Hallahan & Mock, 2003; McDonough, Flanagan, & Alfonso, 2017). However, the concept of an ability–achievement discrepancy was later included when a student of Kirk's, by the name of Barbara Bateman, redefined LD in 1965 (Hallahan & Mock, 2003; McDonough et al., 2017). The idea of an IQ–achievement discrepancy being the hallmark of a child with a LD further gained notoriety in 1975 when the results of the "Isle of Wight" study, conducted by Michael Rutter and William Yule, found that some children performed much lower in reading than was expected given their roughly average intelligence (Rutter & Yule, 1975). The "Isle of Wight" study appeared to confirm the general belief that school psychologists could engage in a "cognitive profile analysis" to assess "unorganized functioning" in children (Beaujean et al., 2018, p. 2).

By school psychologists completing a **cognitive profile analysis,** it was thought that they could determine the underlying presence or absence of a LD and provide a reason or "cognitive dysfunction" for underachievement on academic testing (Beaujean et al., 2018). However, research has consistently drawn into question the reliability and validity of school psychologists engaging in a cognitive profile analysis, finding it to be of little value in the diagnosis and treatment of SLD (Beaujean et al., 2018; Farrell, 2010; McGill et al., 2018). Still, the combination of Bateman's definition for LD, Rutter and Yule's "Isle of Wight" study, and an overall need for more definitive criteria for identifying LD lead to increasing demands for school psychologists to conduct IQ tests. Farrell (2010) writes that "one of the consequences of the Rutter and Yule article is that it encouraged, if not directed, school psychologists to carry out IQ tests when assessing children who were thought to have specific learning disabilities, thus reinforcing their unique and distinctive role" (p. 584).

Although the assessment mandates of the EHCA was the first time that districts were required to provide school psychology services, the federal mandate forced the profession to spend most of, if not all, its time completing IQ and achievement tests (Abramowitz, 1981; Benson, Floyd, Kranzler, Eckert, & Fefer, 2018; Brown, Holcombe, Bolen, & Thompson, 2006; Heiser, Garruto, & Faustino, 2018; Stoiber & Vanderwood, 2008). In years following the EHCA, school psychologists largely advocated that the responsibility of assessor was forced upon the field by the federal government and that the profession would not have imposed such a limited role on themselves (Abramowitz, 1981).

Subsequently, the National Association of School Psychologist's Standards for the Provision of School Psychological Services reflected that school psychologists wanted to reduce the amount of time they spent on assessments (Abramowitz, 1981). Instead, the field advocated for an increase in the amount of time they spent on mental health consultations and the prevention of student learning problems (Abramowitz, 1981). Such advocacy for the prevention of student learning problems was more in line with what Witmer originally proposed for the profession and involved several cornerstones of MTSS. Despite efforts by school psychologists to distance themselves from the roles of assessor and gatekeeper of special education, the field's primary duty continued to involve completing psycho-educational assessments and determining whether a severe discrepancy existed between a student's intellectual ability and achievement.

By school psychologists analyzing and determining whether a severe discrepancy existed between a student's intellectual ability and achievement, their practices began to mirror the traditional **medical model** of training as opposed to a preventative one. The traditional medical model suggested that in order for a child to receive help with their deficits, they must first wait to be diagnosed with a "disability" or "illness" (Remley & Herlihy, 2016). The medical model is in contrast to the preventative model of practice which suggests that many children's deficits can be remediated before a diagnosis is needed (Remley & Herlihy, 2016). The practice of children with learning deficits having to wait to academically fall substantially behind their peers in order to be classified as a child with a disability became known as the **"wait-to-fail"** model. Taken altogether, the history, legislation, and demand to curb SLD numbers using a rigid ability–achievement discrepancy formula made the field of school psychology synonymous with psycho-educational testing rather than placing equal emphasis, if not more emphasis on Witmer's original concepts of prevention using evidence-based interventions within a problem-solving model.

Adoption of the Public Health Model

Ironically, at the time when the educational field was moving toward reactionary practices to identify SLD, it appears that the medical field began to mirror some of Witmer's early concepts with the creation of the public health model in the 1960s (Bruns et al., 2016). The **public health model** emphasized the overall health of the public through epidemiologic methodology, better known as the study, determination, control, and prevention of health problems (Merrill, 2017). More specifically, activities in epidemiology that align with Witmer's early problem-solving process and MTSS include the study of what causes a disease and strategies to prevent illness and the development of a hypothesis to control the illness (Merrill, 2017). Additionally, the practice of epidemiology called for the utilization of evidence-based interventions, and monitoring and evaluating the effectiveness of interventions in preventing and treating the disease (Centers of Disease Control and Prevention, 2018; Dean, 2012; Merrill, 2017) (see Table 1.2). It is not surprising that Witmer's initial ideas may have been inadvertently incorporated into the public health model as Witmer viewed his practice of psychology as "closely related to medicine" (Witmer, 1996, p. 7). Consequently, it was arguably Witmer's past experience as a teacher combined with his view that the practice of psychology was "closely related to medicine" that were influential to preventative practices in education.

FIGURE 1.2 ● Timeline

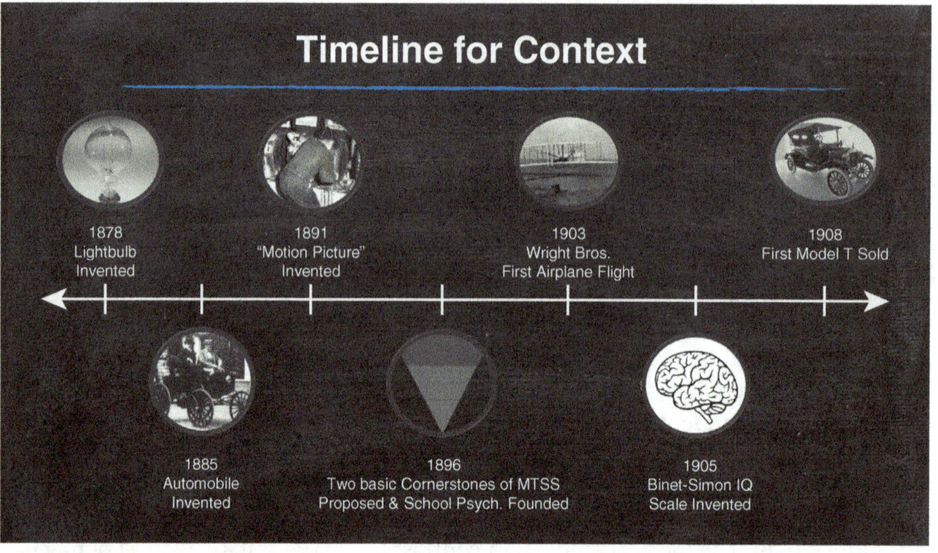

With the central components to epidemiological practices and the public health model involving the study and prevention of disease and illness, Leavell and Clark (1965) outlined primary, secondary, and tertiary levels needed to avoid the contraction and advancement ailments. Primary prevention was designed to promote health and keep medical problems from occurring in the first place through resiliency and protective factors (Ali & Katz, 2016; Schoon, Porta, & Schaffer, 2019). Secondary prevention was

TABLE 1.2 ● Witmer's Clinical Method in Psychology Versus Epidemiology Practices (D'Amato et al., 2011; Merrill, 2017; Witmer, 1907/1996)

Witmer's Proposal	Epidemiology Practices
Investigating the mental development of children, as manifested by mental and moral concerns by means of statistical methods	Investigating and making a judgment on the causes of disease through valid statistical association
Development of hypotheses concerning an appropriate intervention to remediate the child's deficits before a diagnosis is placed on the child. The focus is on prevention.	Development of a hypothesis as to how to best prevent, treat, or control an illness
Development and utilization of evidence-based interventions	Development and utilization of evidence-based interventions
Monitoring and evaluating the effectiveness of interventions at remediating learning and behavioral deficits.	Monitoring and evaluating the effectiveness of interventions at preventing and treating illness.

designed to detect and treat health problems in their early stages before they become too severe and have long-term effects (Ali & Katz, 2016; Schoon et al., 2019). Finally, tertiary prevention was developed to limit further adverse effects of a health problem in its later and more advanced stages (Ali & Katz, 2016; Schoon et al., 2019).

Eventually, Leavell and Clark's different levels of prevention were adopted into a three-tiered triangle, which closely resembled three-tier intervention service delivery models such as RTI and SWBPS (see Figure 1.3). With the medical field adopting a preventative stance toward illness and disease in the 1960s and throughout the 1970s, the field of community-based mental health and psychiatry began to adapt the three-tiered model of prevention into their practices (Ali & Katz, 2016; Schoon et al., 2019). Therefore, while medical and community-based mental health fields appeared to welcome, adopt, and revise preventative models of practice that were similar to what Witmer originally proposed, the field of education increasingly moved toward the reactionary and traditional medical model of practice under "wait-to-fail."

FIGURE 1.3 ● Public Health Model

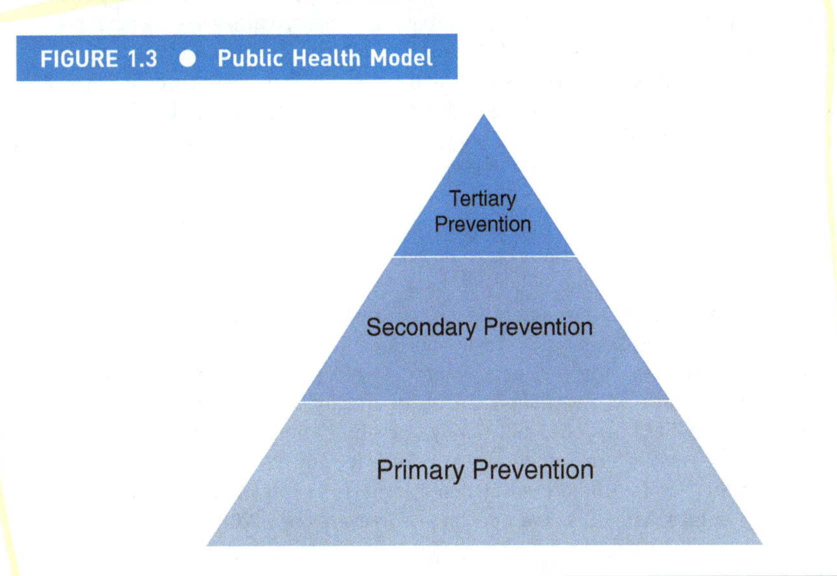

At the time in which community-based mental health was adopting preventative practices and education was adopting the reactionary "wait-to-fail" model, school psychologists could be found working in community-based mental health clinics, residential settings, and in schools (Mordock, 1988; D'Amato et al., 2011). School psychologists often worked in each of these settings as the "school" in school psychology delineates the specialty of practice these psychologists engage in and not the place. Additionally, as mentioned earlier, before 1975 many children with disabilities were educated in residential schools separate from their nondisabled peers (Katsiyannis et al., 2001). With the incorporation of the ability–achievement discrepancy model into EHCA, there was an increased demand for school psychologists to become a mandated practice within public education (Abramowitz, 1981; D'Amato et al., 2011; Mordock, 1988). It was thought that incorporation of the ability–achievement discrepancy model and utilization of school psychologists for psycho-educational testing would impede the flow of children with specific learning disabilities into special education (Cortiella & Horowitz, 2014). Therefore, by the mid-1990s and early 2000s, the ability–achievement discrepancy model was the most widely endorsed method among school psychologists for identifying SLD (Floyd, 2010; Reschly, 2008). Consequently, psycho-educational testing filling a little more than half the workweek and two-thirds of school psychologist's time was devoted to special education classification and placement (Reschly, 2008). Still, school psychologists continued to advocate for a movement away from the severe discrepancy model and better utilization of their time and skills (Box 1.1).

BOX 1.1 COVID-19 AND THE PUBLIC HEALTH MODEL

In late December 2019 and throughout 2020, a mysterious and highly contagious virus emerged that primarily attacked the respiratory system in humans and had no known vaccine or cure (Xie et al., 2020). The emergence and global spread of the disease, which came to be known as coronavirus or COVID-19 for short, globally spread from continent to continent causing millions of people across the world to become sick or pass away (Centers for Disease Control and Prevention, 2020). Due to the dangers that COVID-19 presented, 140,000 out of 148,000 public and private schools suddenly closed across the United States and Canada (National Center for Education Statistics, 2019; Statistics Canada, 2020; Viner et al., 2020). Along with school closure, universities, restaurants, parks, businesses, movie theaters, sporting events, and department stores stopped operations to prevent the spread of the disease.

Little did anyone know it at the time, but they were getting a front row seat of the public health model in action throughout the COVID-19 pandemic. Overall, the goal of the public health model is to promote and "protect the health of people and the communities where they live, learn, work, and play" (American Public Health Association, 2021; para. 1). A main focus of the public health model entails the prevention of disease outbreaks (American Public Health Association, 2021). During the COVID-19 pandemic, all three tiers of the public health model were on full display across the world in an effort to stop the spread of the virus and save lives. As mentioned earlier, initial Tier 1 efforts to stop the spread of COVID-19 involved the closure of schools, universities, businesses, and public places. Additionally, the public was educated about the virus, vulnerable populations who may be exposed to the virus, and how to best protect others from contracting the disease through press briefings and the news. Aside from press briefings and the news, many countries across the world adopted easy-to-remember mottos, such as "Stop the spread. Stay at home. Save lives" (Centers for Disease Control and Prevention, 2020). This motto along with television commercials, billboards, and roadside signs reminded the public of best hygiene practices to prevent the spread of the virus with statements, such as "wash your hands," "cover your face in public," and "stay six feet or two meters apart" (Centers for Disease Control and Prevention, 2020). In addition to these Tier 1 interventions, all family members and friends not residing together were asked to not visit one another and informed by health experts to "stay inside" (Centers for Disease Control and Prevention, 2020).

(Continued)

As a final effort to prevent the spread of COVID-19, grocery stores implemented Tier 1 interventions to protect the general public. Some of the Tier 1 interventions adopted by grocery stores included only allowing a set number of customers to enter at a time, placing tape on the ground in checkout lines to keep customers a safe distance from one another, asking shoppers to wear masks, and increasing sanitization and cleaning efforts. Finally, countries across the world worked diligently to universally screen as many individuals as they could in the community for exposure to COVID-19 (Centers for Disease Control and Prevention, 2020). Taken altogether, Tier 1 efforts during the COVID-19 pandemic were designed to prevent the spread of the virus and were to be ubiquitously adopted and practiced by all individuals residing in a community.

Despite Tier 1 efforts keeping the majority of people safe from contracting COVID-19, some individuals required more intensive interventions and supports. Therefore, Tier 2 supports were designed for individuals who were at increased risk for COVID-19, showed symptoms of the virus, or had traveled during the outbreak (Centers for Disease Control and Prevention, 2020). For these individuals, the standard protocol involved them having to self-quarantine for fourteen days and separate themselves from family members who reside in their home (Centers for Disease Control and Prevention, 2020). If individuals were feeling ill and needed medical assistance, they were advised to contact their primary medical doctor, rest, drink plenty of liquids, and take over-the-counter medications, such as acetaminophen (Centers for Disease Control and Prevention, 2020). Their response to these interventions and supports was progress monitored by having these individuals check in regularly with their primary care physician (Centers for Disease Control and Prevention, 2020).

Finally, Tier 3 efforts in response to COVID-19 were designed for the few individuals within a community who did not respond to previous intervention efforts and supports. These individuals were considered at extreme risk for dying or having lifelong complications as a result of the virus. At Tier 3, individuals who contracted the virus were admitted to hospital where they received interventions and supports, such as practicing breathing exercises with a respiratory therapist, receiving extra oxygen, being administered fluids through an IV, and receiving antiviral or steroid medications, such as remdesivir or dexamethasone (Centers for Disease Control and Prevention, 2020). In extreme cases, individuals were placed on ventilator (Centers for Disease Control and Prevention, 2020). For those individuals who did not respond to Tier 3 interventions and supports, many either developed a disability, such permanent respiratory damage, or passed away.

Although the COVID-19 pandemic significantly impacted the quality of life for many people across the world, it also provided global insight into the public health model. Being familiar with this model to prevent disease outbreaks or adapting it for use in schools is critical to providing best evidence-based supports and interventions. Through using such an approach in the schools, educators are placing them in the best place to succeed not only academically but throughout their life. Overall, the public health model and the intervention service delivery models used in the schools that mirror it seek to prevent diseases, learning, or behavioral deficits from emerging.

A Road Sign During the COVID-19 Pandemic

Movement Away From the Severe Discrepancy Model

Despite the field of education utilizing an ability–achievement discrepancy model to impede the flow of children being classified as learning disabled, the disability category continued to grow substantially. Ironically, from 1976 to 2000, children classified as having a SLD grew by more than 300% (Cortiella & Horowitz, 2014; Heward et al., 2017). In addition to failing to impede the flow of children being classified as learning disabled, scholars and educators began to note several prominent limitations to the ability–achievement discrepancy model.

First, an obvious limitation of the ability–achievement discrepancy model was its tendency to disqualify children in need of special education services and, on the contrary, qualify children who were not truly disabled (Beaujean et al., 2018; Fletcher, Lyon, Fuchs, & Barnes, 2019; Hale, 2008). Scholars have pointed out that a major flaw in the ability–achievement discrepancy model was that it denied children with disabilities access to services because the cognitive difficulties that led to the learning problem also depressed the child's IQ score (Fletcher et al., 2019; Hale, 2008; Restori, Katz, & Lee, 2009). Due to the child's overall IQ score being depressed as a result of significant cognitive deficits, they were less likely to display the substantial discrepancy needed to qualify for special education services.

For example, in a district requiring that a student display a 22-point discrepancy between their cognitive and achievement testing scores, a child with an IQ score of 125 (very high range) and an achievement score of 102 (average range) in reading comprehension could qualify for special education services. However, a child with an IQ score of 83 (low average range) and an achievement score of 67 (extremely low range) in reading comprehension could not qualify for special education services. Taken altogether, under the ability–achievement discrepancy model, a child with significantly lower than average intelligence and achievement scores could be denied special education services, while a child with average to significantly above average intelligence and achievement scores could qualify for special education services as a child with a SLD.

A second criticism of the ability–achievement discrepancy model was that it made early identification and intervention of children with SLD challenging (Alfonso & Flanagan, 2018; Restori et al., 2009). Using the discrepancy model, young children experiencing academic difficulties often did not demonstrate the significant difference needed between their IQ and achievement test scores to meet eligibility as a child with a SLD. Therefore, young students often had to continue to fail for several years before their achievement scores fell significantly below their IQ in order to qualify for special education services (Alfonso & Flanagan, 2018; Restori et al., 2009). For example, under the ability–achievement discrepancy model, the average age at which students were identified as having a reading disability and eligible for special education was ten years or about third to fourth grade (Al Otaiba, Wagner, & Miller, 2014). Consequently, under the ability–achievement discrepancy model, younger students with academic deficits often did not receive support for their learning difficulties in earlier grades (Al Otaiba et al., 2014).

A third problem with the discrepancy model, and one that the Isle of Wight study helped reinforce, is the general perception among school psychologists and educators that IQ and achievement in the general population are perfectly correlated (Beaujean et al., 2018; Farrell, 2010). To clarify, many educators widely believed that children with an average IQ should have reading scores proportionate with their chronological age (Beaujean et al., 2018; Farrell, 2010). Therefore, children with high IQs would be expected to have reading ages above that of their chronological age, and children with lower IQ would be expected to have reading ages below that of their chronological age (Beaujean et al., 2018; Farrell, 2010). Despite the general perception among psychologists and educators that IQ test scores and achievement are perfectly correlated, the two are not. In fact, it is estimated that approximately 50%–60% of student achievement is related to variables beyond intelligence such as motivation, early learning opportunities, and effective instructional practices (Borghans, Golsteyn, Heckman, & Humphries, 2016; Farrell, 2010; Restori et al., 2009).

A fourth limitation of the ability–achievement discrepancy model is that it leads educators and school psychologists to believe that IQ tests can and should be utilized to prescribe interventions to students to best match their specific cognitive profile (Beaujean et al., 2018; Fletcher & Miciak, 2017; Kearns & Fuchs, 2013). Contrary to common belief, there remains a lack of compelling evidence demonstrating that cognitive assessments can be effectively utilized to suggest effective interventions for struggling learners that will help them succeed academically (Beaujean et al., 2018; Fletcher & Miciak, 2017; Kearns & Fuchs, 2013). By school psychologists recommending interventions based on cognitive profiles, students may receive the wrong interventions or interventions that lack empirical support. In addition to failing to provide educators empirically supported interventions, the ability–achievement discrepancy model did not provide educators tools to monitor a student's RTI and exit criteria from special education. Consequently, through the ability–achievement discrepancy model, educators did not fully know how much students were benefiting from their instruction and interventions as their progress was not frequently monitored, and students rarely found their way out of special education (Fletcher & Miciak, 2017; Reschly, 2008).

A final criticism of the ability–achievement discrepancy model is that there was little empirical evidence supporting its use in identifying SLD (Maki et al., 2015; Restori et al., 2009; Stuebing et al., 2002; Vellutino, Scanlon, & Lyon, 2000). Consequently, there was no universally accepted and best practice model adopted for its implementation across school districts and across states (Beaujean et al., 2018; Maki et al., 2015). For example, while one district may have required a 20-point discrepancy for determining whether a student qualified for having a SLD, a neighboring school district may have required a 23-point discrepancy. Therefore, a student who qualified for special education services in one school district may not have qualified for special education services in another school district. Additionally, since IQ and achievement tests provide educators a single test score at a single point in time, the repeated measures needed to establish the reliability of whether the child is consistently underperforming on standardized instruments cannot be determined (Restori et al., 2009). To establish the type of consistency needed to determine whether a child is underperforming, a child's RTI must be monitored over time as Witmer originally proposed.

Response to Intervention and the Problem-Solving Process

Due to ongoing concerns with the discrepancy model, the National Joint Committee on Learning Disabilities (NJCLD) wrote a letter to the Office of Special Education Programs (OSEP) in 1997 to encourage dialogue on best practices for identifying learning disabilities (Preston et al., 2016). Consequently, OSEP responded by forming a committee of researchers, parents, teachers, advocates, and policymakers to identify best possible ways to improve LD eligibility criteria. Subsequently in August 2001 a Learning Disabilities Summit was held by the OSEP of the US Department of Education (Al Otaiba et al., 2014; Preston et al., 2016). The purpose of the summit was to align identification of struggling learners with best evidence-based practices and influence the upcoming NCLB Act (Al Otaiba et al., 2014). A particular emphasis at the summit and in subsequent white papers was placed on children who displayed significant reading deficits and were not receiving adequate support in education. Therefore, scholars and educators argued that there was a critical need to provide children with early preventative interventions rather than waiting for them to fall far enough behind to qualify for help (Al Otaiba et al., 2014).

At the Learning Disabilities Summit, a consensus was reached to incorporate the science of reading intervention with screening and progress monitoring under a three-tiered problem-solving model known as "response to intervention" (Al Otaiba et al., 2014; D'Amato et al., 2011; Maki et al., 2015). Ironically, this three-tiered model appeared to borrow from the public health model's three tiers of preventative practice and incorporated several of Witmer's early ideas including the problem-solving process, progress monitoring, and utilization of evidence-based interventions. Along the lines of evidence-based interventions, the passage of NCLB Act strongly recommended the use of "scientifically based research" over 100 times, suggesting that the teaching methodologies and interventions utilized to assist children should have garnered empirical support (No Child Left Behind, 2002).

By the 2004 reauthorization of Individuals with Disabilities Education Act (IDEA), the federal government introduced the "response to intervention" (RTI) statue, which shifted emphasis away from the utilization of IQ and achievement tests to determine whether a child has SLD and instead suggested the following:

A. When determining whether a child has a SLD as defined in Section 1401 of this title, a local education agency shall not be required to take into consideration whether a child has a severe discrepancy between achievement and intellectual ability in oral expression, listening comprehension, written expression, basic reading skill, reading comprehension, mathematical calculation, or mathematical reasoning [{20 USC 1414(b) (6)}].

B. In determining whether a child has a SLD, a local educational agency may use a process that determines if the child responds to scientific, research-based intervention as a part of the evaluation procedures described in paragraphs (2) and (3) [{20 USC 1414(b) (6)}].

In addition to setting forth these regulations, nearly 30 years after the Federal Register incorporated the discrepancy approach in the identification of students with learning disabilities, the US Department of Education's OSEP distanced themselves from using of intelligence and achievement measures (Federal Register, 2006, p. 46651; VanDerHeyden & Burns, 2010). The department wrote that there is "no current evidence that such assessments are necessary or sufficient in identifying SLD. Furthermore, in many cases, these assessments have not been used to make appropriate intervention decisions" (Federal Register, 2006, p. 46651; VanDerHeyden & Burns, 2010).

Although the federal register statement initially appears to discredit the utilization of IQ and achievement tests for determining whether a child qualifies for special education services, the federal definition of SLD maintained that it is a disorder of "psychological processes" that manifests itself in an "imperfect ability to listen, think, speak, read, write, spell or do mathematical calculations" (Individuals with Disabilities Act, 2004). Consequently, the Federal Register's (2006) statement continues to state that the Department of Education:

> *Permits, but does not require, consideration of a pattern of strengths and weaknesses, or both, relative to intellectual development, if the evaluation group considers that*

information relevant to an identification of SLD. In many cases, though, assessments of cognitive processes simply add to the testing burden and do not contribute to interventions. (p. 46651)

Even though RTI has garnered considerable support, it appears that psycho-educational testing will still play a role in school psychology practice. Intelligence tests are a central component of assessing children for intellectual disability and remain objective measures that are not subject to the same bias as teacher ratings or grading (Floyd, 2010). Additionally, psycho-educational tests, especially IQ scores, have accumulated significant evidence for predicting socially important variables such as grades in school, years of schooling, job performance, income, learning outcomes in college and work, and social status (Butler, Pentoney, & Bong, 2017; Floyd, 2010).

Perhaps, the most important reason why IQ and achievement measures will continue to play a role in school psychology practice is that these measures continue to improve. Therefore, these assessments may eventually provide considerable insight into the cognitive processes that are affecting a child's learning. As a result, cognitive measures could help explain why interventions have largely been proven ineffective at remediating learning deficits for some children. For example, recent studies have suggested that understanding the fundamental cognitive processes that underlie reading, math, and writing disabilities and may be critical in the identification of such impairments (Kudo, Lussier, & Swanson, 2015; Peng, Wang, & Namkung, 2018). Finally, IQ and achievement measures may continue to play a role in school psychology practice as educational scholars have cited several limitations to implementing RTI. These limitations include difficulty establishing criteria for what evidence-based interventions should look like across different subject areas and grade levels, vague criteria on how to implement RTI with fidelity, and RTI being an inadequate stand-alone process for identification of specific learning disabilities (Hale, 2008; Hale et al., 2008; Preston et al., 2016). Ultimately, these limitations involving RTI, along with the fact that the current definition for LD includes a disorder in one or more of the "basic psychological processes," led the final federal regulations to state that:

RTI is only one component of the process to identify children in need of special education and related services. Determining why a child has not responded to research-based interventions requires a comprehensive evaluation [...] An RTI process does not replace the need for a comprehensive evaluation. (Federal Register, 2006, pp. 46646–46647)

The overlying principle of the 2006 regulations was to ensure that RTI was only one component of the evaluation process and that the data gathered do not rely solely on one single procedure for determining SLD (Federal Register, 2006). Therefore, the general impression is that the majority of students will respond to RTI-tiered instruction at the 1, 2, or 3 levels and remain in the general education curriculum. For the few students who do not respond to intervention, a psycho-educational evaluation may assist in determining whether the child is disabled. Therefore, if RTI was attempted and was unsuccessful in helping the child to overcome the problem, a psycho-educational evaluation would reveal the deficits in the basic psychological processes that cause a SLD.

Integration of Intervention Service Delivery Models Under MTSS

The incorporation of the "RTI statute" into IDEA 2004 and the reinforcing statement from the Federal Register in 2006 clarified the federal government's stance on the overuse of cognitive and achievement measures in identifying learning disabilities. Interestingly, IDEA 2004 never once utilized the term "response to intervention," but Vaughn and Fuchs (2003) suggest that the origins of RTI came from a 1982 National Research Council study on an approach to identify students with learning disabilities. Additionally, evidence exists that the term "response to intervention" has its terminology roots in an article by Frank Gresham (1991) in which he utilized the term "resistance to intervention" as a new method of assessing behavior disorders.

Although Gresham's article on "resistance to intervention" better aligns to the improved identification behavioral disorders in children, the term appears to have been altered to "response to intervention" to signify the idea that children without learning deficits tend to respond to evidence-based interventions provided, whereas children who do not may have significant learning impairments. Either way, Gresham's article and his focus on the improved selection and implementation of behavioral interventions appear to be an early precursor to the intervention service delivery model of School-Wide Positive Behavior Support (SWPBS).

The humble beginnings of SWPBS began in response to concerns over the use of aversive and humiliating procedures utilized to manage behaviors for individuals with developmental disabilities (Hieneman, 2015). However, in education, SWPBS was viewed as a means to proactively address the needs of students with significant behavioral concerns. SWPBS' appeal was significantly bolstered from 1987 to 1992 by a $670,000 grant from the US Department of Education National Institute on Disability and Rehabilitation Research (Johnston, Foxx, Jacobson, Green, & Mulick, 2006). The grant provided a consortium of universities funding to research and expand the applicability of SWPBS (Johnston et al., 2006). By 1997, SWPBS was incorporated into the amended version of the IDEA to improve school culture and utilize evidence-based strategies to proactively address the behavioral needs of students (Johnston et al., 2006). Although SWPBS initially had focused on children with developmental and behavioral disabilities, its appeal in proactively addressing problem behaviors and promoting a positive school climate led to it being incorporated as a general education initiative (Johnston et al., 2006).

Like RTI, SWPBS adopted a three-tier triangular model in which interventions increase in intensity and duration, and children do not respond to supports provided. Additionally, like RTI, SWPBS was largely refined throughout the 1990s and gained prominence throughout the 2000s. As both RTI and SWPBS grew in popularity throughout the 2000s, there was an increased push to integrate both of these intervention service delivery models under one general model in what would become known as MTSS.

The initial push for the integration of RTI and SWPBS arose primarily from three assumptions. First, an extensive literature base documented that lower academic achievement may lead to problem behaviors and that problem behaviors tend to lead to lower academic achievement (Kremer, Flower, Huang, & Vaughn, 2017; Madigan, Cross, Smolkowski, & Strycker, 2016). Evidence suggests that there is a 12.5% prevalence rate of children with co-occurring academic and behavior problems and that increased disruptive behavior frequently inhibits academic success, likely as a result of reduced instructional time (Taylor, Kilgus, & Huang, 2018). Additionally, studies have found that academic, behavioral, and emotional problems appear more stable the longer they go undetected and untreated. Due to academic achievement and behavioral deficits appearing to be related, attempting to address both through separate intervention systems rather than through combined approaches may not be as effective (McIntosh & Goodman, 2016). For example, attempting to address a child with academic and behavioral deficits through RTI, as opposed to RTI and SWBPS together, may not fully support the youth's areas of deficit.

Secondly, McIntosh and Goodman (2016) point out that proponents of integrating RTI and SWPBS under MTSS realized that each of these intervention service delivery models share many common underlying theories and features. Consequently, it was thought that by pointing out the similarities between RTI and SWPBS that school staff would be more likely to adopt both models under MTSS. Educators can better adapt to systems-level change when pointing and focusing on the similarities between two intervention service delivery models, rather than pointing out their differences (McIntosh & Goodman, 2016. By school districts introducing and integrating both intervention service delivery models under MTSS, as opposed to adopting each as a separate large initiative, educators may view that task of implementing them as less daunting (Freeman, Miller, & Newcomer, 2015; McIntosh & Goodman, 2016).

Finally, the integration of academic and behavior support efforts may lead to more efficient use of resources (Eagle et al., 2015; Preston et al., 2016). By combining and displaying how RTI and SWBPS initiatives address interrelated challenges as opposed to competing initiatives, a strong case can be made for funding and sustaining an integrated RTI and SWBPS models under MTSS (McIntosh & Goodman, 2016). This is opposed to proposing RTI and SWBPS and separate initiatives, which may seem like a daunting and costly undertaking to educators. Therefore, by integrating RTI and SWBPS under MTSS, resources will be allocated more effectively, time managed more efficiently, concepts will be better understood, and cost to schools will be minimized. Each of these assumptions led to MTSS gaining popularity among educators and educational scholars as a powerful model for best-assisting children socially, emotionally, behaviorally, and academically.

Conclusion

MTSS has its foundations in early school psychology practice and the problem-solving model proposed by Lightner Witmer in 1896. Witmer developed the problem-solving model after his experiences as a teacher and noting that although some of his students appeared capable and motivated remained unable to learn course content. Despite the basic components of MTSS being proposed by Witmer in the late 1800s, the preventative practice model was not fully embraced until the signing of the ESSA in 2015. MTSS is viewed by educators, scholars, and policymakers as a framework for preventing learning, behavior, and social-emotional difficulties early on as opposed to letting the child fail before receiving help for their deficits. MTSS "houses" three-tiered intervention service delivery models which seek to prevent children from experiencing learning and behavioral difficulties in school and in life. These intervention service delivery models seek to help students by providing them evidence-based interventions and supports in the areas of learning, behavior, mental health, and suicide prevention and intervention. To determine whether children are responding to the supports provided in these intervention service delivery models, data are frequently collected, and progress is monitored.

The idea of systemically providing children increasing levels of intervention and supports to remediate their deficits is similar to that of the public health model. Under the public health model, individuals who do not respond to interventions provided receive increasing levels of interventions and supports in hopes of ameliorating their illness and disease early on. Intervention service delivery models operate in a similar fashion in providing students with learning, behavior, or social-emotional challenges increasing levels of support in hopes of remediating their deficits before they lead to special education placement. Understanding the history of where MTSS and intervention service delivery models come from forms the foundation of the MTSS "house."

Discussion Questions

1. How do you think Lightmer Witmer's early career as an English and history teacher influenced his development of the problem-solving process and the profession of school psychology?
2. Do you believe that there was a need to move away from using the severe discrepancy model? Why or why not?
3. As a future educator, how does it make you feel knowing that it took nearly 30 years to endorse RTI over the severe discrepancy model?
4. Do you think academic achievement deficits influence the way a child behaves or feels about themselves? Why or why not?

Components of MTSS

Learning Objectives

After reading this chapter, you should be able to:

- Identify the four pillars of Multi-Tiered Systems of Support.
- Describe the three tiers of varying levels of evidence-based supports.
- Define universal screening.
- Explain progress monitoring.
- Discuss the importance of data-based decision-making.

The Four Pillars of MTSS

Although MTSS is now a common term used in schools today, it was not always a buzzword known to educators. One of the earliest known uses of the term "multi-tiered systems of support" came out of the state of Kansas in 2008 as an effort to reduce confusion over initiatives to shift from standard response to intervention (RTI) to school-wide RTI (Kansas Technical Assistance Network, 2012; Pullen, van Dijk, Gonsalves, Lane, & Ashworth, 2018). Since then, the term has evolved to encompass a model that "houses" two or more intervention service delivery models or "systems," such as RTI and school-wide positive behavior support (SWPBS). As mentioned in the previous chapter, the evolution of MTSS encompassing two or more intervention service delivery models was due to a growing recognition that critical components of response to intervention and SWPBS often mirrored and complemented one another (Freeman, Miller, & Newcomer, 2015). Such mirroring provided an outlet for initial efforts to merge common elements of RTI and SWPBS under MTSS (Eagle, Dowd-Eagle, Snyder, & Holtzman, 2015). Another reason for joining intervention service delivery models under MTSS is that a growing body of research suggests that integrated approaches under MTSS are associated with greater improvements in both academic and behavioral outcomes (Eagle et al., 2015; Stewart, Benner, Martella, & Marchand-Martella, 2007).

Intervention service delivery models, such as RTI and SWPBS, easily integrate and align under MTSS by sharing the four common components or "pillars." These four pillars comprise the framework of building an effective MTSS "house" and include (1) varying levels of preventative evidence-based supports; (2) universal screening; (3) progress monitoring; and (4) data-based decision-making (Freeman et al., 2015; Harn, Basaraba, Chard, & Fritz, 2015; National Association of School Psychologists, 2016). Descriptions of the four pillars that form the framework of the MTSS "house" can be found below.

Pillar 1: Varying Levels of Evidence-Based Supports

Like the three-tiered pyramid found in the public health model, the first critical element to building an effective MTSS "house" includes varying levels of evidence-based supports and instructional practices. Through varying levels of evidence-based supports and instructional practices, students are assigned to tiers (e.g., Tier 1, Tier 2, and Tier 3) that increase in intensity and duration based on their lack of responsiveness to interventions at a prior level (Schaffer, 2017). Typically, evidence-based supports and instructional practices are delivered in the form of interventions and programs.

As mentioned in chapter 1, **evidence-based interventions** consist of treatments or supports that have been peer-reviewed and demonstrate empirical support for effectiveness (D'Amato et al., 2011; King & Coughlin, 2016). Similarly, **evidence-based programs** have demonstrated empirical support but consist of many interventions, tend to be standardized, and are often sold commercially. An example of an evidence-based intervention would be using flash cards to help students with sight word recognition. An example of an evidence-based program would be using Road to the Code to teach early literacy skills. Evidence-based interventions and programs are used to varying degrees of intensity across the three tiers. The least intense interventions and programs are implemented at Tier 1, and the most intense interventions and programs are implemented at Tier 3 (Wexler, 2017). The following paragraphs briefly outline the varying levels of evidence-based supports across all intervention service delivery models that fall under MTSS.

Tier 1, or universal supports, refer to interventions and services that are available to all students across the academic, behavioral, or social-emotional domains (Gresham, Reschly, & Shinn, 2010; Harn et al., 2015; National Association of School Psychologists, 2016). Therefore, Tier 1 refers to the core curriculum and interventions delivered to all students and has a high likelihood of bringing most students to acceptable levels of proficiency (Averill & Rinaldi, 2011). Examples of Tier 1 supports include implementation of the core literacy curriculum, teaching and defining school rules and expectations, and employing a classroom-wide mental wellness program. Approximately 80%–85% of students are expected to respond to interventions at the Tier 1 level (Gresham et al., 2010; Harn et al., 2015; Wexler, 2017).

Tier 2, or targeted supports, is made available to some students who need additional interventions to assist them in overcoming their academic, behavioral, or social-emotional deficits (Wexler, 2017). Tier 2 services supplement core instruction and provide students with more time and opportunities to practice the skills they are struggling with (Wexler, 2017). Interventions and supports at Tier 2 are designed to require low effort from school personnel and tend to be structured around standardized protocol or prescribed curricula (Drevon, Hixson, Wyse, & Rigney, 2018; Joyce-Beaulieu & Sulkowski, 2020). At Tier 2, children tend to receive interventions and programs through push-in or pull-out groups (Schaffer, 2017). **Push-in group intervention** refers to small group instruction that occurs in the child's classroom, while **pull-out**

group intervention refers to group support that is provided outside the student's classroom (Simonsen, Britton, & Young, 2010). Both push-in and pull-out groups at Tier 2 supplement the core learning and behavioral curriculum. According to Kilanowski (2010), supplemental instruction involves delivering instruction to students outside of the core curriculum and features standard protocol interventions or programs. Therefore, supplemental interventions at Tier 2 are provided in addition to core Tier 1 instruction.

As mentioned, supplemental instruction at Tier 2 tends to involve the use of standard protocol interventions and programs (Kilanowski, 2010). **Standard protocol interventions and programs** provide educators standardized and readily available supports to address the most common weaknesses experienced by students (King & Coughlin, 2016). An example of a standard protocol program at Tier 2 would be Great Leaps for developing reading fluency in children or First Step to Success to assist at-risk children in meeting behavior expectations. Pending on the intervention service delivery model being implemented, typically three to eight children are placed in a group and receive services three to five times a week for thirty to forty-five minutes. Interventions and supports at this tier may include small group reading intervention, small group counseling, or behavior skills training (Harn et al., 2015; National Association of School Psychologists, 2016). Approximately 10%–15% of students receive Tier 2 interventions or services (Gresham et al., 2010; Wexler, 2017).

Finally, Tier 3, or tertiary interventions, are designed for 1%–5% of students with severe or chronic deficits that are beyond the capacity of Tier 1 or Tier 2 intervention efforts (Sugai & Horner, 2008; Wexler, 2017). Like Tier 2, Tier 3 is designed to supplement Tier 1 instruction and supports. However, unlike Tier 2, Tier 3 interventions and supports are only delivered through pull-out services and instruction. Therefore, Tier 3 interventions and supports are more intense and rigorous than those provided at Tier 1 or Tier 2 (Shinn & Walker, 2010; Wexler, 2017). Due to the intensity and individualization of interventions at Tier 3, supports are generally delivered to students through a problem-solving approach as opposed to the standard protocol method used at Tier 1 and Tier 2 (King & Coughlin, 2016). The problem-solving method utilizes specific and individually designed assistance to meet student's needs (King & Coughlin, 2016). For example, through the problem-solving method, although two students may be showing the same behavioral deficits, they may react differently to the interventions and supports provided. Therefore, each student may need their own specific set of interventions to assist them in remediating their unique challenges. Examples of Tier 3 interventions and services may include individualized instruction, FBA/BIP development, or one-to-one intensive counseling.

Traditionally, varying levels of preventative evidence-based supports and interventions within intervention service delivery models have been viewed as a three-tiered right-side-up triangle. However, a better understanding for how they operate may be to turn the triangle upside down and view them flowing from least to most intense interventions (see Figure 2.1). Such a view may be familiar to educators and in line with least restrictive environment as the upside-down triangle follows a continuum of services from least to most intense interventions. Additionally, a better understanding of how intervention service delivery models operate may be provided by turning the triangle upside down as they can be viewed as a funnel providing most children Tier 1 support, some children Tier 2 support, and very few children Tier 3 support (see Figure 2.2). Figure 2.3 shows the foundation of MTSS, and the first pillar in constructing the MTSS "house."

FIGURE 2.1 ● Turning the Triangle Upside Down

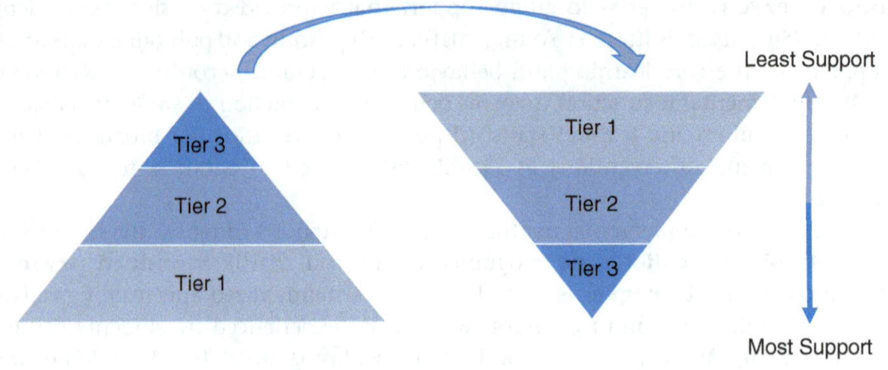

FIGURE 2.2 ● Viewing Intervention Service Delivery Models as a Funnel

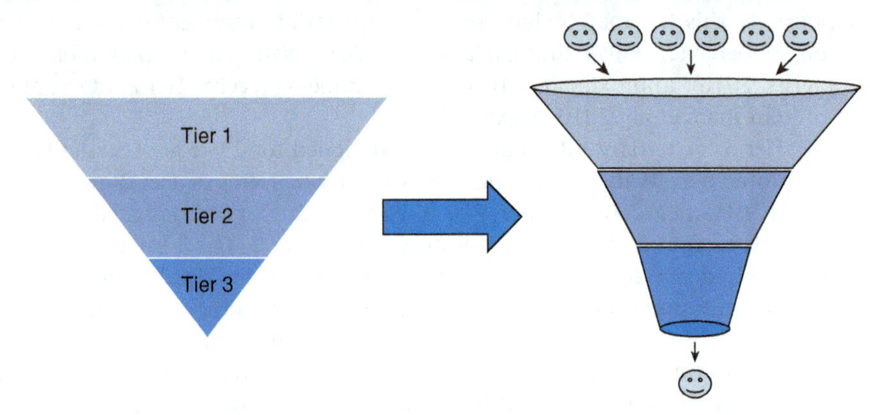

FIGURE 2.3 ● The Foundation to Constructing the MTSS "House" and Pillar 1

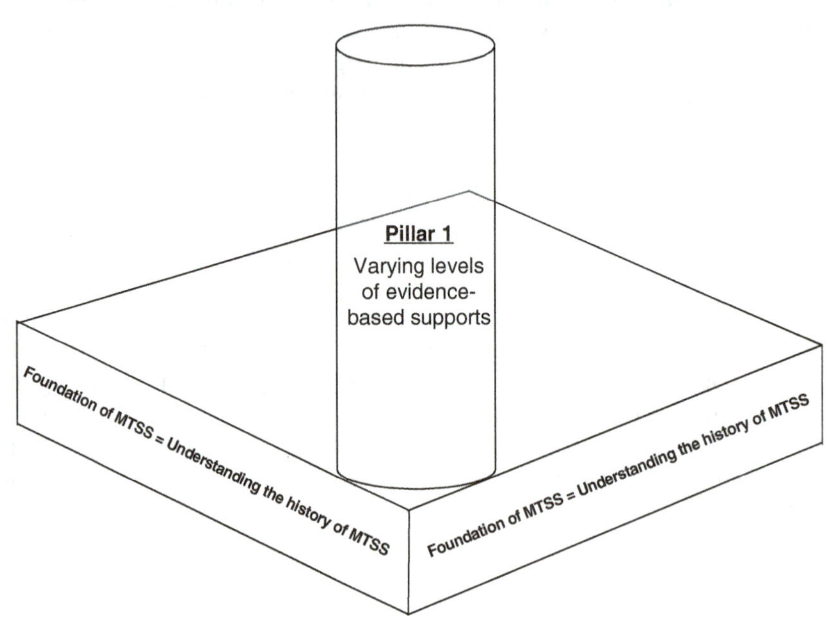

Pillar 2: Universal Screening

A second critical component, or "pillar," in facilitating an effective MTSS framework involves the use of **universal screening**. Similar to the fields of medicine and public health, universal screeners provide a quick and cost-efficient method for identifying students who may require additional interventions or supports (Pentimonti, Walker, & Edmonds, 2017). Universal screening involves the brief systemic assessment of the school population to determine children who are not responding to Tier 1 interventions and is the first step in identifying children at-risk for academic, behavioral, or social-emotional deficits (National Association of School Psychologists, 2016; Pentimonti et al., 2017). Universal screening the entire school population typically takes place in the fall, winter, and spring of each school year and is known as benchmarking (Jenkins, Hudson, & Johnson, 2007; Pentimonti et al., 2017). It is important to consistently administer universal screeners at predetermined times because some students may perform within the typical range at the start of the school year but struggle and fall into the at-risk range as the year progresses (Pentimonti et al., 2017).

Several features define universal screeners. First, universal screeners tend to be curriculum-based measures. **Curriculum-based measures (CBM)** are measures that are used by educators to quickly determine the level and rate of performance in acquiring necessary skills or content knowledge (Van Norman & Christ, 2016). CBMs are extremely sensitive to systemic change in student learning and provide ongoing insight as to whether the student is meeting basic grade-level expectations (Schaffer, 2017; Van Norman & Christ, 2016).

Second, measures used for universal screening should be selected to target skills appropriate to the grade level and be indicative of overall functioning in the area they are measuring, such as reading fluency (Arden & Pentimonti, 2017; Pentimonti et al., 2017). In other words, universal screeners should be aligned to the curriculum and measure the basic skills of what educators want students to know given that curriculum. Therefore, educators should administer universal screeners that are relevant in the area and grade levels taught. For example, a school should not have teachers administer a universal screener in early reading skills, such as letter-naming, to eighth-grade students who have more than mastered the skill. Likewise, a school should not have teachers administer universal screeners to students that are too advanced for their grade level, such as screening kindergarteners in comprehension before they can identify all the letters of the alphabet.

The third feature of universal screeners is that they are quick to administer and efficient to score (Pentimonti et al., 2017). Typically, administration time for most universal screeners is under ten minutes and rarely exceeds fifteen minutes (Schaffer, 2017). Universal screeners are designed to be quick to administer and score to make them less costly to districts compared to more comprehensive measures.

The fourth characteristic of universal screeners is that they must be valid and reliable tools that are extremely sensitive to measuring small degrees of change or growth in student performance (Pentimonti et al., 2017; Schaffer, 2017). In other words, universal screeners should be psychometrically sound and measure what they are designed to assess. Additionally, universal screeners should demonstrate that they are reliable measures through consistently showing their effectiveness for measuring minute learning and behavioral outcomes.

A final feature of universal screeners is that they allow for comparison to **national and local norms** (Pentimonti et al., 2017; Schaffer, 2017). To elaborate, universal screeners should enable users to compare student performance to children of the same age across the nation to determine whether they are meeting expectations (Schaffer, 2017). Additionally, if a district does not want to compare a student to national norms, they can compare the youth to how the student is performing on the universal screener to other students of the same age in the district by developing local norms.

Aside from the characteristics of universal screeners, such measures serve three primary purposes. As previously discussed, the first purpose of universal screening is to detect deficits early on to provide children timely and effective evidence-based interventions to overcome areas of concern. The second purpose is to provide data on the effectiveness of the core curriculum and whether students are responding appropriately to the curriculum put into place. The final purpose of universal screening is to reveal whether a core program is being delivered effectively by instructors.

Universal screening may be able to provide insight on the effectiveness of the core curriculum by showing whether a Tier 1 program is meeting the needs of students. For example, a district has selected Harcourt as a Tier 1 reading program to teach children in first-grade reading comprehension. However, after fall and winter universal screening, the district notices that 70% of its students continue to fall in the at-risk range in reading comprehension. Consequently, the district reconsiders whether Harcourt is an effective Tier 1 program for teaching its students in the area of reading comprehension. It has generally been recommended that if more than 20%–30% of students are found to be at-risk during fall, winter, or spring benchmarking, that core instructional practices at Tier 1 may need strengthening (Arden & Pentimonti, 2017; Bartholomew & De Jong, 2017).

As mentioned, aside from indicating whether a program is effective at meeting the needs of students, universal screening may reveal whether a core program is being delivered effectively by teachers. For instance, within a school district, universal screening results show that most students are responding as expected to Harcourt reading instruction. However, further evaluation reveals that one classroom across the district has 60% of its students being deemed at-risk for reading comprehension deficits. As a result, educators may question whether the program is being implemented effectively and as outlined. When evaluating universal screening results, Pentimonti et al. (2017) suggest educators ask several questions of which include:

- Do most students appear to be benefiting from the core program as indicated by universal screening?
- What percentage of students require additional intervention beyond the Tier 1 supports being provided?
- Have the universal screening numbers changed from one benchmarking period to the next (e.g., winter to spring)?
- If students appear to not benefit from the core program as indicated by universal screening results, what factors may be contributing to the ineffectiveness of the program (e.g., core program is not a good fit for students' needs, core program is too difficult for teachers to implement with fidelity, instructors failing to understand or lacking training in how to utilize the program)?
- Is the universal screening measure a valid and reliable tool in the area it is assessing students in? In other words, does the universal screener measure what it is designed to measure, and has the universal screener demonstrated in the scholarly literature that it is a trustworthy assessment of the construct it is measuring?
- Are those administering the universal screener properly trained and comfortable in using it?

Aside from all these questions, it is important for educators to understand that no single measure, whether used for universal screening or progress monitoring, is currently comprehensive enough to examine students for all areas of educational risk. Nonetheless, screeners have been or are being developed to identify the academic, behavioral, and social-emotional needs of students. Examples of some of these measures include Aimsweb's Reading CBM,

Behavior and Emotional Screening System (BESS), Devereux Student Strengths Assessment-Mini (DESSA-Mini), and Systemic Screening for Behavior Disorders (SSBD) (Schaffer, 2017). Figure 2.4 shows the second pillar needed to build the MTSS "house."

FIGURE 2.4 • The Second Pillar Needed to Construct the MTSS "House"

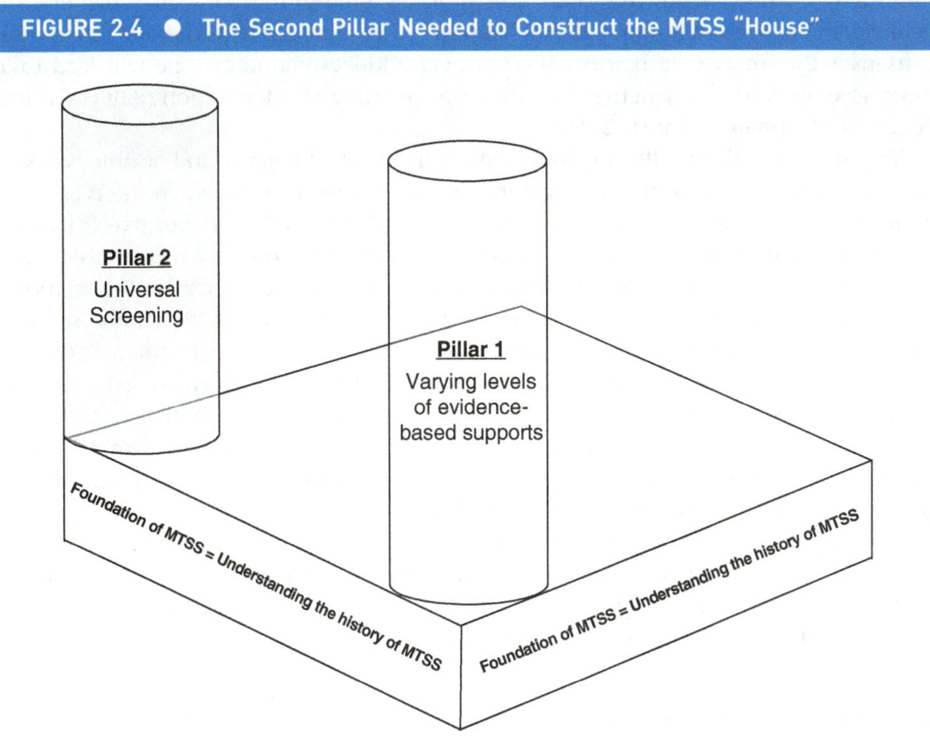

Pillar 3: Progress Monitoring

Another feature of an effective MTSS framework utilizes **progress monitoring**. Progress monitoring involves the repeated assessment of skills and strategies learned to determine whether a child is responding to the interventions and services being provided (Shapiro, 2013). Progress monitoring takes place at Tier 2 and Tier 3 of MTSS. Several features characterize measures used for progress monitoring. First, progress monitoring, measures should be brief, valid, and reliable (Pentimonti et al., 2017). Next, assessments used for progress monitoring should be administered at regular intervals (Pentimonti et al., 2017). For example, at the Tier 2 level, progress monitoring tends to occur on a weekly or biweekly basis; while at the Tier 3 level, progress monitoring tends to occur on a weekly basis (Christ, Zopluoglu, Monaghen, & Van Norman, 2013; Pentimonti et al., 2017; Shapiro, 2013). A final characteristic of progress monitoring tools is that the data collected from them can be used to inform instructional decisions on whether the interventions being provided are working. For example, through collecting progress monitoring data over time, teachers can graph a student's performance and calculate the growth the student has made in response to the interventions being provided. Additionally, educators can determine whether the student is on track toward remediating their learning or behavioral deficits or whether the child is in need of another intervention or more intense support.

To best determine whether students are making enough progress, there has been a general call by scholars to collect at least 12–14 weeks of data for measures of academic progress, such as Aimsweb's Reading CBM or easyCBM Reading (Ardoin & Christ, 2009;

Ball & Christ, 2012; Shapiro, 2013; Van Norman & Christ, 2016). This recommendation would mean that for a student who is receiving intensive supports at Tier 3 level and being progress monitored on a weekly basis, 12 to 14 data points should be collected before a decision can be made as to whether the interventions provided are working. Although the time period for collecting progress monitoring data on screeners for behavioral and social-emotional deficits appears to be less stringent, there tends to be a consensus that more data points collected over a longer period of time will lead to a more accurate read as to whether the child is responding to intervention (Ball & Christ, 2012; Van Norman & Christ, 2016).

The ongoing call for collecting more data points over a longer period of time is based on findings that progress monitoring outcomes are highly unstable when interventions occur over periods of less than two months (Ball & Christ, 2012; Van Norman & Christ, 2016). Over a shorter period of time, progress monitoring tools may be unstable measures of a student's response to intervention because they are very sensitive to variations in performance attributed to examiner characteristics, delivery of directions, setting, and difficulty of content across measures (Ball & Christ, 2012; Van Norman & Christ, 2016). Due to these variables not being accounted for, the widely accepted belief that six to eight data points are enough to make an adequate decision of whether a student is responding to the supports provided is inaccurate. It is generally viewed that by collecting 12–14 weeks of data, a more stable read can be obtained on whether the student is truly responding to intervention (Shapiro, 2013). On the contrary, by failing to collect more data points over longer periods of time, students may prematurely be pulled from interventions they may have responded to or, even worse, the student could be quickly streamlined into receiving special education services (Van Norman & Christ, 2016). Figure 2.5 shows the third pillar needed to build the MTSS "house."

FIGURE 2.5 ● The Third Pillar Needed to Construct the MTSS "House"

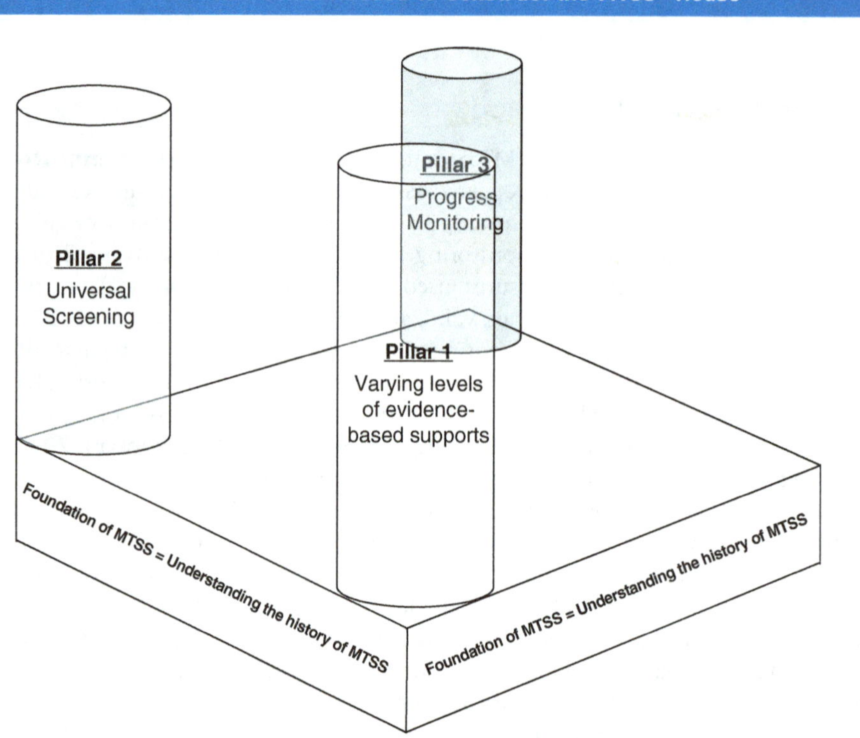

Pillar 4: Data-Based Decision-Making

Finally, the proper implementation of MTSS involves making effective data-driven decisions. Before delving into what data-based decision-making entails, it is important to understand what data are in an educational context. Lai and Schildkamp (2013) defined educational data as information that is collected systemically and organized to represent some aspect of schooling. Data not only include information on assessment and student achievement but also encompasses both qualitative and quantitative data on the functioning of the school (Schildkamp, Poortman, Luyten, & Ebbeler, 2017). Some types of data collected by schools include input data (e.g., student background data), context data (e.g., information about the building or district), and process data (e.g., teacher interviews and classroom observations) (Schildkamp et al., 2017). Arguably, the most familiar type of data to educators is output data, such as student achievement data (Schildkamp et al., 2017).

In addition to the different types of data collected by school districts, data on school and district functioning and student achievement can be either formal or informal. Examples of formal data include curriculum-based measures, computer-adaptive tests, state exams, behavior rating scales, medical records, and student attendance data. Examples of informal data include classroom observations, teacher-developed assignments, tests, student work samples, teacher reports, school projects, staff interviews, district-developed staff questionnaires, and parent feedback. Each of these sources of data may play varying levels of importance in making data-based decisions at the district, school, class, and student levels.

Data-based decision-making refers to the continual process of collecting and interpreting data to alter and improve instructional and behavioral practices to best benefit learners (Prenger & Schildkamp, 2018). The term "decision" in data-based decision-making indicates that a variety of actions can be undertaken on the basis of data, such as adapting instruction and curriculum, setting goals, evaluating the effectiveness of programs and interventions, improving policy, and reallocating time, funds, and resources (van Geel, Keuning, Visscher, & Fox, 2016). Modern-day data-based decision-making in education can be attributed to an approach pioneered by Deno and Mirkin in 1977 called data-based program modification (DBPM) (Espin, Wayman, Deno, & McMaster, 2017). In DBPM, data-based systemic procedures were used to evaluate the effectiveness of interventions for students experiencing difficulties in school (Espin et al., 2017). Similar to Witmer's problem-solving process outlined in chapter one, DBPM assumed that interventions designed to assist students are "hypotheses" that need to be "empirically tested" before a decision could be made about whether they were effective (Espin et al., 2017). For comparison, recall that Witmer's original proposal called for the development of "hypotheses" concerning appropriate intervention. Additionally, Witmer's proposed evaluating the intervention or "hypothesis" to establish an evidence-base as to whether it was effective at remediating the child's area of deficit.

Since 1977, the importance of data-based decision-making being incorporated into everyday educational decisions and instructional practices has been increasingly highlighted by educational law and policy. More and more data are being used to evaluate district and school performance, teacher effectiveness, instructional methodology, and student achievement. With so much pressure and accountability being placed on data, educators have become wary, defensive, and exasperated by mere mention of the word—"data." However, the use of data has numerous and profound benefits for educators and students. At the district and school level, data can be used to determine if yearly improvement goals are being met in the areas of academics, behavior, and attendance based on student learning results from state tests, universal screening data, discipline data, and school attendance records. Additionally, data can be used to determine if core programs are effective at meeting state learning standards. For example, after using the core math program TouchMath, a district notes that 80% of students are meeting expectations during winter benchmarking, and first quarter student report cards further bolster universal screening results in that most students are responding to the curriculum.

At the classroom level, data allow educators to prioritize their time to target areas most needed (Hamilton et al., 2009; Schildkamp et al., 2017). For example, after reviewing universal screening results from the school psychologist and evaluating student performance on a recent quiz, a teacher may realize that a number of her students are still performing in the at-risk range on single-digit addition. Therefore, the teacher may decide to spend additional time re-teaching critical components to single-digit addition as opposed to moving onto double-digit addition. Additionally, teachers may use data, such as student interviews, homework, classroom observations, and in-class assignments, to improve their instruction, set learning goals, pace their lessons, differentiate instruction, and provide individual students and the class feedback on their learning progress (Prenger & Schildkamp, 2018; Schildkamp et al., 2017).

Finally, at the student level, data can be used to identify student strengths, weaknesses, and provide student feedback. This student feedback is critical to advancing the understanding of concepts taught, providing focus on areas of improvement, and differentiating instruction to meet learner's needs. For example, a teacher may write comments and correct errors on a student's research report or write down an example of how to correctly solve a problem on a child's homework. Additionally, progress monitoring data may provide insight on whether a student is responding to interventions being implemented or whether a change in supports is needed.

Data and data-based decision-making are critical in building and maintaining the overall quality of education. In regards to MTSS and interventions service delivery models, both formal and informal data play a significant role and support one another in determining whether a student is in need of more support or whether an intervention being provided is effective. Typically leading data-based decisions in the context of MTSS and movement of students to higher or lower levels of support in three-tier intervention service delivery models is the utilization of curriculum-based measures. Supplementing the formal data of curriculum-based measures may be informal data such as student work samples, discipline reports, nurse office visits for somatic complaints, and teacher report.

For example, after universally screening a class in mathematics, one student in the class was found to be at risk and in need of Tier 2 targeted intervention in hopes of remediating her math deficits. Before recommending the student to Tier 2, the school's child study team holds a meeting with the student's teacher to go over the results of the student's universal screening data and brainstorm possible interventions and supports available to the student. To further support the universal screening results, the teacher brings with him samples of the student's work on single-digit addition and subtraction, a recent quiz, and provides a verbal report. Each further bolsters why the student is in need of Tier 2 math support and which intervention may be best to remediate the child's deficits. Therefore, in this case, the student's informal data further add to the universal screening data that this student is in need of additional support.

On the contrary, in rare instances, formal universal screening data may identify a student at risk but informal data provided by the teacher may not support that the student is at risk and in need of Tier 2 intervention. In cases such as these, there are a number of factors that could be attributed to the student performing below expectations such as student motivation, whether the student was feeling well at the time screened, examiner characteristics, and delivery of directions (Ball & Christ, 2012). Therefore, both formal and informal data are vital in providing insight in moving students to higher or lower levels of support within intervention service delivery models. In the following chapters, discussions will be held on how to effectively use data to move students through the tiers of the four most common intervention service delivery models: RTI, SWPBS, social-emotional RTI, and suicide prevention and intervention. Figure 2.6 shows the fourth pillar needed to construct the MTSS "house."

FIGURE 2.6 ● The Fourth Pillar Needed to Construct the MTSS "House"

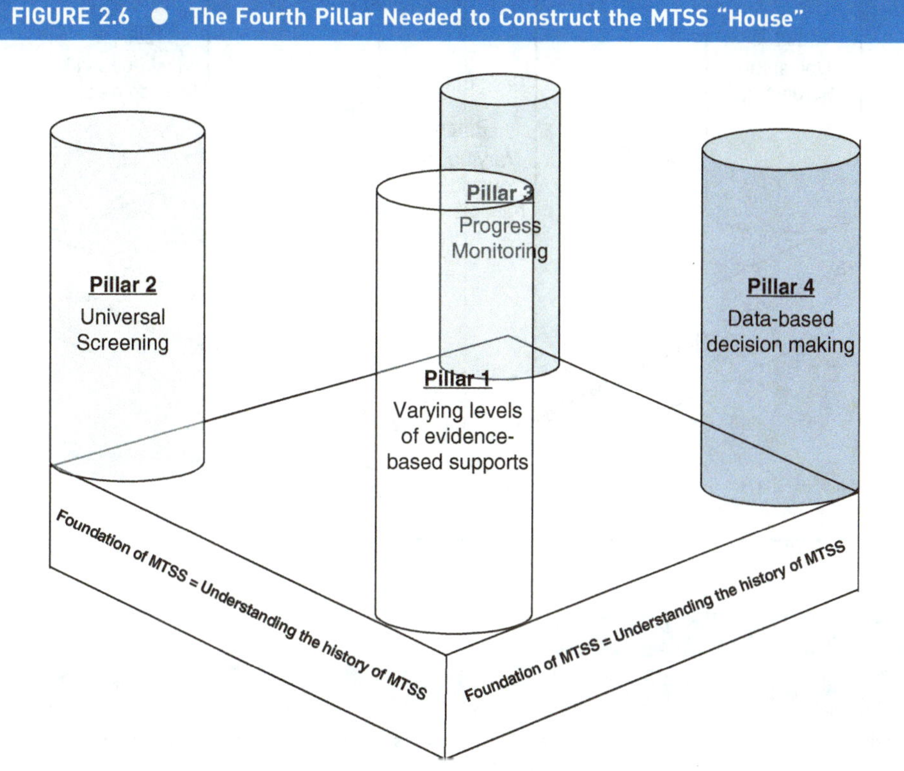

Conclusion

Understanding, outlining, and implementing the four "pillars" that link all intervention service delivery models is critical to building MTSS. Without each of the pillars being implemented accordingly across intervention service delivery models, a true MTSS framework is not able to be executed properly. Therefore, in order to link intervention service delivery models and align them under MTSS, it is vital that the four pillars of varying levels of preventative evidence-based supports and interventions, universal screening, progress monitoring, and data-based decision-making are put into place. Figure 2.7 shows all the pillars linked together to form the framework to the MTSS house. Table 2.1 provides a brief summary of all the pillars in the MTSS "house."

FIGURE 2.7 ● All the Pillars Linked Together to Form the Framework to the MTSS "House"

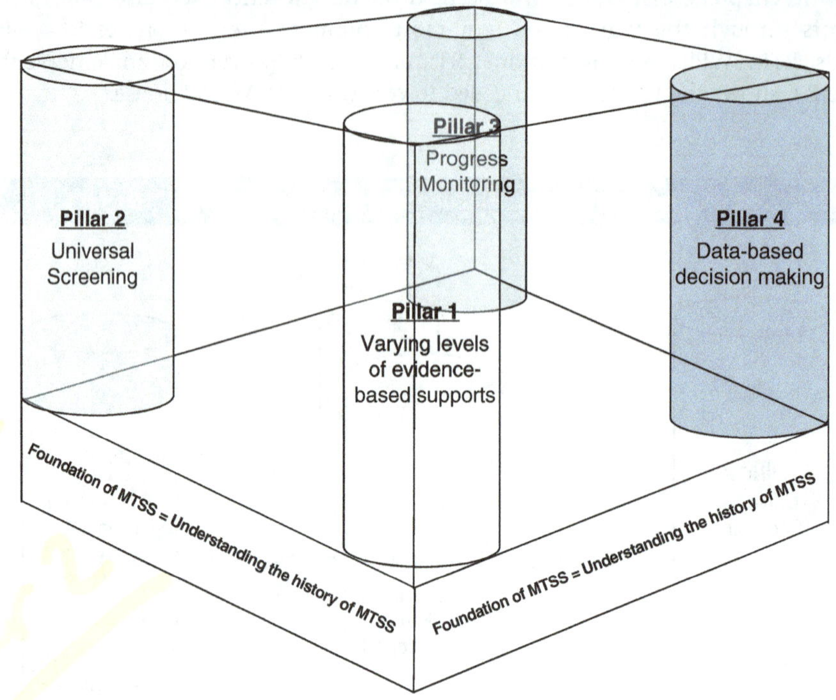

TABLE 2.1 ● Summary of the Four Pillars of MTSS

Four Pillars of MTSS	
• **Varying levels of preventative evidence-based supports and interventions** **Pillar 1** 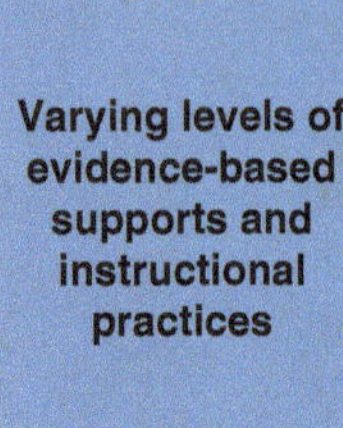 	***Levels of evidence-based supports and interventions within an intervention*** *service delivery model are based on student need and include the following:* • ***Universal Interventions (Tier 1):*** *80%–85% of children will respond to Tier 1 interventions that apply to ALL students and tend to be more generalized interventions and less specific (i.e., general class reading instruction, posting classroom rules, teaching mental wellness skills to all children, etc.).* • ***Targeted Interventions (Tier 2):*** *10%–15% of students will not respond to Tier 1 interventions and as a result may require more intensive supports under Tier 2. Tier 2 interventions tend to occur outside of core instruction time three to five times per week with groups of three to six children receiving more intense and explicit instruction (i.e., reading groups, behavior support groups, or social-emotional support groups). Group intervention time varies from 20 to 40 minutes.* • **Intensive Interventions (Tier 3):** 1%–5% of students will not respond to Tier 2 interventions and as a result may require tertiary support. Tier 3 interventions tend to occur outside core instruction in which the student is pulled from the classroom and receives 1:1 instruction in their area of deficit. Recommended tertiary intervention time is 45–60 minutes, five days per week.

Four Pillars of MTSS

- Universal Screening

Pillar 2

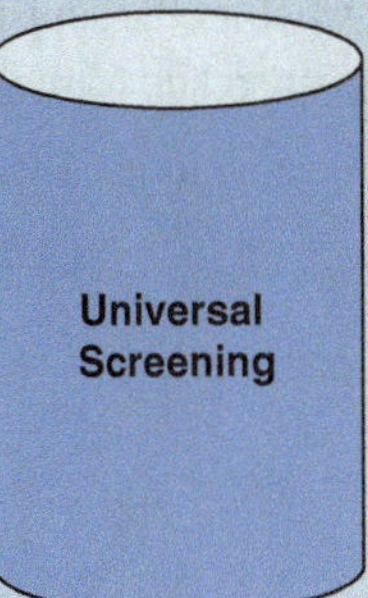

Universal screening is typically conducted three times per year and is used to identify or predict children who may be at risk for poor learning outcomes or developing social, emotional, or behavioral deficits. Universal screeners are typically brief (under eight minutes to administer) and completed by all students at a grade level to determine which students are at risk.

- Progress Monitoring

Pillar 3

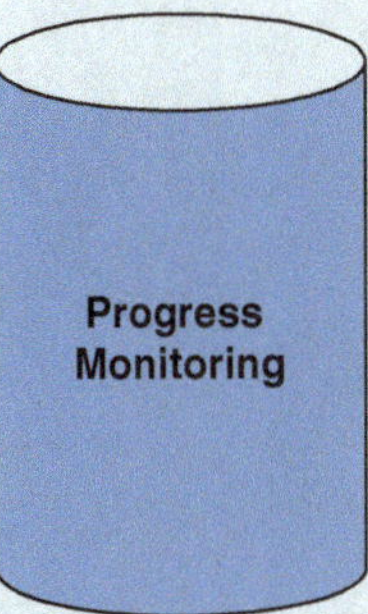

Progress monitoring provides an ongoing assessment to evaluate whether an at-risk student is benefiting from more intense levels of intervention (Tier 2 or Tier 3). At the Tier 2 level, progress monitoring should take place on a bimonthly basis or more. At Tier 3, progress monitoring should occur on a weekly to biweekly basis.

- Data-Based Decision-Making

Pillar 4

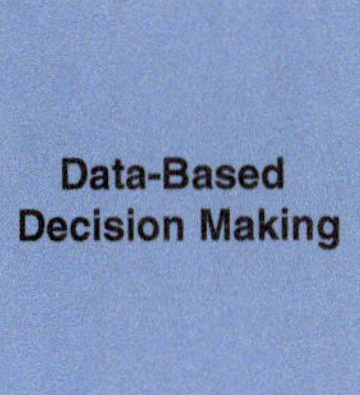

Data-Based Decision-Making entails the ongoing process of collecting and using screening, progress monitoring, and other forms of data (grades, office referrals, etc.) to make decisions about whether a student is benefiting from their instruction, movement to within a three-tiered intervention service delivery model, and disability determination. If the data indicate that a student is not responding to the interventions provided, a change in the supports and strategies used may be warranted or, after all interventions have been exhausted fail, a special education referral may be considered.

Discussion Questions

1. Why do you think it is important to have varying levels of evidence-based supports and interventions available to children?
2. Do you think universal screening is an effective method for identifying children who may need additional interventions or supports? Why or why not?
3. Why do you think it is important to compare student performance to national or local norms within a school district?
4. How can progress monitoring be used to inform instructional decisions on whether the supports being provided are helping struggling learners?
5. Why is it important for educators to make decisions based on data?

Response to Intervention

Learning Objectives

After reading this chapter, you should be able to:

- Define response to intervention (RTI).
- Differentiate between Tier 1, Tier 2, and Tier 3 of RTI.
- Argue the importance of instructing students across three tiers of intervention.
- Explain the importance of data collection and data-based decision-making under RTI.
- Identify the critical components of data-based decision-making.
- Summarize how to incorporate culturally responsive practices into RTI.

Background

In the previous chapters, the history of RTI and the differences between MTSS and intervention service delivery models were discussed. Additionally, an overview was provided of the four pillars that align and link all intervention service delivery models forming the framework of the MTSS house. If the four pillars that link intervention service delivery models form the framework of MTSS, intervention service delivery models form the four walls and include: response to intervention (RTI), school-wide positive behavior support (SWPBS), social-emotional RTI, and suicide prevention and intervention. In this chapter, a focus will be placed on describing one of the earliest intervention service delivery models and the first wall of the MTSS "house," namely, RTI.

The following chapters will cover the intervention service delivery models of SWPBS, social-emotional RTI, and suicide prevention and intervention. Accompanying the descriptions of the intervention service delivery models in each chapter of this book are flowcharts located in the appendices. These flowcharts show how models of intervention service delivery function as "systems" under MTSS. Recall that intervention service delivery models function as "systems" under MTSS as they provide educators a "systemic" outline for implementing supports, evaluating student progress, and making data-based decisions on student performance. Furthermore, readers in this chapter and in the following chapters will gain a further understanding of how the four pillars of multi-tiered systems of support are common across all intervention service delivery models. Finally, readers will be able to understand how the four intervention service delivery models and four pillars integrate and are housed under MTSS. Figure 3.1 shows how RTI forms one wall of the MTSS "house."

FIGURE 3.1 ● RTI Forming the First Wall of the MTSS "House"

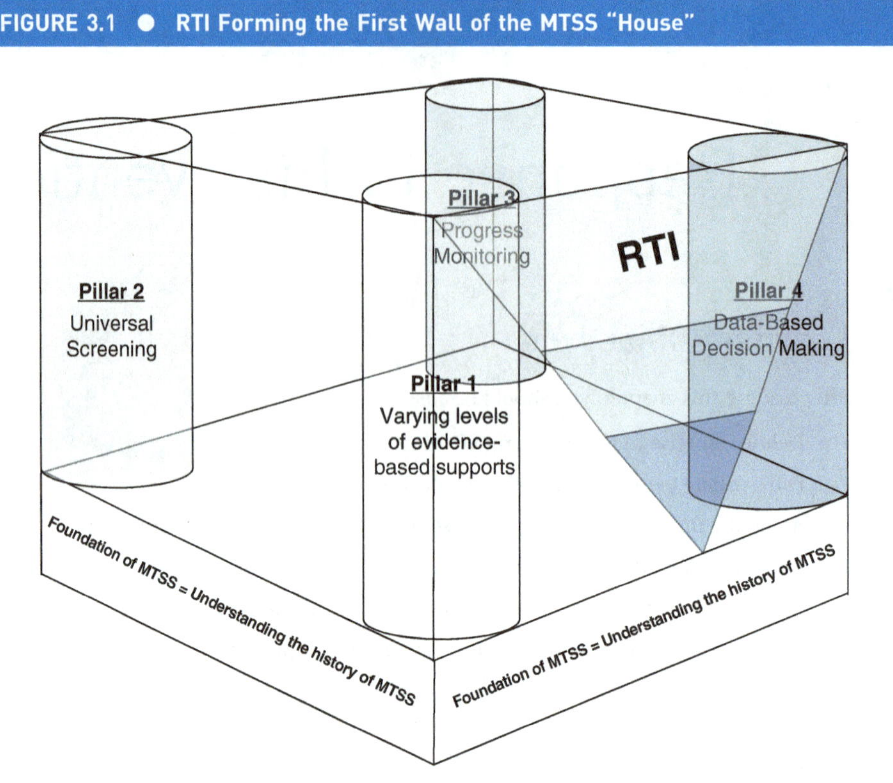

Introduction to Response to Intervention

Throughout their educational careers, many students experience difficulty in one area of academics or another. However, continued chronic failure and difficulty acquiring a specific set of skills despite receiving evidence-based instruction could be indicative of a child having a learning disability (Fuchs et al., 2015). Although continued chronic failure and difficulty acquiring a specific set of skills may be indicative of a learning disability, educators should consider other factors first as to why a child is struggling, such as an intervention being implemented incorrectly or the intervention not being a good fit for the child. These factors will be discussed in greater detail in chapter seven of this book. For now, readers should note that both children who need more repetition and practice and those with learning disabilities represent an extremely heterogeneous group of students. Academically, these children may have difficulty in the areas of reading, writing, and mathematics. Each of these areas can significantly hinder their understanding in classes that utilize these skills and in daily life, such as completing basic addition and subtraction in technology class, counting change at a grocery store, or filling out a job application.

Although children who need more repetition and practice show some of the same characteristics as those with learning disabilities, the signature characteristic of students with learning disabilities is severe low achievement despite receiving effective evidence-based instruction (Fuchs et al., 2015). Other characteristics of children with learning disabilities include problems with reasoning, memory, listening, social skills, self-esteem, telling right from left, and processing visual or auditory information (Fuchs et al., 2015). Luckily for many students with learning difficulties, their deficits can be remediated to prevent more severe consequences, such as disability placement, failing grades, and even school dropout. Due to the growing recognition that many students learning deficits can be remediated early on in their academic careers, RTI has grown in popularity.

The academic area most often targeted by schools that implement RTI revolves around early reading. Early reading is often targeted by schools because approximately 90% of all children identified as learning disabled are referred for special education due to reading difficulties (Heward, Alber-Morgan, & Konrad, 2017). Despite reading posing an area of difficulty for so many children, scholars and studies have generally found that approximately 80%–90% of students with reading challenges can overcome their deficits if they receive appropriate evidence-based instruction (Bock, 1998; Kilapatrick, 2015). With such promise for remediating reading deficits, RTI has expanded to assist students in other academic areas including mathematics and writing. Although RTI remains the most well-known intervention service delivery model, educators still struggle considerably in understanding what it is and how it differs from MTSS.

RTI is a triangular, three-tiered intervention service delivery model that is part of the general education curriculum and whose focus is on providing quality evidence-based instruction and remediating academic deficits for students having difficulty in reading, writing, or mathematics (Al Otaiba et al., 2019). RTI is based on the concept that all students should be ensured high-quality instruction and that universal screening, early identification, and evidenced-based interventions can reduce and prevent future learning delays (Al Otaiba et al., 2019; Gresham, MacMillan, Beebe-Frankenberger, & Bocian, 2010). Goals of RTI include bringing all students to proficiency, increasing the quality of general education programming and outcomes, avoiding the misclassification of students who have lapses in their knowledge as learning disabled, and ensuring that those students receiving special education services truly require that level of intensive academic support (Bohanon, Gilman, Parker, Arnell, & Sortino, 2016; Heward et al., 2017; Shinn, 2007). At present, RTI is implemented in every state across America, but models may vary considerably across states, districts, and schools (Al Otaiba et al., 2019; Little, Marrs, & Bogue, 2017). RTI's significant variability across states, districts, and schools may be due to educators being resistant to change, not receiving adequate training in RTI, not having enough resources to implement RTI properly, and lack of appropriate guidance from policymakers. Despite these shortcomings, RTI presents as a promising intervention service delivery model to identify struggling students early, provide them with evidence-based interventions, and monitor their response to the interventions being provided (Al Otaiba et al., 2019).

Description of Response to Intervention Tiers

Tier 1

Tier 1 of RTI is designed to deliver academic interventions and supports to all students in the general education classroom with approximately 80%–85% of students responding to the intervention (Forman & Selman, 2011; Wexler, 2017). Instruction at Tier 1 is evidence-based and less intensive than Tier 2 and Tier 3. Additionally, instruction at

Tier 1 is delivered to all students through the core curriculum and supplemental instruction (Bartholomew & De Jong, 2017). At this tier, instruction is differentiated to meet the needs of students who are performing as expected and those who may be having some difficulty with the core curriculum. **Differentiated instruction** refers to teachers tailoring the classroom environment, instructional practices, and teaching environments to create appropriately different learning experiences for students with different interests, needs, readiness, and learning profiles (Heward et al., 2017). For example, one way in which teachers may differentiate their instruction for all learners is through a tiered lesson. A tiered lesson involves the teacher breaking up students into three groups to work on follow-up activities or assignments at the basic, middle, and high difficulty levels after the teacher has presented the basic lesson to the whole class (Heward et al., 2017).

Within RTI, all students are universally screened during the typical benchmarking periods of fall, winter, and spring of each school year. Data from universal screening are used to plan for the instructional needs of all students and to decide if any students fall in the at-risk range. Students who are found to be in the at-risk range are generally referred to Tier 2. As mentioned earlier, if more than 20%–30% of students are found to be at-risk during fall, winter, or spring benchmarking, core instructional practices at Tier 1 may need strengthening (Arden & Pentimonti, 2017; Bartholomew & De Jong, 2017).

Tier 2

Tier 2 of RTI focuses on the 10%–15% of students who have been identified at-risk for not meeting proficiency at Tier 1 (Sugai & Horner, 2009; Wexler, 2017). Consequently, these students require supplemental instruction that is more rigorous and intense than Tier 1 instruction. Supplemental instruction involves delivering instruction to students outside of the core curriculum and features standard protocol interventions or programs (Kilanowski, 2010). Therefore, supplemental interventions at Tier 2 are provided in addition to core Tier 1 instruction. As mentioned in the previous chapter, standard protocol interventions and programs provide educators standardized and readily available supports to address the most common weaknesses experienced by students (King & Coughlin, 2016). An example of a standard protocol program at Tier 2 would be Great Leaps for developing reading fluency in children.

At Tier 2, supplemental instruction tends to involve either providing groups of 5–8 students push-in or pull-out supports (Harlacher, Sanford, & Nelson, 2014). As mentioned earlier push-in group intervention involves either the teacher or content specialist delivering interventions within the classroom to help a small group of students remediate their deficits in reading, writing, or mathematics (Harlacher et al., 2014; Kilanowski, 2010). For example, a math specialist may push into a second-grade classroom during the school day to provide supplemental math instruction using evidence-based interventions and programs. Push-out group intervention involves students leaving the general education classroom to receive supplemental instruction through a specialist or teacher. For instance, three kindergarten students may relocate to the reading specialist's room to receive supplemental instruction in letter-word identification.

The general time allotted for push-in or pull-out supplemental instruction is between 30 and 35 minutes for 3–5 times per week. The duration of interventions and programs being implemented at Tier 2 last between 8 and 15 weeks (Harlacher et al., 2014; Kilanowski, 2010). Finally, at Tier 2 of RTI, students are typically progress monitored on a biweekly or weekly basis with 12–14 weeks of data being recommended before it is recommended a child change intervention or be recommended to receive Tier 3 supports (Harlacher et al., 2014). Students who respond to Tier 2 interventions are moved back into Tier 1 and only provided core instruction. In the event where students do not respond to Tier 2 interventions, the school may either look into whether another Tier 2 intervention is available or recommend to Tier 3 interventions and supports. It is generally viewed that students who do not respond to intervention at Tier 2 are considered to have severe and long-standing deficits that cannot be remediated through Tier 2 interventions.

Tier 3

Finally, Tier 3 of RTI consists of 1%–5% of students (Shinn & Walker, 2010; Sugai & Horner, 2009). These students did not respond to Tier 2 interventions and have long-standing learning difficulties that exceed the capacity of Tier 1 or Tier 2 interventions (Shinn & Walker, 2010). In order to remediate these longstanding difficulties, Tier 3 focuses more explicit instruction that is highly structured and is delivered for 45–120 minutes every day (Harlacher et al., 2014). Interventions at Tier 3 are delivered in exceedingly small pull-out groups of one to three students by a content specialist or special education teacher (Harlacher et al., 2014). At Tier 3, it is recommended that interventions are delivered to students for a duration of over 20 weeks with progress monitoring occurring on a weekly or twice-weekly basis (Ardoin & Crist, 2009; Ball & Christ, 2012; Harlacher et al., 2014; Shapiro, 2013; Van Norman & Crist, 2016).

Like Tier 2, interventions provided Tier 3 are supplemental to Tier 1 core instruction. Therefore, students at Tier 3 receive their Tier 3 interventions and supports on top of their core Tier 1 supports. Unlike Tier 2, where interventions and programs tend to be standard protocol supports, supports at Tier 3 in RTI tend to utilize a problem-solving approach individualized to the student's specific area of deficit (see the previous chapter). Students who respond to Tier 3 interventions are moved back into Tier 1 and are subsequently only provided core Tier 1 instruction. In the event where students do not respond to Tier 3 interventions, the school may either look into whether another Tier 3 intervention is available or determine whether a referral to special education is needed. Table 3.1 summarizes the critical elements found in a three-tier RTI model.

TABLE 3.1 • Critical Elements Found in a Three-Tier RTI Model

Elements	Tier 1	Tier 2	Tier 3
Type of Instruction	Core Classroom Instruction	Targeted Small Group Instruction	Intense Individualized Instruction
Size of instructional group	Whole-class	5–8 students	1–3 Students
Instructional time	Per school schedule	30–45 minutes; 3–5 days a week	45–120 minutes; 5 days a week
Duration of intervention	All school year	8–15 weeks	20+ weeks
Instruction provided by	Teacher	Teacher or content specialist	Content specialist or special education teacher
Frequency of screening/ progress monitoring	3 times per year (Universal screening)	Biweekly or weekly (Progress monitoring)	Weekly or twice weekly (Progress monitoring)
Number of data points collected	3	12–14 (if collected on a weekly basis)	12–14 (if collected on a weekly basis)
Length of data collection	3 times throughout school year	12–14 weeks (at least)	12–14 weeks (at least)

Source: Adapted from Harlacher et al. (2014).

Data Collection and Data-Based Decision-Making Under RTI

As mentioned in the previous chapter, when evaluating data to inform instructional practices and determine whether children are meeting learning objectives, educators should consider data from both formal and informal measures. Under MTSS, two of the most important pieces of initial data that can be used to determine if students are meeting learning outcomes are universal screeners and progress monitoring measures. Through analysis of universal screening and progress monitoring data, decisions can be made to determine whether a child is responding to instruction or intervention, if the child is in need of a more intense levels of intervention, or whether a change in intervention approach or a referral to special education may be needed (Christ, Zopluoglu, Monaghen, & Van Norman, 2013; Prenger & Schildkamp, 2018).

When using universal screeners and progress monitoring tools to determine whether a child is in need of more intense levels of intervention or is meeting learning objectives, often educators utilize a predefined cut-point score. A **cut-point** score is a score that is used to determine whether a student is at-risk for poor academic and behavioral outcomes (Schaffer, 2017). For universal screening, students whose scores fall below the predefined cut-point typically receive more intensive intervention services at the Tier 2 level in addition to still receiving core instruction (Schaffer, 2017). Students whose scores fall at or above the cut-point receive only core Tier 1 instruction. For example, a district may determine that students falling below the 25th percentile on a universal screener to be considered at-risk for reading fluency deficits. Therefore, the district may recommend that any student falling below the 25th percentile receive more intensive Tier 2 supports to remediate their deficits in reading fluency.

Table 3.2 illustrates how a school district would utilize a cut-point score to determine second-grade students who are at-risk for reading fluency deficits. In the example, the district has decided to abide by the publisher's recommendation that students that fall below the 25th percentile are at-risk for reading fluency deficits compared to their same-age peers. Upon locating the 25th percentile column and moving to the next column over to the right, it is viewed that students reading below 35 words per minute fall below the cut-point. Consequently, these students can be considered in the at-risk range for needing more intensive supports in the area of reading fluency.

TABLE 3.2 ● Cut-Point for Words Read Correct (WRC) on Second-Grade Reading Fluency Universal Screener

Percentile	Words Read Correct
90	115
75	88
50	62
25	***35***
10	17

Once students are referred to more intense interventions at Tier 2 or Tier 3, a cut point may be used during progress monitoring to determine whether the student has demonstrated adequate RTI, whether to change interventions, or whether to move the student to more or less intensive services (Bernhardt & Hebert, 2017). Although the cut-point may be used to determine whether typical students are responding adequately to interventions at Tier 2 and Tier 3, a better and more individualized option is to calculate whether a child is making enough progress in closing the gap between current and expected performance using a student's weekly **rate of improvement (ROI)** or growth rate (Schaffer, 2017).

By calculating a student's individualized ROI, a determination can be made as to how slow or fast that particular student is responding to the interventions provided. In other words, a student's individual rate of improvement determines how much growth the student is making on a weekly basis toward achieving their goal and is used when national goals may be too ambitious for them to reach. For example, Table 3.3 shows that in order for a student who is reading an average of 88 words read correct at winter benchmark to meet the spring benchmark goal of 106 words read correct, they would have to have a rate of improvement 1.22 words per week at the 50th percentile. Although increasing 1.22 words per week to meet the national spring benchmark goal of 106 words read correct is expected for typically performing students, it may be too ambitious of a goal for students who are underperforming in reading fluency and need either Tier 2 or Tier 3 support. Therefore, an individual goal should be calculated.

TABLE 3.3 ● Rate of Improvement Needed to Meet Spring Grade 2 Benchmark for Oral Reading Fluency

Percentile	Winter Words Read Correct	Spring Words Read Correct	National Rate of Improvement
90	140	156	1.14
75	115	131	1.19
50	***88***	***106***	***1.22***
25	64	82	1.31
10	39	59	1.17

The formula for calculating an individual goal for a child involves noting the number of weeks left in a school year and multiplying them by the national rate of improvement at the 50th percentile (Shapiro, 2008). After obtaining the product from the aforementioned formula, add the child's benchmark or baseline score to obtain the child's individual goal. For example, if 36 weeks are left in a school year, a student's individual goal could be calculated by multiplying the 36 weeks left in the school year by the national AIMSweb ROI of 1.22 to obtain a product of 43.92 words read correct. After obtaining the product of 43.92 words read correct, add the student's fall benchmarking words read correct to 43.92. Therefore, if the student only read two words correct at fall benchmarking, add this number to 43.92. Consequently, the resulting total of 45.92 words read correct per minute yields the student's individualized end of the year goal (see Table 3.4 and Figure 3.2).

TABLE 3.4 ● Progress Monitoring Data

Student X Progress Monitoring Data: Oral Reading Fluency														
Date	*09/12*[a]	*09/19*	*09/26*	*10/02*	*10/09*	*10/16*	*10/23*	*10/30*	*11/07*	*11/14*	*11/21*	*11/28*	*12/04*	*12/11*
Corrects	2	0	1	1	1	2	2	3	3	3	4	3	5	5
Errors	4	6	5	5	6	8	8	8	10	13	13	12	11	14

[a]benchmark score.

FIGURE 3.2 ● Goal Calculation

22 (National ROI)
X 36 (Weeks left in school year)
43.92

43.92
\+ 2 (Fall benchmark score)
45.92 (Spring goal words read correctly)

In order to make appropriate data-based decisions and determine if students are responding to interventions, educators will need to know if at-risk students are making enough progress to meet their goals and catch up to their typically performing peers. To determine whether at-risk students are responding to interventions and on track to meeting their goals, an important step in data-based decision-making involves calculating an individual rate of improvement. Calculating a student's individualized rate of improvement involves subtracting the student's highest data point score from their lowest data point score and then dividing the difference in scores by the number of data points collected. After obtaining this quotient, multiply it by a standard deviation between 1.5 and 2.0. Given that at-risk students must catch up to their peers, the ROI that must be obtained for these students needs to be higher than their typically developing peers (Shapiro, 2008). By multiplying the quotient by a standard deviation between 1.5 and 2.0, an ambitious rate of improvement can be set for the student to determine if they can catch up to their peers.

In setting an ambitious rate of improvement using the tables above, Student X's highest data point of five would be subtracted from his lowest data point of 0, yielding a difference of five. Subsequently, the difference of five would be divided by the 14 data points collected, yielding a quotient of 0.357. In this case, the obtained quotient of 0.357 would then be multiplied by a standard deviation of 1.5 to obtain a product or average words the Student X is gaining per week, of 0.54. Therefore, in the example provided above, Student X is only gaining an average of 0.54 words per week. When compared to his typically developing peers' average words gained per week of 1.22, it is found that Student X is not making enough progress to catch up to his peers. Therefore, an important data-based decision must be made to either alter the interventions in place or recommend Student X to Tier 3 support. Figure 3.3 provides the steps needed to calculate an individual student's rate of improvement based on Student X's performance.

FIGURE 3.3 ● Rate of Improvement Calculation

Rate of Improvement Calculation

1) **Subtract the highest data point from the lowest data point**
   - **5 – 0 = 5**
     (Highest data point) – (Lowest data point)

2) **Divide answer from step 1 into the # of data points collected**
   - **5/14 = 0.357**

3) **Multiply your answer from step 2 by a standard deviation between 1.5 and 2.0 to obtain the words the child is gaining per week (preferably use the standard deviation at the 50th percentile).**
   - **0.357 x 1.5 = 0.54** (Gaining 0.54 words per week)

4) **Compare student to the average words per week students his/her age are making at the 50th percentile.**
   - **0.54** (Gaining 0.54 words per week; Average is 1.22 words per week = minimal progress being made)
   - **In this case, Student X is making minimal progress.**

5) **Determine whether to change intervention, refer to a higher tier, or refer to special education evaluation if the student is at Tier 3.**

Culturally Responsive Practices and RTI

Defining Culturally Responsive Practices

Within any intervention service delivery model under MTSS, such as RTI or SWPBS, incorporation of culturally responsive practices and instruction should be of prominent focus. While **culture** is defined as the customary beliefs, material traits, and social forms held by racial, religious, or social groups, **culturally responsive practices and instruction** is defined as a pedagogy that both empowers and recognizes that students are both similar to, but also uniquely different from, one another (Ford & Kea, 2009; Kieran & Anderson, 2019). Consequently, culturally responsive practices and instruction takes into account the diverse intellectual, social-emotional, ethnic, religious, language, customs, and beliefs of all learners to best ensure student success (Ford & Kea, 2009; Kieran & Anderson, 2019). Within culturally responsive practices and instruction, educators recognize that certain aspects of human identity, such as gender, race, socioeconomic status, and disability, interact and intersect with one another to shape the lived experiences through interlocking systems of bias and inequality (Carey, Yee, & DeMatthews, 2018).

Over the past 50 years, there has been growing recognition and emphasis placed on culturally responsive practices within education due to the growing diversity of students making up schools. For example, in 1972, 78% children attending school in the United States were predominantly white (Ford & Kea, 2009). By 2016, the number of public school students identifying as white decreased to 50%, while 25% of students identified as being Hispanic or Latino (National Center for Education Statistics, 2016). The remaining 25% of students comprising public schools include children who are Black, Native American, and Asian and Pacific Islander (National Center for Education Statistics, 2016). These trends of increasing ethnic diversity of students within the US public schools are projected to continue. Despite the increasing ethnic diversity of public schools in the United States, most staff interacting with students are white. For example, 86% of school psychologists, 82% of teachers, and 79% of school counselors are white (American School Counselors Association, 2020; Goforth et al., 2021; United States Department of Education, 2016).

Within schools, students with disabilities and children from ethnically diverse backgrounds traditionally have not received equal and equitable opportunities to succeed. These unequal and unequitable opportunities have left many of these children to disproportionality be retained, placed into special education, drop out of school, or obtain poor grades compared to their peers (Artiles, Bal, & King-Thorius, 2010; Kieran & Anderson, 2019; Sanford et al., 2020). However, RTI encompasses promising features, such as tiered systems of academic support and universal screening, to quickly identify and provide academic remediation to students in need rather than waiting for them to fail, receive inadequate support, and ultimately be placed into special education (Artiles et al., 2010; Sharma & Christ, 2017).

Under well-outlined RTI models, access and equitable distribution of resources, interventions, and curricula are critical to student success. Consequently, one of the goals of RTI is to prevent diverse learners from inappropriately being placed into special education (Artiles et al., 2010; Sharma & Christ, 2017). Inappropriate placement into special education might narrow diverse students' chances of future learning opportunities because disability identification is associated with higher school dropout rates, reduced access to higher education programs, and increased risk of compounding multiple marginalities, such as having a disability but also being Black (Artiles et al., 2010; Sharma & Christ, 2017). To incorporate culturally responsive practices and instruction into RTI, and MTSS as a whole, educators must develop six salient characteristics.

1. *Socialcultural consciousness:* Educators must understand that one's way of thinking, behavior, and being are influenced by race, socioeconomic status, language, and disability. Consequently, within RTI, educators must continuously engage in self-analysis and reflective thinking to examine their own sociocultural identity (Artiles et al., 2010; Sharma & Christ, 2017).

2. *An affirming attitude toward children from culturally different backgrounds:* Educators should inspect and confront negative attitudes they might have toward culturally diverse learners and students with disabilities (Artiles et al., 2010; Sharma & Christ, 2017).

3. *Commitment and skills to act as agents of change:* Educators should understand the change process and obstacles to change (Sharma & Christ, 2017). Therefore, educators must develop skills for collaboration and ways of dealing effectively with issues and problems with a basis in cultural and learning differences (Artiles et al., 2010; Sharma & Christ, 2017).

4. *Constructivist views of learning:* Educators should believe that all students and capable of learning and hold a high expectation for all students, regardless of their cultural or learning differences (Artiles et al., 2010).

5. *Learning about students:* Educators must take the time to learn about their students, their experiences, and their home lives and surrounding community and use this information in teaching, support services, learning, and assessment (Artiles et al., 2010).

6. *Culturally responsive teaching, support services, and counseling strategies:* Educators should help students learn and grow by building on students' cultural and learning strengths to create an inclusive school environment where each student feels a sense of empowerment, membership and value (Artiles et al., 2010; Sharma & Christ, 2017).

Incorporating Culturally Responsive Practices into RTI

Across each tier of RTI, educators can incorporate culturally responsive practices in many ways. First and foremost, educators should consider the instructional materials and assessments used to increase students' interest and proficiency in what they are being taught (Kieran & Anderson, 2019). For example, educators should note that many well-known booklists used by teachers and schools to select texts predominately suggest titles that depict white or animal characters and are often written by white or authors without disabilities (Sharma & Christ, 2017). Consequently, many of these texts may be unappealing to students from ethnically diverse backgrounds or who have a disability. Luckily, there are many other booklists available to help teachers select culturally relevant texts that have won awards, such as the Corretta Scott King Book Awards for texts written by Black authors and the Tomás Rivera Mexican Children's Book Award, for books that depict the experiences of Latino and Hispanic Americans (Sharma & Christ, 2017).

Outside of selecting culturally relevant materials within RTI, educators should consider how to place vocabulary and big ideas into context with relevant examples (Kieran & Anderson, 2019). For instance, in teaching a diverse group of seventh graders about reading poetry, this author introduced the lesson and key vocabulary by having students guess at whether a key term or quote was used by a poet, rock star, or hip-hop artist. For students who are English Language Learners, educators should be attuned to how complex terminology and words used outside of routine use may be confusing, difficult to recognize, and intimidating.

For example, Sanford et al. (2020) note that attainment of mathematics skills may be difficult for English Language Learners not because they do not have the ability to grasp the concepts being taught but often because they struggle with technical terms associated with mathematics. These technical terms might include symbolic language, such as zero or dollars, and polysemous vocabulary, such as the side of a cube versus the side of a rectangle. Consequently, these students may need early, explicit, and intense instruction to prevent the development of ineffective strategies that may lead to lifelong learning deficits in mathematics (Sanford et al., 2020).

In order to best assist culturally diverse students in taking an interest in the curriculum, educators need to carefully consider their students' interests, display empathy for learning differences, and create a safe space and time for children to ask questions. Educators should note that students from some cultural backgrounds may be very comfortable with raising their hands to participate in class and ask questions. On the contrary, those from other cultures may be reluctant to participate or ask questions due to believing that responding to the whole class is a form of showing off or asking a question is a form of weakness (Au, 2009). At Tier 2 and Tier 3 of RTI, students who are reluctant to participate or ask questions may feel increasing pressure due to supports being provided in a small group or individual format.

Finally, under culturally responsive practices and instruction, educators should utilize multiple measures to assess student progress beyond paper and pencil tasks (Kieran & Anderson, 2019). Teachers may best assess student progress utilizing traditional methods, such as exams, assignments, and homework, and non-traditional measures, such as curriculum-based measures, student observation, projects, presentations, and journaling (Kieran & Anderson, 2019). Ultimately, throughout each Tier of RTI, educators have an opportunity to remediate learning deficits, offer expansive opportunities to diverse learners, and provide culturally responsive teaching and support services.

Conclusion

RTI is an intervention service delivery model that helps to ensure all children receive differentiated high-quality instruction in the general education classroom through evidence-based interventions (Heward et al., 2017). The basic premise of RTI is that students who do not respond to Tier 1 core instruction increasingly receive more intense instruction to remediate learning difficulties early on before they become significant and long-standing academic deficits. Although RTI is not designed to be used specifically for the identification of learning disabilities and is more concerned with offering students quality evidence-based instruction, a child's failure to respond to intervention may suggest evidence of a disability in preventing adequate learning (Al Otaiba et al., 2019; Heward et al., 2017). Lack of response to an intervention may suggest evidence of a disability because RTI eliminates instructional quality as being a viable explanation for poor academic growth (Heward et al., 2017). In other words, RTI seeks to ensure that quality differentiated instruction is delivered to all students and that poor instructional practices are eliminated.

Educators should note that although a child's lack of response to an intervention may suggest evidence of a disability, other factors as to why the child is not responding to the intervention should be considered first, such as whether the intervention is being implemented as it is intended or whether the support in place is a good fit for the child. Lastly, when implementing RTI, educators should make sure to engage in culturally responsive teaching and supportive practices. Figure 3.4 displays a checklist for RTI and the systemic decisions to be made in regards to moving students throughout the RTI Tiers to provide quality differentiated instruction. Similarly, Appendix A displays a flow-chart of RTI. When viewing Appendix A, recall the discussion in Chapter 2 in that the traditional three-tier right-side-up triangle has been flipped upside down to resemble a funnel flowing from least intensive interventions and supports to most intense interventions and supports.

FIGURE 3.4 ● RTI Checklist

Tier 1
A *For all students:* ✓ Implement core curriculum ✓ Conduct universal screening by using curriculum-based measures like aimswebPlus and evaluate data ✓ **If student meets grade level standard, continue to implement the core curriculum at Tier 1A** ✓ **If student does not meet grade level standard (scores below 25th percentile on curriculum-based measure and/or not maintaining passing grades in subject area), proceed to Tier 1B**
B *For students who are not meeting grade level standard first attempt the following:* ✓ Differentiate and re-teach critical components of instruction ✓ Check attendance and medical status (hearing, vision, outside diagnosis) ✓ Consult with parents and provide them interventions to implement at home ✓ Track data for four to six weeks and document evidence-based interventions and instructional tactics used ✓ Meet with the child study team to evaluate data and determine whether Tier 2 interventions are needed ✓ **If student responds to interventions and makes adequate progress, return to Tier 1A** ✓ **If student does not make adequate progress or is not on grade level, provide the student Tier 2A interventions**

FIGURE 3.4 ● (Continued)

Tier 2
A *For students who have not responded to Tier 1:* ✓ Implement and monitor Tier 2 interventions (interventions should take place 3-5 times per week for 30–45 minutes) ✓ Collect at least 12–14 bi-weekly or weekly progress monitoring data points ✓ Use push-in or pull-out groups to implement interventions and supports ✓ Implement interventions and supports for 8–15 week cycles ✓ Continue with core curriculum (Tier 1) on top of Tier 2 interventions with adjustments to student's schedule ✓ Meet with the child study team to determine whether the student is responding to intervention(s) ✓ **For students who have made adequate progress in Tier 2, return to Tier 1A** ✓ **For students who have not made adequate progress, proceed to Tier 2B (If no alternative Tier 2 intervention is available, move to Tier 3A).**
B ✓ Implement and monitor another Tier 2 intervention in area of deficit if there is one available ✓ Collect 12–14 curriculum-based measure data points on a weekly or bi-weekly basis to determine whether the student is responding to the new Tier 2 intervention ✓ Meet with the child study team to evaluate data and determine whether Tier 3 interventions are needed ✓ **If student responds to interventions and makes adequate progress return to Tier 1A** ✓ **If student does not make adequate progress or is not on grade level, proceed to Tier 3A interventions**
Tier 3
A *For students who have not responded to Tier 2 supports:* ✓ Implement and monitor Tier 3 interventions for 45–120 minutes of instruction 5 times per week ✓ Collect at least 12–14 data points on a weekly basis ✓ Pull the student out of the classroom to provide interventions and supports ✓ Implement interventions and supports in 20+ week cycles ✓ Meet with child study team to evaluate data and determine whether the student is responding to intervention(s) ✓ **If student responds to interventions and makes adequate progress return to Tier 1A** ✓ **If student does not make adequate progress or is not on grade level, proceed to Tier 3B (If no alternative Tier 3 intervention is available, meet with CST to determine if a special education referral is needed)**
B ✓ Implement and monitor another Tier 3 intervention in area of deficit if there is one available ✓ Collect 12–14 curriculum-based measure data points on a weekly or bi-weekly basis to determine whether the student is responding to the new Tier 3 intervention ✓ Meet with the child study team to evaluate data and determine whether the student is responding to intervention(s) ✓ **If student responds to interventions and makes adequate progress, return to Tier 1A** ✓ **If student does not make adequate progress or is not on grade level, determine if a special education referral is needed**

CASE EXAMPLE

RESPONSE TO INTERVENTION

Child Background

Habib Abbar is a second-grader at Dundas Middle School in Dayton, Ohio. He currently resides with his parents, Karima and Akbar, and older brother, Korbin. The primary language spoken in the home is Arabic. Mrs. Abbar is employed as an accountant, and Mr. Abbar works as a banking executive.

Per parent report, Habib was born one month premature and at birth was jaundiced. Consequently, he received light therapy and remained in the hospital for one-week. No other complications during pregnancy, delivery, or birth were noted. Developmental milestones were reported to be reached within expected limits with Habib sitting up at six months, walking and talking at 13 months, and speaking short sentences at two years. Habib's parents indicate that he was potty trained by age three and continue to remain dry at night. To date, Habib is reported in good health.

Mr. and Mrs. Abbar note that Habib is a well-behaved and kind child who enjoys school. Despite enjoying school, Mr. and Mrs. Abbar believe that Habib is falling behind his peers in reading. Habib's teacher, Mr. Smith, elaborated on Habib's difficulties noting that he appears to be struggling in his ability to sound out words. More specifically, Habib's difficulties in sounding out words have greatly impacted his ability to read with speed and accuracy. From all the information provided, it appears that Habib is struggling in the area of reading fluency. A review of Habib's social history revealed that his father has a specific learning disability in reading.

Response to Intervention

RTI is an intervention service delivery model that seeks to ensure that all students receive high quality instruction in reading, writing, and mathematics (Schaffer, 2017; Sugai & Horner, 2009). Through RTI, evidence-based interventions and supports are utilized to prevent and remediate academic deficits before they turn into severe and long-standing learning problems.

Tier 1

Tier 1 of RTI is designed to deliver academic interventions and programs to all students in the general education classroom with approximately 80%–85% of students responding to such interventions (Forman & Selman, 2011; Sugai & Horner, 2009). At Tier 1, Habib's school has selected the Open Court Reading Comprehensive Curriculum to teach students critical components of reading, such as phonics, fluency, and word knowledge (What Works Clearninghouse, 2014). Every year, Habib's elementary school completes universal screening in the fall, winter, and spring. After spring screening, Habib's aimswebPlus' Oral Reading Fluency score placed him in the 9th percentile and in the Well Below Average range. Additionally, Habib's teacher noted that he performed poorly on a recent reading test. As a result of Habib's poor performance on the universal screener and additional data provided by his teacher, the child study team recommended that Habib be placed into a Tier 2 small group reading program.

Tier 2

Tier 2 of RTI is designed for the 10%–15% of students who have been identified as "at-risk" and are in need of supplemental instruction to become proficient in any given academic area (Shinn & Walker, 2010; Wexler, 2017). At Tier 2, Habib was placed into the Great Leaps Reading Fluency Program with four other students, and his progress was monitored on a biweekly basis. While in Great Leaps, Habib was instructed in sound awareness, letter recognition and phonics, and high frequency sight words and phrases (Begeny et al., 2010). He also was provided stories to practice oral reading (Begeny et al., 2010). Despite efforts to remediate Habib's reading difficulties, progress monitoring data and teacher report indicated that Habib made little progress. Consequently, at the child study team meeting, it was recommended that Habib receive Tier 3 supports.

Tier 3

Tier 3 of RTI is dedicated for students in need of intensive supports and is comprised of 1%–5% of students (Shinn & Walker, 2010; Wexler, 2017). At Tier 3, Habib received individualized instruction in developing his reading fluency using the program, Read Well. While taking part in the Read Well curriculum, Habib learned about letter/sound associations, word parts, and multisyllabic word fluency (What Works Clearinghouse, 2010). On a weekly basis, his progress was monitored. Although Habib took part in Read Well, his progress monitoring data indicated that he still continued to fall in the Well-Below Average range. Consequently, Habib was referred to the Committee on Special Education to determine whether he qualifies as a student with a specific learning disability.

Discussion Questions

1. What is the overall goal of RTI?
2. In your own words, explain the differences between Tier 1, Tier 2, and Tier 3 of RTI?
3. Why is it important to use cut-point score in determining whether a student is at-risk for poor academic and behavioral outcomes?
4. Explain how a rate of improvement may assist in informing whether a child is making enough progress in responding to an intervention.
5. How would you incorporate culturally responsive practices both into your profession and into RTI efforts?
6. Use the chart below to calculate the student's rate of improvement.

Student X Progress Monitoring Data: Oral Reading Fluency

Date	*09/12*[a]	*09/19*	*09/26*	*10/02*	*10/09*	*10/16*	*10/23*	*10/30*	*11/07*	*11/14*	*11/21*	*11/28*	*12/04*	*12/11*
Corrects	3	8	10	9	16	20	25	29	36	34	40	48	41	45
Errors	2	1	4	5	7	3	10	12	10	13	15	17	14	19

[a]benchmark score.

School-Wide Positive Behavior Support

Learning Objectives

After reading this chapter, you should be able to:

- Define school-wide positive behavior support (SWPBS).
- Differentiate between Tier 1, Tier 2, and Tier 3 of SWPBS.
- Describe the five main reasons why students engage in in challenging behaviors.
- Differentiate between minor and major behavior infractions that are used in making data-based decisions.
- Identify formal systemic screening and progress monitoring measures that can be used to make data-based decisions in regards to student behavior.
- Summarize how to incorporate culturally responsive practices into SWPBS.

Introduction to School-Wide Positive Behavior Support

When asked about major job stressors that lead to teacher burnout, educators have long named student disciplinary problems and classroom disturbances (Berg & Cornell, 2016; Friedman, 1995). Each year, approximately 3.5 million students in the United States are suspended from school at least once (Fetterman, Ritter, Morrison, & Newman, 2020). Moreover, it is estimated that one in three students will be suspended from school between their kindergarten and twelfth grade year (Shollenberger, 2015).

Of the students facing school discipline most often, Latino and Hispanic youth are 1.5 times more likely to be suspended from school than white children (Seroczynski & Jobst, 2016). Moreover, Black students are more than three times more likely to be expelled or suspended than white children (United States Department of Education Office for Civil Rights, 2014). Lastly, the United States Government Accountability Office (2018) reports that schools suspend children with disabilities at rates more than twice as high as children without disabilities. Given these statistics, schools who have adopted and are implementing SWPBS are attempting to both reduce student disciplinary referrals and the disproportionality in which such referrals are given.

Students who exhibit externalizing behaviors often have a negative effect on how schools and classrooms function in regards to student learning and achievement, decorum of other students, teacher and student engagement, instructional practices, and educator turnover rate. **Externalizing behaviors** can be defined as negative conduct that is directed outwardly toward others and is considered *undercontrolled* (Hunter, Chenier, & Gresham, 2014). In other words, externalizing behaviors occur when a child has difficulty self-regulating or inhibiting his or her actions to the point where such behaviors consistently disturb others around them (Hunter et al., 2014). Examples of externalizing behaviors include hyperactivity, impulsivity, defiance, speaking out of turn, yelling, and verbal and physical aggression. Such behaviors are characteristic of attention-deficit/hyperactivity disorder (ADHD), oppositional defiant disorder (ODD), and conduct disorder (CD). Most recent estimates suggest that approximately 19.6% of youth between ages 13 to 18 have either ADHD or a disruptive behavior disorder, such as ODD or CD, and about 9.6% of youth who are diagnosed with one of these disorders present with a severe impairment (Merikangas et al., 2010; National Alliance on Mental Health, 2019).

Children who enter adolescents with a history of defiant and aggressive behavior are at increased risk for poor grades, dropping out of school, being arrested, abusing alcohol and drugs, and dying at a young age (Heward et al., 2017). Fortunately, like academic deficits, conduct problems in children can often be remediated through evidence-based interventions and supports that promote prosocial behavior, embrace a warm and caring school culture, and increase student engagement in their educational environment. SWPBS or Positive Behavior Support (PBS) for short seeks to accomplish each of the aforementioned goals and is considered the second wall in building the Multi-Tiered Systems of Support (MTSS) "house." Figure 4.1 shows SWPBS forming the second wall of the MTSS "house." A detailed description of SWPBS follows.

FIGURE 4.1 ● SWPBS Forming the Second Wall of the MTSS "House"

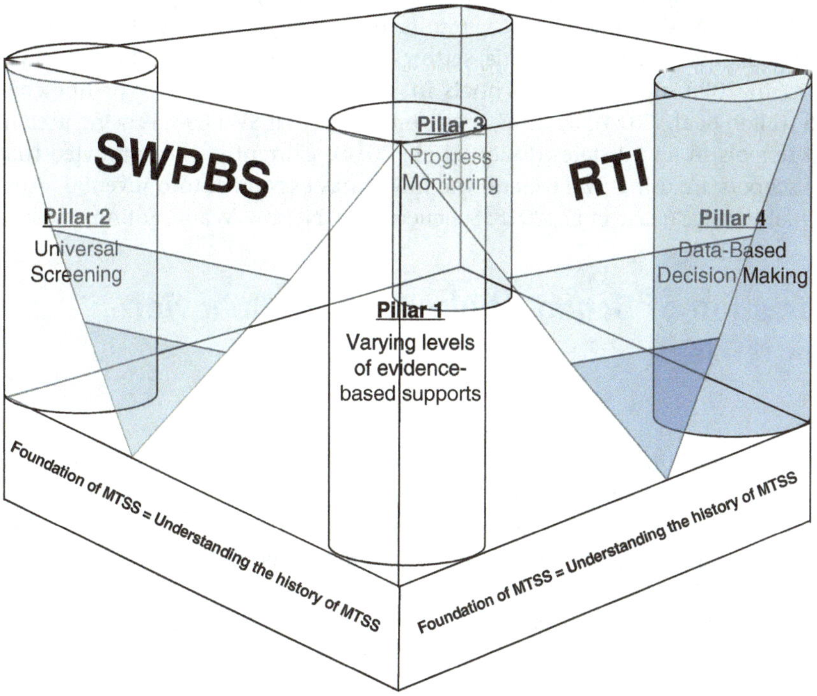

School-Wide Positive Behavior Support (SWPBS) or Positive Behavior Support (PBS) for short is a triangular three-tiered intervention service delivery model focused on improving school culture and the individual behavior of all students (Fallon, McCarthy, & Sanetti, 2014; Gage, Lee, Grasley-Boy, & George, 2018). Like all intervention service delivery models, SWPBS is based on the public health framework discussed in chapter 1 and employs a continuum of supports and interventions to prevent and address challenging behaviors in children (Fallon et al., 2014). More specifically, SWPBS focuses on preventing and intervening in children who present with externalizing behaviors. To adequately prevent negative externalizing behavior from occurring, SWPBS places special emphasis on (1) building a schools capacity to implement preventative behavioral interventions through a continuum of positive behavior support, (2) improving a school's climate and culture leading to school improvement, (3) making data-based decisions to effectively promote prosocial behavior, and (4) intervening for students who are not responding to those interventions (Fallon et al., 2014; Gage, 2015). Essential components to SWPBS include establishing and teaching clear expectations to all students, providing students opportunities to practice these expectations, positively reinforcing desired behavior, and establishing non-punitive consequences for problem behavior (Wienen et al., 2018).

Empirical evidence shows that implementation of SWPBS has led to positive student and school-level outcomes with improvements in school climate, bullying and peer victimization, academic achievement, and student behavior (Gage et al., 2018). Additionally, SWPBS has shown that it can reduce student suspensions, expulsions, and office discipline referrals (ODRs) (Gage et al., 2018; Wienen et al., 2018). By utilizing a preventative behavior approach instead of reactionary disciplinary practices, such as suspensions or expulsions, schools decrease their risk for alienating students, causing emotional harm, and elevating school drop-out rates (Gage et al., 2018; Sprick & Borgmeier, 2010). Additionally, research has shown that suspensions and expulsions have a negative effect on student behavior and learning because they reduce the amount of instruction and class-time students receive, reduce engagement in school, decrease academic achievement, and considerably increase the odds of a student dropping out of school and being arrested in early adulthood (Gage et al., 2018).

Due to SWPBS' showing promising results in over 30 years of use, its implementation across school, juvenile, and residential settings continues to grow (Fallon et al., 2014). For example, in 2008, nearly 8,000 schools in 40 states were adopting or implementing SWPBS (Fallon et al., 2014). By 2013, it was estimated that SWPBS was being used in over 18,000 schools in all 50 states (Fallon et al., 2014). Currently, it is estimated that over 25,000 schools are using SWPBS, and the model has expanded into juvenile justice and residential settings (Gage et al., 2018; Scheuermann, Nelson, Wang, & Bruntmyer, 2015).

Description of School-Wide Positive Behavior Support Tiers

Tier 1

Similar to response to intervention (RTI), SWPBS involves three tiers of interventions and supports that increase in intensity and duration as students do not respond to such interventions (Noltemeyer, Palmer, James, & Wiechman, 2019). At Tier 1 of SWPBS, primary prevention and intervention strategies are utilized to foster a warm, caring, and safe school environment for all students (Noltemeyer et al., 2019). Approximately 80%–85% of students are expected to respond to Tier 1 supports, which typically involve all school staff members working together to foster, embrace, and model school expectations, routines, and positive mottos (Horner & Sugai, 2015; Lewis, McIntosh, Simonsen, Mitchell, & Hatton, 2017). For example, at the beginning of each class, a teacher may recite with the class the school's motto of being "safe, respectful, and responsible." The teachers may then go over scenarios in which they saw students acting in a safe, respectful, and responsible manner as they came into the classroom or model for students what safe, respectful, and responsible behavior looks like.

A positive school motto should be easy to remember and involve three to five behavioral expectations that are positively stated (OSEP Technical Assistance Center, n.d.). To increase familiarity with positive school mottos and behavior expectations, posters may be placed around the school showing what each expectation consists of, such as in the school cafeteria or in a busy school hallway. Both the school motto and behavior expectations should be explicitly taught across settings (e.g., cafeteria, gym, classroom, playground) and reinforced by a school-wide reinforcement system, such as a token economy (Gage, 2015). At the classroom level, Tier 1 includes effective and efficient classroom management strategies that include the use of high classroom structure, increased contingent praise, prompting for expectations, and increased opportunities to respond to meet these expectations (Gage, 2015). Table 4.1 provides an example of a positive school motto that could be placed on a poster to review classroom expectations. Table 4.2 shows a matrix of behavioral expectations using the school motto across the classroom, school lunchroom, and hallway settings.

TABLE 4.1 • School Motto and Explanation of Expectations

Be Safe	• Keep hands, feet, objects, and items to self • Use materials appropriately
Be Respectful	• Use polite and kind words like please, thank you, and excuse me • Raise your hand and wait your turn • Participate in class discussion and respond appropriately
Be Responsible	• Return classroom materials back where you found them • Turn in homework and classwork at the appropriate time • Keep your desk clean and tidy

TABLE 4.2 • Matrix of Behavioral Expectations

Motto	Classroom Expectations	Lunchroom Expectations	Hallway Expectations
Be Safe	• Keep hands, feet, objects, and items to self • Use materials appropriately • Walking feet only	• Keep hands, feet, objects, and items to self • When lunch monitor's hand is up in the air, listen for directions • Remain seated until dismissed • Walk at all times	• Walk on the right side of the hallway • Walk-in a single file line if you are with your class • Use one step at a time on stairwells • Walking feet only and hands to self • Stay with your group

(Continued)

TABLE 4.2 ● Matrix of Behavioral Expectations *(Continued)*

Motto	Classroom Expectations	Lunchroom Expectations	Hallway Expectations
Be Respectful	• Use polite and kind words like please, thank you, and excuse me • Raise your hand and wait your turn • Participate in class discussion and respond appropriately • Avoid bringing your cell phone to class or keep cell phone turned off during school hours	• Use polite and kind words like please, thank you, and excuse me • Do not cut others in the lunch line • Raise your hand and wait your turn if you need something • Use your indoor voice	• Avoid talking in the hallway • Hold the door open for your classmates • Avoid cutting others in line • Do not touch or grab posters or artwork on hallway walls • Keep cell phones in locker during school hours
Be Responsible	• Return classroom materials back where you found them • Turn in homework and classwork at the appropriate time • Keep your desk clean, neat, and tidy	• Remember to bring your lunch, your lunch money, or to know your lunch # • Carry your belongings and lunch carefully	• Bring your belongings to your next class • Avoid talking in the hallway • Make sure your backpack is zipped when walking down the hallway

Outside the classroom setting, schools can support positive behavior in the hallways by having school staff monitor high traffic areas where students may engage in bullying or where altercations occur and reward positive behavior (Lewis et al., 2017). For example, if a teacher observed a student holding open a door for another peer, they may reward that student for good behavior by providing them a ticket that would count toward purchasing a prize at the end of the week. Finally, a positive behavior environment can be fostered by sending a newsletter home to parents explaining behavioral expectations, modeling appropriate behavior for students, and providing students specific feedback on good behavior. For example, a teacher may provide specific feedback by saying "I like the way you are sitting with your hands and feet to yourself." This is opposed to simply saying "good job," which is vague and does not inform the student what they are doing a good job at.

Finally, two commonly used Tier 1 programs for teaching students prosocial behavior include the **Good Behavior Game (GBG)** and **Zones of Regulation**. GBG is a classroom-based behavior management support for elementary school students. The game assigns students to teams that are balanced based on gender, disruptive behavior, and socially isolated behavior (Foley, Dozier, & Lessor, 2019). Classroom rules are posted and reviewed. Each team is rewarded if team members commit a total of four or fewer violations of the classroom rules during game periods. Children who played the GBG showed lower rates of drug and alcohol use disorders, regular smoking, antisocial personality disorder, delinquency and incarceration for violent crimes, suicide ideation, depression, and use of school-based services among students who had played the GBG (Bowman-Perrott, Burk, Zaini, Zhang, & Vannest, 2016; Foley et al., 2019). Lastly, the GBG has shown to be an effective intervention across cultures, and languages (Mitchell, Tingstrom, Dufrene, Ford, & Sterling. 2015; Nolan, Jenson, & Houlihan, 2014). Moreover, the intervention has been used effectively with students who speak English as a

Second Language and with urban students whose families are facing financial hardship (Mitchell et al., 2015; Nolan et al., 2014).

The Zones of Regulation Program is an 18-lesson curriculum for children ages four and above that utilizes a cognitive behavioral approach to teach self-regulation by categorizing the ways children may feel and states of alertness they may experience (Zones of Regulation, 2019). The ways children feel and the state of alertness they experience are concentrated into four zones: blue, green, yellow, and red (Kuypers, 2011; Zones of Regulation, 2019). The blue zone is utilized to signify a low state of alertness and down feelings, such as a child who is experiencing boredom or feeling sad. The green zone is used to describe a calm state of alertness and signify feelings of happiness or content. The yellow zone is used to describe elevated emotions and a heightened state of alertness, such as a child experiencing stress, nervousness, or silliness. Finally, the red zone signifies extremely heightened states of alertness and intense emotions, such as anger, rage, or devastation (Zones of Regulation, 2019). Through taking part in the curriculum and learning about the "zones," students become more aware and independent of controlling their emotions and actions, managing their sensory needs, inhibiting their impulses, and improving their ability to solve conflicts (Kuypers, 2011; Zones of Regulation, 2019). Although the Zones of Regulation Program is popular among schools, evidence is extremely limited in the scholarly literature as to its effectiveness and no large studies exist with the program being implemented with students from various ethnic backgrounds.

Tier 2

Tier 2 of SWPBS provides interventions and supports to approximately 10%–15% of students who have not responded to Tier 1 efforts (Drevon, Hixson, Wyse, & Rigney, 2018; Horner & Sugai, 2015). These students tend to display low magnitude and persistent behavioral deficits, such as engaging in off-task, non-compliant, or disruptive behaviors or occasionally being verbally and physically aggressive (Gage, 2015; Lane, Oakes, Ennis, & Hirsch, 2014). Like RTI, Tier 2 supports in SWPBS are added to Tier 1 supports to assist students who are at-risk for developing more severe problems. In the case of SWPBS, Tier 2 supports and interventions are consistent with school-wide expectations, involve explicit instruction, focus on providing students additional structure, present students opportunities to practice and receive feedback on newly acquired skills, provide a higher rate of positive recognition, and involve parent/guardian communication (Drevon et al., 2018). Consequently, children at Tier 2 may greatly benefit from interventions that offer them explicit expectations and feedback such as a check-in/check-out (CICO) or a behavior contract.

A **check-in/check-out** is a multi-component behavior intervention that typically consists of five defining features (Drevon et al., 2018). First, a student checks in with the CICO mentor upon arriving at school. The CICO can be a teacher, school psychologist, counselor, or staff member who can provide guidance and support to the student. During check-in, the mentor reviews behavioral expectations and goals with the student. Second, the student receives a daily progress report form to take to his or her classes. After checking in with the CICO mentor, the student receives both oral feedback and written input on the daily progress report to inform the student whether they are meeting behavioral expectations. Third, the student checks out with his or her CICO mentor at the end of the school day to review behavioral performance (Drevon et al., 2018). If the student met their goal on the daily progress report, they earn an incentive or tangible reward (such earning a preferred object or item as a prize or being able to spend time with a preferred staff member). Finally, the daily progress report is sent home to parents/guardians to sign off on to increase home-school collaboration. CICO has been shown to be an effective intervention for reducing student discipline referrals and increasing student compliance in children from white American, Black, Hispanic, and Latino backgrounds (Drevon et al., 2018; Hawken, Bundock, Kladis, O'Keeffe, & Barrett, 2014; Toms, Campbell-Whatley, Stuart, & Schultz, 2018). Figure 4.2 shows a CICO daily progress form for an elementary school student (Box 4.1).

FIGURE 4.2 ● Example of a Check-In/Check-Out

Check-in/Check-out

Student Name:
Date:________   **3 = Excellent 2 = Good 1 = I know I could do better**

**Teachers please have student complete with you briefly at the end of class and initial. You may add comments for good behavior or areas of improvement if you wish.*

Period	Peaceful			Responsible			Respectful			Teacher Comments
Check-in with Point Person morning										
	3	2	1	3	2	1	3	2	1	Teacher initials________
	3	2	1	3	2	1	3	2	1	Teacher initials________
Check-in w/ Point Person before lunch										I need to earn_____ out of_____ points to get my reward.
	3	2	1	3	2	1	3	2	1	Teacher initials________
	3	2	1	3	2	1	3	2	1	Teacher initials________
	3	2	1	3	2	1	3	2	1	Teacher initials________
	3	2	1	3	2	1	3	2	1	Teacher initials________
Check-in w/ Point Person end of day										I need to earn_____ out of_____ points to get my reward.

For earning my points I can choose from the following rewards/privileges	
• ____________	• ____________
• ____________	• ____________
• ____________	• ____________
• ____________	• ____________

Additional space for teacher comments:

____

____

Parent Signature: ____________
Date: __________

Teacher/Point Person Signature: ____________
Date: __________

BOX 4.1 CHECK-IN/CHECK-OUT SYNOPSIS

Ricardo Alfarez is a sixth-grader at Elm Middle School in Chicago, Illinois. Due to Ricardo struggling to meet behavioral expectations set by the school, he recently began receiving additional support through a CICO. Ricardo's behavioral progress and implementation of his CICO are overseen by his gym teacher, Mr. Heaggans. Ricardo looks up to Mr. Heaggans because he is athletic but also because he is very nurturing and supportive. Each day before school, Ricardo checks in with Mr. Heaggans to review desired behaviors and expectations and subsequently sets goals for himself in order to make sure he is ready to take on the day. Before Ricardo leaves for his classes, Mr. Heaggans hands him a blank daily progress report form. As Ricardo attends each of his classes throughout the day, he hands his daily progress report form to his teachers before the start of class and receives feedback on how he did during each class period.

At the end of the school day, Ricardo heads down to Mr. Heaggans office to check-out and review his behavioral performance. During the check-out session, Mr. Heaggans provides Ricardo highly effective praise and recognition along with additional coaching and guidance on meeting behavioral goals if it is needed. If Ricardo earns all the necessary points throughout the school day, he earns his reward, which entails playing basketball with Mr. Heaggans. If Ricardo does not earn all his points needed to obtain his reward, constructive feedback is given, and he is reminded that he can try to earn all his points again the next day to obtain his reward.

A **behavior contract** is a formal written agreement between a child and school staff member to outline the expectations of the student, teacher, and occasionally parents to help the student succeed in school. Behavior contracts have been used for more than 50 years to influence positive behavior change (Bailey, Wolf, & Phillips, 1970). Within SWPBS, behavior contracts are utilized as a useful Tier 2 intervention because they seek the student's insight for establishing expectations, as opposed to just school staff, and work with the child to establish the conditions on which the student is rewarded. Major features of behavior contracts include clearly stating the behavioral expectations to accomplish behavior change, including rewards and incentives for adhering to the contract, consequences for not meeting agreed-upon expectations, and a plan for maintaining desired behavior (Bowman-Perrott, Burke, de Marin, Zhang, & Davis, 2015).

When used as an independent Tier 2 intervention, behavior contracts have been found to have a moderate effect on changing student behavior (Bowman-Perrott, Burke, Zhang, & Davis, 2015). Therefore, some studies suggest that behavior contracts may more beneficial when paired with other Tier 2 interventions, such as a CICO or the program First Step to Success. A meta-analysis of 18 studies by Bowman-Perrott et al. (2015) found that behavior contracts are beneficial for students regardless of grade level, gender, ethnicity, or disability status. Findings from Bowman-Perrott et al. (2015) suggest that behavior contracts are more effective in reducing inappropriate behaviors than increasing appropriate behaviors. See Figure 4.3 for an example of a behavior contract.

FIGURE 4.3 ● Behavior Contract

Behavior Contract

Name:________________ Date:________________

My goals are to:

1. ______________________________

2. ______________________________

When I meet my goals, I will earn:

1. ______________________________

2. ______________________________

If I do not reach my goals, I will lose the following opportunities/privileges:

3. ______________________________

4. ______________________________

I can do the following to help me reach my goals:

1. ______________________________

2. ______________________________

Teacher signature:____________ Student signature:____________

Parent signature:____________

Although Tier 2 of SWPBS consists of interventions that may assist some students in meeting behavior expectations, there are programs, like First Step to Success or Social Academic Intervention Groups (SAIG) that may also greatly assist at-risk children. **First Step to Success** is an early intervention program that is designed to assist children who are at-risk for developing aggressive and antisocial patterns of behavior (Gage, 2015; What

Works Clearinghouse, 2012). The program is geared toward students in grades kindergarten through three and uses a trained behavior coach who works with each student, teacher, and parents for approximately 50–60 hours over a three-month period (Gage, 2015).

First Step to Success has shown great promise in assisting students in meeting behavior expectations, increasing socially appropriate behavior, and engaging children academically (Gage, 2015). In a study involving 200 children in which 72% of participants were Hispanic, Black, Native American, Asian, multiracial, and Pacific Islander, First Step to Success was found to be a successful program at reducing aggressive and antisocial patterns of behavior in youth (Walker et al., 2009). Additionally, more recent study involving three Latino English language learners in a California elementary school found that a culturally adapted version of First Step to Success was successful at reducing problem behaviors (Castro-Olivo, Preciado, Le, Marciante, & Garcia, 2018).

Social Academic Intervention Groups are based on the CIRCLE format (where children sit in a circle to build a sense of belongingness) and restorative practices, which seek to repair relationships that have been damaged (Franklin, Harris, & Allen-Meares, 2013). There are two themes to SAIG: classroom survival skills, which are and emotional management skills (Franklin et al., 2013). Classroom survival skills of SAIG are geared more toward students displaying externalizing behaviors and involve lessons that teach students listening skills, following instructions, ignoring distractions, making connections, and accepting consequences. Emotional management skills groups tend to fit better as a Tier 2 intervention under social-emotional RTI and are geared more toward students with difficulties managing their internalizing feelings. Students in these groups learn about feeling recognition, expression of feelings, coping with anger, and self-soothing strategies (Franklin et al., 2013).

Tier 3

Tier 3 of SWPBS is designed for one to five percent of students who do not respond to Tier 2 interventions and supports (Horner & Sugai, 2015). These students tend to have persistent and severe maladaptive behavior patterns that may endanger themselves, others, or cause significant classroom disturbances (e.g., students who are verbally and physically aggressive or students who frequently are non-compliant). Consequently, Tier 3 interventions and supports are individualized and designed to address the specific function of the behavior (Gage, 2015). At Tier 3 of SWPBS, practices include assessing why behaviors are occurring, developing behavior support plan to address difficult behaviors, implementing the behavior support plan, and connecting parents and students to services in the community that may further address student behavior deficits (Horner & Sugai, 2015; Lewis et al., 2017).

An essential component to Tier 3 of SWPBS is that a behavior support team meet to outline the preferences and individual needs of the student (Horner & Sugai, 2015). This behavior support team should consist of individuals who know the student well and include the school psychologist, a general education teacher, school counselor, administrator, and, if possible, a special education teacher proficient at behavior management. The purpose of the behavior support team is to develop a functional behavior assessment for the student (FBA). If the FBA reveals a need for additional interventions and supports, a behavior intervention plan (BIP) is devised.

A **functional behavior assessment** is a systemic process for gathering information to determine why a student may be engaging in challenging behavior (Gage, 2015; Heward, Alber-Morgan, & Konrad, 2017). The first step to completing an FBA is to define the behavior(s) in concrete, observable, and measurable terms. By defining behavior(s) in concrete, observable, and measurable terms, educators are better able to notice target behaviors and track them. For instance, a concrete observable, and measurable way to define physical aggression may be as follows: "any incident in which the child engages in hitting, kicking, or pushing peers." The behavior in this example is defined concretely because it is explained in short terms that are observable to educators. To elaborate, educators can see the child engaging in the behaviors of hitting, kicking, and pushing peers. This is opposed to a behavior being defined in terms that are long, vague, or do not accurately depict what the difficult behavior looks like.

After defining the target behavior(s) in an FBA, it is vital for educators to obtain a baseline of the behavioral occurrences by measuring their frequency, intensity, and duration (Gage, 2015; Heward et al., 2017). The frequency of the behavior can be defined as how often the behavior occurs (Gage, 2015; Heward et al., 2017). For example, a teacher may assess how often the behavior occur in a week, day, or hour. Duration can be defined as how long the behavior episode lasts (Gage, 2015; Heward et al., 2017). For instance, does the behavior last for a few minutes or for a few hours? Finally, the intensity of the behavior is defined as the severity of the behavior. For example, a child engaging in lightly pushing a peer is engaged in less intense behavior than a child who severely injures his peers by pushing them.

The final step of completing an FBA looks into the antecedents (what is occurring or taking place before the behavior(s) occurs and the immediate consequences of the child engaging in the behavior (e.g., a consequence of the child engaging in verbal outbursts in class is that they obtain the immediate attention of their peers). By looking into the antecedents and consequences of the child engaging in maladaptive behavior(s), a hypothesis can be formed as to why the behaviors are taking place. Generally, it has been viewed that there are five primary reasons that students may be engaging in problem behavior. These five primary reasons can be easily remembered by the acronym TEAMS and include the following motives for engaging in challenging behavior: tangible, escape, attention, medical, and sensory (Durand & Crimmins, 1988; McCurdy, Skinner, & Ervin, 2017). A description of each of these motives is provided in the following paragraphs.

The first letter in the TEAMS acronym is "T," suggesting that children may engage in challenging behavior(s) to obtain "tangible" items (Durand & Crimmins, 1988; McCurdy et al., 2017). For example, a child may engage in physical aggression to intimate another student to give them a toy. Another example would be a child engaging in verbal aggression to obtain a snack.

The next letter in the TEAMS acronym is "E," standing for "escape." Children may engage in challenging behavior(s) to escape or avoid certain tasks, activities, locations, or people (Durand & Crimmins, 1998; Gage, 2015; Heward et al., 2017). For example, a student may engage in the non-compliant behavior of putting his head down when presented with a math test to escape or avoid completing the exam. Another example would be a young child running out of the classroom to avoid reading instruction.

The third letter is "A," which stands for "attention." Aside from engaging in maladaptive behavior(s) to obtain objects/items or escape/avoid situations, children may engage in challenging behaviors to obtain attention (Durand & Crimmins, 1998; Heward et al., 2017; McCurdy et al., 2017). For instance, a child may make noises or insulting jokes during class to obtain attention from his or her peers in the form of laughter. Another child may engage in physical aggression to obtain the attention of his or her teacher.

The fourth letter in TEAMS is "M," which suggests that a child may engage in difficult behavior(s) for "medical" reasons (Durand & Crimmins, 1998; Gage, 2015; Heward et al., 2017). A student may engage in the non-compliant behavior of refusing to participate during group instruction due to being tongue-tied or experiencing hearing deficits. Another example would be a student constantly getting out of his or her seat to get a drink due to having diabetes. Lastly, a child may engage in non-compliant behavior due to experiencing significant motivational deficits as a result of suffering from depression.

Finally, the last letter is "S," which indicates that children may engage in maladaptive behaviors for "sensory" reasons (Durand & Crimmins, 1998; Heward et al., 2017; McCurdy et al., 2017). For instance, a child with autism may cover their ears when the school bell rings and run out of the classroom due to it being too loud. Another child who has low vision may touch objects or items to obtain sensory input of what they look and feel like. It is worthy to note that challenging behaviors a child engages in may be due to a number of factors outlined by the TEAMS acronym. For example, a child may engage in running out of the classroom both for sensory reasons and to escape a non-preferred environment. In addition to looking into why the behavior(s) occurs, it is important for educators to consider where the behavior is taking place most often. For example, a student may constantly engage in speaking out of turn in math class. However, that same student may not engage in talking out of turn in art class due to enjoying the content being covered. Table 4.3 provides a summary of the five reasons why students engage in challenging behaviors.

TABLE 4.3 • Typical Reasons Why Challenging Behaviors Occur Using the TEAMS Acronym (Durand & Crimmins, 1988; McCurdy et al., 2017)

1. **Tangible**	Challenging behavior(s) occur to obtain desired objects or items
2. **Escape**	Challenging behavior(s) occur to avoid non-preferred tasks, activities, locations, or people
3. **Attention**	Challenging behavior(s) occur to obtain the attention of others, whether it be positive or negative
4. **Medical**	Challenging behavior(s) occur due to medical reasons
5. **Sensory**	Challenging behavior(s) occur due to sensory reasons

After completing an FBA to determine why a behavior(s) is taking place and what circumstances are maintaining behavioral concerns, the child study team may decide to develop a behavior intervention plan. A **behavior intervention plan** is a plan that provides educators specific interventions and supports to utilize when a child is engaging in maladaptive behavior(s). For example, the plan may include interventions such as modeling how to appropriately obtain teacher attention instead of talking out of turn or teach the student how to engage in deep breathing when becoming upset. The goal of a behavior intervention plan is for students to be able to replace maladaptive behaviors with more socially appropriate ones and generalize these more appropriate behaviors across settings and contexts (Pennington, Simacek, McComas, McMaster, & Elmquist, 2018). Additionally, the goal of a behavior intervention plan is for the child to maintain behavioral changes even after the plan is discontinued (Pennington et al., 2018). Research has shown that use of FBAs and BIPs across educational, residential, and juvenile detention center settings increases child engagement, on-task behavior, self-monitoring practices (Collins & Zirkel, 2017). Additionally, research shows that FBAs and BIPs decrease disruptive and non-compliant behavior (Collins & Zirkel, 2017).

Aside from an FBA and BIP, Tier 3 supports and services for students with behavioral difficulties may involve individual counseling by a school psychologist and include establishing wraparound support for the child. Wraparound support services attempt to assist the student by connecting family, schools, and community partners in a problem-solving relationship to best help the youth in overcoming their behavioral deficits (Gopalan et al., 2017). Wraparound support is based on the idea that services and supports should be flexible in meeting the needs of students and families (Gopalan et al., 2017). Overall, the goal of wraparound supports is to increase school, community, and family involvement to best assist everyone executing interventions and supports for the student with integrity.

Unlike RTI, data-based decision-making is less stringent and formalized in SWPBS. Educators may utilize a multitude of measures to universally screen and progress monitor student behavior. Typically to universally screen and progress monitor students for behavioral outcomes, both schools and researchers have turned to ODRs or systemic screening measures. The more common of the two measures utilized to screen and progress monitor students for behavioral outcomes involve the use of ODRs. In the upcoming sections, the utility of ODRs and systematic screening measures ability to track student behavior and allow schools to make adequate data-based decisions will be discussed.

Data Collection and Decision-Making Under SWPBS

Office Discipline Referrals

Office discipline referrals (ODRs) can be defined as written records of behavioral problems that violate school discipline codes (Cavanaugh, 2016). ODRs are often used as an indicator of schoolwide behaviors and overall school climate because they have been generally viewed as a useful, efficient, and valid source of data for school-wide data-based decision-making (Cavanaugh, 2016; Flannery, Fenning, Kato, & Bohanon, 2011). Additionally, to a lesser extent, ODRs have demonstrated that they can be a valid indicator of individual student behavioral performance (Cavanaugh, 2016; Flannery et al., 2011).

At the individual student level, several advantages come with schools utilizing ODRs for data-based decision-making. First, schools are already tracking ODRs regularly on students and as such ODRs are a time-saving method for evaluating and planning behavior support for students (Cavanaugh, 2016; McIntosh, Campbell, Carter, & Zumbo, 2009). Second, ODRs may provide more realistic data on low-frequency, high-intensity behaviors than conducting having staff complete observations of the class or student (McIntosh et al., 2009). To elaborate, it would be difficult for a school psychologist or school counselor to observe a classroom and directly encounter low frequency, high-intensity behaviors, such as severe physical aggression. This is because behaviors are less likely to occur when staff are present and may not occur on a daily basis. Therefore, ODRs offer a more realistic glimpse into student behavior as it occurs throughout the school year.

Third, ODR data can be utilized to answer a broad range of questions by behavior support teams on a schoolwide level (Cavanaugh, 2016; McIntosh et al., 2009). For instance, ODR data can be indicative of the overall climate of the school and inform educators as to whether most students are meeting school-wide expectations. For example, if a school finds that only 40% of their students have only zero to one ODRs when the expected percentage of students responding to Tier 1support is 80%, then a critical look may be needed to adjust Tier 1 interventions. Therefore, ODR data may be critical in helping target and evaluate school-wide reform efforts to ensure that the supports being provided are effective (Cavanaugh, 2016; McIntosh et al., 2009). Additionally, ODR data may help educators identify and track school-wide patterns of problem behavior. For example, perhaps it is noted that several fights have taken place in the cafeteria hallway over the past month after fifth period. As a result, the school principal may decide that more school staff are needed to monitor the cafeteria hallway during certain times of the day. A final advantage of using ODRs for data-based decision-making is that these data are cost-effective and take no additional time to score (Cavanaugh, 2016; McIntosh et al., 2009). In other words, the district does not have to purchase anything extra to provide them ODR information as it is already being tracked and documented. Furthermore, unlike rating scales, ODR data does not have to be tabulated and scored.

Before a school can utilize ODRs to universally screen and progress monitor student behavior, violations of school conduct should first be broken down into minor and major infractions. **Minor infractions** involve violations of school conduct that are documented but do not lead to an ODR or result in administrative action (Cavanaugh, 2016). Examples of minor infractions include running down the hall, coming to class unprepared, being off-task, or talking out of turn. **Major infractions**, better known as major ODRs, are infractions that lead to ODRs and result in administrative action (Cavanaugh, 2016; McIntosh et al., 2009). Administrative action for students who receive a major ODR may result in a conference with the child's parents, school restitution, detention, or suspension. Some examples of behaviors that may lead to major ODRs include bullying, fighting, harassment, inappropriate language, and property destruction (Cavanaugh, 2016; Flannery et al., 2011; Taylor, Kilgus, & Huang, 2018).

It is important to note that minor infractions, such as disrupting class or coming to class unprepared, may lead to major ODRs if the behaviors are repeated frequently. However, there is no clear consensus among scholars or educators as to how many minor infractions equate to a major ODR (Cavanaugh, 2016; Flannery et al., 2011; McIntosh et al., 2009; Taylor et al., 2018). Therefore, it is important for schools and school administrators to clearly outline for staff which behaviors are considered minor infractions, which behaviors lead to major ODRs, and how many minor infractions lead to a major ODR.

Once schools have clearly defined the difference between minor infractions and major ODRs, they can use major ODRs to universally screen and progress monitor students under SWPBS. It has generally been accepted that SWPBS is effective when approximately 80%–85% of students in a school receive zero to one major ODRs, 10%–15% receive two to five major ODRs, and 1%–5% receive six or more major ODRs (Cavanaugh, 2016; Flannery et al., 2011; Taylor et al., 2018). In a similar vein, it has generally been accepted that by the end of the school year, students who have zero to one major ODRs present no to little risk of presenting with chronic discipline problems, students with two to five major ODRs present with some risk for developing chronic discipline problems, and students with six or more major ODRs are at high-risk for developing chronic discipline problems (Cavanaugh, 2016; Flannery et al., 2011; McIntosh et al., 2009; Taylor et al., 2018). The common cut-point for recommending a child receive Tier 2 support is two or more major ODRs per year (Taylor et al., 2018). Moreover, the common cut-point for recommending a child is in need of Tier 3 supports is six or more major ODRs per year (Taylor et al., 2018).

The final step in using major ODRs to make data-based decisions is appropriately documenting, filing, and summarizing them to evaluate school-wide and individual trends in student behavior. One system that has been developed to assist districts in documenting, filing, and summarizing ODRs is known as the **school-wide information system (SWIS)**. SWIS is a web-based system developed to collect, summarize, and utilize student behavior data for decision-making (Cavanaugh, 2016; Ervin, Schaughency, Matthews, Goodman, & McGlinchey, 2007). By using SWIS, educators can obtain information on the average ODRs per day per month, the percentage of students across tiers who present with a behavioral risk, and view patterns in individual student problem behavior.

In using ODRs to recommend students to higher levels of support, schools should use caution to not advance the child too quickly through Tier 2 or 3 before the supports put into place have a chance to work. For example, a student may receive two ODRs during the first three months of school, and as a result, may be referred to Tier 2 interventions and supports. At Tier 2, the supports provided may involve group behavior counseling paired with a CICO. However, during the first two weeks of supports being put into place, the student receives five more major ODRs. In this case, it would not be favorable to remove the child from the Tier 2 supports being provided to receive Tier 3 interventions because the child has not had an ample chance to respond to those supports offered at Tier 2.

Similarly, it is advised that interventions and supports be implemented for their suggested time frames before a switch in intervention takes place or the student is recommended to a higher level of support. For example, perhaps a classroom survival skills group at Tier 2 is devised to run for twelve weeks before the program is completed by students. A determination of whether the student moves onto another intervention or onto Tier 3 should not be made prematurely six to eight weeks into the classroom survival skills group being implemented. It would generally be recommended that the child complete the group rather than the support being terminated early. Therefore, schools must exercise caution and restraint in moving students who are at-risk through Tier 2 and onto Tier 3 too quickly before they have a chance to respond to the interventions being put into place. Educators should consider that it may take a child time to learn appropriate behavior if all that has been modeled for them in the home environment, neighborhood around them, and even in the school setting are inappropriate ways to meet their needs. Moreover, the longer a child has demonstrated maladaptive behaviors over time, the more resistant the behaviors may be to intervention. Therefore, educators must be patient in trusting that an appropriately outlined SWPBS model is designed to best help students succeed and understand that in cases where such students are not successful ample supports and recommendations will be provided for the student.

Finally, educators should be aware that although major ODRs provide a great deal of information on school-wide and individual behavior patterns, there are possible limitations in the reliability and validity of such data being used as the sole measure to make data-based decisions. Among the most evident reasons why major ODRs may not serve as the best means for universally screening students for future behavioral problems is that they are based on a "wait-to-fail" model. In other words, students must exhibit multiple behavioral episodes and receive multiple major ODRs before being identified at-risk instead of receiving help before their actions lead to administrative action (Cavanaugh, 2016). For example, a student may receive one major ODR in October and may not receive another three major ODRs until April. As a result, the chances of remediating a child's behavioral deficit early on are considerably delayed.

In addition to major ODRs possibly employing a "wait-to-fail" model to assist students at-risk, their sensitivity has been drawn into questions as to whether they are able to accurately identify many students who are at-risk (Taylor et al., 2018). Major ODRs may lack sensitivity in accurately identifying many students who are at-risk for chronic behavior problems because they tend to only detect students after they have experienced a significant level of difficulty over a prolonged period of time (Taylor et al., 2018). In going back to the "wait-to-fail" model, a student may display several minor conduct infractions, such as disrupting class or non-compliance, on a weekly basis but only receive one major ODR because these infractions occur in different classrooms, settings, and with different staff. Therefore, although the student is presenting with infractions that may be interrupting his or her learning and the learning of others, intervention may be delayed due to it being a frequent, low-level infraction across various settings and contexts. For these reasons, some scholars have argued that in order to truly universally screen and progress monitor students for behavioral deficits, consideration should be given to tracking both minor infractions along with major ODRs (Cavanaugh, 2016).

Finally, the use of major ODRs are subjective to personal opinion and bias. If major ODRs are not defined in clear and concise terms, there is increased chance in how staff will interpret and respond to violations. For example, one staff member may interpret a child playfully shoving a peer as a minor infraction of school discipline policy, warn the student, and note it as physical contact. However, another staff member may interpret the same incident as a major ODR and send the child down to the principal's office to face administrative consequences.

A number of other factors may play a role in how a staff member responds to student behavior in regards to viewing an incident as a minor infraction or viewing and incident as a major ODR. These factors may include whether an educator hold biases toward the student based on their race, gender, religious affiliation, previous encounters with the child, and prior experiences with the child's family (e.g., Does the child come from a family that has a poor relationship with the school? Does the child have siblings who are often in trouble with teachers? Is the family well regarded by educators?). To further illustrate this point, consider that it has long been documented that in the United States, racial disparities exist in how students are disciplined for their actions. Typically, Black students and students from marginalized backgrounds continue to be disciplined at higher rates than white students. In a study involving 1,666 elementary schools and 483,686 ODRs, Black boys were found to be given major ODRs at a rate of 1.25 times as often as their white counterparts (Smolkowski, Girvan, McIntosh, Nese, & Horner, 2016). Additionally, Black girls were found to be given major ODRs at a rate of 1.73 times more than white females (Smolkowski et al., 2016). Despite the general consensus that ODRs are a useful and fairly valid measure to make data-based decisions, each of these glaring shortcomings continues to draw their utility into question as to whether they should be used the sole measures to universally screen and progress monitor students in SWPBS. Table 4.4 summarizes the advantages and disadvantages of using ODRs in making adequate data-based decisions under SWPBS.

TABLE 4.4 • Advantages and Disadvantages of Using Major ODRs for Data-Based Decision-Making

Advantages of Using Major ODRs	Disadvantages of Using Major ODRs
Can be used as an indicator of both school climate and individual student behavior	Employs a wait-to-fail model of intervening in student behavior
Can identify patterns of school-wide and individual student behavior	Lacks sensitivity by not considering minor infractions
Cost-effective	At times unclear on what is a minor infraction versus what is a major ODR
Efficient	Subject to personal bias and opinion

Systemic Screening Measures

Due to the limitations of using major ODRs in identifying and monitoring students at-risk for behavior deficits, there have been calls to utilize more formal universal screening and progress monitoring tools. Consequently, researchers have advocated for combining the use of major ODRs with universal screening and progress monitoring measures. By combining major ODRs with universal screening and progress monitoring measures, scholars believe that schools may be better able to effectively and efficiently identify the greatest number of students who are in need of behavioral support (Cavanaugh, 2016; Taylor et al., 2018). Universal screeners used in SWPBS are quick evidence-based measures that are utilized to evaluate all students within a school and proactively identify those who may be in need of additional behavioral support. Typically, it is advised that universally screening students for behavior deficits take place three times a year in the fall, winter, and spring.

Aside from universal screeners, scholars have called for schools to utilize progress monitoring measures. Like in RTI, progress monitoring in SWPBS involves the brief repeated assessment of students to determine whether they are responding to the behavioral supports and interventions being provided. To determine if students are at or remain at-risk for a behavior disorder, cut points are utilized. For example, a universal screener may use a cut-point indicating that students who score ten and above are deemed at-risk for developing chronic behavior problems. On the contrary, students who fall below the cut-point are within expected limits and are not considered at-risk. The following sections will introduce four common measures for screening and progress monitoring students for behavior deficits.

Systemic Screening Measures

Student Risk Screening Scale-Internalizing and Externalizing (SRSS-IE)

One of the most popular free universal screening and progress monitoring measures used in SWPBS involves the **Student Risk Screening Scale-Internalizing and Externalizing**. The SRSS-IE is an adapted version of the Student Risk Screening Scale (SRSS) which was originally developed to detect maladaptive externalizing behavior in elementary school students (Drummond, 1994; Taylor et al., 2018). The adapted version of the SRSS added additional items to increase the tool's utility in measuring patterns of internalizing problems. Therefore, the SRSS-IE includes a total of 12 items and takes approximately one to three minutes per student to complete (30–40 minutes per class of 20 students). The first seven items of the SRSS-IE are devoted to externalizing maladaptive behaviors that may be best addressed under SWPBS and include the following: (1) steal; (2) lie, cheat, sneak; (3) behavior problem; (4) peer rejection; (5) low achievement; (6) negative attitude; (7) aggressive behavior (Drummond, 1994; Taylor et al., 2018). The next five items of the SRSS-IE are devoted to internalizing problems that may be best addressed under the intervention service delivery model of social-emotional RTI and are as follows: (1) emotionally flat; (2) shy, withdrawn; (3) sad, depressed; (4) anxious; (5) lonely (Oakes, Lane, & Ennis, 2016; Taylor et al., 2018).

In completing the SRSS-IE, teachers utilized a four-point Likert-type scale to rate the frequency with which students display each behavior (Taylor et al., 2018). Teacher responses range from 0 (never) to 3 (frequently). SRSS-IE scores are then calculated by obtaining the sum of item ratings within the internalizing and externalizing scales (Taylor et al., 2018). Higher scores are indicative of more problematic behavior. The SRSS-IE comes in an elementary and middle-high school versions. For the elementary school SRSS-Externalizing scale (SRSS-E), cut score risk levels are as follows: 0–3 (low), 4–8 (medium), and 9–21 (high). For the elementary SRSS-Internalizing scale, cut score risk levels are as follows: 0–1 (low), 2–3 (moderate), and 4–15 (high) (Oakes et al., 2016;

Taylor et al., 2018). The SRSS-IE, and even more its predecessor the SRSS, are well-established screening and progress monitoring measures that has been utilized to predict short-term (1.5 years) and long-term (10 years) negative academic and behavioral outcomes for children (Oakes et al., 2016; Taylor et al., 2018).

Social, Academic, and Emotional Behavior Risk Screening (SAEBRS)

The **Social, Academic, and Emotional Behavior Risk Screening (SAEBRS)** is a brief universal screening tool for students displaying both behavioral and emotional risk (Taylor et al., 2018). The SAEBRS takes approximately one to three minutes per student (about 30–40 minutes for a class of 20) to complete and is designed to be used across grades K-12 for up to five times per year (Taylor et al., 2018). The SAEBRS consists of 19 items that are divided into three subscales: Social Behavior (six items), Academic Behavior (six items), and Emotional Behavior (seven items). Summing the items yields a Total Behavior Scale score that indicates whether students are at high-risk for behavioral deficits.

Raters of the SAEBRS identify how frequently the student has displayed behaviors over the course of the previous month using a 4-point Likert scale (0 = never, 1 = sometimes, 2 = often, 3 = often, 4 = almost always) (Kilgus, Taylor, & von der Embse, 2018; Taylor et al., 2018). Higher scores on the SAEBRS are indicative of more positive and appropriate behavior. Cut scores indicating whether students fall in the at-risk range are as follows: Total Behavior Scale: <36, Social Behavior: <12, Academic Behavior: <9, and Emotional Behavior: <16 (Kilgus et al., 2018). Research on the SAEBRS supports its use as a valid, reliable, and diagnostically accurate tool in identifying students at behavioral and emotional risk (Kilgus et al., 2018; Taylor et al., 2018). Therefore, the SAEBRS is viewed as a useful tool in universally screening and students under both SWPBS and social-emotional RTI. It is worthy to note that the SAEBRS is only designed as a universal screening measure and is not a progress monitoring tool.

Behavioral and Emotional Screening System (BESS)

The **Behavioral and Emotional Screening System** is an abbreviated, standardized, and norm-referenced version of the Behavioral Assessment System for Children, third edition (Kilgus et al., 2018). The BESS is utilized as a universal screener that consists of 25–30 items and comes in a teacher, child, and parent form and takes approximately five to ten minutes per student to complete (about 100–200 minutes to complete for a class of 20 students). The teacher and parent form are available for children ranging in age from three through five. The student form is designed for children in grades three through twelve edition (Kilgus et al., 2018).

Scores from the BESS are derived from the following four areas: Externalizing Problems, Internalizing Problems, School Problems, and Adaptive Skills. Scores on the aforementioned four areas are derived from a four-point Likert scale from 0 (Never) to 3 (Almost Always) and summed to yield a raw single score that is indicative of behavioral and emotional risk (Kilgus et al., 2018). Raw scores on the BESS are converted to *T* scores with a mean of 50 and a standard deviation of 10. Higher scores on the BESS suggest more concerns regarding general behavior and emotional functioning with *T* scores being classified into three levels of risk, including normal ($T < 60$), elevated ($T = 61–70$), and extremely elevated ($T > 70$) (Kilgus et al., 2018). Like the other measures mentioned in this chapter, the BESS can be utilized to universally screen students with behavioral risk under SWPBS and emotional risk under social-emotional RTI.

Behavior Intervention Monitoring Assessment System 2 (BIMAS-2)

The **Behavior Intervention Monitoring Assessment System 2 (BIMAS-2)** is a universal screener, progress monitoring, and intervention planning measure of behavioral, social, and emotional functioning in children and adolescents ages 5–18 years (McDougal, Bardos, & Meier, 2016). The BIMAS-2 is a nationally standardized and norm-referenced assessment that is available in two versions: BIMAS Standard and BIMAS Flex. The BIMAS Standard includes 34 items that are used for universal screening of behavior and comes in three forms: teacher, parent, and student (Behavior Intervention Monitoring System 2; McDougal et al., 2016). The 34 items on the BIMAS-2 include three Behavioral Concern Scales of which include conduct, negative affect, and cognitive attention and two Adaptive Scales, including social and academic functioning (Behavior Intervention Monitoring System 2; McDougal et al., 2016). On the Behavioral Concern and Adaptive Scales, cut scores are identified through the use of *T*-scores. For the Behavioral Concern Scales, *T*-scores that are above 70 fall in the high-risk range (Jenkins et al., 2014). *T*-scores between 60 and 69 fall within the some-risk range (Jenkins et al., 2014). Lastly, *T*-scores below 60 fall within the low-risk range (Jenkins et al., 2014). For the Adaptive Scales, *T*-scores higher than 60 are classified as a strength. *T*-scores between 41 and 59 are classified as typical, and finally *T*-scores below 40 are identified as a concern (Jenkins et al., 2014). The BIMAS-2 Standard takes approximately five to ten minutes to complete.

The BIMAS-2 Flex is an optional progress monitoring extension of the BIMAS-2 Standard version that is utilized to target specific interventions for concerns identified with the standard form (Behavior Intervention Monitoring System 2; Jenkins et al., 2014). Like the BIMAS-2 Standard, the BIMAS Flex comes in teacher, parent, and student forms. The BIMAS-2 Flex is unique in that it allows users to customize items that are specific to student need for progress monitoring (BIMAS-2, n.d.). The BIMAS-2 presents as a promising universal screening and progress monitoring tool for children who present with externalizing and internalizing challenges.

Culturally Responsive Practices and SWPBS

Utilization of SWPBS provides a three-tiered framework to teach appropriate behavior to all students and remediate behavior deficits in children. When implemented with fidelity and in considering the needs of diverse learners, SWPBS should increase opportunities for students to learn about school expectations and decrease the disproportionality of school disciplinary practices toward ethnically diverse learners and students with disabilities. Through SWPBS, schools should strive to create a culture with a shared vision, beliefs, and behavior expectations that ensures students who are not from the dominant culture do not experience "unintentional slights," which can devalue their backgrounds and diminish school connectedness (Fetterman et al., 2020). Therefore, SWPBS efforts that are culturally responsive hold great promise for reducing the use of punitive disciplinary practices that are ineffective and contribute to the inequitable treatment of ethnically diverse students and students with disabilities (Fetterman et al., 2020).

In seeking support for incorporating culturally responsive practices into SWPBS, the *PBIS Cultural Responsiveness Field Guide: Resources for Trainers and Coaches* serves as a strong and free reference for educators (Leverson, Smith, McIntosh, Rose, & Pinkelman, 2019). In the guide, Leverson et al. (2019) outlines five core components of cultural responsiveness that can be incorporated into SWPBS: (1) identity, (2) voice, (3) supportive environment, (4) situational appropriateness, and (5) data for equity.

Identity

Identity refers to teachers and other school staff's ability to possess a self-understanding of their identity and an awareness of how that influences their surrounding environment and the individuals within that environment (Fetterman et al., 2020). Therefore, educators should reflect on how their identity is comprised of multiple aspects, such as their race, ethnicity, disability status, gender identity, language, marital status, religion, and socio-economic status (Fetterman et al., 2020; Leverson et al., 2019). By educators reflecting on how their identity is comprised of multiple aspects, they can become familiar with their way of viewing the world and own biases. To become more familiar with their identity and worldview of diverse learners, educators can engage in journaling and ask themselves what biases they may hold and how did they form those biases?

Voice

Voice refers to students, their families, and those within the school community having the opportunity to provide information and feedback on their cultural values and histories in the school setting (Leverson et al., 2019). For example, the school may provide students, family members, and those in the community opportunities to examine and give feedback on school-wide expectations and rules before implementing them (Leverson et al., 2019). By providing opportunities to examine and give feedback, school-wide expectations and rules can be revised to reflect the values of the surrounding community and culture. Moreover, by providing students, families and those in the community a voice, educators can reflect and examine rules for a reflection of dominant cultural values that may need explicit teaching. Subsequently, educators can provide materials for families to assist them in defining and teaching behavior expectations in the home in ways that fit their needs (Leverson et al., 2019). In seeking out feedback from students, families, and the surrounding community, language and modes of delivery should be taken into account. For example, letters sent home should ideally be in the language spoken in the home and consideration should be given as to how families respond best to providing feedback, such as through written form, telephone interview, and school conferences.

Supportive Environment

A supportive environment refers to whether or not students feel welcomed and safe in their schools (Fetterman et al., 2020). To make school environments more culturally responsive, art, and artifacts should be on display that reflect the heritage, values, interests, and expectations of the different cultures and ethnicities represented in the school (Leverson et al., 2019). Educators can also make school environments more culturally responsive by posting images of successful people from underrepresented groups and encourage students to share elements of their culture and family history in class (Leverson et al., 2019). Moreover, school posters defining expectations and reward tickets are both in English and other languages that comprise the school. For example, a school may have a bull as a mascot but have a large Spanish speaking population. To incorporate the school mascot into the reward tickets given out, educators might refer to the tickets as "toro tickets" on one side and "bull bucks" on the other to reflect both the Spanish and English languages. Finally, within the classroom, teachers should ensure that all students can see their cultures, histories, home language, and lives through posters, materials, and class expectations (Leverson et al., 2019).

Situational Appropriateness

Situational appropriateness can be defined as staff's recognition that certain behaviors that are expected in a school setting may differ from those considered appropriate in community or home environments (Fetterman et al., 2020; Leverson et al., 2019). Consequently, classroom routines and expectation are taught explicitly and are connected to both the students' prior knowledge and home lives and school-wide systems (Leverson et al., 2019). Where home and school expectations are different, explanations are provided to both the student and the family as to why there is difference between the two environments. For example, in many cultures, it is appropriate to have overlap in a conversation where a person makes a point or speaks while another person is talking (Leverson et al., 2019). Although speaking over or alongside a person to make a point in some cultures shows engagement in the conversation such behavior may be seen as talking out of turn by some educators. Consequently, educators should ensure that the student and family understand why it might be viewed as talking out of turn by teachers and seek to find a common ground with the family and student in understanding some of the school rules in place (Leverson et al., 2019).

Data for Equity

Data for equity entails schools using data to determine whether instruction and interventions used in SWPBS and within other interventions service delivery models, such as RTI, are effective for students from all backgrounds (Fetterman et al., 2020). Consequently, if there are a disproportionate number of students from ethnic backgrounds receiving minor and major ODRs compared to their white peers, schools should utilize the data to inform practice and make alterations within the three tiers of SWPBS accordingly. Data-based teams should research their communities to determine which ethnic groups are represented within the broad federal race categories and use this information to make practices more culturally responsive (Leverson et al., 2019).

In reviewing data, school teams should develop norms that entail discussing issues of race and culture openly and respectfully (Leverson et al., 2019). Additionally, Leverson et al. (2019) note that data-based teams should not talk in code, such as using terms like "those kids" or "those types of children don't listen" in referring to youth who may be struggling behaviorally. Additionally, Leverson et al. (2019) note that teams should be committed to examining the data and focusing on alterations within SWPBS that are within their sphere of influence and avoid making judgements about students or families. Therefore, teams examining data should be purposeful in looking into inequitable data first from a systems level perspective (i.e., what could our school be doing better?) rather than viewing it as an issue with an individual student or family (i.e., that student's parents let them get away with everything). In order to keep educators informed about behavioral data, teams should distribute data in their core reports by race, ethnicity, and disability status at least quarterly. To assist teams in using data for making equitable decisions, McIntosh, Barnes, Eliason, and Morris (2014) released a free guide entitled *Using discipline data within SWPBIS to identify and address disproportionality: A guide for school teams.*

Conclusion

SWPBS is a three-tier intervention service delivery model "housed" under multi-tiered systems of support. The goal of SWPBS is to create a warm, caring, and welcoming school environment that promotes positive behavior and provides increasing levels of interventions and supports for students who have difficulty managing their behavior. For students who do not respond to interventions and supports under SWPBS, a special education referral may be needed to determine underlying difficulties that the child may be experiencing in maintaining their behavioral challenges. In over 30 years of implementation, SWPBS has expanded across school, residential, and juvenile detention facilities and is currently being used internationally to address behavioral challenges in children, increase academic engagement, and teach prosocial behaviors.

Although major ODRs have been primarily used to screen and progress monitor students for behavioral deficits, many scholars have argued that more formalized tools should be combined with major ODRs to best identify students at-risk conduct deficits. At present, a number of valid and reliable tools for universally screening and progress monitoring student behavior are available. For universal screening, the SRSS-IE, BESS, SAEBRS, SSBD, and BIMAS-2 may be utilized. For progress monitoring, the SRSS-IE, SSBD, and BIMAS-2 are available. It is worthy to note that many screening and progress monitoring tools available briefly assess for both behavioral and emotional risk and can be used in SWPBS or social-emotional RTI. Finally, in implementing SWPBS, Leverson et al. (2019) note that five components can be incorporated to increase cultural responsiveness of which include identity, voice, supportive environment, situational appropriateness, and using data for equitable decision-making. Table 4.5 summarizes the critical elements found in SWPBS. Figure 4.4 provides a checklist for SWPBS with suggested interventions and decision points. Lastly, Appendix B provides a flow-chart of SWPBS.

TABLE 4.5 ● Critical Elements Found in a SWPBS

Elements	Tier 1	Tier 2	Tier 3
Type of support provided	Whole school & class behavior support	Targeted behavior interventions & supports	Intense behavior interventions & supports
Interventions provided	Classroom and school expectations posted Teaching and modeling of expectations Ticket reward system for positive behavior Positive school motto Newsletter home to parents outlining behavior expectations	Check-in/Check-out Behavior contract Daily behavior report card Group counseling with three to six students (if needed)	FBA/BIP Wrap-around support 1:1 counseling (if needed)
Duration of Intervention	All school year	School determined or lasts the length of the counselling program No less than eight weeks	School determined or lasts length or length of counseling No less than ten weeks
Instruction or intervention provided by	Teacher and/or school counselor	School staff Counseling: school counselor and/or school psychologist	FBA-BIP developed by the behavior support team and implemented by school staff Counseling with the school psychologist
Frequency of screening/ progress monitoring	3 times per year (Universal screening)	Bi-weekly or weekly (Progress monitoring)	Weekly or twice weekly (Progress monitoring)
Number of data points collected	3	School determined but preferably 12 to 14 data points if using a formal progress monitoring measure. Also consider number of major office discipline referrals in determining progress.	School determined but preferably 12 to 14 data points if using a formal progress monitoring measure. Also consider number of major office discipline referrals in determining progress.

FIGURE 4.4 ● SWPBS Checklist

School-Wide Positive Behavior Support (See Appendix B for Flow Chart on School-wide Positive Behavior Support)
Tier 1
A *For all students, implement core behavior expectation/school rules by:* ✓ Teaching three to five behavior expectations through the school mission statement, posters, and Good Behavior Game ✓ Informing parents of classroom and school rules/expectations through the school website and newsletters ✓ Reinforcing positive behaviors through specific verbal praise, special privileges, and a ticket reward system ✓ Supervising high frequency areas where problem behavior occur (i.e. crowded hallway, cafeteria, foyer) ✓ Building rapport with students and families through after school programs, events, and phone calls home to report positive behavior ✓ Universally screening students using measures such as the Behavior Intervention Monitoring Assessment System-2 (BIMAS-2), Behavioral and Emotional Screening System (BESS), and/or office discipline referrals ✓ **If student meets grade level behavior expectations continue to implement the core behavior curriculum at Tier 1A** ✓ **If student does not meet behavior expectations, proceed to Tier 1B**
B *For students who are not meeting grade level behavior expectations, attempt the following before proceeding to Tier 2:* ✓ Differentiate instruction; re-teach class and school rules ✓ Check attendance and medical status (outside diagnosis, hearing, and vision that may be impacting behavior) ✓ Consult with parents over behavior concerns and review behavior expectations ✓ Note any changes to home environment that may be affecting child's social, emotional, or behavioral well-being (death of loved one, birth of sibling, divorce etc.) ✓ Meet with the child study team to evaluate data and determine whether Tier 2 intervention(s) are needed ✓ **If student responds to interventions and makes adequate progress return to Tier 1A** ✓ **If student does not make adequate progress or is not on meeting behavior expectations, provide the student Tier 2A interventions (Review minor and major office discipline referrals; Refer to Tier 2 after two or more office discipline referrals or if screening data indicates student is at-risk)**
Tier 2
A *Fro students who have not responded to Tier 1 supports:* ✓ Schedule parent-teacher conference ✓ Develop and implement check-in/check-out (CICO) ✓ Use tangible rewards with CICO ✓ Track data on CICO to determine if intervention is working ✓ Progress monitor student using BIMAS-2, BESS, or other measure on a bi-weekly basis ✓ Continue to monitor office discipline referrals ✓ Meet with child study team to evaluate data and determine student progress after eight to ten weeks ✓ **For students who have made adequate progress in Tier 2, return to receiving Tier 1A interventions and supports only** ✓ **For students who have not made adequate progress, proceed to Tier 2B (If no alternative Tier 2 intervention is available, move to Tier 3A).**

FIGURE 4.4 • (Continued)

B ✓ Combine CICO with behavior contract, daily report card, or another intervention

✓ Provide child social skills or problem-solving group counseling consisting of 3–6 students using programs such as Skillstreaming or First Step to Success (counseling sessions should be held two times per week)

✓ Continue to progress monitor on a bi-weekly basis and monitor office discipline referrals

✓ Meet with child study team to evaluate data and determine whether Tier 3 intervention(s) are needed

✓ **If student responds to interventions and makes adequate progress return to Tier 1A**

✓ **If student does not make adequate progress, try another Tier 2 intervention or proceed to Tier 3A**

Tier 3

A *For students who have not responded to Tier 2 supports:*

✓ Develop a functional behavior assessment (FBA) and behavior intervention plan (BIP) (if needed)

✓ Contact outside agencies for wraparound services and supports

✓ Refer student for individual counseling with school psychologist using cognitive behavior therapy, dialectical behavior therapy, or other counseling method

✓ Track progress on a weekly basis using BIMAS-2, BESS, office discipline referrals or other measure

✓ Meet with child study team to evaluate data and determine if adequate progress has been made

✓ **If student responds to interventions and makes adequate progress return to Tier 1A**

✓ **If student does not make adequate progress, proceed to Tier 3B**

B ✓ Implement and monitor another Tier 3 intervention in area of deficit if there is one available

✓ Collect 12–14 curriculum-based measure data points on weekly or bi-weekly basis to determine whether the student is responding to the new Tier 3 intervention

✓ Meet with the child study team to evaluate data and determine whether the student is responding to intervention(s)

✓ **If student responds to interventions and makes adequate progress return to Tier 1A**

✓ **If student does not make adequate progress, edit and revise the FBA/BIP and attempt to re-implement before moving towards a special education referral in needed**

CASE EXAMPLE

SCHOOL-WIDE POSITIVE BEHAVIOR SUPPORT

Child Background

Aniyah is a fifth-grader at Ellis Middle School in Lansing, Michigan. She currently resides with her mother, Latoya Smith, and two older sisters, Brianna and Vivienne. Aniyah's father, Brian Jackson, and mother divorced when Aniyah was in third-grade, and she has not spoken to her father for the past two-years. During the week, Miss Smith is employed as a direct support professional and helps care for individuals with developmental disabilities at a group home. Miss Smith's job often requires her to work at night or mandates her to come in during weekends. Consequently, Aniyah and her sisters are often cared for by their grandparents.

Aniyah was born at 42 weeks gestation and delivered via C-section. At birth she weighed seven pounds, two ounces. Per Mrs. Smith, developmental milestones were reported as follows: walked alone 15 months, spoke first words: 13 months, spoke first sentences: 28 months, and was potty-trained by 36 months. At present, Aniyah is reported to be in good health. Her family history is noteworthy for her father being diagnosed with antisocial personality disorder. Mrs. Smith describes her daughter as good natured but noted that she does have a "mean streak."

Aniyah's teacher, Mrs. Burns, agrees with Mrs. Smith's report that Aniyah has a "mean streak." She noted that Aniyah's behavior can be disruptive to the classroom routine and often intimidates other students. Overall, Aniyah displays with the behaviors of verbal and physical aggression. Verbal aggression can be defined as any incident in which Aniyah swears, screams, or makes derogatory remarks toward others in an attempt to avoid non-preferred tasks/activities or obtain objects/items she wants. Physical aggression can be defined as any incident in which Aniyah attempts or successfully completes hitting, kicking, punching, or slapping others in an attempt to obtain objects/items she wants.

School-Wide Positive Behavior Support

SWPBS is a three-tier intervention service delivery model that attempts to create a warm and welcoming school environment (Gage et al., 2018; Sugai & Horner, 2008). A central ternate of SWPBS is to prevent and intervene appropriately to address maladaptive externalizing behaviors that children might display, such as verbal or physical aggression (Sugai & Horner, 2008; Gage et al., 2018).

Tier 1

Tier 1 of SWPBS is designed to foster a safe, positive, and caring school community (Lewis et al., 2017). Typically, 80%–85% of students are responsive to these efforts (Horner & Sugai, 2015; Sugai & Horner, 2008). At Aniyah's school, educators have worked together to develop a school motto, expectations, and routines. These school-wide expectations are posted in the hallways and in classrooms. To help students demonstrate prosocial behaviors, a positive phrase has been developed and states that "Ellis' school students SOAR." The acronym, SOAR, is catchy and fits well with the school mascot of the Ellis bald eagle. Moreover, this acronym can be found in the school motto of "Be **S**afe. Be resp**O**nsible. **A**nd be **R**espectful."

Every Friday morning, Aniyah's class recites the school motto and subsequently provides examples when a classmate "SOARED" by displaying safe, responsible, or respectful behavior. In addition to the school motto, a school-wide token economy has been put into place to reward students who are caught engaging in safe, responsible, and respectful behavior. For example, earlier in the school year, when Aniyah's principle observed her holding the door open for another student, she was rewarded with an Ellis Elite school token for respectful behavior. At the end of the week, these tokens can be exchanged for prizes and treats at the school bookstore.

Aside from using a token economy, school staff help to foster a safe and positive school environment by monitoring crowded areas and hallways where problem behaviors often occur. For example, at the beginning and end of each day, school staff increasingly monitor entranceways where students gather and bullying tends to take place. Moreover, school staff model appropriate behaviors for students and provide specific feedback when students are behaving appropriately. Finally, Aniyah's teacher is using the GBG as a classroom-based behavior management program.

In spite of all the Tier 1 interventions and supports being put into place, Aniyah continued to display both verbal and physical aggression. By combining major ODRs with universal screening data, Aniyah's school identified several means in which students with behavioral concerns could be referred to Tier 2 supports. Students who receive at least two major ODRs, four minor infractions, or have scored in the some to high risk range on the BIMAS-2 are referred to Tier 2. Three weeks into the start of the school year, Aniyah has obtained two major ODRs. Additionally, fall universal screening data using the BIMAS-2 indicated that she fell in the some risk range for developing future significant behavior deficits. As a consequence of Aniyah's ODRs and score on the BIMAS-2, the child study team met and referred Aniyah to Tier 2 of SWPBS.

Tier 2

For the 10%–15% of students who have not benefited from Tier 1 supports and interventions within SWPBS, Aniyah's school uses a CICO program (Horner & Sugai, 2015). At the start of each day, Aniyah visits the school counselor's office to check-in and pick up her daily progress report form. After reviewing the day's behavioral goals and how many points she will need to receive her end of the day reward, Aniyah attends her first period class. During lunch, Aniyah once again visits her school counselor to check-in with how she is progressing throughout the day and receive feedback and support. Finally, at the end of the day, Aniyah checks-out with her school counselor to review her performance throughout the day and to see if she earned enough points to earn a prize. While in Tier 2, Aniyah's progress will be monitored on a bi-weekly basis by reviewing her scores on the BIMAS-2. Additionally, Aniyah's major ODRs will continue to be tracked.

After eight weeks of participating, the CICO program, Aniyah's BIMAS-2 progress monitoring data indicated that she continued to fall in the high-risk range. Additionally, Aniyah received one additional ODR since the CICO program began. Consequently, the child study team met and agreed to discontinue the check-in/check program. Subsequently, the CST team thought that Aniyah may benefit from taking part in a school developed social academic intervention group for students displaying aggressive or defiant behaviors. Additionally, Aniyah's counselor worked with her in developing a behavior contract. After attending the social academic intervention group for ten weeks, Aniyah's biweekly progress monitoring scores indicated that she continued to fall in the high risk-range. Moreover, she received four minor classroom infractions, which resulted in one major ODR. Consequently, the child study team reviewed Aniyah's progress and recommended her for Tier 3 interventions and supports.

Tier 3

Approximately 1%–5% of students do not respond to Tier 2 interventions and programs and are in need of Tier 3 support (Horner & Sugai, 2015; Sugai & Horner, 2008). At Tier 3, the school psychologist lead child study team in writing up a FBA for Aniyah. Through the FBA, the team determined that Aniyah tends to engage in verbal aggression to escape or avoid non-preferred tasks or activities, such as reading. Additionally, it was determined that Aniyah engages in both verbal and physical aggression for tangible reasons. For example, Aniyah often engages in physical aggression to obtain objects/items she wants, such as bracelets, trinkets, and toys from her peers.

After completing the FBA, the team decided to put a behavior intervention plan into place in hopes of remediating Aniyah's maladaptive deficits. At Tier 3, Aniyah's progress was tracked using the BIMAS-2 on a weekly basis. Additionally, Aniyah's ODRs were closely monitored. After eight weeks of the BIP being put into place, Aniyah made significant gains on her BIMAS-2 scores and only had two minor classroom infractions. Consequently, the CST team decided to keep Aniyah on her BIP for an additional eight weeks. By the eighth week after the CST met, Aniyah's BIMAS-2 scores fell in the low risk range, and she had no further infractions. As a result, the CST team determined to start fading Aniyah's interventions within her BIP to effectively transfer her back into Tier 1 supports only.

Discussion Questions

1. What is the overall goal of SWPBS?
2. What four areas does SWPBS place emphasis on in preventing and intervening in externalizing behaviors?
3. In your own words, explain the differences between Tier 1, Tier 2, and Tier 3 of SWPBS?
4. What are the differences between a functional behavior assessment and a behavior intervention plan?
5. What are the five major reasons why children engage in challenging behaviors?
6. What is the difference between a minor and major disciplinary infraction?
7. Why is it important for schools to use more formal measures in universally screening and progress monitoring students with potential behavior concerns?

Social-Emotional RTI and Embedding Trauma-Informed Practices

Learning Objectives

After reading this chapter, you should be able to:

- Explain the reasons why children turn to educators for mental health support.
- Summarize the five areas of core competency of social-emotional learning.
- Describe the overall goal of social-emotional response to intervention (RTI).
- Differentiate between Tier 1, Tier 2, and Tier 3 of social-emotional RTI.
- Compare social-emotional RTI to social-emotional RTI with embedded trauma practices.
- Define trauma.
- Identify universal screening and progress monitoring tools used for data-based decision-making within social-emotional RTI.
- Summarize how to incorporate culturally responsive practices into social-emotional RTI.

Background on Children's Mental Health Services

The previous two chapters covered the earliest intervention service delivery models that comprise two of the walls to building a sound Multi-Tiered Systems of Support (MTSS) framework, namely, response to intervention and school-wide positive behavior support. This chapter will focus on a newer model of intervention service delivery that makes up the third wall of the MTSS house called social-emotional RTI. Recall that all intervention service delivery models are connected and supported under the house of MTSS by the four pillars of varying levels of evidence-based interventions and supports, universal screening, progress monitoring, and data-based decision-making. These four pillars are equally prevalent and important in newer models of intervention and service delivery, such as social-emotional RTI and suicide prevention and intervention.

In the early 2000s, the suggestion of developing an intervention service delivery model to meet the social-emotional needs of children began to gain momentum (Gresham, 2005). This concept grew out of the fact that students exhibiting social-emotional challenges were either underserved or unserved by mental health systems and school districts in the United States (Gresham, 2005; Tibbets, 2013). Aside from being underserved, children who display with elevated levels of internalizing and externalizing behaviors in early and middle childhood often experience underachievement in school, bullying, victimization, substance use and abuse, and even mortality (Arby et al., 2017).

As a consequence of children with social-emotional deficits being underserved and often experiencing underachievement, many scholars and policymakers realized that by not preventing emotional and behavioral deficits, considerable money was being expended on reactionary treatments that were not adequately helping children with such concerns (Arby et al., 2017; Gresham, 2005; Tibbets, 2013). To illustrate, the latest estimates suggest that emotional and behavioral health disorders among children cost the United States $247 billion annually in treatment, special education services, incarceration, and decreased productivity (Bardach et al., 2014). Furthermore, a recent analysis revealed that benefits of implementing programs that promote mental wellness and prevent social-emotional concerns outweigh the costs of not doing so by a factor of 11:1 with an average net present value per 100 participants of $618,380 (Belfield et al., 2015).

Despite the staggering cost of childhood mental health disorders, the Centers for Disease Control and Prevention (2019) and National Association of School Psychologists (2015) report that one out of five children have a diagnosable mental health condition and approximately 80% of children do not receive appropriate treatment for their condition (Farmer, Burns, Phillips, Angold, & Costello, 2003; Langer et al., 2015). Of the 20% of children who do receive treatment for social-emotional difficulties, approximately 70%–80% receive mental health support in school settings (Farmer et al., 2003; Langer et al., 2015). In fact, children were found to be 21 times more likely to visit school-based centers for mental health concerns over community-based centers (Juszczak, Melinkovich, & Kaplan, 2003). Moreover, systemic reviews have found that school-based practitioners are more effective at improving the social-emotional learning (SEL) outcomes of students than nonschool practitioners (Durlak, Weissberg, Dymnicki, Taylor, & Schellinger, 2011; Maras, Thompson, Lewis, Thornburg, & Hawks, 2015).

Although children are more likely to visit and receive help from school-based mental health practitioners, the average delay between the child's onset of mental health symptoms and intervention is approximately 8–10 years (National Alliance on Mental Health, 2019). This is in light of over 50% of all lifetime cases of mental illness beginning by age 14 and 75% by age 24 (National Alliance on Mental Health, 2019). Given these statistics, it is imperative for parents, educators, and policymakers to advocate and ensure increased access to school-based mental health practitioners to provide children adequate mental health support.

Reasons Why Children Turn to Educators for Support

There are generally several reasons why children seek out teachers, administrators, and school-based mental health practitioners, such as school psychologists and school counselors, over community-based practitioners. First, educators and school-based practitioners tend to be close in physical proximity to the child (Maras et al., 2015). Since educators and school-based practitioners are located within the schools themselves, they likely have the ability to provide the child "on the spot" and "in the moment" counseling or behavioral remediation when the child is having difficulty (Maras et al., 2015). On the contrary, community-based clinicians do not have the same immediate access to children to provide counseling and support when they are experiencing difficulties.

Aside from being close to children in physical proximity, educators and school-based clinicians are easily accessible compared to outside practitioners (Maras et al., 2015). In some cases, school-based practitioners offer and provide the only mental health services for children in a community. For example, Figure 5.1 shows that many states and counties across America have little to no licensed psychologists to support children outside the school setting (American Psychological Association, 2016). Further analysis revealed that approximately 66.4 counties across the United States had no more than five psychologists, and 74.6% of counties had no more than ten psychologists (American Psychological Association, 2016).

FIGURE 5.1 • Hot Spot Analysis on the Number of Licensed Psychologists, 2012–2015 (American Psychological Association, 2016)

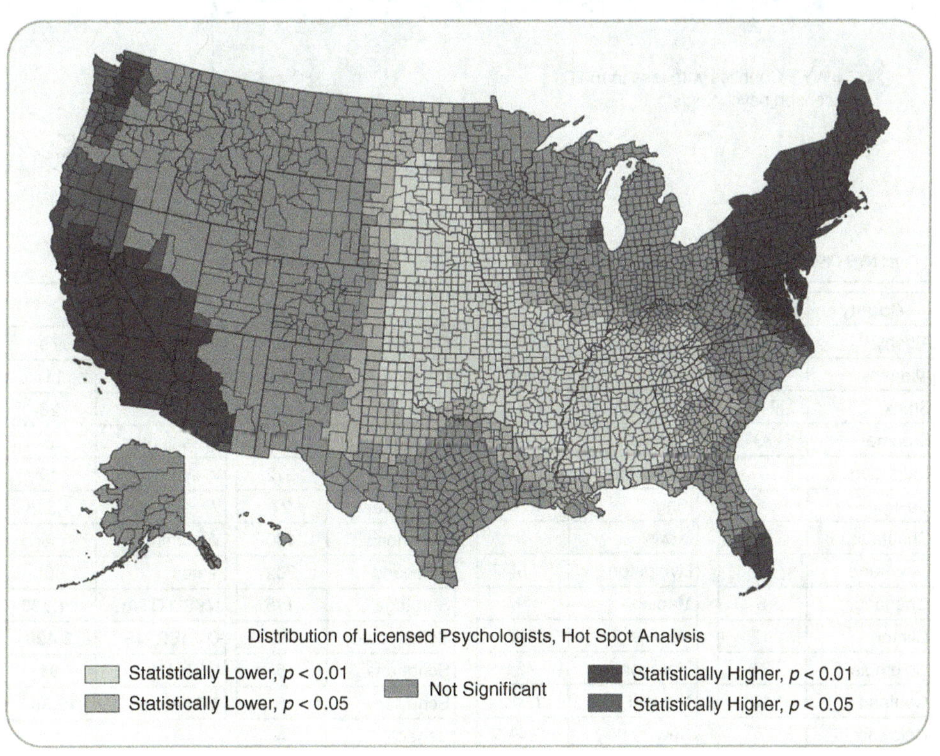

Even in states where there appears to be an adequate number of licensed psychologists to meet the mental health needs of children, like New York, a closer look at Figure 5.2 reveals that 32 out of 62 counties (53%) have less than 20 licensed psychologists (NYS Office of Professions, 2021). Additionally, the number of licenses issued in New York State for the title of psychologist decreased from 572 to 507 from 2019 to 2020 (NYS Office of Professions, 2021). Finally, although some counties across the United States appear to have an adequate number of licensed psychologists, only a fraction of these psychologists treat children or possess specialized training in the treatment of children (NYS Office of Professions, 2021; Swick & Powers, 2018).

FIGURE 5.2 ● New York State Counties With Less Than 20 Licensed Psychologists

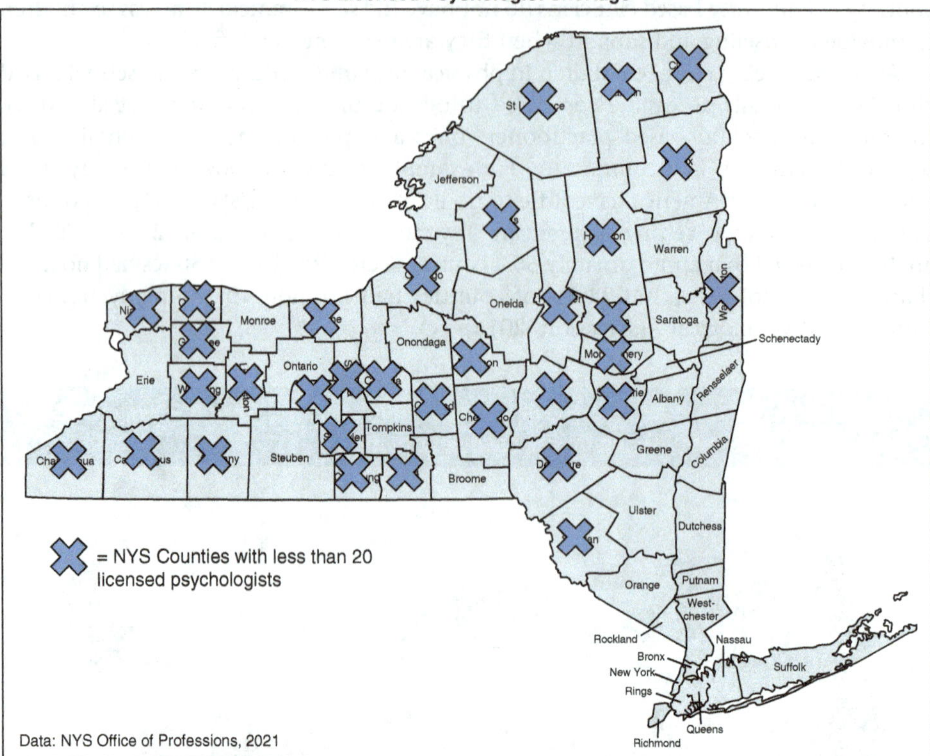

County	Number
Albany	247
Allegany	13
Bronx	217
Broome	73
Cattaraugus	6
Cayuga	4
Chautauqua	5
Chemung	8
Chenango	6
Clinton	12
Columbia	31
Cortland	10
Delaware	7
Dutchess	176
Erie	333
Essex	12
Franklin	5
Fulton	10
Genesee	6
Greene	14
Hamilton	1
Herkimer	1
Jefferson	20
Kings	1,087
Lewis	3
Livingston	14
Madison	16
Monroe	385
Montgomery	5
Nassau	1,322
New York	3,447
Niagara	19
Oneida	49
Onondaga	225
Ontario	38
Orange	107
Orleans	3
Oswego	8
Otsego	14
Putnam	59
Queens	612
Rensselaer	27
Richmond	140
Rockland	202
Saratoga	115
Schenectady	56
Schoharie	5
Schuyler	5
Seneca	4
Steuben	26
St. Lawrence	18
Suffolk	911
Sullivan	19
Tioga	10
Tompkins	79
Ulster	117
Warren	26
Washington	5
Wayne	10
Westchester	1,318
Wyoming	2
Yates	5
NYS TOTAL	**11,730**
OTHER US	**3,498**
NON-US	**81**
TOTAL	**15,309**

One of the biggest reasons children seek out educators and school-based mental health practitioners over outside mental health clinicians may be due to their level of comfort with them (National Association of School Psychologists, 2015; Swick & Power, 2018). Due to frequently coming into contact with children in the school setting, it is likely that educators and school-based practitioners have developed a personal connection or are familiar with the student already (National Association of School Psychologists, 2015; Swick & Power, 2018). For example, often educators and school-based mental health practitioners are notified early when the child starts showing signs of social-emotional concerns or students frequently seek out assistance from school-based mental health practitioners. To that point, another reason why children and parents may seek out educators and school-based mental health practitioners over a community-based professional is that there appears to be reduced stigma involved in seeking out school-based practitioners (Swick & Power, 2018). Possible contributing factors to children and families seeking out educators and school-based practitioners over community-based clinicians are that these practitioners have a sound understanding of how school systems function and how student behavior and mental health impact their ability to be successful in school. Moreover, schools are familiar environments to families and students as opposed to community-based clinics and hospitals (Swick & Power, 2018).

Finally, even if children have access to clinicians outside the school setting, the cost of accessing such a practitioner may be too big a barrier for parents to overcome (Cuellar, 2015; Swick & Power, 2018). Often insurance may not fully cover counseling sessions or limit the child to a number of sessions before parents have to take on the costs of counseling themselves (Cuellar, 2015; Swick & Power, 2018). Not surprisingly, data from the National Survey of children with Special Health Care Needed revealed that 25% of parents reported the reason they did not obtain mental health care for their child was due to services costing too much (DeRigne, Porterfield, & Metz, 2009; Swick & Power, 2018). In contrast to nonschool-based mental health providers, school-based mental health services are provided to the child at no additional cost to parents.

For all the aforementioned reasons, schools are ideal places to promote mental wellness, prevent mental illness, and provide ongoing support to students at critical times throughout their life. As a consequence of growing concerns over student mental health, the idea of having a three-tiered intervention service delivery model to foster children's mental wellness became particularly appealing to schools, parents, and policymakers. Therefore, the Every Students Succeeds Act (ESSA) provides administrators and schools opportunities to prioritize the development of social-emotional skills in children (Eklund, Kilpatrick, Kilgus, & Haider, 2018). More specifically, ESSA requires states to develop systems of accountability that not only included two indicators of student academic achievement but also at least one indicator of school quality or student success in areas such as school climate or SEL.

Social-Emotional Learning

Social-emotional learning was largely introduced and defined in the book *Promoting Social and Emotional Learning: Guidelines for Educators* (Elias et al., 1997). Since then, there have been many proposed definitions of SEL, but one of the most accepted descriptions states that SEL is:

> *the processes through which children and adults acquire and effectively apply the knowledge, attitudes, and skills necessary to understand and manage emotions, set and achieve positive goals, feel and show empathy for others, establish and maintain*

positive relationships, and make responsible decisions. (Collaborative for Academic, Social, and Emotional Learning [CASEL], 2019, para. 1)

Development of SEL in children is generally characterized by five areas of core competency including: (1) self-awareness, (2) social awareness, (3) self-management, (4) relationship skills, and (5) responsible decision-making (Eklund et al., 2018; Moy & Hazen, 2018). **Self-awareness** is the ability to recognize one's own emotions, values, and thoughts and how each may influence behavior (Eklund et al., 2018). **Self-management** has been described as the ability to successfully regulate emotions, thoughts, and behaviors in different situations and across different contexts (Eklund et al., 2018). **Social awareness** entails whether one can take on the perspective of others and empathize with them (Eklund et al., 2018). **Relationship skills** consist of an individual's ability to establish and maintain healthy and rewarding relationships with diverse groups and individuals (Eklund et al., 2018). Finally, **responsible decision-making** requires the ability to make constructive choices about social interactions and personal behavior based on social norms, ethical standards, and safety concerns (Eklund et al., 2018).

Each of these core competencies in SEL is viewed as interrelated to one another and critical to children developing positive coping strategies and displaying prosocial behaviors. In order to promote SEL, educators should identify and build on existing supports and strengths for SEL. Additionally, educators should develop a shared vision that integrates SEL with academic learning for all students and establishes partnerships with parents to enhance children's social-emotional competence (Greenberg, Domitrovich, Weissberg, & Durlak, 2017). Finally, educators should establish resources for professional development that builds SEL awareness for staff and students and incorporate SEL into their everyday teaching (Greenberg et al., 2017).

For example, during a history lesson on colonization of America, a teacher may incorporate components of SEL by asking students to describe how Native Americans may have felt about the arrival of Europeans and being moved off their land. This particular activity involves students further developing the core SEL competency of social awareness. The lesson may further assist students in developing their self-awareness by asking them to reflect on how their own personal values, beliefs, and experiences may affect their view of others.

The benefits of incorporating SEL into schools include improved student outcomes in academics, behavior, and academic engagement. Additional benefits of incorporating SEL into schools include increases in graduation rates and lower rates of school dropout (Eklund et al., 2018; Moy & Hazen, 2018). A long-term outcome of schools implementing SEL interventions includes students having greater social-emotional competence. Greater social-emotional competence has been linked to college and career readiness, good family and work relationships, and improved mental health (Greenberg et al., 2017). Lastly, a recent national survey of teachers revealed that 95% believe that SEL is teachable, and 97% indicated that SEL can benefit students from all socioeconomic backgrounds (Bridgeland, Bruce, & Hariharan, 2013).

As a consequence of these promising findings, many states have adopted SEL standards and have sought out social-emotional RTI to help meet these goals (Dusenbury & Weissberg, 2018). For example, in 2011 only one state, Illinois, articulated SEL competencies through twelfth grade (Dunsenbury & Weissberg, 2018). However, by 2018, over 12 states articulated SEL competencies through twelfth grade (Dunsenbury & Weissberg, 2018). Despite children's mental health being increasingly highlighted by policymakers and SEL gaining in popularity, there is a significant lack of information available in the implementation of social-emotional RTI. Consequently, there is considerable variability in how social-emotional RTI and SEL interventions are being implemented across schools (Dursenburty & Weissberg, 2018).

Although social-emotional RTI is in its infancy stages and significant variability exists in how or to what extent it is implemented, it is arguably the most closely linked model of intervention service delivery to public health. This is because the ultimate goal of the public health model is to improve the overall well-being of the general population. As mentioned at the beginning of this book, even though the public health model was initially developed to prevent the spread of disease and physical illness in the general population, it was eventually adopted by the psychiatric community (Leavell & Clark, 1965). Therefore, it appears there was an understanding that improvement in the general population's well-being meant not only preventing physical ailments from occurring and spreading but also included the prevention and early treatment of social-emotional concerns (Greenberg et al., 2017). Ironically, both the prevention and early treatment of physical and social-emotional concerns incorporated practices from epidemiology to inhibit the spread or advancement of the disease. As discussed, some of these practices have their foundations in Witmer's problem-solving model and are mirrored in every intervention service delivery model, including social-emotional RTI. The remainder of this chapter will discuss social-emotional RTI and provide readers a detailed outline of this intervention service delivery model. Figure 5.3 shows social-emotional RTI forming the third wall to the MTSS "house."

FIGURE 5.3 • Social-Emotional RTI and Embedding Trauma-Informed Practices Forming the Third Wall of the MTSS "House"

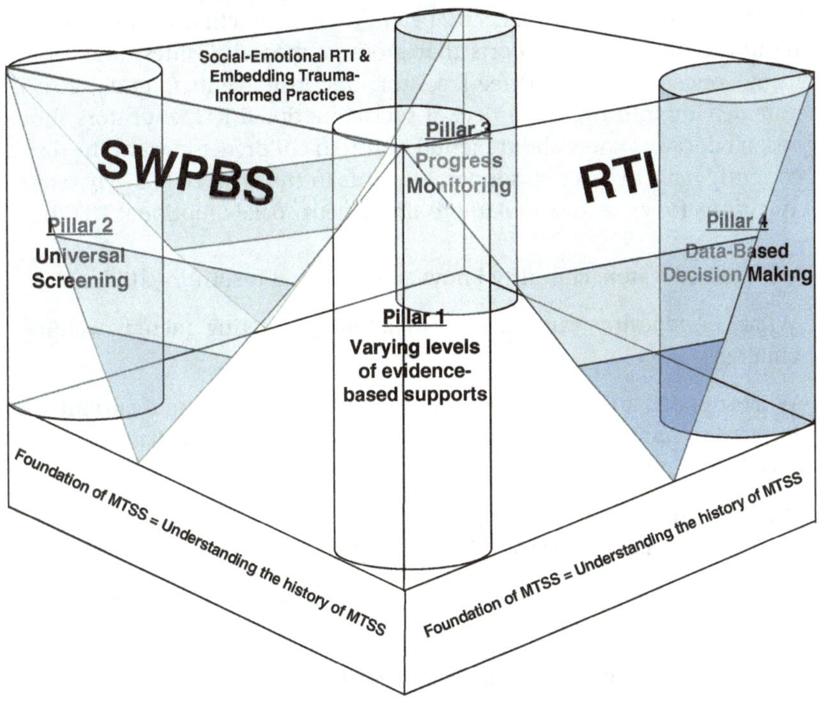

Introduction to Social-Emotional RTI

Just as RTI and SWPBS have increasingly become ways in which to identify and intervene with students who have academic and behavior difficulties, **social-emotional RTI** has been developed to promote mental wellness, prevent mental illness, and identify children at-risk for social-emotional deficits. Therefore, while SWPBS focuses on externalizing behaviors, such as physical aggression, verbal aggression, and acts of defiance, social-emotional RTI attends to children presenting with internalizing concerns (Gresham, 2007; Tibbets, 2013). Examples of internalizing concerns include social withdrawal, somatic complaints, negative thoughts, poor self-esteem, episodes of sadness, and bouts of nervousness. Unlike externalizing deficits, which are directed outwardly toward others and considered *undercontrolled*, **internalizing concerns** are directed inwardly at the individual and considered *overcontrolled* (Hunter, Chenier, & Gresham, 2014). In other words, children presenting with internalizing concerns attempt to overcontrol internal emotions or thoughts to an excessive and maladaptive extent (Hunter et al., 2014). Both schools and mental health providers tend to overlook children presenting with internalizing concerns and do not recommend them for intervention because their behaviors often do not clash with behavioral expectations set by teachers, administrators, parents, or law enforcement (Hunter et al., 2014; Tibbets, 2013). Consequently, social-emotional RTI continues to gain momentum as an intervention service delivery model to prevent and treat children presenting with social-emotional concerns.

As with every intervention service delivery model, social-emotional RTI consists of three tiers with a specific focus of teaching students mental wellness strategies and providing support to children with social-emotional concerns (Greenberg et al., 2017; Gresham, 2005). A key goal of social-emotional RTI is to foster the development of the five SEL competency areas discussed earlier (Greenberg et al., 2017). Social-emotional RTI seeks to develop the five SEL competency areas in children by systematically delivering interventions and supports that promote mental wellness and remediating internalizing concerns through three levels of support (Greenberg et al., 2017). However, before delving into the three tiers of social-emotional RTI, educators should first identify what educators know about mental health in children and what the district and school currently have in place to support students in the areas of SEL. Therefore, some helpful questions for educators looking to implement social-emotional RTI include:

1. What do educators currently know about mental health in children?
2. What do educators currently know about promoting mental wellness in children?
3. What supports and interventions does the district and school currently have in place to promote mental wellness in children and remediate social-emotional concerns?
4. What tier do existing supports and interventions that are currently being implemented fall into (Tier 1, Tier 2, Tier 3)?
5. Why is it believed the supports and programs currently being implemented fall into the tier selected?
6. Are the district and school consistently implementing these supports and interventions on a daily basis at each tier?
7. How are the district and school consistently implementing these supports and interventions on a daily basis at each tier?

8. Are the supports and interventions currently being implemented evidence-based? In other words, has research-proven them to be effective at promoting mental wellness or remediating social-emotional concerns?
9. Are the supports and interventions currently being implemented culturally and developmentally appropriate?
10. What other supports and interventions do school-based mental health staff know about that may greatly benefit students in the areas of promoting mental wellness and remediating social-emotional deficits?
11. Is the school currently screening for social-emotional concerns and progress monitoring students with social-emotional concerns?
12. How much are the district and school utilizing school-based mental health professionals to engage in supporting children's social-emotional needs?
13. Has the district or school assessed what factors may be limiting school-based mental health professional's time in implementing social-emotional RTI and providing guidance and support to both district staff and students?

After considering each of these questions, districts and schools can best position themselves to start constructing a sound social-emotional RTI model. By utilizing the guiding questions above, educators can compare what they currently have in place to what is needed at each tier of social-emotional RTI to properly implement it. Critical to the implementation of social-emotional RTI is whether schools are adequately seeking insight from their school-based mental health staff and utilizing their time effectively to set up the model. By highly involving school-based mental health staff to lead efforts in outlining and implementing social-emotional RTI, tiered interventions and supports have a better chance at being constructed accordingly and implemented with fidelity. Therefore, it is vital that school-based mental health practitioners fully understand what each tier of social-emotional RTI entails and what is needed at each tier to appropriately implement it.

Description of Social-Emotional RTI Tiers

Tier 1

Many components of Tier 1 of social-emotional RTI are similar and blend together with that of SWPBS. Tier 1 supports and interventions within social-emotional RTI are implemented with the goal of preventing mental health concerns which might act as a barrier to academic achievement. Therefore, these supports and interventions focus on the promotion of mental wellness for all students with approximately 80%–85% of students expected to respond to such interventions (Ziomek-Daigle & Heckman, 2019). Like Tier 1 of SWPBS, a central component to preventing both mental and behavioral health concerns is the creation of a warm, welcoming, and caring school environment that students feel safe in (Lester & Cross, 2015).

Schools can create an environment that promotes mental wellness by positively outlining behavioral expectations, implementing a positive school motto to teach behavioral expectations, modeling prosocial behaviors, rewarding prosocial and positive behaviors through a token economy, and holding in-service trainings for educators to recognize the basic signs of students struggling with social-emotional problems (Moy & Hazen, 2018). Social-emotional RTI supplements existing interventions covered under

Tier 1 of SWPBS by teaching students how to appropriately label and express their feelings, enter new groups and establish relationships, adapt and cope with stressful situations, overcome adversity without lasting difficulties, and develop awareness and respect for other's feelings and perspectives (Greenberg et al., 2017; Moy & Hazen, 2018).

Each of these areas can be incorporated into everyday teachings. Earlier, it was discussed how a teacher may include several components of SEL into a lesson on the colonization of the United States. Another activity may involve students working together on problem-solving activities or games that involve cooperation, perspective-taking, and respectfully expressing one's thoughts and feelings. For example, a science lesson may involve students working in pairs to see which pair can complete an electrical circuit the fastest. After the students have completed the activity, the teacher may conclude the lesson by having students review difficulties they may have encountered during the activity and whether there were differences in opinion over how to complete the task. The teacher may then have students describe how they overcame differences in opinion and tie it into how scientists studying conductivity have to work in teams every day to advance the field.

Other than classroom lessons and activities that incorporate SEL, teachers may include familiar games in their classroom with some minor alterations in rules of playing the game. To illustrate, the teacher may create social-emotional *Jenga* by simply writing different emotions on blocks (Gotay, 2013; Hasbro, 2017). Emotions may include feelings such as happy, sad, scared, jealous, and nervous. When playing the game, upon students pulling out a block with an emotion on it, the student then describes to their partner what that emotion means and how it makes them feel. A similar activity can be developed using the children's game *Don't Break the Ice* (Gotay, 2013; Hasbro, 2017). In addition to games, the teacher may have a bookshelf that students can access during downtime or silent reading that includes books on promoting mental wellness and coping with social-emotional difficulties. Some books that teachers may want to consider in promoting SEL include *Don't Feed the WorryBug* by Andi Green (2011) and *In My Heart: A Book of Feelings* by Jo Witek (2014). Educators can find a list of over 40 children's books on mental health by visiting the Child Mind Institute's website (Cicero, n.d.).

Aside from incorporating lessons and games that promote SEL at the Tier 1 level, teachers may model for students how to complete brief mindfulness activities independently. **Mindfulness** is a therapeutic technique that assists individuals in becoming aware of the present moment by acknowledging one's feelings, thoughts, and bodily sensations (Sapthiang, Van Gordon, & Shonin, 2019). Incorporation of mindfulness activities has been shown to decrease children's levels of anxiety, depression, hostility, intrusive thoughts, and stress (Sapthiang et al., 2019). Teachers may easily integrate mindfulness activities into a student's daily routine by modeling and having students participate in deep breathing activities, meditation, or even yoga. Teachers may even have set times during the day in which students can practice mindfulness activities, such as when students enter the classroom at the beginning of the day or at the end of the school day.

In addition to these activities that promote mental wellness, teachers and schools may want to incorporate playing calming classical or acoustic music at the beginning or end of the day to create a comforting environment and have a "cool-down corner" in their classroom. A **cool-down corner** is a designated place in the classroom where children who are sad, nervous, or upset can go to calm down, feel comfortable, and de-stress. Cool-down corners typically involve a number of objects, items, and activities to assist children in calming down including pillows, bean bag chairs, books, stress balls, noise canceling headphones, blankets, and fidget toys. Cool-down corners provide students, who are having a difficult time, a safe place to head to and provide them activities and objects to engage in to appropriately cope with their emotions.

Aside from these more informal strategies of building SEL and mental wellness at Tier 1, a number of programs have been developed to foster prosocial behaviors in students and develop healthy coping strategies. SEL programs tend to share three common features: (1) increasing students' knowledge of socially and emotionally competent behavior, (2) utilization of social and emotional competence in daily interactions with others, and (3) reliance on social and emotional competence to prevent disruptive, antisocial, or harmful behaviors (Moy & Hazen, 2018). Two programs that can be used at Tier 1 to develop SEL competency and promote mental wellness in students are Second Step and Promoting Alternative Thinking Strategies (PATHS).

Second Step is a Tier 1 SEL program designed to promote interpersonal and intrapersonal competencies and reduce the development of behavioral, social, and emotional problems in children in preschool through eighth grade (Moy & Hazen, 2018). The program is influenced by social learning theory, cognitive behavioral therapy (CBT), and social information processing (Moy & Hazen, 2018). Second Step is designed to be implemented over the course of 22–28 weeks with lessons focusing on emotion management, empathy, problem-solving, and friendship skills (Moy & Hazen, 2018). The curriculum can be delivered by classroom teachers or school mental health providers. Lessons usually begin with warm-up activities that are followed by an audiovisual media presentation (Moy & Hazen, 2018).

Research has demonstrated that students who participated in Second Step demonstrate increased prosocial outcomes and social-emotional skills (Espelage, Low, Polanin, & Brown, 2015; Moy & Hazen, 2018). For example, a study conducted by Espelage et al. (2015) involving 3,658 students found that the Second Step middle-school program significantly reduced homophobic name calling and increased social-emotional competence. The Second Step program is available in both English and Spanish and has been implemented with students from a wide variety of ethnic and cultural backgrounds (Espelage et al., 2015; Low, Cook, Smolkowski, & Buntain-Ricklefs, 2015; Moy & Hazen, 2018).

Aside from Second Step, **Promoting Alternative Thinking Strategies** is a Tier 1 school-based program designed to improve children's ability to discuss and understand emotions, promote social competencies, and manage behavior (Humphrey et al., 2016). The PATHS program can be delivered to students in kindergarten through sixth grade and is designed to be implemented by classroom teachers (Humphrey et al., 2016). The program is delivered two to three times weekly with each lesson lasting 30–40 minutes (Humphrey et al., 2016). PATHS targets five domains including self-control, emotional understanding, positive self-esteem, relationships, and interpersonal problem-solving skills (Humphrey et al., 2016). Lessons cover topics such as identifying and labeling feelings, controlling impulses, understanding other's perspectives, and reducing stress (Humphrey et al., 2016). The curriculum includes parent materials to extend learning into the home environment. The PATHS program is often used in conjunction with the Good Behavior Game known as PATHS to PAX (Humphrey et al., 2016).

PATHS is only one of fourteen interventions to be designated as a "model program" by the Center for the Study and Prevention of Violence (Humphrey et al., 2016). Multiple studies have demonstrated PATHS effectiveness on increasing social-emotional competence, mental health, and academic attainment for children from a wide variety of ethnic and cultural backgrounds (Crean & Johnson, 2013; Humphrey et al., 2016). The PATHS program is available in the following languages: German, Croatian, Chinese, French, Swedish, Dutch, Welsh, and Portuguese (Crean & Johnson, 2013; Humphrey et al., 2016; Novak, Mihić, Bašić, & Nix, 2017).

Tier 2

Tier 2 interventions and supports are provided to the 10%–15% of children who display social-emotional concerns that are not adequately being addressed by Tier 1 services alone (Ziomek-Daigle & Heckman, 2019). Like other intervention service delivery models, supports at Tier 2 of social-emotional RTI tend to be of lower intensity than Tier 3, provide additional opportunities to practice and receive feedback on new skills, include parent/guardian communication, are flexible, and are structured around a standardized protocol or prescribed curricula (Drevon, Hixson, Wyse, & Rigney, 2018; Joyce-Beaulieu & Sulkowski, 2020).

Supports at Tier 2 are designed to be short-term and generally occur over the course of six to twelve weeks (Joyce-Beauliue & Sulkowski, 2020). However, as available interventions and supports for internalizing concerns have lagged behind those for externalizing disorders, time frames for implementation may vary. Likewise, time frames for progress monitoring within social-emotional RTI may vary and will be discussed in greater detail later on in this chapter along with universal screening. For now, educators are urged to follow the suggested implementation timelines outlined by prescribed programs when implementing Tier 2 interventions and supports. For example, a Tier 2 social-emotional program may require students to receive group counseling every week for 12 weeks. Therefore, it is generally recommended that a student complete the program before deeming it ineffective and pulling the child from the intervention prematurely.

Currently, cognitive-behavioral interventions (CBIs) appear to be the most common form of targeted supports for children with internalizing problems (Hunter et al., 2014). However, due to these interventions being time-consuming and requiring the services of a school-based mental health professional, many of these supports are beyond those offered by a classroom teacher. Consequently, educators have sought Tier 2 interventions that may both offer additional support to children with internalizing concerns and that can be quickly implemented by classroom teachers. Tier 2 interventions that may be implemented by teachers include a social-emotional check-in/check-out and a coping card.

Although a check-in/check-out has generally been used to assist at-risk students for behavioral disorders, there is some evidence to support the use of an adapted check-in/check-out (CICO) with students with internalizing disorders (Dart et al., 2015; Eklund, Kilgus, Izumi, DeMarchena, & McCollom, 2021; Hunter et al., 2014). Like the check-in/check-out utilized for students with externalizing deficits, a CICO coordinator is assigned for the student to check-in with throughout the school day. The CICO coordinator should be a teacher the student is comfortable with and who can be trusted for the student to rely on during difficult times throughout the day (Dart et al., 2015). For the **social-emotional check-in/check-out**, the student should check-in with the CICO coordinator in the morning, in the afternoon, and at the end of the school day.

During the initial check-in, the CICO coordinator should inquire how the student is feeling and then, based on the student's answer, respond accordingly. For example, if the student replies that they are doing well, the CICO coordinator may simply remind the child that they and other school staff are there for them throughout the school day and point out various healthy coping strategies the student can use during times in which they are having difficulty. For example, the teacher may model and remind the student of the strategies of deep breathing or counting to ten. In the event the student indicates that they are not feeling well during morning check-in, the teacher may briefly go over some healthy coping strategies and have the student practice one or two of them. For example, the teacher may have the student briefly write about their feelings in a journal or have them discuss what activities make them feel good to overcome negative thoughts.

Subsequently, the teacher may then ask how the student feels after partaking in the journaling activity and remind them that they will check-in again at the middle and end of the school day to see how it went. If the student indicates that they are still not feeling well despite the teacher having the child partake in journaling or deep breathing, the teacher can ask the student if they would like to talk in more detail to a school-based mental health practitioner. The teacher should follow the same sequence of responses for the afternoon and end of the day check-in pending on how the student responds they are feeling.

Aside from utilizing a social-emotional CICO, educators may find **coping cards** a particularly quick, flexible, and easy to implement intervention for students at risk for social-emotional concerns. Coping cards are small index-sized cards that children can carry with them in their pocket to remind them of particular triggers that may cause them to feel upset and provide them coping strategies learned for overcoming internalizing distress, such as using deep breathing (Wenzel, 2018). Additionally, these cards may provide children a list of one to two people to talk to when they are experiencing difficulties coping with their emotions (Wenzel, 2018). Since each child experiences different situations that may cause negative feelings, coping cards are a versatile intervention that can easily be tailored to the child's needs.

Coping cards help reinforce concepts taught to children for dealing with internalizing distress and provide children a reminder of how they can control their feelings (Wenzel, 2018). Children who utilize coping cards effectively may obtain a sense of accomplishment that they are in control of their emotions and possess strategies to help them cope with their feelings in a healthy and independent manner (Wenzel, 2018). For children who are prone to losing small index cards, teachers or school mental health practitioners may consider having the student screenshot a picture of their coping card on their cell phone or tablet, tape coping cards to the inside of their binder, or utilize an electronic application, such as Toolbox Coping Cards, to design, store, and carry the coping card (Edmunds, 2015). Figure 5.4 provides an example of a coping card (Box 5.1).

FIGURE 5.4 • Coping Card

Coping Card

Some events, activities, and settings that may make me upset include:

1) Gym
2) Tests or Exams

My body may be telling me I am upset when:

1) I feel hot and sweaty
2) I feel lightheaded
3) I feel like I want to cry

When I begin to feel upset, I can:

1) Practice deep breathing
2) Write in my journal
3) Talk to Ms. V

BOX 5.1 COPING CARD SYNOPSIS

Giovanna Sampognaro is a ninth-grade student at Thompson Ranch High School in Albuquerque, New Mexico. Increasingly, she has been experiencing bouts of nervousness as her unit test in English is quickly approaching. Due to Giovanna becoming worried when she knows there is an upcoming test, her school counselor, Mrs. Sztandera, recommended that she try using a coping card to remind her of things she can do to make herself feel better. On the coping card, Giovanna outlines events, activities, and settings that make her worried or upset, such as gym class or when she has to take exams. She then details how her body may tell her that she is starting to become worried, such as feeling like she is about to cry or becoming lightheaded. Finally, Giovanna notes things she can do to make herself feel better, such as practicing deep breathing or writing in her journal.

Giovanna makes multiple copies of her coping card and places them on the inside of each of her subject binders at school. Upon taking her seat in English class, she begins to feel like she is about to cry and becomes increasingly nervous. However, instead of feeling overwhelmed by her emotions, she quickly opens up her English binder, reads over her coping card, and is reminded that she can quietly practice deep breathing to make herself feel better. After practices deep breathing, Giovanna begins to feel better, and her English class begins. She realizes that there are very simple things that she can do to cope with her bouts of nervousness and smiles.

In addition to a social-emotional CICO and coping cards, Tier 2 supports for children with internalizing concerns consist of group counseling. Group counseling at Tier 2 typically involves three to ten students and consists of standardized programs that are run by either a school psychologist or school counselor (Joyce-Beaulieu & Sulkowski, 2020; Schultz et al., 2012). Two standardized programs that are used for group counseling within social-emotional RTI are Skillstreaming and the Penn Resilience Program.

Skillstreaming is a widely used prosocial and emotional management program based on social learning theory. The program is available for 4–18-year-old children and available at three instructional levels, including early childhood, elementary school, and adolescence (Raffaele Mendez, 2016). The number of lessons in Skillstreaming varies by age with 40 in early childhood, 60 in elementary, and 50 in adolescents (Raffaele Mendez, 2016). Broad subject areas covered by Skillstreaming include anger and conflict management, life skills and character development, and SEL (Raffaele Mendez, 2016). Subject areas are further divided into six skill areas: (1) social or classroom skills, (2) school-related skills, (3) friendship-making skills, (4) ways to deal with feelings, (5) alternatives to aggression, and (6) skills for dealing with stress (Raffaele Mendez, 2016). Overall, Skillstreaming has shown promise in decreasing disruptive behaviors and developing social skills in children (Raffaele Mendez, 2016).

A more targeted Tier 2 social-emotional program for children and adolescents experiencing episodes of sadness includes the Penn Resilience Program. The **Penn Resilience Program** is a 12-week curriculum designed to teach cognitive, behavioral, and social skills to children aged 10–14 years to prevent symptoms of depression in children or to remediate risk for depression (Macklem, 2011; Sapthiang et al., 2019). Since its inception, the Penn Resilience Program is utilized to build resilience competencies in youth in the areas of self-awareness, self-regulation, and optimism. The program seeks to build these resilience competencies through games, discussions, role-playing, cartoons, and short stories (Macklem, 2011; Sapthiang et al., 2019). Interestingly, the Penn Resilience Program can be used as both a Tier 1 or Tier 2 program (Macklem, 2011). At Tier 1, the program can be used in a classroom of 15–30 students (Macklem, 2011). At Tier 2, the program can be used in a group of three to six students (Macklem, 2011).

Studies suggest that the Penn Resilience Program has demonstrated some efficacy for improving resilience in adolescents, reducing depression, and decreasing anxiety (Bastounis,

Callaghan, Banerjee, & Michail, 2016; Brunwasser, Gillham, & Kim, 2009; Macklem, 2011; Sapthiang et al., 2019). A small literature base exists for the Penn Resilience Program being adapted to work with Black and Latino middle school children in overcoming feelings of sadness (Cardemil, Reivich, & Seligman, 2002). Additionally, the program has been adapted to help children in Mainland China overcome episodes of sadness (Yu & Seligman, 2002). Readers can learn more about the Penn Resiliency Program and request materials by visiting the University of Pennsylvania Positive Psychology Center website.

Tier 3

Tier 3 of social-emotional RTI is designed for the one to five percent of students who display significant social-emotional concerns and may require sustained individualized counseling and supports to address their long-standing difficulties (Ziomek-Daigle & Heckman, 2019). These students have not responded to the standard protocol interventions offered at Tier 2 and are at considerable risk for developing a mental health disorder that affects their educational and daily life functioning. Therefore, unlike students at Tier 2 whose needs can be addressed by relatively simple interventions and manualized programs and supports, children at Tier 3 require intensified supports that are individualized to their specific areas of deficit (Joyce-Beaulieu & Sulkowski, 2020; Ziomek-Daigle & Heckman, 2019). To elaborate, whereas Tier 2 counseling programs like Skillstreaming address a broad array of social-emotional concerns, counseling programs at the Tier 3 level, like Coping Cat, are narrower in scope and are designed to address specific internalizing deficits, such as anxiety. Consequently, services at Tier 3 are designed to treat children who present with the highest mental health care needs outside of special education (Joyce-Beaulieu & Sulkowski, 2020; Tibbets, 2013). Therefore, counseling and intervention services at Tier 3 tend to be delivered by school psychologists with lower-level interventions and supports being delivered by school counselors or teachers.

Due to many children with social-emotional deficits presenting with both internalizing and externalizing concerns concurrently, these children may be in need of a multifaceted support plan that may include behavioral and emotional interventions (Joyce-Beaulieu & Sulkowski, 2020). Therefore, children at Tier 3 of social-emotional RTI may require both individualized counseling alongside a behavior intervention plan if they are also presenting with significant externalizing concerns. Along with a behavior intervention plan, school psychologists providing counseling at this tier should develop a counseling treatment plan for the child.

Treatment plans are documents that utilize a child's strengths to deal with presenting concerns and assist the child in reaching or achieving identifiable goals (Jones-Smith, 2019). Although treatment plans are frequently used outside school settings, these documents remain underutilized by school-based practitioners. Overall treatment plans help guide the counseling and intervention process and are considered a "living document" that can be changed to meet the child's goals and needs (Jones-Smith, 2019). Treatment plans may prove particularly useful for school-based mental health practitioners because they serve the following three purposes:

1. Ensuring that counseling is grounded in best evidence-based practice and is likely to succeed (Jones-Smith, 2019; Seligman & Reichenberg, 2014).
2. Specifying goals to help school-based mental health practitioners track process, determine whether goals are being met, and, if not, revising and improving the plan (Jones-Smith, 2019; Seligman & Reichenberg, 2014).
3. Providing structure and direction to the counseling process by helping practitioners and children develop shared and realistic expectations for treatment (Seligman & Reichenberg, 2014).

Due to the individualized nature of Tier 3 supports and counseling services, treatment planning provides a vital road map for school-based practitioners, children, parents, and educators in indicating how the clinician and student will proceed at the start of services and reach their destination at the conclusion of counseling. Therefore, treatment planning may provide some comfort and closure to all stakeholders in the child's life as the counseling process is outlined accordingly, goals are developed to address the child's needs, and a direction is provided to best assist the child in overcoming their deficits (Jones-Smith, 2019). A large part of having an effective treatment plan involves possessing knowledge of evidence-based counseling and therapeutic programs at the Tier 3 level of social-emotional RTI. Two such programs designed to remediate children at risk for chronic and severe mental health disorders are the Coping Cat program and the Prevention of Depression (POD) Teen Achieving Mastery over Stress (TEAMS) program, also known as the POD-TEAMS Depression Prevention Program.

Although many interventions and supports at Tier 3 are designed to be delivered individually to students, other manualized Tier 3 counseling programs are designed to address a specific area of deficit that is relevant to several children through group therapy. One such program that utilizes an individualized or group counseling format to address the specific social-emotional needs of children is the Coping Cat program. The **Coping Cat program** is a 16-session manualized counseling curriculum designed for children aged seven to thirteen who are exhibiting signs and symptoms of anxiety disorders (Lenz, 2015; Schaffer, 2017). Each session lasts approximately 50 to 60 minutes and can be delivered individually or with a group of up to five students (Schaffer, 2017). As children progress throughout each counseling session, they learn to recognize thoughts, feelings, and bodily actions associated with anxiety through psychoeducation, exposure tasks, cognitive restructuring, and problem-solving (Lenz, 2015).

A recent meta-analysis by Lenz (2015) revealed that Coping Cat is significantly more effective for treating anxiety symptoms in youth than no treatment at all and slightly more effective than alternative similar programs and interventions. Aside from these promising results, an extension of the Coping Cat program has been released for children ranging in age from 14 to 17 known as the **C.A.T. project** (Kendall, Crawford, Kagan, Furr, & Podell, 2018). The Coping Cat program is available in languages other than English including: Spanish, Chinese, Hungarian, Japanese, and Norwegian (Lenz, 2015).

While Coping Cat and the C.A.T project address children who are at risk for anxiety disorders, the **POD-TEAMS Depression Prevention Program** is a manualized counseling curriculum designed to assist children at risk for depression (Raffaele Mendez, 2016; TEAMS/POD Intervention Team, 2003). The POD-TEAMS program is based on CBT and was adapted from the Coping with Stress course (Raffaele Mendez, 2016; TEAMS/POD Intervention Team, 2003). The program consists of eight weekly, ninety-minute group sessions and six-monthly, ninety-minute continuation sessions (Gladstone, Beardslee, & Diehl, 2015). The curriculum focuses on communication skills, cognitive restructuring, and developing skills for interpersonal problem-solving (Gladstone et al., 2015).

The POD-TEAMS Depression Prevention Program was developed for adolescents ranging in age from 13 to 17, who have already experienced an active depressive episode or are at risk for depression due to showing resistance to previous interventions, having a parent or sibling who is depressed, or reporting frequent bouts of sadness. For students suffering from an active episode of depression, as opposed to being at risk, the closely related Coping with Depression for Adolescents program has been developed (Garvik, Idsoe, & Bru, 2014). Previous studies have indicated that adolescents tended to benefit most from taking part in the POD-TEAMS program when the curriculum was provided during "moments of wellness" (Weersing, Jeffreys, Do, Schwartz, & Bolano, 2017).

Aside from manualized counseling programs, such as the Coping Cat and POD-TEAMS Depression Prevention Program, school-based mental health providers may opt to provide nonmanualized individual **cognitive behavior therapy (CBT)** at Tier 3. CBT is an evidence-based treatment that brings together two systems of therapy: cognitive therapy and behavior therapy (Joyce-Beaulieu & Sulkowski, 2020; Raffaele Mendez, 2016). The main purpose of cognitive behavior therapy is to assist individuals in understanding how their thoughts lead to feelings and how their feelings influence their behaviors (Joyce-Beaulieu & Sulkowski, 2020; Raffaele Mendez, 2016). CBT seeks to challenge and change unhelpful and negative thoughts that may lead to poor emotional and behavioral regulation. Although CBT was originally utilized as an adult-orientated treatment, clinicians began using it with children in the 1980s (Raffaele Mendez, 2016).

As can be inferred by the manualized counseling programs discussed, CBT has many applications in remediating many internalizing concerns children present with, such as youth experiencing sadness or nervousness. For children whose needs and presenting symptomology are so unique, individual counseling using CBT might provide a vital route to effectively managing and remediating the child's concerns. CBT is a widely utilized and well-liked counseling approach by practitioners in and outside of school settings because of its brief and flexible format. CBT tends to be implemented between 10 and 20 weekly or biweekly sessions with the average number of therapy sessions attended being 16 (Clark et al., 2015). The length of sessions can vary between 50 to 60 minutes or be further shortened to fit better into the school day (Clark et al., 2015). Overall, CBT has shown great promise in assisting children in remediating maladaptive thoughts and behaviors in relation to sadness, nervousness, phobias, and impulsivity (Joyce-Beaulieu & Sulkowski, 2020; Raffaele Mendez, 2016).

Social-Emotional RTI With Embedded Trauma Practices

In recent years, childhood trauma has been increasingly focused on by educators and educational scholars. This increased in focus is for good reason. Childhood trauma is often a considerable risk factor for an array of mental health concerns, such as anxiety, depression, suicide, and even physical ailments, such as heart attack, stroke, and obesity (Felitti et al., 1998; Kerker et al., 2015). Additionally, traumatic events have been shown to alter brain structure and functioning (Ormiston, Nygaard, & Heck, 2020). Estimates suggest that as many as 68% of children experience at least some form of traumatic event (Copeland, Keeler, Angold, & Costello, 2007).

Trauma can be defined as a real or perceived experience that is significantly distressing and causes feelings of fear, terror, or helplessness (Felitti et al., 1998; Kerker et al., 2015). Traumatic events can take many forms including overt acts that potentially cause harm or threaten to cause harm to a child, such as physical abuse, psychological abuse, and sexual abuse (Ormiston et al., 2020). Additionally, traumatic events can take on the form of failing to provide for the basic physical, emotional, or educational needs of a child, such as lack of adequate supervision or exposure to a violent environment (Ormiston et al., 2020). Finally, traumatic events can be caused by natural or human disasters, such as hurricanes or acts of terrorism. Due to educators recognizing how trauma can impact children's learning, behavior, and social-emotional well-being, many schools have adopted trauma-informed approaches and supports to meet the needs of students.

Trauma-informed approaches and supports in schools include preventing adverse events and experiences from occurring by building individual capacity for self-regulation, supporting the individuals experiencing adverse effects from trauma, and avoiding retraumatizing affected individuals (von der embse, Rutherford, Mankin, & Jenkins, 2019). Each of these components can be built into an existing social-emotional RTI model. However, before delving into what social-emotional RTI with embedded trauma practices looks like, it is hard to do so without mentioning the impact adverse childhood experiences (ACEs) have on a person's overall mental and physical health.

Adverse Childhood Experiences

Adverse childhood experiences, or ACEs for short, are potentially traumatic events that occur in childhood between 0 and 17 years of age (Felitti et al., 1998; Oral et al., 2016). Examples of ACEs include sexual abuse, emotional and physical neglect, parental separation or divorce, and exposure to a caregiver suffering from mental illness (Felitti et al., 1998; Kerker et al., 2015). In one of the largest studies conducted on ACEs, over 17,000 participants completed a questionnaire that inquired about child abuse and exposure to household dysfunction while growing up (Felitti et al., 1998). Results indicated that approximately 67% of respondents reported being exposed to at least one ACE. Of those exposed to at least one ACE, 87% reported having two or more ACES (Felitti et al., 1998).

Arguably, the most interesting finding of the original ACE study by Felitti et al. (1998) was that respondents who had an ACE score of four or more appeared to be at significantly increased risk for developing mental and physical health concerns. For example, an ACE score of four or more increased the risk of a person experiencing depression by 460% and the possibility of committing suicide by 1220% (Felitti et al., 1998; Ranjbar & Erb, 2019). Moreover, an ACE score of four or more was attributed to an increased likelihood of acquiring chronic pulmonary lung disease by 390% and choric bronchitis by 400% (Felitti et al., 1998; Rajbar & Erb, 2019). Finally, an ACE score of six or more increased the likelihood of heavy drinking by 280% and drug use by 370% and Rajbar and Erb (2019).

Part of the reason for higher ACE scores resulting increased risk for developing mental and physical ailments is due to toxic stress (Felitti et al., 1998). **Toxic stress** has been defined as exposure to severe and prolonged stress in the absence of protective factors, such as safety, security, social support, or appropriate coping techniques (Kerker et al., 2015). Toxic stress may result in children being overloaded with stress hormones and keep them in a flight, fright, or freeze response, which could disrupt developing brain circuits (Kerker et al., 2015). Ultimately, exposure to frequent and chronic ACEs can result in neurobiological changes, as well as structural and functional alterations in the brain (Kerker et al., 2015).

Consequently, studies have generally found that exposure to trauma in childhood is associated with lower academic achievement and test scores, depressed IQ scores, impaired working memory, delayed language and vocabulary, poor attention span, increased impulsivity, and low self-esteem (Berg, 2019; Perfect, Turley, Carlson, Yohanna, & Saint Giles, 2016). Fortunately, due to the growing interest in childhood trauma, an increasing number of interventions and programs have been developed to specifically incorporate trauma-informed practices, interventions, and programs into social-emotional RTI. The reason for integrating trauma-sensitive practices and programs within existing intervention service delivery models, such as social-emotional RTI, is because such integration is likely to increase the sustainability of interventions and supports (Berg, 2019).

By incorporating trauma-sensitive practices and programs into social-emotional RTI, educators are less likely to be discouraged by the idea of implementing "yet another" intervention service delivery model in their schools (Zakszeski, Ventresco, & Jaffe, 2017). Therefore, embedding trauma-sensitive practices and programs into social-emotional RTI may be an efficient, feasible, and effective way of promoting student mental health and school success (Zakszeki et al., 2017). For purposes of this text and to specifically highlight components of incorporating trauma-sensitive practice into social-emotional RTI, a brief outline of implementation across the three tiers of social-emotional RTI has been provided.

Tier 1

In incorporating trauma-sensitive practice within social-emotional RTI, likely a broad array of existing, low-intensity strategies are being implemented by the school for all students regardless of emotional or behavioral concerns (Berg, 2019). These strategies likely blend together universal supports and interventions across both SWPBS and social-emotional RTI. Therefore, schools implementing these strategies likely have created a warm, caring, and safe school environment through posting school rules, modeling school expectations, having a school motto, and using the Good Behavior Game. In addition to these practices, schools incorporating a trauma-sensitive approach teach children to appropriately label and express their feelings, establish relationships, develop respect for differing perspectives, and utilize self-soothing techniques when upset, such as listening to music or practicing deep breathing (Moy & Hazen, 2018).

Trauma-sensitive schools and educators consider how emergency drills may impact a child with trauma to relive their scariest memories. For example, care is taken in considering how a smoke alarm may impact a child who has survived a house fire. Consequently, educators talk with families and the child to best assist them in preparing for an upcoming emergency drill. Similarly, trauma-sensitive schools at Tier 1 consider how assignments, readings, and certain environments may lead to children reliving frightening memories. For instance, perhaps a child avoids an assignment having them draw their family and tell who each member is due to it leading them to think about their father who was physically abusive toward them.

Finally, Tier 1 of embedding trauma-sensitive practices into social-emotional RTI may include universal training for all school staff regarding trauma and the effects of trauma on children (Zakszeski et al., 2017). When training school staff, school mental health practitioners should use a trauma-informed approach. A trauma-informed approach to training school staff will help them to: (1) realize the effects of trauma on the child, the child's family, and on the greater community; (2) recognize the signs and symptoms of trauma, such as confusion or difficulty concentrating; (3) identify trauma triggers, such as certain sounds or smells; (4) respond by integrating knowledge about trauma into school policies, procedures, and practices; (5) resist in re-traumatization through the unitization of universal supports that create a caring and safe school climate, teach emotional regulation techniques, and provide instruction on feeling recognition and appropriate expression (Zakszeski et al., 2017).

Under trauma-informed training, educators should be made aware of groups who at higher risk of encountering adverse childhood experiences. Groups of students who may be more at risk of encountering ACEs include students with disabilities, LGBTQ youth, children from military and veteran families, children who are homeless or whose families are facing economic hardship, youth residing in neighborhoods with high crime rates, and youth who have fled war-torn countries (Herrenkohl, Hong, & Verbrugge, 2019). As with social-emotional RTI without trauma-sensitive practices in place, social-emotional RTI with embedded trauma-informed practices still universally screen children for social-emotional deficits using measures like the DESSA-mini or BIMAS-2. Interventions and supports at Tier 1 of social-emotional RTI with embedded trauma-informed practices are designed for all students with 80%–85% of students responding to these services.

Tier 2

Tier 2 of social-emotional RTI with embedded trauma-sensitive practice simply means adding trauma-based programs and supports into the existing social-emotional RTI framework. For example, a school might be implementing the Penn Resilience Program as a Tier 2 program for children at risk for experiencing episodes of sadness. However, for students who have experienced trauma and are showing social-emotional concerns, the Penn Resilience Program might not be the best fit. To best assist students who have been exposed to traumatic events and may be experiencing episodes of sadness, increased nervousness, or risky behavior, the **Support Students Exposed to Trauma (SSET)** program may prove useful as an alternative Tier 2 program.

The SSET program is a manualized curriculum that seeks to help children between 10 and 14 years of age who have been exposed to traumatic events learn how to manage their distress (Schultz et al., 2012; Support Students Exposed to Trauma, n.d.). Although the program has been designed for children between 10 and 14 years of age, the authors indicate that it will likely work well with students in fourth to ninth grade (Schultz et al., 2012; Support Students Exposed to Trauma, n.d.). The program consists of a ten-lesson curriculum and is run by either a teacher or school counselor in groups consisting of eight to ten students (Schultz et al., 2012; Support Students Exposed to Trauma, n.d.). To best assist educators, the SSET program has been designed to be used in situations where there is limited support from school-based mental health clinicians (Schultz et al., 2012; Support Students Exposed to Trauma, n.d.).

Each SSET lesson typically lasts approximately an hour and is largely based in strategies and techniques utilized in CBT, such as identifying maladaptive thinking (Support Students Exposed to Trauma, n.d.). The SSET program utilizes many CBT strategies and techniques due to CBT having the most empirical evidence for treating traumatized youth (Farmer & Chapman, 2016; Hunter et al., 2014). Lessons teach children about common reactions to trauma, how to challenge maladaptive thinking, relaxation techniques, and problem-solving skills (Support Students Exposed to Trauma, n.d.). Like social-emotional RTI without embedded trauma-sensitive practice, children involved in social-emotional RTI with embedded trauma-sensitive practice should be progress monitored on a biweekly basis. Moreover, interventions and programs at Tier 2 of social-emotional RTI with embedded trauma-informed practices are designed for the 10%–15% of students who did not respond to Tier 1 supports.

Tier 3

Tier 3 of social-emotional RTI with embedded trauma-sensitive practice is designed for the one to five percent of students experiencing significant emotional or behavioral problems as a result of being exposed to trauma. For children who have been exposed to substantial ACEs, typical Tier 3 programs like Coping Cat may not prove as useful due to being less attuned to trauma-informed practices. To address deeply engrained trauma in students who have not been responsive to Tier 2 efforts, the **Cognitive Behavioral Intervention for Trauma in Schools (CBITS)** program has shown strong evidence (Franco, 2018). Although related to the SSET curriculum and based on CBT, CBITS is designed to be used by skilled school or community-based mental health practitioners, such as school psychologists, clinical psychologists, or mental health counselors (Cognitive Behavioral Intervention for Trauma in Schools, n.d.; Franco, 2018).

The CBITS curriculum takes place on a weekly basis over the course of ten weeks and consists of groups of six to eight children aged 10–15 (Franco, 2018). Each session is one-hour long and utilizes CBT techniques such as psychoeducation, relaxation, cognitive restructuring, and exposure (Cognitive Behavioral Intervention for Trauma in Schools, n.d.). Aside from the ten group sessions, the program consists of one to three individual sessions, two parent psychoeducational sessions, and one teacher educational session (Cognitive Behavioral Intervention for Trauma in Schools, n.d.; Franco, 2018). Overall, CBITS teaches participants about six CBT techniques: (1) education about reaction to trauma; (2) relaxation training; (3) cognitive therapy; (4) real-life exposure; (5) stress or trauma exposure, and (6) social problem-solving (Franco, 2018). For children who are five to eleven years of age, the **Bounce Back Program** has been developed and is based on CBITS.

CBITS has been adapted to assist children from diverse backgrounds in overcoming trauma and traumatic experiences with much work of adaptation being completed with Black, Latino, Native American, and Hispanic communities (Allison & Ferreira, 2017; Cognitive Behavioral Intervention for Trauma in Schools, n.d.; Morsette, Swaney, Stolle, & Schuldberg, 2009). Outside of the English language, CBITS is available in Arabic and Spanish (Cognitive Behavioral Intervention for Trauma in Schools, n.d.). A study by Allison and Ferreira (2017) involving 23 Latino youth, ages 10–14, found that CBITS was a practical and effective program for Spanish-speaking youth who have been exposed to stress and trauma. Another study by Morsette et al. (2009) involving 48 Native American students in sixth grade found that CBITS significantly reduced PTSD symptoms and trauma in these youth.

As an alternative to CBITS, trauma-focused cognitive behavior therapy (TF-CBT) may prove useful as a Tier 3 counseling approach. TF-CBT is typically completed in individualized 60–90 minute sessions that take place over the course of 12–16 weeks (Franco, 2018; Murray, Cohen, Ellis, & Mannarino, 2008). School psychologists and counselors using TF-CBT emphasize the use of exposure, stress management, parental treatment, and cognitive processing and reframing (Franco, 2018). TF-CBT has been shown to reduce internalizing and externalizing symptoms in traumatized youth (Franco, 2018; Murray et al., 2008). When implementing counseling programs and curriculums at Tier 3, it is important for school-based practitioners to connect with outside clinicians to provide wraparound support and additional services.

In addition to connecting with outside clinicians to provide wraparound support, school-based mental health practitioners implementing CBITS, TF-CBT, or another individual or group counseling methodology must utilize culturally responsive practices in providing services to students. Consequently, school-based mental health professionals should reflect and develop an awareness of their own cultural values and biases, strive to understand the worldview of the child and family they are working with, and educate themselves on the customs and beliefs of different cultural and ethnic groups that they frequently work with (Zigarelli, Jones, Palomino, & Kawamura, 2016).

Data Collection and Decision-Making Under Social-Emotional RTI

Just as social-emotional RTI is in its infancy stages so is the development of screening and progress monitoring measures under the model. Fortunately for educators, many screening and progress monitoring measures used for students exhibiting externalizing concerns and covered under SWPBS also possess scales that assess children for internalizing concerns under social-emotional RTI. For example, the Student Risk Screening Scale-Internalizing and Externalizing is a screening and progress monitoring measure for both behavioral and social-emotional deficits. Although the SRSS-IE assesses both internalizing and externalizing deficits, it is considered to be a problem-focused instead of a strengths-based measure. In other words, measures like the SRSS-IE focus solely on reducing negative symptomology and target negative outcomes. This is opposed to being a strength-based screening tool that targets positive outcomes of the child to promote growth in less developed areas (Kilpatrick, Maras, Brann, & Kilgus, 2018).

Not surprisingly, there are many more social-emotional screeners and progress monitoring measures that are problem-focused instead of strengths-based. However, it has been found that by including strengths in social-emotional screeners instead of just focusing on deficits that teachers may be more accepting of the validity and usefulness of such measures (Kilpatrick et al., 2018). One such measure that utilizes a strengths-based approach to assessing social-emotional competence in children is the Devereux Student Strengths Assessment-Mini (DESSA-mini).

Devereux Student Strengths Assessment-Mini (DESSA-mini)

The **DESSA-mini** is a norm-referenced, strengths-based social-emotional scale that can be utilized as a universal screener or progress monitoring measure for children in kindergarten through eighth grade (Kilipatrick et al., 2018). For adolescents in grades nine through twelve, the DESSA-High-School Edition mini (DESSA-HSE mini) has been created. Both the DESSA-mini and DESSA-HSE mini are shorter forms of the longer and more comprehensive DESSA. Due to the DESSA being 72-items and impractical for screening purposes, the DESSA-mini was developed as a shortened version to save educators time and financial resources (Maras et al., 2015). The DESSA-mini consists of four brief, eight-item parallel forms that can be completed by teachers or other school staff to assess social awareness, optimistic thinking, relationships skills, goal-directed behavior, personal responsibility, decision-making, and self-management in students (Kilipatrick et al., 2018; Maras et al., 2015). Items on the DESSA-mini are strengths-based, positively worded, and rated on a five-point scale based on how often the student has demonstrated each behavior in the past four weeks. Examples of DESSA-mini items include how often the child makes a suggestion or request in a polite way and how often the child shows appreciation for others (Kilipatrick et al., 2018).

Ratings on the DESSA-mini items yield a single score known as the Social-Emotional Total to indicate the child's level of social-emotional competence. Scores on the DESSA-mini are reported as T-scores, which have a mean of 50 and a standard deviation of 10 (Kilpatrick et al., 2018; Maras et al., 2015). Higher scores on the DESSA-mini suggest areas of strength, and lower scores suggest an area of need. Therefore, T-scores of 60 and above are considered strengths. T-scores of 41–59 are considered typical scores (Kilpatrick et al., 2018; Maras et al., 2015). Lastly, T-scores of 40 and below are described as needs for instruction. Students whose Social-Emotional Total falls below the 25th percentile are considered at high risk and in need of additional social-emotional support beyond the core interventions provided at the Tier 1 level (Kilpatrick et al., 2018; Maras et al., 2015). Overall, the DESSA-mini presents as a promising screener and progress monitoring measure for students displaying with social-emotional or behavioral deficits. Better yet, unlike other measures that are used three times per year for universal screening, the DESSA-mini has been found to be relatively stable over time (Kilpatrick et al., 2018). Consequently, the measure does not need to be re-administered for universal screening beyond fall benchmarking (Kilpatrick et al., 2018).

Strengths and Difficulties Questionnaire

The **Strengths and Difficulties Questionnaire (SDQ)** is a brief, norm-referenced universal screener for social, emotional, and behavioral concerns in children aged 2–17. The instrument is not recommended as a progress monitoring tool, but the measure has shown good psychometric properties when used as a universal screener (Deutz et al., 2018; Jenkins et al., 2014). The SDQ consists of 25 items across five subscales with each subscale consisting of five items. The SDQ subscales include: Emotional Symptoms, Conduct Problems, Hyperactivity/Inattention, Peer Relationship Problems, and Prosocial Behavior (Deutz et al., 2018; Jenkins et al., 2014).

A Total Difficulties score can be generated by summing all the scores except the Prosocial Behavior Subscale. Across these subscales, the SDQ asks parents, teachers, or the student via self-report to what extent both positive and negative attributes of the child were true in the past six months. Informants rate items on the SDQ using a three-point scale. Item scores rated zero indicate attributes are "not true" of the child. Item scores rated one suggest that attributes are "somewhat true" of the child. Finally, items scores rated two suggest attributes that are "certainly true" of the child. The Total Difficulties score ranges from 0 to 40 with each one-point increase corresponding with an increase in the risk of a child developing a mental health disorder (Deutz et al., 2018; Jenkins et al., 2014). Suggested cut-off scores and risk ranges for the SDQ vary based on whether the parent, teacher, or student form was utilized. Cut-off and risk ranges can be found by visiting the SDQ website at www.sdqinfo.org. Finally, the SDQ and scoring for the measure are available for free on the assessment's website.

Culturally Responsive Practices and Social-Emotional RTI

Research indicates that children from culturally and linguistically diverse backgrounds experience a higher prevalence of mental health problems when compared to white youth (Alegria et al., 2008; Castro-Olivo, 2017). Children from culturally and linguistically diverse backgrounds may be at higher risk and experience a higher prevalence of mental health concerns due to encounters with discrimination, systemic oppression, being more likely to reside in neighborhoods with more crime and violence, fleeing war-torn countries, and facing acculturative stress (Goforth, Nichols, Stanick, Shindorf, & Holder, 2017). **Acculturative stress** is defined as stress or the psychological impact of adapting to a new culture, whereas **acculturation** is defined as the process by which an individual adopts, acquires, and adjusts to a new cultural environment (Goforth et al., 2017; Jones, 2014). Both teachers and school-based mental health professionals should familiarize themselves with acculturative stress because it has been associated with mental health problems developing in children (Goforth et al., 2017; Jones, 2014). Studies have found that individuals who dissociate from the majority culture, as well as their native culture, tend to face the highest levels of acculturative stress (Goforth et al., 2017; Jones, 2014).

To best assist culturally diverse students throughout social-emotional RTI, educators should seek to develop cultural humility, awareness, knowledge, and skills in working with diverse learners. **Cultural humility** is the ability to self-reflect on one's values and beliefs (Goforth et al., 2017). By reflecting on one's values and beliefs, educators can develop self-awareness and in turn recognize their own biases and stereotypes that they might hold about diverse learners (Goforth et al., 2017; Ratts, Singh, Nassar-McMillan, Butler, & McCullough, 2016). From there, educators should seek to develop knowledge on how their assumptions, values, beliefs, and bias contribute to their worldview and may influence their teaching or school-based mental health practices (Goforth et al., 2017; Ratts et al., 2016). Additionally, educators should seek to develop knowledge about the student population and families that they work with through consulting books, scholarly literature, professional development, and community resources (Goforth et al., 2017; Ratts et al., 2016). Finally, through becoming knowledgeable about their student population, educators have developed the skills needed to deliver culturally responsive supports and interventions that promote mental wellness and prevent social-emotional concerns (Goforth et al., 2017).

Many of the culturally responsive supports and adaptations suggested for SWPBS can be implemented at Tier 1 of social-emotional RTI. For example, to potentially reduce acculturative stress, educators could make basic modifications to the school environment, such as displaying artifacts and artwork from the various ethnicities that make up the school. Teachers can also infuse lessons, content, and classroom materials with positive depictions and role models from the different ethnicities and disabilities that comprise the school. Moreover, both teachers and school-based mental health professionals may receive training on how to best promote mental wellness in diverse learners (Goforth et al., 2017). For example, some Asian cultures may view mental health concerns or difficulties as an imbalance of ying and yang (Castro-Olivo, 2017; Ratts et al., 2016). Consequently, at Tier 1, teachers may incorporate yoga, meditation, and even tai chi into the beginning and end of the school day to help students maintain a balance between ying and yang (Shrestha, Lautenschleger, & Soares, 2020) Finally, educators should be made aware that social-emotional concerns do not display the same across cultures. For instance, many Arab cultures may present feelings of sadness or nervousness through the expression of physical symptoms or somatic complaints (Goforth et al., 2017). Therefore, educators can consult with the school nurse to investigate whether frequent reports of stomachaches or headaches have a medical cause or whether they may be due to an underlying and unaddressed mental health concern.

At Tier 2 and Tier 3 of social-emotional RTI, a number of considerations and adaptations can be made for culturally diverse learners. First and foremost, school-based mental health practitioners should familiarize themselves with how different cultures in their school view social-emotional concerns. Subsequently, for diverse students in need of additional Tier 2 or Tier 3 support, school-based mental health practitioners may want to complete a multicultural interview with the family. For example, the Jones (2009) Intentional Multicultural Interview Schedule can be used to uncover:

- The conditions or circumstances the child and their family entered the United States.
- Whether the family and child have experienced racism and oppression.
- Everyday challenges the family has to deal with.
- The family and child's thoughts about group or individual counseling.
- The family and child's view of mental health and wellness.
- The difficulties the family and child have encountered in adapting to a new home or residing in a new country.
- Whether stress has been brought upon the family because the child appears to be adapting and adopting to a new culture faster than their parents.

After completing a multicultural interview with the family and child, school-based mental health staff can obtain a better understanding and idea of what counseling approach or Tier 2 or Tier 3 program may best assist the child. Often in working with students from diverse backgrounds, cultural adaptations may need to be made to existing counseling programs or methodologies. **Cultural adaptations** are defined as the modification of an existing intervention, such as changing the materials, cultural references, or language, in order to make the intervention more compatible with a specific population (Lauricella, Valdez, Okamoto, Heim, & Zaremba, 2016).

For example, this author had the opportunity to counsel an adolescent with a mild intellectual disability who was also a devout Muslim. In counseling this student, adaptations were made to the counseling curriculum to best account for the child's cognitive abilities and religious beliefs. Consequently, the tenets of Islam and a Quran with pictures were incorporated into cognitive behavioral therapy sessions. From this example, school-based mental health professionals should note that in working with students from multicultural backgrounds, religion, and community resources can greatly assist in adapting practices. Overall, teachers and school-based mental health practitioners can relatively easily adapt programs and supports within social-emotional RTI to best benefit multicultural learners.

Conclusion

Students with social-emotional concerns present educators with some of their greatest challenges due to their internalizing difficulties being challenging for teachers to recognize and provide assistance. Up until the last twenty years, there was little structure in delivering interventions and supports to children who presented with mental health care needs in the schools, and these students often went underserved or unrecognized. With a growing focus on preventative efforts, schools are increasingly turning to three-tiered models to deliver evidence-based interventions and supports to children presenting with and without social-emotional challenges. Increasingly, schools and teachers are incorporating wellness activities and trauma-informed practices into their everyday routines to promote SEL and development. Likewise, school counselors and school psychologists are turning to evidence-based screeners, progress monitoring measures, and interventions to best support and provide for children in need of more intensive supports.

In utilizing evidence-based interventions and programs with students, educators should take into account their student population and the diverse needs of multicultural learners. In doing so, educators should be aware that some students from diverse backgrounds may be at higher risk for and experience more mental health concerns due to encounters with discrimination, oppression, being more likely to reside in neighborhoods with more crime and violence, fleeing war-torn countries, and facing acculturative stress. Educators should make cultural adaptations throughout the three tiers of social-emotional RTI to best provide for diverse learners in their schools. By providing children adequate support under social-emotional RTI, students will be placed in the best position to learn the material presented to them. Table 5.1 summarizes the critical elements found in social-emotional RTI. Figure 5.5 provides a checklist for social-emotional RTI with suggested decision points and interventions. Similarly, Appendix C provides a flowchart on social-emotional RTI.

TABLE 5.1 • Critical Elements Found in Social-Emotional RTI

Elements	Tier 1	Tier 2	Tier 3
Type of support provided	Whole school and class social-emotional support	Targeted social-emotional interventions, supports, and counseling	Intense social-emotional interventions, supports, and counseling
Interventions provided	Classroom and school expectations posted Teaching and modeling of expectations Ticket reward system for positive behavior Positive school motto Newsletter home to parents outlining behavior expectations	Social-emotional check-in/check-out Coping Card Group counseling with three to six students	Intensive 1:1 or group counseling Develop a counseling treatment plan Wraparound support FBA/BIP (if co-occurring behavior problems present)
Duration of intervention	All school year	Six to twelve weeks or lasts length counseling program	Lasts length of the counseling program
Instruction or intervention provided by	Teacher and/or school counselor	Counseling: school counselor and/or school psychologist	Counseling with the school psychologist
Frequency of screening/ progress monitoring	3 times per year (Universal screening) 1 time per year for DESSA-mini	Biweekly or weekly (Progress monitoring)	Weekly or twice weekly (Progress monitoring)
Number of data points collected	3	School determined but preferably 12–14 data points if using a formal progress monitoring measure or length of counseling program.	School determined but preferably 12–14 data points if using a formal progress monitoring measure or length of counseling program.

FIGURE 5.5 ● Social-Emotional RTI Checklist

Social-Emotional Response to Intervention
(See Appendix C for Flow-chart on Social-Emotional Response to Intervention)

Tier 1

A *Promote mental wellness for all students by:*

- ✓ Teaching social expectations and developing positive peer relationships through character development sessions, school motto, posters of positive interactions, perspective taking, and anti-bullying initiatives
- ✓ Incorporating the five social-emotional learning components of self-awareness, social awareness, self-management, relationship skills, and responsible decision making into everyday lessons and teaching practice
- ✓ Teaching students about mental wellness and how to maintain mental wellness through mindfulness activities, deep breathing, and programs such as Second step and Promoting Alternative Thinking Strategies (PATHS)
- ✓ Educating all staff on the warning signs of social-emotional concerns, trauma, and trauma sensitive practice
- ✓ Universally screening all students for social-emotional concerns using instruments, such as the Behavior Intervention Monitoring system-2 (BIMAS-2) or Devereux Student Strengths Assessment-mini (DESSA-mini)
- ✓ Examining screening results and identifying at-risk youth
- ✓ **If student shows no social-emotional concerns, continue to implement interventions at Tier 1A**
- ✓ **If student shows social-emotional concerns, proceed to Tier 1B**

B *For students who appear to have some minor social-emotional concerns:*

- ✓ Note frequency of somatic complaints, nurse referrals, negative self-talk
- ✓ Contact parents
- ✓ Note any changes to the home environment that may be affecting the child's social, emotional, or behavioral well-being (death of a loved one, friend moving away, birth of a sibling, divorce etc.)
- ✓ Meet with child study team to evaluate data and determine whether Tier 2 intervention(s) are needed
- ✓ **If student responds to interventions and makes adequate progress return to Tier 1A**
- ✓ **If student does not make adequate progress, provide the student Tier 2A interventions**

Tier 2

A *For students who have not responded to Tier 1 supports:*

- ✓ Conduct a child study team meeting
- ✓ Utilize after-school programs to promote positive interactions with peers and adults
- ✓ Refer the child for small group counseling using programs such as Skillstreaming, The Penn Resiliency Program, Support for Students Exposed to Trauma (counseling should take place one to two times weekly and consist of 3–6 students)
- ✓ Utilize a social-emotional check-in/check-out, coping card, or social stories
- ✓ Track progress using the DESSA-Mini, BIMAS-2, or other measure on a bi-weekly basis
- ✓ Meet with the child study team to determine if adequate progress has been made
- ✓ **For students who have made adequate progress in Tier 2, return to receiving Tier 1A interventions and supports only**
- ✓ **For students who have not made adequate progress, proceed to Tier 2B (If no alternative Tier 2 intervention is available, move to Tier 3A).**

B

- ✓ Implement and monitor another Tier 2 if there is one available
- ✓ Track progress using the DESSA-Mini, BIMAS-2, or other measure on a bi-weekly basis
- ✓ Meet with the child study team to evaluate data and determine whether Tier 3 interventions are needed
- ✓ **If student responds to interventions and makes adequate progress return to Tier 1A**
- ✓ **If student does not make adequate progress, proceed to Tier 3A interventions**

FIGURE 5.5 ● (Continued)

Tier 3
A *For students who have not responded to Tier 2 supports:* ✓ Develop a functional behavior assessment (FBA) and behavior intervention plan (BIP) if child is displaying externalizing behavior along with internalizing concerns ✓ Develop school-based counseling treatment plan ✓ Provide intensive 1:1 or small group counseling with school psychologist ✓ Contact wraparound services ✓ Seek outside support if student poses risk to self-or others ✓ Track progress on a weekly basis using DESSA-Mini, BIMAS-2, or other measure on a weekly basis ✓ **If student responds to interventions and makes adequate progress return to Tier 1A** ✓ **If student does not make adequate progress, proceed to Tier 3B (If no alternative Tier 2 intervention is available, meet with CST to determine if a special education referral is needed)**
B ✓ Edit FBA/BIP, counseling treatment plan or both ✓ Continue wraparound and intensive counseling services ✓ Meet with the child study team to evaluate data and determine whether the student is responding to the intervention(s) ✓ **If student responds to interventions and makes adequate progress return to Tier 1A** ✓ **If student does not make adequate progress, determine if a special education referral is needed**

CASE EXAMPLE

SOCIAL-EMOTIONAL RTI WITH EMBEDDED TRAUMA-INFORMED PRACTICE

Child Background

Justin is currently a fourth-grader at Williams Elementary School in Buffalo, NY. At present, he resides with his parents, Anna and Joe Thompson. His father is employed as a nurse practitioner at Saint John's Hospital, and his mother works as a science teacher at Jacobs High School.

Per parent report, Justin was the product of a thirty-nine week pregnancy, and at birth he weighed six pounds, seven ounces. During pregnancy, Justin's mother reported that she was induced due to having gestational diabetes. Despite Mrs. Thompson being induced, Justin was born healthy with no complications. Developmental milestones were reported as follows: stood up without support: ten months, walked: one-year, spoke first words: one-year, spoke first sentences: one-and-a-half years, and potty-trained: three-years.

Overall, Mrs. Thompson reported concerns in Justin's social-emotional development. More specifically, she noted that Justin appears to cry more easily compared to his peers, withdrawal from his friends and classmates, and complain of having stomach and headaches despite his primary care physician ruling out any medical concerns. Mrs. Thompson first began to notice a change in Justin's demeanor that last spring when his father began working longer hours at the hospital after receiving a promotion. Additionally, around the same time last year, Justin found his grandmother unconscious as a result of a heart attack.

Justin's teacher noted similar concerns to Mrs. Thompson, adding that Justin's grades are declining, and he is increasingly crying. More specifically, Justin's teacher noted four areas of concern of which include: episodes of sadness, withdrawal, somatic complains, and requesting to call his grandmother. Episodes of sadness can be defined as any incident in which Justin cries or verbally expresses that he is "sad" or "feels like crying." Withdrawal can be defined as any incident in which Justin avoids engaging in group projects with his peers by putting his head down or sits alone during lunch. Somatic complaints can be defined as any incident in which Justin complains of having a stomach or headache or goes down to the nurse's office. Finally, requesting to call his grandmother is defined as any incident in which Justin requests to call his grandmother during instruction to check on her well-being.

Social-Emotional RTI With Embedded Trauma-Informed Practice

To promote mental wellness and prevent students from developing social-emotional concerns, like Justin, his school has implemented social-emotional RTI with embedded trauma-informed practices. In brief, social-emotional RTI is an intervention service delivery model under MTSS that focuses on building social-emotional competency in children and providing increasing levels of support for children who do not respond to efforts to build such competency (Joyce-Beaulieu & Sulkowski, 2020).

Tier 1

Tier 1 of social-emotional RTI is designed to teach mental wellness and appropriate social-emotional coping strategies to all children in school. Typically 80%–85% of students are responsive to these efforts (Joyce-Beaulieu & Sulkowski, 2020). At Justin's elementary school, a number of easy-to-implement interventions, strategies, and efforts have been made to increase the social-emotional competence of both students and school staff.

One of the strategies employed by Justin's school involves four staff in-service trainings per year to raise awareness for mental wellness strategies, signs of mental illness in children, trauma-informed practices, and SEL. Each of these in-service trainings focuses on how to implement strategies and techniques highlighted by the Collaborative for Academic, Social, and Emotional Learning (CASEL) in the five SEL areas of: self-awareness, self-management, social awareness, relationship skills, and responsible decision-making (Collaborative for Academic, Social, and Emotional Learning [CASEL], 2019). These in-service training are typically given to school staff through the school psychologist and school counselor.

Aside from conducting in-service trainings, Justin's school has implemented a number of simple techniques to promote a safe, comforting, and caring environment to foster mental wellness in children. The first of these techniques involves the school playing calming music over the intercom system at the beginning and end of each school day. Secondly, the school has a number of posters reminding students of coping strategies to use when they are upset, such as deep breathing and muscle tension and relaxation.

In addition to these strategies, teachers have the rules clearly posted in the classroom that reflect the five

SEL areas outlined by CASEL. For example, a classroom rule may indicate that the child "will make good choices," and a teacher-led discussion or storybook could reinforce the components of "responsible decision-making" as outlined by CASEL. Moreover, after Justin's teacher was trained in trauma and SEL, she developed a "cool-down corner" to be used by students when they are feeling upset, sad, or scared. In the cool-down corner, Justin's teacher has placed pillows, bean bag chairs, books, magazines, squishy balls, and noise canceling headphones. Finally, Justin's school uses the program, Second Step, program to teach students about feeling management, feeling recognition, and problem-solving.

Despite all these interventions and strategies in place, Justin's Social-Emotional Total score on the DESSA-mini revealed that he fell below the 25th percentile and in the "needs instruction" category. As a result of Justin falling below the 25th percentile during universal screening, he was considered to be at high risk for developing or presenting with social-emotional concerns. Therefore, the child study team met, and Justin was placed into Tier 2 of social-emotional RTI.

Tier 2

Tier 2 interventions and supports are designed for the 10%–15% of students who have been identified at-risk on social-emotional universal screeners, such as the DESSA-mini (Joyce-Beaulieu & Sulkowski, 2020). At Tier 2, Justin was placed in a weekly small group counseling program consisting of six students who were exposed to trauma and led by the school counselor. To best address Justin and his peers' presenting concerns in experiencing episodes of sadness, the Support for Students Exposed to Trauma was selected. In addition to taking part in the SSET curriculum, Justin's school counselor helped him to develop a coping card and taught him how to use it. Finally, a social-emotional check-in/check-out was utilized so that Justin may check in with his teachers to discuss how the day is going and how he is feeling. Throughout the twelve weeks that Justin attended SSET, his progress was monitored on a biweekly basis using the DESSA-mini. Despite receiving Tier 2 interventions and supports, Justin's score on the DESSA-mini suggested that he continued to be at risk and in need of more intensive social-emotional support. Consequently, the CST team met and decided that Justin was in need of Tier 3 interventions and supports.

Tier 3

Tier 3 interventions and supports are designed for the 1%–5% of students who not responded to Tier 2 efforts (Joyce-Beaulieu & Sulkowski, 2020). At Tier 3, Justin was placed in small group counseling consisting of three students displaying severe bouts of sadness as a result of trauma. The group met with the school psychologist on a weekly basis and followed the CBITS curriculum.

Additionally, the school psychologist and school counselor worked together to locate an outside social worker and mental health counselor to provide Justin with additional counseling and wraparound support. For the ten weeks that Justin attended CBITS, his progress was monitored on a weekly basis using the DESSA-mini. Results continued to show that Justin fell in the at risk range. Additionally, Justin's teacher reported that his grades continued to fall and that she saw little decrease in Justin's display of episodes of sadness, withdrawal, somatic complains, and desire to contact his grandmother during instruction. Consequently, the child study team met and determined that Justin would be referred for a special education evaluation and possible classification as a student with an emotional disability.

Discussion Questions

1. What are some reasons that children turn to educators or school-based mental health professionals for support?
2. Why is it important for children to incorporate SEL into the school day?
3. How does social-emotional RTI differ from SEL?
4. What are some examples of Tier 1 supports and programs that may assist in preventing mental illness and promoting mental wellness in children?
5. How might trauma or a child's exposure to traumatic events affect their learning and mental health?
6. Why is it important for educators to universally screen students for potential mental health concerns?
7. What are some culturally responsive practices that you can adopt in your classroom or school to promote the mental well-being of ethnically diverse students?

Suicide Intervention and Prevention

Learning Objectives

After reading this chapter, you should be able to:

- Describe suicide and behaviors associated with suicide based on the Columbia Classification Algorithm of Suicide Assessment.
- Explain what the interpersonal psychological theory of suicide proposes.
- Differentiate between Tier 1, Tier 2, and Tier 3 of suicide prevention and intervention.
- Restate the warning signs of suicidal behavior in youth.
- Identify risk and protective factors of youth suicide.
- Identify data collection measures and questions that may be helpful in screening students who are suspected of being at-risk for suicide.
- Summarize how to incorporate culturally responsive practices into suicide prevention and intervention efforts.

Introduction to Suicide Prevention and Intervention

Suicide is now ranked as the second leading cause of death in the United States for children and young adults ages 10–24 (Hedegaard, Curtin, & Warner, 2018). In fact, across all age groups, the Centers for Disease Control and Prevention reported a 30% increase in suicide in the United States from 2000 to 2016 with rates reaching their highest levels in two decades for youth ages 15–19 (Hedegaard et al., 2018; Miron, Yu, & Wilf-Miron, 2019). It is estimated that one-fourth of visits to pediatric emergency departments are due to youth presenting as suicidal (Sheridan et al., 2015). Despite this, less than half of emergency departments are prepared to address the increasing rates of suicide in youth (Lo, Bridge, Shi, Ludwig, & Stanley, 2020). In an examination of 1,613 emergency room visits for suicidal thoughts or attempted suicide, it was noted that only

2% of children and teens under the age of 18 were admitted to the hospital (Burstein, Agostino, & Greenfield, 2019; Nickerson, Breux, Schaffer, & Samet, 2021). Given these alarming statistics, it is imperative that educators are prepared to prevent and intervene during episodes of suicidal crisis.

Although suicide prevention and intervention might seem like a natural extension of social-emotional RTI, the procedures, practices, and steps for preventing and intervening in youth suicide are distinct and unique. These steps are distinct and unique from social-emotional RTI because, as readers are aware, not every child who experiences social-emotional concerns is suicidal or has considered suicide. Moreover, as will be discussed in greater detail, the reasons for youth committing suicide may not simply be linked to underlying mental health concerns across cultures but rather due to other factors, such as losing the respect of family or community members or even due to historical discrimination (Chu, Khoury, Bahn, Bongar, & Goldblum, 2017).

In fact, whereas 90% of individuals who have attempted suicide in the general population have an underlying psychiatric disorder, only around 30% of Asian Americans with past attempts have no history of mental illness (Chu, Chi, Chen, & Leino, 2014; Chu et al., 2017). Moreover, it was found that the other half of Asian Americans who have attempted suicide are characterized by a nonpsychiatric subtype relating to sociocultural factors, such as attempting to commit suicide due to discrimination, family conflict, low acculturation, or medical problems (Chu et al., 2014).

As a result of the distinctive protocol and unique circumstances in which youth may consider or attempt suicide, an increasing number of scholars, educators, and government organizations have attempted to conceptualize suicide prevention and intervention under a three-tiered framework (Breux & Boccio, 2019; Breux & Samet, 2019; Miller, 2014; Miller, Eckert, & Mezza, 2009; Nickerson et al., 2021; Singer, Erbacher, & Rosen, 2018). The use of a three-tiered framework to prevent suicide and reduce suicide risk in schools is one that is modeled off the public health approach to suicide prevention and intervention (Breux & Boccio, 2019; Singer et al., 2018). Moreover, the World Health Organization (WHO), Centers of Disease Control and Prevention, and Association of State and Territorial Health Officials (ASTHO) have all advocated for a public health approach to preventing and intervening in suicide (Stout, Hindman, & Heinan, 2016; WHO, 2012).

Despite educators being aware of the seriousness of suicide, many are not aware that they have a legal responsibility to prevent and intervene upon suspecting or finding out that a youth is suicidal (Miller, 2014). Educators should be aware that in incidents in which a student has died by suicide, school staff have legally been held responsible when they did not report that a child posed a threat to themselves or other children (Miller, 2014). Moreover, due to the severe consequences of a child taking their own life, 32 states have mandated suicide prevention training for school personnel (American Foundation for Suicide Prevention, 2020). Despite these mandates, only 25% of high school principals were able to accurately identify their state law for suicide prevention (Smith-Millman & Flaspohler, 2019). With rates of suicide among youth continuing to increase, school administrators, teachers, and school-based mental health practitioners need to handle suicide seriously and in line with best evidence-based practice.

Despite the personal and professional ramifications student suicide has on educators, prevention and intervention of it remains on the back burner for many districts with other educational initiatives taking priority. It is easy for educators to forget about the very real dangers and consequences of a child engaging in or completing suicide when student grades, school budget, parent-teacher conferences, and even personal matters require attention. However, with suicide rates on the rise and social media exposing student suicide, educators should be prepared to best assist children who are thinking about or prepared to take their own life.

Suicide is defined as death that results from deliberate self-injurious behavior with any intent to die as a result of the behavior (Posner, Brodsky, Yershova, Buchanan, & Mann, 2014; Posner, Oquendo, Gould, Stanley, & Davies, 2007). Many theories have been proposed as to why individuals commit suicide. However, one of the most well supported and accepted theories is the interpersonal-psychological theory of suicide, which posits that in order for a person to carry out a suicidal behavior, individuals have to exhibit a high degree of suicidal desire and have developed the capability to carry out a self-directed lethal act (Burke, Hamilton, Ammerman, Stange, & Alloy, 2017). Central to the interpersonal psychological theory of suicide is that suicidal desire is best predicted by the individual believing that they are a significant burden on those around them combined with the individual feeling socially isolated despite wanting to be connected with others (Burke et al., 2017). Finally, this theory suggests that individuals who commit suicide have acquired the capability to complete the act due to reduced aversion or fear of death and to the physiological experience of pain. Each of these factors acting together significantly increases the likelihood of an individual attempting or completing suicide.

Although most educators are familiar with the term suicide and contributing factors as to why a child may take his or her own life, the act of killing oneself represents only one component among a continuum of suicidal behaviors (Posner et al., 2007). Due to the complex nature of one taking their own life and behaviors leading up to suicide, defining suicide and actions associated with it has been a source of contention for educators and scholars. Still, school staff and mental health practitioners need to be clear in their understanding of the act of suicide, the continuum of behaviors associated with it, and how to define such terms to avoid confusion. Fortunately, the **Columbia Classification Algorithm of Suicide Assessment (C-CASA)** provides educators and mental health practitioners suggested set terms and definitions to utilize in understanding and clearly relaying information regarding suicide.

Columbia Classification Algorithm of Suicide Assessment

The development of the C-CASA was originally intended to aid the Food and Drug Administration in assessing the link between suicidal behavior and anti-depressants (Posner et al., 2007). However, educators and school-based mental health practitioners may find the classification system useful in providing a common language to understand the range suicidal behaviors students may engage in. The C-CASA provides definitions of suicidal behavior and assists practitioners in distinguishing between suicidal events, non-suicidal events, and potentially suicidal events (Posner et al., 2007).

To date, the C-CASA remains one of the most well-known and accepted classification systems for suicidality and the protocol's definitions for suicidal behavior were adopted by the Centers for Disease Control and Prevention in 2011 (Posner et al., 2011). School mental health practitioners and administrators may want to consider the adaptation of the C-CASA categories into their school and district-wide suicide prevention and intervention manuals to formulate a common language regarding suicide and behaviors associated with suicide. School-based clinicians can utilize the C-CASA as a standardized measure to differentiate between individuals who self-injure in an attempt to die versus those who self-injure for non-suicidal reasons (Posner et al., 2007). Having such a classification system in place may further assist school-based practitioners in coordinating efforts with outside clinicians and hospitals to obtain help for the child.

A description of suicide and behaviors associated with suicide based on the C-CASA follows. *Some of the examples that are provided based off of the C-CASA may be graphic to the reader but in light of better understanding suicide and suicidal behavior they have been provided.*

Completed suicide is described as a self-injurious behavior resulting in fatality and is associated with some intent to die as a result of engaging in the behavior. Therefore, if there is any intent to die associated with the behavior, then the act is considered suicide (Posner et al., 2014). The intent to die can be either explicitly stated by the individual or inferred. An examples of suicide include a child who hangs himself and leaves a note stating his intent to die. The intent of the latter action can be inferred from the severity of the act. In the United States, 6,769 youth between 10 and 24 years of age died by committing suicide in 2017 (Centers for Disease Control and Prevention, 2017). The three most common means to commit suicide in the United States include use of firearms, suffocation (including death by hanging), and poisoning (including drug overdose) (Kochanek, Murphy, Xu, & Arias, 2019).

Attempted suicide is defined as a potentially self-injurious behavior that is associated with some intent to die as a result of the behavior (Posner et al., 2007, 2014). A suicide attempt may be explicit or implicitly inferred and may or may not result in actual injury to the child. For instance, a child who purposely points a gun at his chest, shoots himself, and survives is an example of attempted suicide. Before and after the incident the child did not explicitly indicate an intent to die, but the intent can be inferred that the child was attempting to commit suicide based on the severity of the behavior (Posner et al., 2007, 2014). Approximately 7.4% of high school students engaged in at least one suicide attempt, and 2.4 made an attempt that required medical attention in the past year (Breux & Boccio, 2019). For perspective, this means that in a high school with 1,000 students, it is possible that within one year approximately 74 students attempted to commit suicide and around 25 students will make an attempt to take their own life that results in medical attention.

An **interrupted attempt** involves a child taking steps toward suicide but the behavior is stopped by others before the potential for harm has begun (Posner et al., 2007, 2014). An attempt is considered interrupted if injury does not occur to the individual. If injury to the child takes place as a result of their actions to commit suicide, the child's behavior is considered a suicide attempt rather than an interrupted attempt (Posner et al., 2007, 2014). For example, an interrupted attempt might involve a parent walking in on child about to cut her wrist. Consequently, the child stops the act before injury occurs. In this case, the child has caused no harm to themselves due to the attempt being interrupted. However, if the child attempted to cut her wrist and successfully scratched the surface of her skin before her parent interrupted the behavior, the act would be considered a suicide attempt (Posner et al., 2007, 2014).

An **aborted or self-interrupted attempt** entails a child taking steps to self-injure but stopping themselves before any injury occurs. If not for the child abandoning the suicide attempt, it would have occurred causing self-harm (Posner et al., 2007, 2014). If an injury to the child occurs as a result of their actions, the incident becomes a suicide attempt. To illustrate, a child steals a bottle of pills from the nurse's office and plans to ingest the bottle at the end of the school day. However, on the way home from school, the child changes his mind and throws the bottle of pills in the trash can. On the contrary, if on the way home from school the child swallows fifteen pills from the bottle, throws the bottle out, and becomes sick, the behavior is considered a suicide attempt (Posner et al., 2007, 2014).

Preparatory acts toward suicidal behavior are described as incidents in which the child takes steps toward making a suicide attempt (Posner et al., 2007, 2014).

Preparatory acts involve either assembling the method to kill oneself or preparing for one's death by suicide (Posner et al., 2014). Examples of preparatory acts include giving away valuable possessions, writing a suicide note, saying final goodbyes to loved ones, purchasing a gun, or locating a high jumping point to commit suicide (Posner et al., 2014). Approximately 13.6% of students in grades nine through twelve indicated that they made a plan to commit suicide (Breux & Boccio, 2019).

Suicidal ideation involves passive or fleeting thoughts about wanting to be dead or active thoughts about killing oneself (Posner et al., 2007, 2014). Active thoughts of suicidal ideation may involve a child reporting to his teacher that he is thinking about hanging himself in the janitor closet. Passive thoughts of suicidal ideation may involve free-floating thoughts or ideas about wanting to be dead but failing to act on these feelings. For example, during reading instruction the child suddenly begins experiencing thoughts of dying. Recent studies suggest that suicidal ideation may begin as early as age three with an increase in thoughts about death occurring around age twelve (Glenn et al., 2017; Whalen, Dixon-Gordon, Belden, & Barch, 2015). Nationally, among children aged 5–18, suicidal thoughts and attempts led to more than 1.1 million emergency room visits in 2015 (Burnstein et al., 2019). This was up from about 580,000 in 2007 according to CDC data (Burnstein et al., 2019).

Non-suicidal self-injurious behavior involves a student engaging in self-harm that deliberately results in injury or the potential for injury to oneself (Posner et al., 2014). The behavior must be outside the realm of socially accepted forms of self-injury, such as tattooing and body piercing (Posner et al., 2014). With non-suicidal self-injury, there is no implicit or explicit suicidal intent (Posner et al., 2014). Some examples of self-injurious behavior include a child cutting herself to bleed as a form of self-punishment or a person burning themself to feel alive.

Finally, educators and school mental health professionals may simply not have enough information to determine whether the event involved deliberate suicidal behavior or ideation (Posner et al., 2007). Although there may be reason to suspect the possibility of suicidal behavior, there may not be enough information to determine with confidence whether the behavior was suicidal in nature. For instance, a child may have stabbed himself in the neck with a pen but there is not enough information to determine whether there was intent to commit suicide or whether the behavior was simply self injurious in nature. When asked about the incident, the child fails to respond as to whether the act is suicidal or not and indicates that he "doesn't want to talk about it." Therefore, the not enough information category is designed for incidents in which an injury was sustained on a place on the body that is consistent with deliberate self-harm or suicidal behavior (e.g., neck, wrists), without any information on how the injury was received (Posner et al., 2007).

Through using a classification system of suicidal behavior like the C-CASA, educators and school-based mental health practitioners will have a common language and understanding of suicide and the continuum of behaviors associated with it. Having such a common language is essential for clearly relaying information among school-based mental health practitioners, medical staff, and outside clinicians. These common terms and definitions are critical to avoid any confusion over suicide or attempted suicide and may streamline support for the child during a time of crisis. The remainder of this chapter focuses on suicide prevention and intervention as a three-tiered intervention service delivery model and makes up the final wall of the MTSS "house." Figure 6.1 shows suicide prevention and intervention as the fourth wall to the MTSS "house." A detailed description of the model follows.

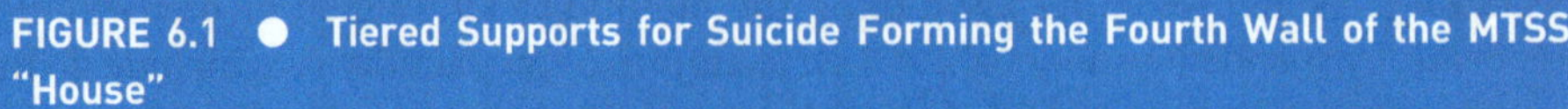

FIGURE 6.1 ● Tiered Supports for Suicide Forming the Fourth Wall of the MTSS "House"

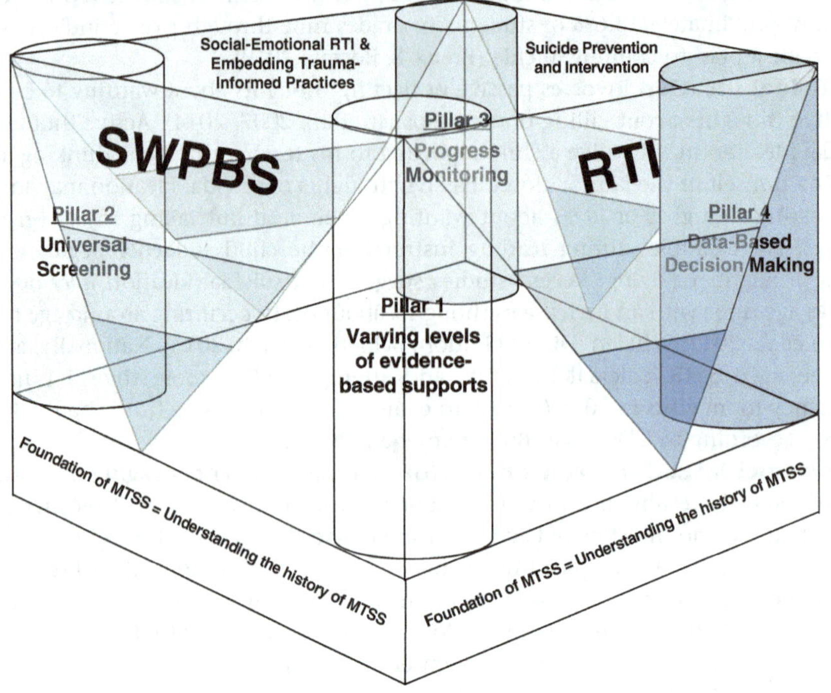

Description of Tiers Under Suicide Prevention and Intervention

Due to suicide becoming an increasing concern across the United States, there has been growing interest in developing a three-tiered intervention service delivery model to address suicide prevention and intervention in youth (David-Ferdon et al., 2016; Singer et al., 2018). Consequently, as both youth and adult suicide rates continued to climb, in 2016 the CDC recommended that a "public health approach" be utilized to prevent suicide (David-Ferdon et al., 2016). Such a model was recommended as it targets the general population in a proactive fashion before suicide is imminent. This is as opposed to the former approach that was based off the medical model in which only those with significant mental health concerns may have been concurrently treated for suicide. For example, under the medical model, children and adults may have received treatment for suicidality alongside their primary presenting concerns of depression, anxiety, conduct disorder, or substance abuse. However, for children and adults who may not have had such diagnosis or whose concerns were not severe enough to warrant a diagnosis, treatment of suicide and suicidal behavior was limited (David-Ferdon et al., 2016).

At present, scholarly literature is just starting to present with suggestions for schools to develop a three-tiered intervention service delivery model that focuses on suicide prevention and intervention (Miller, 2014; Singer et al., 2018). However, what has been proposed so far provides the basis for an intervention service delivery model that proactively addresses suicide as a public health concern that is affecting the everyday lives of children in school. Therefore, suicide prevention and intervention is a three-tiered intervention service delivery model that seeks to prevent and decrease incidents of suicide and suicidal behaviors in youth through best preventative practices.

Although social-emotional RTI promotes mental wellness and attempts to remediate mental health concerns in youth, suicide prevention and intervention is considered a separate and distinct intervention service delivery model (Miller, 2014; Singer et al., 2018). Suicide prevention and intervention is a distinct and unique intervention service delivery model because it is geared to raise awareness, prevent, and intervene for a subset of children who may be not only at-risk for social-emotional concerns but who are also experiencing suicidal ideation or behavior. Therefore, as mentioned earlier, suicide prevention and intervention operates out of the idea that not all children who are experiencing social-emotional concerns or engaging in self-injurious behaviors are suicidal. Consequently, a distinct intervention service delivery model is needed prevent suicide and assist those few students who are suicidal (Brown & Plener, 2017; Miller, 2014).

Unlike the previous intervention service delivery models that provide expected percentages of students at each tier (e.g., Tier 1: 80%–85%, Tier 2: 5%–10%, Tier 3: 1%–5%), suicide prevention and intervention does not allocate such percentages. The objective of suicide prevention and intervention is to increase awareness of youth suicide and provide increasing levels of support to the very few students who may be presenting with suicidal behavior (Miller, 2014; Singer et al., 2018). By adopting suicide prevention and intervention as an intervention service delivery model, schools are attempting to better outline, address, and support students who are at-risk or are contemplating suicide. A discussion of the supports and services provided at each Tier of suicide prevention and intervention follows.

Tier 1

Educators will be glad to know that Tier 1 of suicide prevention and intervention builds on universal supports already in place through school-wide positive behavior support (SWPBS) and social-emotional response to intervention (Miller, 2014; Singer et al., 2018). Moreover, like any intervention service delivery model, Tier 1 supports for suicide prevention and intervention are delivered to the entire school population, regardless of whether students are at-risk of suicide or not. As with SWPBS, creating a warm, caring, and comforting school environment is a critical component to preventing youth suicide. A culture that models and emphasizes respect, empathy, and kindness for one another lays the foundation for children feeling cared about and viewing school as a safe zone even when other areas of their lives may not feel as safe (NASP School Safety and Crisis Response Committee, 2015). Recall that the interpersonal psychological theory of suicide suggests that individuals who feel socially isolated and like they are a burden on others appear to be at-risk for suicide (Burke et al., 2017). Therefore, having a positive school climate that fosters inclusivity, diversity, and welcomes student opinions is critical. Not surprisingly, many Tier 1 supports offered through SWPBS to reduce problem behaviors, such as bullying, are equally valuable to suicide prevention and intervention. Likewise, Tier 1 interventions and supports through social-emotional RTI, such as mindfulness and deep breathing, may play a vital role in reducing youth suicide and suicidal behaviors by teaching children how to appropriately cope with negative feelings. Interestingly, it is estimated that 90% of individuals who die by suicide have an underlying mental illness (National Alliance on Mental Health, 2022). Therefore, it is especially important for schools to teach children mental wellness strategies and prosocial behaviors.

Aside from elements of SWPBS and social-emotional RTI being incorporated into suicide prevention and intervention at Tier 1, universal supports at this level include educating staff regarding youth suicide, known as gatekeeper training (Singer et al., 2018). **Gatekeeper training** involves dissemination of information on youth suicide in regards to demographic information, statistics, risk factors, protective factors, warning signs, misunderstandings, vulnerable populations, and minorities (Breux & Boccio, 2019). Some populations that may be at increased risk for suicide include students who identify as LGTBQ, disabled, or ethnic minority status (e.g., Native American). In addition to disseminating information on youth suicide, gatekeeper training promotes help-seeking behavior for students, teaches educators how to respond effectively to at-risk students, and informs them how to connect at-risk children to appropriate school and community-based resources through activities, behavioral rehearsal, and role play (Breux & Boccio, 2019; Singer et al., 2018). Gatekeeper training may also involve providing educators an understanding of the continuum of suicidal behaviors under the C-CASA and incorporate such language into a readily available school or district suicide prevention and intervention manual (Breux & Boccio, 2019; Singer et al., 2018). School suicide manuals and protocols should be available to all staff at Tier 1 and personnel responsible for carrying out these plans should be identified during gatekeeper training.

Existing gatekeeper training programs vary in duration, ranging from one hour to two days and modality of delivery with both online and live training options available (Singer et al., 2018). Additionally, gatekeeper trainings range in their target audience with most programs available, such as the Lifelines Suicide Prevention Program, focusing on middle and high school teachers and students. Other programs, such as Applied Suicide Intervention Skills Training (ASIST), have been implemented with a kindergarten through twelfth-grade audience of caregivers, teachers, or other community members (Singer et al., 2018). Finally, other Gatekeeper training programs are specifically designed for students. For example, the Youth Aware of Mental Health Program is designed for students ages 14–16 to provide an overview of suicide and warning signs of suicide (Breux & Boccio, 2019).

Of the many gatekeeper training programs available, only Signs of Suicide and the Youth Aware of Mental Health curriculum have been shown to reduce suicidal behavior (Singer et al., 2018). Even more surprising, is that out of all the gatekeeper and social-emotional programs available, only the Good Behavior Game has been shown to reduce both suicidal behavior and ideation in youth (Breux & Boccio, 2019; Singer et al., 2018). Still, for educators looking for a cost-effective suicide gatekeeper program, the Society for the Prevention of Teen Suicide offers one for free on their website entitled *Making Educators Partners in Youth Suicide*. Lastly, the Lifeguard Workshop by the Trevor Project is a free online training program that helps educators identify the challenges faced by LGBTQ individuals, recognize the warning signs of suicide, and respond to someone who is in crisis (The Trevor Project, 2019). The Lifeguard Workshop is listed in the Suicide Prevention Resource Center/American Foundation for Suicide Prevention best practice registry for suicide prevention (The Trevor Project, 2019).

In addition to gatekeeper training, it is important for school staff to receive supplemental education and information on the warning signs of suicidal behavior in children. Although often confused with risk factors, warning signs are different. The main difference is that warning signs indicate that a youth is at immediate risk of suicide and are considered the earliest detectable signs that identify heightened risk (Hazelden Betty Ford Foundation, 2019). These signs suggest that without interruption, the youth may engage in suicidal behavior within minutes, hours, or days after them appearing. This is opposed to risk factors which increase the likelihood of a child engaging in suicidal behavior and take place over a longer period, such as a year to a lifetime

(Hazelden Betty Ford Foundation, 2019). Risk factors will be discussed in more detail in Tier 2 of suicide prevention and intervention, but some examples include having a friend commit suicide or being physically abused.

At Tier 1, all staff members should be trained and become familiar with the warning signs of suicidal behavior in youth. One acronym that may prove useful in helping educators remember and recognize warning signs of suicidal behavior in youth is known as FACTS, which stands for Feelings, Actions, Changes, Threats, and Situations (Hazelden Betty Ford Foundation, 2019). The incorporation of FACTS into school in-service training and district suicide manuals at Tier 1 is key to educators becoming familiar and recognizing the signs of an imminent suicidal crisis. Figure 6.2 provides brief outline of FACTS (Hazelden Betty Ford Foundation, 2019).

FIGURE 6.2 • FACTS From the Hazelden Betty Ford Foundation (2019)

Feelings:

- Hopelessness: feeling like things are bad and won't get any better
- Fear of losing control, going crazy, harming himself/herself or others
- Helplessness: a belief that there's nothing that can be done to make life better
- Worthlessness: feeling like an awful person and people would be better off if they were dead
- Hating themselves, feeling guilty or ashamed
- Being extremely sad and lonely
- Feeling anxious, worried or angry all the time

Actions:

- Drug or alcohol abuse
- Talking or writing about death or destruction
- Aggression: getting into fights or having arguments with people
- Recklessness: doing risky or dangerous things

Changes:

- Personality: behaving like a different person, becoming withdrawn, tired all the time, not caring about anything, or becoming more talkative, outgoing
- Behavior: can't concentrate on school or regular tasks
- Sleeping pattern: sleeping all the time or not being able to sleep at all, or waking up in the middle of the night or early in the morning and not being able to get back to sleep
- Eating habits: losing your appetite and/or overeating and gaining weight
- Losing interest in friends, hobbies, and appearance, or in activities or sports previously enjoyed
- Sudden improvement after a period of being down or withdrawn

Threats:

- Statements like "How long does it take to bleed to death?"
- Threats like "I won't be around much longer" or "Don't tell anyone else...you won't be my friend if you tell!"
- Plans like giving away favorite things, studying about ways to die, obtaining a weapon or a stash of pills: the risk is very high if a person has a plan and the way to do it
- Suicide attempts like overdosing, wrist cutting

Situations:

- Getting into trouble at school, at home, or with the law.
- Recent loss through death, divorce, or separation; the break-up of a relationship; losing an opportunity or a dream; losing self-esteem
- Changes in life that feel overwhelming
- Being exposed to suicide or the death of a peer under any circumstances

Source: Hazelden Betty Ford Foundation (2019) Lifelines Curriculum.

Finally, at Tier 1, educators and especially administrators should ensure that the school is following proper and standard protocol in identifying, storing, and securing objects, items, and materials that students may utilize during a suicide attempt. Common rooms and locations that may store hazardous materials that students may utilize to harm themselves include the school nurse's office, janitor's closet, science lab, technology room, or even the art teacher's classroom. Each of these rooms and locations may contain objects and materials that at-risk students can utilize to attempt or commit suicide. Therefore, it is important at Tier 1 for school administrators to work with their school staff to ensure and reinforce that all objects and materials that can cause harm to students are properly stored and put away to reduce the chances of a suicidal crisis emerging.

Tier 2

Tier 2 helps to identify subpopulations of students who are at higher risk for suicidal behavior than the general population but who are not at imminent risk of completing suicide. This tier is designed for students who may be at-risk for suicidal behavior due to expressing a desire to commit suicide but failing to have a concrete plan to complete the act or having some identifiable risk factor. For example, the student may indicate that they "don't want to live anymore" but when asked if they have a plan in place to take their own life, they respond "no" or with a vague answer "I guess I would try and find some pills or something."

Identifiable risk factors for suicide can be understood as occurring along a continuum that includes individual, relationship, and cultural/environmental factors (Breux & Samet, 2019). This continuum starts at the individual level and encompasses a person's psychology, biology, and social history. Risk factors at this level include poor coping skills, substance use, depression, prior experiences with death and trauma, and impulsive or aggressive responses to stress. The risk for suicide is also influenced by a person's relationships with their family, friends, peers, and mentors (Breux & Samet, 2019). Factors that may increase suicidal risk at the relationship level include interpersonal violence, bullying, abuse or sexual assault, family separations, being exposed to suicide by others, and loss of an important friend, family member, or mentor (Breux & Samet, 2019). Finally, cultural/environmental factors, include having access to the means to kill oneself, the perception of social acceptability of suicide in popular culture or among a peer group, codes of silence that discourage reaching out to adults for assistance, poor coordination of services, lack of social connectedness, and limited access to care (Breux & Samet, 2019). Out of all the risk factors mentioned, educators should note that attempted suicide is the strongest predictor of subsequent death by suicide (Breux & Boccio, 2019; Miller, 2014).

Even if educators are unaware of whether a student has identifiable risk factor, a child may have been identified as a youth with significant externalizing or internalizing concerns through prior screening. Subsequently, a school-based mental health practitioner may follow-up with a brief suicide screener or comprehensive risk assessment to determine whether the child is at-risk for wanting to take their own life, has a plan in place to do so and has access to materials to complete the act (e.g., access to guns, knives, cleaning supplies, high jumping points, or medications). For example, unknown to a teacher, a student's parents may be going through a divorce causing significant family dysfunction in the home. Upon being universally screened for internalizing concerns using the Strengths and Differences Questionnaire, the child's ratings identify the youth at is at-risk and in need of further support. After the school-based mental health practitioner contacts the family regarding the student's elevated ratings on the SDQ, it uncovered that the child's parents are going through a divorce, and the recent changes have been hard on the child. The school-based mental health practitioner may then decide to follow-up with the student using a screener or comprehensive risk assessment to determine whether the child is at risk for suicide, how the student's identifiable risk factors, such as divorce, are influencing their feelings, and what action(s) to take next to best support the youth. Table 6.1 outlines risk and protective factors for youth suicide. A further discussion on informal and formal screeners for suicide can be found in the data-based decision-making section of this chapter.

TABLE 6.1 • Risk and Protective Factors of Youth Suicide

Risk Factors of Youth Suicide	Protective Factors of Youth Suicide
• **Mental Health:** Depressive disorders, substance abuse or dependence, anxiety disorders, personality disorders, difficulty regulating emotions, external locus of control	• **Mental Health:** Emotional well-being, internal locus of control, resilience, coping skills, ability to perceive, understand, and manage emotions.
• **Personal Characteristics:** Hopelessness, low self-esteem, loneliness, impulsivity, self-injurious behavior, bullied at school, risky sexual behavior, delinquency, low frustration tolerance, having a disability, withdrawn, lonely, anxious, fearful, and non-adaptable temperament.	• **Personal Characteristics:** Hopeful, good social and communication skills, close friends, connected to others, good self-esteem, adaptable temperament, frustration tolerance and emotional regulation, involved in positive outside activities, clubs, and/or sports
• **Family History:** Parent suicide or suicidal behavior or parental mental health problems, parent divorce, death of a parent or close relative, problems in parent/child Relationship	• **Family History:** Little or no history of parental suicide or mental health problems, parents married or maintained an amicable relationship, family support or connectedness to family, strong relationships with parents and parental involvement
• **Interpersonal Problems:** Difficulty getting along w/others at school, work, or in the community	• **Interpersonal Relations:** Gets along and maintains relationships with others at school, work, or in the community
• **Access:** Access to firearms, medications, jumping sites (rooftops and buildings), drugs, or alcohol.	• **Access:** No or restricted access to firearms, medications, jumping sites (rooftops and buildings), drugs or alcohol.

Source: Adapted from Center for Mental Health Services, Substance Abuse and Mental Health Services Administration (SAMHSA) (2012). *Preventing suicide: A toolkit for high schools* (HHS Publication No. 02-2650).

After the student has been screened for suicide by a school-based mental health practitioner, and it is deemed that the child presents with some risk factors related to suicide but is not at imminent risk (student does not have a concrete plan to commit suicide or immediate access to materials to commit suicide), Tier 2 encompasses a number of interventions to assist the child. Arguably, one of the easiest interventions both educators and school-based mental health practitioners can utilize to assist children who are at-risk of suicide includes the development and use of a safety plan (Breux & Samet, 2019; Stanley & Brown, 2012). A **safety plan** is a prioritized written list of coping strategies and sources of support children can use if they have been deemed at-risk for suicide (Stanley & Brown, 2012). These coping strategies and sources of support can be used before or during a suicidal crisis and are put into the child's own words in an easy-to-read format. The coping strategies and sources of support implemented in a safety plan are derived by working with the child to obtain student buy-in as opposed to simply dictating to the child what is in their plan (Stanley & Brown, 2012). To develop a safety plan, Stanley and Brown (2012) recommend that school-based mental health practitioners should help the child:

1. Recognize their own warning signs of an impending suicidal crisis. For example, some children may notice that when they are feeling suicidal they tend to think about killing themselves or have thoughts of death. Other students might notice that they engage in negative self-talk (e.g., "I am a failure." "I wish I was not here anymore."), feel hopeless, or feel disengaged and withdrawn from their peers and activities
2. Identify internal coping strategies to distract themselves from suicidal thoughts (i.e., engaging in deep breathing, listening to music, reading, drawing, practicing yoga, etc.)
3. Utilize social contacts to distract from suicidal thoughts by identifying individuals and settings where socialization occurs. For example, students should identify close contacts inside and outside of the school who they can talk to when they are feeling upset. These close contacts may not necessarily know the child has or is experiencing a suicidal crisis. Additionally, children can identify places inside and outside of the school that encourage socialization, such as the school gymnasium, going to a local coffee shop, sporting event, or place of worship.
4. Generate a list of family members or friends who may help resolve the crisis (child reveals to close family or a friend that they are experiencing a suicidal crisis). The individuals are very close to the individual and are aware that the child is at-risk of suicide or has had thoughts of suicide. Therefore, the child can openly feel safe talking to them if they are in a suicidal crisis. These individuals might be made up the same people from number three but the main difference is that individuals in number four are aware of the child being at-risk of suicide in the past or having thoughts of suicide, whereas individuals in group three might not be aware.
5. Contact mental health professionals or agencies to help (seeking school psychologist, counselor, or social worker for assistance)
6. Reduce the potential for lethal means (reduce access to guns, medication, high jumping points, sharps, etc.).

The use of safety planning as a viable and easy-to-implement intervention for students at-risk for suicide is growing schools. School-based mental health practitioners tend to like safety planning as an intervention because it is relatively easy to develop and only takes approximately 20–40 minutes to complete (Stanley & Brown, 2012). Additionally, educators like safety planning because it provides children a set of prioritized contacts and coping strategies to utilize when feeling upset or experiencing a suicidal crisis. Finally, after being developed, students can use their safety plan rather independently or with simple prompts. Consequently, the intervention is not difficult to implement or time-consuming for educators. For students who are prone to losing a paper version of their safety plan, there are applications that allow them to be stored on phones or tablets, such as the MY3 suicide prevention application.

In addition to safety planning, Tier 2 consists of school-based practitioners providing at-risk students and caregivers psychoeducational interventions and information on community-based service providers who may further assist the child. **Psycho-education** for youth at-risk for suicide might involve providing the child and their caregiver's information and resources on suicidality and teaching them about how to utilize a safety plan at home (Breux & Samet, 2019; Singer et al., 2018). If the child has an accompanying mental health disorder or has been identified at-risk for having an accompanying internalizing or externalizing concern, school-based practitioners may also educate caregivers and the child on their condition and provide some basic interventions that can be implemented in the home.

Psycho-education may help dispel common myths and misconceptions regarding suicidal behavior for caregivers. For example, caregivers might be concerned that by asking the child about suicide, the school-based practitioner has increased the likelihood of the child thinking about or attempting to take their own life. During psycho-education, the school-based practitioner can address caregiver concerns by indicating that talking about suicide has not been found to increase suicide risk and that asking about suicide may actually reduce suicidal ideation (Dazzi, Gribble, Wessely, & Fear, 2014).

Finally, Tier 2 might involve having the student partake in a suicide prevention program or a program that addresses areas of significant concern, such as **Coping and Support Training (CAST)** or the POD-TEAMS Depression Prevention Program discussed in the previous chapter. CAST is a school-based small group counseling program for children 14–19 years of age (Singer et al., 2018). The program is designed to assist youth in overcoming suicide risk factors including depressive symptoms, hopelessness, anger, anxiety, and substance abuse by introducing coping strategies and a sense of personal control over negative feelings (Singer et al., 2018). The CAST program involves twelve 55-minute sessions over the course of 6 weeks and is designed to be implemented by teachers or school-based mental health practitioners (Signer et al., 2018).

Tier 3

Tier 3 of suicide prevention and intervention targets students who are at high-risk for committing suicide. These students may have a prior history of suicidal behavior, self-identify as suicidal, or may have been identified by others as high risk due to their suicidal thoughts and behaviors (Breux & Boccio, 2019; Miller, 2014; Singer et al., 2018). Children at Tier 3 tend to have experienced suicidal ideation in the past month or are actively having frequent and intrusive thoughts about death, dying, and killing themselves (Breux & Boccio, 2019; Miller, 2014; Singer et al., 2018). These students likely have developed a concrete and well thought out plan to commit suicide and have access to materials to complete the act. Finally, these students may display a reduced aversion to death, show little fear of dying, and have made preparatory acts in readying themselves for suicide (giving away personal possessions, writing a suicide note, etc.).

For example, while completing a risk assessment with the school-based mental health practitioner, a student who is at imminent risk for suicide might say:

> *I am no longer afraid to die and have often thought about being dead for the past year. I am not even afraid to tell you my plan for going away forever because the world would be better off without me. I know my father leaves his gun cabinet unlocked during hunting season, and I located the bullets in the basement last month. My parents will be going on vacation in two weeks, and I think that would be the best time for me to leave this world behind. I have been visiting my family and friends to see them one last time before I take my life. I even visited my Uncle who I have not seen since last summer.*

In the above example, the child indicates that he frequently thinks about dying, appears to have little fear of death, has established a concrete plan to kill themself, is in the process of preparing to die, and has access to materials to complete the plan. All these factors play into determining whether a student is in need of Tier 2 or Tier 3 supports. The main difference between a student at Tier 2 and one at Tier 3 is that a student at Tier 3 is at imminent risk of committing suicide, has a detailed method to complete the act, has access to materials to attempt suicide, and is showing one or more the warning signs under FACTS discussed in Tier 1 (Breux & Boccio, 2019; Miller, 2014; Singer et al., 2018). A child at Tier 2 may have expressed a desire to die but is not showing warning signs under FACTS, has not developed a detailed plan to commit suicide, and has limited access to materials that may place them at high risk for suicide. In the event where this is the first time a child has openly expressed suicidal ideation or intent, the suicide screener will play a vital role in determining whether the child is at Tier 2 or Tier 3. Either way, all suicidal threats should be handled seriously.

Although working with a student who is at high-risk for suicide is extremely scary for educators and school-based mental health practitioners, efforts at Tier 1 and Tier 2 levels of suicide prevention and intervention can greatly reduce the chances of children reaching this point. Additionally, educators may find comfort in the fact that there is time to assist youth who are suicidal and, contrary to common belief, suicide is rarely an impulsive act in childhood. In fact, research has found that generally youth plan their suicide attempts in advance with the average length of time between a child's first serious thought of suicide and attempt to take their own life being approximately one year (Singer et al., 2018). Therefore, effective suicide prevention and intervention service delivery model is vital to establishing set protocols and procedures revolving around youth suicide.

In the event a student is at imminent risk for suicide, Tier 3 efforts are devised to ensure student safety, inform caregivers, minimize distress, and link students to the appropriate level of care outside the school, such as a hospital setting or mental health facility. In-service training for school-based mental health practitioners on these specific topics is key to developing a well thought out plan to work with students at imminent risk of suicide. First and foremost, efforts at this tier should ensure that the child is not left alone and does not have access to materials in the immediate surroundings to hurt themselves or attempt suicide (Stone et al., 2017). Common items in the school environment that a student may use to hurt themselves or commit suicide include pencil sharpeners, letter openers, pens, pencils, paper cutters, medications, high jumping points, or chemicals.

In addition to these more evident items that at-risk students may utilize in an attempt to take their own life, educators should consider non-traditional objects that students may use. These items may include the tape cutter at the end of a dispenser, shoelaces, staples, garbage bags, and even cords to window blinds, fans, radios, or other electronic equipment. Each of these objects can be either used to penetrate skin, swallowed, or utilized for suffocation, and each should be kept out of the reach of a child experiencing a suicidal crisis. Finally, school-based mental health practitioners and administrators should be aware and keep track of local "hot spots," which may be popular places for individuals to attempt or complete suicide, such as bridges, tall buildings, cliffs, or isolated parks (Stone et al., 2017). Although this list may seem extensive, it is better for educators, and especially school-based mental health practitioners, to take advanced precautionary measures to eliminate any risk.

When a suicidal crisis arises, it is important for educators to work together and have a plan to ensure the student's safety. Such a plan should be outlined prior to a crisis emerging and may involve educators each taking on a role to best support the child in need. For example, after a school psychologist heads down to retrieve a student who is experiencing suicidal thoughts, the school counselor may assist by completing a sweep of the immediate area outside and inside the school psychologist's office and remove any items the student may utilize to harm themselves. Additionally, the teacher's aide in the classroom may remain with the student and help the school psychologist escort the child back to the office to ensure the youth's safety and well-being. Once down in the office, the school psychologist may administer a suicide screener to the student to determine the level of risk and develop a further course of action. Additionally, the school psychologist may either work to develop a safety plan with the student or take the student through their suicide safety plan if one already exists.

Educators should be aware that while suicide tends not to be an impulsive act from the first thoughts of taking one's life to the act of attempting suicide, suicidal crisis is just that: a crisis (Stone et al., 2017). In other words, high-risk students have likely long thought, planned, and are ready to commit suicide. For a student expressing a desire to take their own life, educators should be prepared and plans should be in place to reduce the probability of a possible attempt being successful. The CDC indicates that when individuals are in a suicidal crisis the interval between deciding to act and attempting suicide can be as little as five to ten minutes (Stone et al., 2017). Additionally, people tend not to substitute a different method to commit suicide when a highly lethal method is unavailable or difficult to access (Stone et al., 2017). Therefore, by limiting access to lethal methods, educators are increasing the time interval between students deciding to act and the actual suicide attempt (Stone et al., 2017). This time is critical in providing school-based mental health practitioners an opportunity to assist the student in overcoming their suicidal urges. These urges may arise because the student is feeling considerable stress, sadness, or anxiety and such feelings tend to pass when provide time, adequate support, and ensured safety.

After eliminating access to lethal items, ensuring the student's safety, and developing a course of action, school-based mental health practitioners may work with the school administrator to contact the youth's parents (Breux & Samet, 2019). It may greatly help school-based mental health practitioners or administrators to have a script of what to say to parents or bullet points in order to deliver a clear, concise, and reassuring message to caregivers. Before revealing the specifics of how the events unfolded concerning the suicidal crisis, school-based mental health practitioners or administrators should first assure parents that their child is safe and that school personnel are there to help them. Subsequently, school-based mental health practitioners or administrators should keep information over the phone brief and notify caregivers that they can speak at greater length concerning the incident in person. The rationale for being brief on the phone concerning suicidal behavior is that caregivers may be experiencing considerable shock or have difficulty processing the idea that their child has a desire to take their own life. Too much information over the phone may further overwhelm, confuse, or upset caregivers.

After speaking with the parent over the phone, Tier 3 efforts consist of school-based mental health practitioners and administrators working with the local hospital, community mobile mental health unit, or outside mental health agency to ensure the child is connected with outside support (Breux & Samet, 2019; Breux, Samet, Nickerson, & Schaffer, 2018). Schools should work with parents and outside providers to ensure that the child is being safely transported to a facility that can further address their mental health care needs. Additionally, the student should be reassured that the school will be there to support them and address any questions the student has. Lastly, school-based mental health practitioners, with caregiver permission, may want to supply outside agencies and practitioners' information on the student in regards to risk factors, warning signs, likes, dislikes, interests, suicide screening information, and a copy of their safety plan.

Arguably, the most overlooked component of Tier 3 involves school-based mental health practitioners properly following up with parents, outside providers, and the student to develop a re-entry plan for the child to return to school (Breux et al., 2018). The development of such a plan is essential to the student's safety and successful transition back into the educational environment. Moreover, development of such a plan often needs to take place quicker than school-based mental health practitioners think. Surprisingly, although the number of adolescents who experience a psychiatric hospitalization increased by nearly 300% over the past 20 years, the average hospitalization duration has continued to decrease dramatically (White, LaFleur, Houle, Hyry-Dermith, & Blake, 2017). Additionally, it has been found that within three months after discharge for hospitalization, the risk of suicide is higher than at any other time in the child's life (Chung et al., 2017). Therefore, school-based mental health practitioners must work diligently and be prepared to collaborate with stakeholders in transitioning the child back into the school.

In order to best transition the student back into the educational environment, school-based mental health professionals may first want to obtain permission from the child's parents to communicate with the hospital, outside providers, and even the student. Additionally, school-based clinicians may wish to request permission to attend treatment plan meetings or the hospital discharge conference (Hazelden Betty Ford Foundation, 2019). By attending treatment plan meetings and the discharge conference, school psychologists or counselors can obtain critical information on the child's current condition, interventions utilized, medications prescribed, and current prognosis. Moreover, school-based mental health practitioners can coordinate efforts with outside clinicians to best assist the child upon their reentry into the school system.

Aside from attending treatment plan meetings and the hospital discharge conference, school-based clinicians and administrators should consult with caregivers and involve the student in their school re-entry plan meeting. During this meeting, it is important to discuss what the student feels is needed to make the transition successful and what school staff can do to help the child (Hazelden Betty Ford Foundation, 2019). Moreover, discussions should be held on how to handle assignments the student has missed without penalty, modifying the child's schedule and course load to reduce stress, and arranging before or after school tutoring to help the youth catch up on lessons missed (Breux et al., 2018). A plan should also be created on how the student can explain their absence to peers and how it will be explained to the child's teachers (Breux et al., 2018). Finally, efforts should be made to establish contact with outside mental health professionals the child may be seeing and enroll the child in Tier 3 school-based counseling, such as the POD-TEAMS Depression Prevention Program (Breux et al., 2018).

Helping Students At-Risk for Suicide Program

Not many formal programs exist that that train school-based mental health practitioners and administrators in developing a standardized procedure to assess and manage suicide risk in youth. Although gatekeeper training programs prepare educators to recognize the warning signs of suicide in youth and subsequently refer them for help, these programs do not delineate a set of standardized steps that school-based mental health clinicians or administrators can follow to manage suicide risk (Nickerson et al., 2021). Consequently, the Helping Students at Risk for Suicide program (HSAR) was developed by Breux et al. (2018) to provide evidence-based practice and tools for school-based mental health professionals to use when intervening with students who demonstrate a possible risk for suicidal behavior (Nickerson et al., 2021). Therefore, HSAR program is designed to be a Tier 2 and Tier 3 one-day professional workshop for school psychologists, school counselors, and school administrators to guide their practice and understanding for working with youth at risk for suicide. As outlined by Breux et al. (2018), the objectives of the HSAR workshop are to:

1. Increase familiarity with a best practice process to assist students who are having suicidal thoughts or behavior
2. Understand the need for pre-planning and standardized procedures for helping students at risk for suicide
3. Identify the importance of collaboration and shared decision-making in managing students at risk for suicide
4. Practice with suicide assessment and safety planning tools

Although the HSAR program is still early in its development and implementation, the workshop has been given to educators across New York State. Results of initial pilot testing of the program indicate that HSAR fills a training need that gatekeeper programs do not address in preparing school-based mental health practitioners and administrators in working with students who are at higher risk for suicide (Nickerson et al., 2021). Continued expansion of the HSAR program is still in development, but early pilot testing results are promising for application beyond New York State (Box 6.1).

BOX 6.1 THE FOREVER 27 CLUB

In music, there is an ominous club of endless artists collectively known as the "Forever 27 Club" or simply the "27 Club" (Bellis, Hughes, Sharples, & Hardcastle, 2012) The club consists of a laundry list of musicians, such as Jimi Hendrix, Janis Joplin, and Amy Winehouse, who passed away too early through homicide, substance abuse, transportation-related accidents, or suicide (Bellis et al., 2012). Over the past three decades, the cultural phenomenon and mystery of the 27 Club grew in recognition and was often cited in scholarly journals, social media, the news, and magazines (Bellis et al., 2012). Arguably, the most well-known member of the 27 Club, and the one who helped to propel interest in it, was that of Kurt Cobain, lead singer of the rock band Nirvana. In a study of 1489 musicians reaching fame between 1956 and 2006, a study by Bellis et al. (2012) revealed that adverse childhood experiences likely predisposed many famous artists to health-damaging behaviors, such as substance abuse and suicide. Sadly, Kurt Cobain was one of these artists and provides a case study as to how a child's early experiences can possibly influence their behaviors and actions throughout their adolescence and adulthood with dire suicidal consequences.

In evaluating interviews with Cobain and biographies about his life, a twisted tale emerges over how the lead singer of one of the most popular bands in modern history was exposed to many ACES and how he coped with mental health difficulties in youth. Fortunately, since Cobain's death evidence-based treatment for those facing suicidal ideation and childhood mental illness has evolved and a proactive approach is being adopted by schools across America. Below is a comparison of some of the types of questions asked by the ACE study and experiences from Cobain's life before he committed suicide on April 5, 1994. With an ACE score of four or more, a person's odds of committing suicide are 1120% higher than someone with an ACE score of zero (Felitti et al., 1998). From what can be gleaned from these interviews, and his biography, Cobain's ACE score was at least a five or higher.

(Continued)

(Continued)

Prior to Your 18th birthday

1. **Did you often or very often feel that no one in your family loved you or thought you were important or special? Did you ever feel that your family didn't look out for each other, feel close to each other, or support each other (Felitti et al., 1998; Starecheski, 2015)?**

   In speaking about his father (Green et al., 2006):

   - *"I felt like I never really had a father. I've never had a father figure who I could share things with."*
   - *"I was one of the last things of importance on his list."*

2. **Did a parent or other adult in the household often or very often swear at you, insult you, put you down, or humiliate you, or act in a way that made you afraid that you might be physically hurt (Felitti et al., 1998; Starecheski, 2015)?**

   - *"If we were in social situations or at restaurants, my dad would...if I had spilled a glass of water, he'd put me in a head lock and would dig his knuckles into my head and would smack me in the face. I never understood that—why a parent would be so embarrassed by or be so intimidated by what other people would think of you in a restaurant just because your child spills something on accident and would have to punish them for having an accident. That is a weird psychological trip to play on a child because I still put myself down and cuss myself out for knocking things over, and I get really upset with myself because I've been conditioned not to spill things, not to have accidents, to not have human error* (Green et al., 2006)."

3. **Were your parents ever separated or divorced (Felitti et al., 1998; Starecheski, 2015)?**

   - At age 9, Cobain's parents got divorced (Green et al., 2006). In speaking about the divorce Cobain said:

   I had a really good childhood until the divorce and all the sudden my whole world changed. I couldn't face some of my friends at school. I desperately wanted to have the classic typical family. Mother, father. I wanted that security so I resented my parents for quite a few years because of that. (Savage, 1993)

4. **Was your mother or stepmother often or very often pushed, grabbed, slapped, or had something thrown at her (Felitti et al., 1998; Starecheski, 2015)? Was your mother or stepmother sometimes, often, or very often kicked, bitten, hit with a fist, or hit with something hard (Felitti et al., 1998; Starecheski, 2015)?**

   - After Kurt's parents divorced, his mother, Wendy, dated a man by the name of Frank Franich. Upon Wendy beginning to drink more heavily, Mr. Franich broke her arm, and she was subsequently hospitalized (Cross, 2001). After the incident, Cobain's mother refused to press any charges on Mr. Fanich (Cross, 2001). Frequently, Cobain would witness his mother being physically abused by Mr. Fanish (Cross, 2001).

5. **Did you live with anyone who was a problem drinker or alcoholic, or who used street drugs (Felitti et al., 1998; Starecheski, 2015)?**

   - *"One time my mom knew we were smoking pot, and she tried all of these psychological angles to try to get me to stop, and she had some pot. She had some in her jewelry drawer, and I'd sneak some* (Green et al., 2006)."

Data Collection and Decision-Making Under Suicide Prevention and Intervention

At present, best practices on how and when to screen for suicide have not been established. However, combined internalizing and externalizing screeners, such as the SRSS-IE or Strengths and Differences Questionnaire, certainly could help flag students who are showing risk factors for suicide, such as having a depressed mood, losing interest in pleasurable activities, or withdrawing from others. It is worthy to note that unlike universal screening under RTI, SWPBS, and social-emotional RTI, which occurs at Tier 1, suicide screening can occur at Tier 1 or Tier 2 because students may not be screened until some thought, behavior, or significant risk factor was uncovered that lead an educator to believe a child might be considering taking their own life (Singer et al., 2018). When screening students for suicide, districts can adopt an existing measure or formulate their own to universally screen the entire student population at Tier 1 or selectively screen students already known to be at-risk at Tier 2.

This book advocates for the latter approach. A two-step approach involves screening students for social-emotional and behavioral concerns at Tier 1 and subsequently following through to further screen students at-risk for suicide at Tier 2 if significant concerns arise. The rationale for using a two-step process for suicide screening at this juncture of suicide prevention and intervention is simple as this service delivery model is in its infancy stages, and there are not many research-based and validated suicide screeners available to districts (Horowitz, Bridge, Pao, & Boudreaux, 2014). Horowitz et al. (2014) write that "sometimes, suicide risk detection strategies are created for the general public and are then utilized for children and adolescents, even if age-specific validity has not been proven" (p. S172). Aside from there being a limited number of research-based and validated suicide screeners available, students at-risk for social-emotional concerns should be identified through universal screening under social-emotional RTI. Upon being identified by at-risk through social-emotional screening, follow-up inquiries or simply touching base with the student can provide insight as to whether they considered committing suicide.

In order to further screen students who are suspected to be at-risk of suicide, educators can utilize informal and formal measures. Informal means of screening students for suicide might include educators developing a short suicide questionnaire. This questionnaire may be used to ask the student questions regarding suicide and allow for follow up with caregivers and educators to determine the level of risk. Some questions to include in the questionnaire might be:

1. Have you ever considered taking your own life or going to sleep and never waking up?
2. Are you, or have you, ever had thoughts of suicide? (Singer et al., 2018)
3. What do you find yourself thinking about most often?
4. When did you begin having thoughts of taking your own life?
5. Is there an event or point in time when you started really considering taking your own life?
6. Have you ever planned to take your own life or wished that you went to sleep and never woke up?
7. If you have planned to take your own life, can you tell me about the plan in detail?
8. Have you noticed any changes in your behavior since you began feeling this way and can you tell me about those changes?

Aside from informal measures of screening students at-risk for suicide, the gold standard for determining whether a child is considering taking their own life remains the **Columbia-Suicide Severity Rating Scale (C-SSRS)**. The C-SSRS was developed to address inconsistencies and lack of uniformity in identifying suicide and suicidal behavior in individuals (Posner et al., 2011). It is currently the most widely used measure in screening and assessing individuals at-risk for suicide and can be also used to monitor progress over time. The C-SSRS measures risk for suicide across four constructs:

the severity of ideation, the intensity of ideation, behavior, and lethality and classifies range of suicidal ideation and behavior based on the C-CASA (Interian et al., 2017; Posner et al., 2011). The C-SSRS assesses these constructs across ten categories, which require individuals being interviewed to respond either "yes" or "no" to indicate the presence or absence of the behavior (Columbia University, 2022). The ten categories included in the C-SSRS are as follows: wish to be dead, non-specific active suicidal thoughts, active suicidal ideation with any methods (no plan) without intent to act, active suicidal ideation with some intent to act, without a specific plan, active suicidal ideation with specific plan and intent, preparatory acts or behavior, aborted attempt, interrupted attempt, actual non-fatal attempt, and completed suicide (Columbia University, 2022). Through scoring each of these categories, a numerical score can be derived.

The C-SSRS comes in three versions and is available in 114 languages. The *lifetime/recent* version is designed to allow practitioners to gather a lifetime history of ideation and/or behavior (Columbia University, 2022). The *since last visit* version is designed to assess the presence or absence of suicidal thoughts and behaviors since the last administration of the C-SSRS. The *screening* version of the C-SSRS is a six-question shortened version of the full form and is used for screening and progress monitoring of treatment (Columbia University, 2022).

Although a numerical score can be derived from administering the C-SSRS, there are no specified clinical cutoffs provided to determine the level of risk for suicide and clinical judgment must be utilized. The developers of the Columbia cite that no clinical cut-off scores have been suggested due to no study identifying one specific risk factor or set of risk factors as specifically predictive of suicidal behavior or suicide (Columbia University, 2022). However, educators may find the following table from the Center for Deployment Psychology (n.d.) helpful in guiding their decisions when administering the lifetime/recent and since last visit versions of the C-SSRS (see Table 6.2).

TABLE 6.2 ● Center for Deployment Psychology Guidelines (Center for Deployment Psychology, n.d.)

Outcome	Item Endorsement	C-SSRS Categories
Suicidal ideation	Yes	Categories 1–5
Suicidal behavior	Yes	Categories 6–10
Suicidal ideation and behavior	Yes	Categories 1–10

When determining whether a child falls in the low, moderate, or high levels of suicide risk using any version of the C-SSRS, it is useful for educators to consider the following factors: frequency of suicidal thoughts, how long such thoughts have been occurring, whether such thoughts can be controlled, risk factors for the child wanting to commit suicide, view toward death and dying, whether the child has a plan in place, and accessibility of objects/items to complete suicide (Breux et al., 2018). After such factors have been considered, the level of risk can be determined and a course of action can be planned. The following courses of action have been recommended by Breux et al. (2018) based on the severity level of the C-SSRS (see Table 6.3).

TABLE 6.3 • Courses of Action for Level of Suicide Risk (Breux et al., 2018)

Level of Risk	Response
Low	Parent notification; develop safety plan; recommend consultation/counseling with licensed or certified mental health professional for ideation.
Medium	Parent notification, consult with colleagues, develop a safety plan, refer parent/child to community mental health provider. Provide counseling and support in school. Coordinate efforts and follow up with parents and community mental health providers.
High	Parent notification, consult with colleagues, immediate referral to community mental health provider or transition to emergency care (parent or emergency personnel). Coordinate efforts and follow up with parents and community mental health providers.

The C-SSRS is a standardized and validated tool for assessing the risk of suicidal thoughts and behavior in children and adolescents. At present, it remains the gold standard in determining the level of risk for suicide. However, other formal available tools to assess risk for suicide in children include the Beck Scale for Suicide Ideation and Ask Suicide-Screening Questions (ASQ). Although both measures may provide some valuable insight into suicidal behavior and ideation in youth, the C-SSRS remains the most clinically validated, reliable, and well-researched tool available to assess for suicide (Columbia University, 2022). Additionally, the C-SSRS is a versatile tool that is free, available in 140 languages, and widely disturbed among educators, mental health professionals, medical staff, and law enforcement (Columbia University, 2022). For these reasons, the C-SSRS is an ideal tool for screening children and adolescents at-risk for suicide.

Viewing Suicide Through a Cultural Lens

With the growing rates of youth suicide and ethnic diversity of students inside American schools, there is a great need for both teachers and school-based mental health practitioners to not only familiarize themselves with suicide in children but also to do so under a cultural lens. Whereas suicide risk was once predominately associated with men of white descent and Native Americans, there has been an alarming increase in both suicide attempts and ideation among ethnic groups who traditionally presented with decreased risk for suicide, such as Hispanic and Black youth (LaVome Robinson, Droege, Hipwell, Stepp, & Keenan, 2016; Silva & Van Orden, 2018).

For example, an examination of trends by race revealed that while suicidal rates among white children ages 5–11 years significantly decreased between 1993 and 2012, the rate of Black children of the same age committing suicide nearly doubled in the same time frame (Bridge et al., 2015). A study by LaVome Robinson et al. (2016) found that Black girls were almost twice as likely to consider suicide and report frequent thoughts of suicide compared to their white peers. Moreover, the study found that Black girls were more likely to report suicidal ideation at lower levels of depressive severity than white girls, suggesting that suicide across different ethnicities may not necessarily be directly linked to an underlying mental health concern (LaVome Robinson et al., 2016). While suicide rates have increased for Black youth, rates of suicide for American and Alaskan Native youth between 10 and 14 years old are nearly double the rate for all races in that age range (LaFromboise & Malik, 2016).

To remain cognizant of suicide risk in children, it is important for teachers and school-based mental health practitioners to pay attention to the intersectionalities of gender, age, and culture (Clay, 2018). Moreover, it is important for educators, and especially school-based clinicians, to realize that the Westernized view of committing suicide being viewed as a privatized individual act in response to psychological pain and illness does not automatically transcend cultures. For example, suicide in Native American communities is often the result of a youth being disappointed that they have hurt or abandoned loved ones who are dealing with a hardship (LaFromboise & Malik, 2016).

Historical oppression may also play a large role in why some culturally diverse youth may think about or commit suicide believing that there is little room for them to advance in a society that is based on white goals and ideals (Goldston et al., 2008; LaFromboise & Malik, 2016; Wexler & Gone, 2012). **Historical oppression** can be defined as the pervasive, chronic, and intergenerational experiences of oppression that may be normalized, imposed, and internalized into the daily lives of a marginalized group of people (Goldstonet al., 2008; LaFromboise & Malik, 2016; Wexler & Gone, 2012). As readers can see, there are many cultural factors that may influence whether a youth commits or thinks about committing suicide that are outside the westernized purview of mental illness or social-emotional concerns.

Cultural Theory and Model of Suicide

Due to the many other reasons that multicultural individuals may commit suicide, Chu, Goldblum, Floyd, and Bongar (2010), grouped unique cultural suicide risk factors into four major categories: cultural sanctions, idioms of distress, minority stress, and social discord. **Cultural sanctions** are messages of approval or acceptability supported by one's cultures in regards to the acceptability of suicide and unacceptability and shame associated with life events (Chu et al., 2010). For cultures who deem suicide as unacceptable or amoral, such as cultures whose religion deems that suicide is a sin, there is a lower likelihood of suicide. For example, many Black cultures view suicide as unacceptable or amoral versus many Asian cultures who may view suicide as acceptable if the individual committing it dishonored their family (Chu et al., 2010, 2013).

Idioms of distress are defined as cultural variations in an individual's likelihood to express suicidality and the way in which suicide is expressed and methods or means of attempting suicide (Chu et al., 2013). For example, ethnic minorities are less likely to express suicidal ideation than caucasians, a concept known as "hidden ideation." Therefore, the traditional signs of suicide, such as hopelessness and withdrawal, may be less predictive of suicide in Black youth compared to white children. Instead, violence, aggression, anger, irritability, and risk taking behavior may be more symptomatic of suicidal intent among Black children (Chu et al., 2013). Means of committing suicide might also vary in different cultures. While Black and white individuals are more likely to use firearms to commit suicide, Latino, Hispanic, and Asian Americans tend to utilize methods such as hanging, jumping from high spots, suffocating, and poisoning (Chu et al., 2010, 2013).

Minority Stress refers to the stresses and hardships cultural minorities experience because of their social identity or position (Chu et al., 2010, 2013). Minority stressors occur at two levels. The distal level involves discrimination or daily hassles that people of different ethnicities and culture experience every day (Chu et al., 2010, 2013). The proximal level represents the internalization of negative beliefs, stereotypes, and events about one's cultural group (Chu et al., 2010, 2013).

Lastly, **social discord** involves the suicide risk factors of alienation, conflict, or lack of integration with one's community, friends, or family (Chu et al., 2010, 2013).

Although lack of social support has been viewed as a source of suicide risk in literature, there are unique and culturally specific variations in the types of social factors that play a role in suicide risk for sexual and ethnic minority groups (Chu et al., 2010, 2013). For example, many children who come out to their family as gay might experience parental rejection and alienation, which can increase a child's risk for wanting to commit suicide. For Asian American, Latino, and Hispanic children, a risk factor for suicide may be whether these youth feel connected with their family or whether they have brought their family great shame (Chu et al., 2010, 2013).

Culturally Responsive Practices and Suicide Prevention and Intervention

To best incorporate culturally responsive practices into suicide prevention and intervention efforts, educators need to carefully consider the make-up of their student body in regards to age, physical and mental health, sexual orientation, religion, race, ethnicity, cultural beliefs, and disability status. After carefully considering the make-up of their student body, educators should consider whether they currently have a Tier 1 suicide gatekeeper program in place, such as the Signs of Suicide Program and what cultural modifications need to be made to it. Although both the Signs of Suicide program and the Good Behavior Game have had success in decreasing suicide attempts in youth, components of both interventions may not be congruent with the values of certain cultural groups. For example, the Good Behavior Game may be incongruent with the values and teachings of some Native Americans because it includes an element of competition rather than working together (LaFromboise & Malik, 2016). Given the extremely limited number of culturally responsive gatekeeper programs, educators may need input from families and community leaders as to how to best adapt existing programs to prevent suicide in youth.

Likewise, for Tier 2 and Tier 3 interventions and supports under suicide prevention and intervention, educators should consult families within their district as well as cultural and community leaders. In considering how to best prevent and intervene in youth suicide in a culturally competent manner, educators should seek the answers to the following questions:

1. *What is the role of the family in preventing and intervening in suicide?*
   - Educators should explore and determine how families of students that make up their school view suicide and how suicidal behavior or ideation is recognized in their culture. For example, do the families of students in a school denounce suicide or is it more accepted by their culture?
   - Educators should seek to understand whether extended family members are considered important sources of support for a youth who is suicidal. For example, many Latino and Hispanic families turn to extended family in times of need and hold a clear expectation that they be involved in the therapeutic process because of views of interdependence within the family (Goldston et al., 2008).
2. *What unique cultural and historical stressors may be impacting youth and their families in obtaining support for the child in need?*
   - In preventing and understanding suicide through a culturally responsive lens, educators need to develop an understanding of the degree to which the process of acculturation, history of racism, and societal pressures may impact the children they serve. For example, in events where a child is a risk to themselves, Native American youth have involuntarily been taken

away from their parents without family consent and placed in psychiatric emergency care (Goldston et al., 2008). Although the goal is to save the child's life, for many Native American families, having their child taken away is a reminder of the coercive removal of indigenous youth from their parents and placement into church-sponsored industrial schools (Wexler & Gone, 2012).

3. *What cultural mistrust and stigma exists within the school and the surrounding community in regards to suicide and suicidal behavior?*

    - Educators should seek to identify any what cultural areas of mistrust and stigma exist within their schools and in the surrounding community that may impact a family or child from seeking out additional help if suicidal. Schools should strive to create an open dialogue with family and community members to allow cultural considerations to be communicated and heard.

4. *To what degree does religion and spirituality impact the views of children and their family in suicide prevention and intervention efforts?*

    - Many Black cultures view church, religion, and their relationship with God as a strong powerful influence on their everyday life and involvement in their community. Other cultures views toward spirituality may influence the type of coping behaviors they engage in and how help they seek. For example, Native American families may not seek out a mental health professional or medical doctor to help a child who is suicidal. Rather, they may obtain help from a traditional healer or spiritual leader within their tribe.

Conclusion

Suicide prevention and intervention is a newer intervention service delivery model that remains in its infancy stages. However, such a three-tiered intervention service delivery model provides a systemic means to address and reduce suicidal ideation and suicidal behavior in students through well-outlined interventions and supports. By providing educators a familiar three-tier intervention service delivery model to address suicidal behavior and suicide, they will be better prepared with a set protocol to prevent and address youth suicide. In preventing and intervening in youth suicide, educators should consider whether their practices are culturally responsive. Educators can do so by considering the role a family plays in the life of a child who is at-risk for suicide and being aware of unique cultural and historical stressors that may impact the well-being of a youth. Additionally, culturally responsive suicide prevention and intervention efforts seek to obtain information from families in regards to cultural mistrust and stigma in regards to suicide. Additionally, culturally responsive suicide prevention and intervention efforts consider the role that religion plays in suicide prevention and intervention efforts.

Arguably, the best measure for screening and monitoring risk for suicide in youth is the Columbia Suicide Severity Rating Scale. Although the C-SSRS does not provide users clinical cut-off scores to determine suicidal risk, it does provide a standardized set of questions to ask individuals experiencing suicidal ideation or behavior. Through adopting the C-SSRS and suicide prevention and intervention efforts, it is hoped that children's lives will be saved and educators will feel better prepared and organized to work with youth experiencing a suicidal crisis. Figure 6.3 provides a checklist for suicide prevention and intervention with suggested decision points and interventions. Similarly, Appendix D provides a flowchart for suicide prevention and intervention. Figure 6.4 shows how the "pillars" of varying levels of interventions and supports, universal screening, progress monitoring, and data-based decision link together and connect the four walls of the MTSS "house." Finally, Figure 6.5 shows the completion of the MTSS "house."

FIGURE 6.3 • Suicide Prevention and Intervention Checklist

Tier 1
Prevent suicide for all students by:
✓ Educating staff, students, and parents on the risk factors and warning signs of suicidal behavior through recognizing FACTS (Feelings, Actions, Changes, Threats, and Situations)
✓ Defining and educating staff on suicide and the range of suicidal behaviors using the Columbia Classification Algorithm of Suicide Assessment (C-CASA)
✓ Teaching students about mental illness and mental wellness through in-service trainings and programs like Mindwise's Signs of Suicide program (SOS)
✓ Creating a warm, caring, supportive, and welcoming school environment
✓ Universally screening all students for social-emotional concerns using instruments such as the Behavior Intervention Monitoring System-2 (BIMAS-2) or Devereux Student Strengths Assessment-mini (DESSA-mini)
✓ Examining screening results and identifying at-risk youth
✓ Consulting with parents and child if social-emotional concerns are present
✓ **If student does not show risk for suicide continue to implement Tier 1A interventions**
✓ **If student shows some social-emotional concerns that may be indicative of suicidal behavior, refer to Tier 2**
✓ **If there is an immediate or imminent threat of suicide refer the student directly to Tier 3**
Tier 2
For students who have not responded to Tier 1 supports:
✓ Assess risk for suicide using the Columbia-Suicide Severity Rating Scale (C-SSRS) or other means
✓ Develop suicide intervention plan (see Stanley and Brown's Safety Planning Intervention (SPI)
✓ Identify and mobilize a social support system for the child
✓ Keep the child into daily contact with social support system of close family members, friends, and school staff
✓ Provide psycho-education to child's parent/caregiver on information and community resources on suicidality and suicidal behavior
✓ Utilize social skills and replacement behavior/cognition groups such as Coping and Support Training or POD-TEAMS Depression Prevention Program
✓ Track student progress using BIMAS-2, DESSA-mini, or other progress monitoring measure
✓ Involve the child in activities and tasks that they like
✓ **Student no longer shows any risk for suicide, return to 1A**
✓ **If the student does not respond to Tier 2 interventions, refer to Tier 3**
✓ **If there is an immediate or imminent threat of suicide refer the student directly to Tier 3**
Tier 3
For students who have not responded to Tier 2 supports or are at immediate risk of suicide:
✓ Do NOT leave the child alone
✓ Keep the child within your field of vision
✓ Refer to district suicide risk manual/procedures and student's suicide safety plan
✓ If suicide safety plan has not been developed with student yet, develop one
✓ Remove access to all lethal means to commit suicide (guns, knives, chemicals, medicine, letter openers, pens etc.)
✓ Contact parents/guardians
✓ Link student to outside clinician or hospital if needed
✓ Work with outside clinicians/hospital, administration, and parents/guardian to devise school re-entry plan when student is stable
✓ Assist student in making up missed assignments and explaining absence to teachers upon returning to school

FIGURE 6.4 ● Putting the Roof on the MTSS "House"

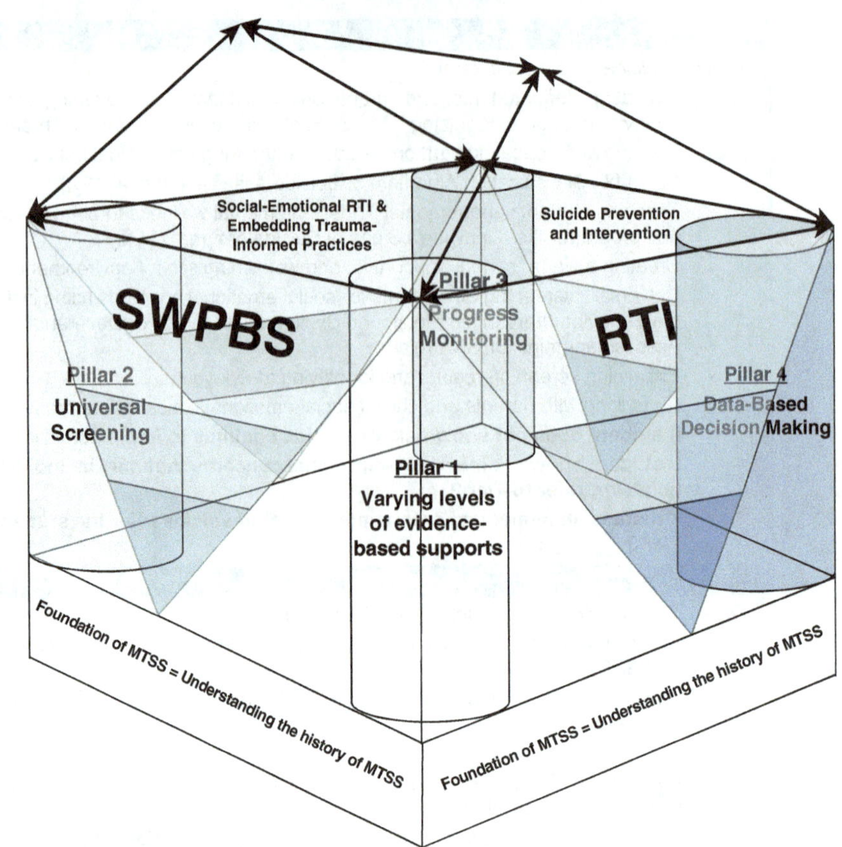

FIGURE 6.5 ● Completed MTSS "House"

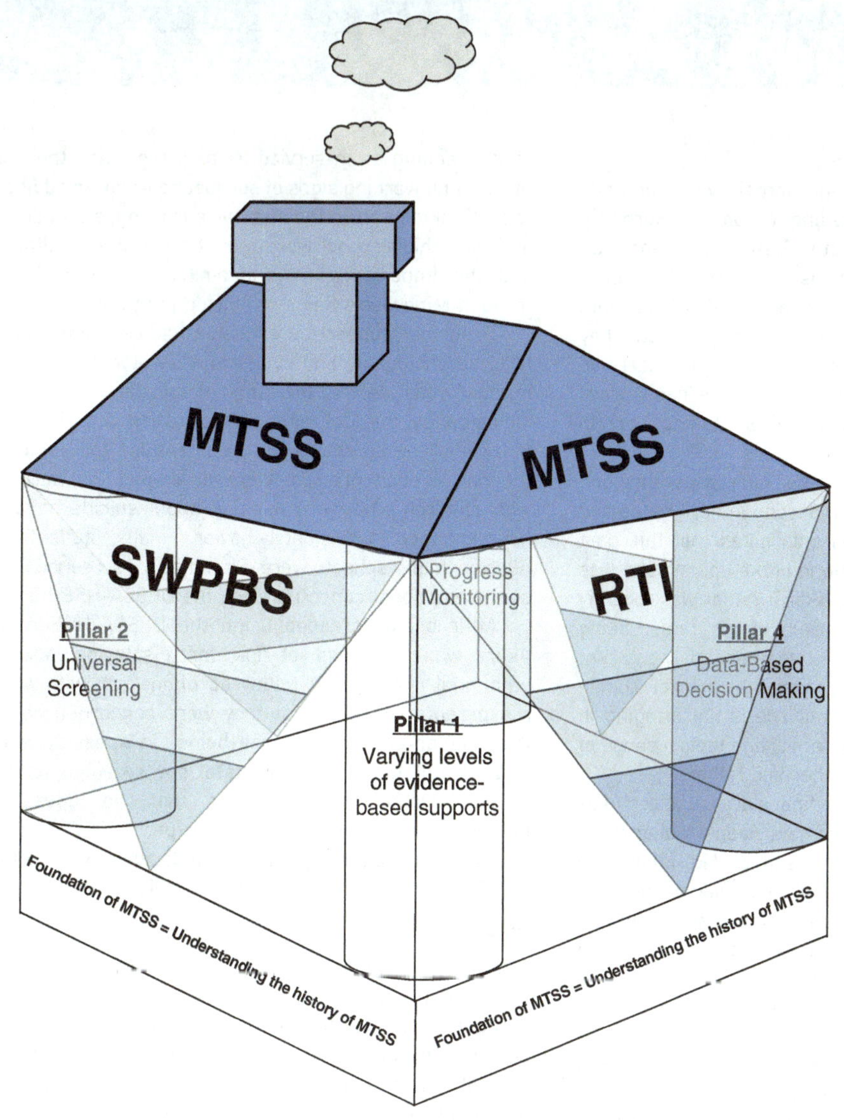

CASE EXAMPLE

SUICIDE PREVENTION AND INTERVENTION

Child Background

Akari is a 16-year-old Hispanic female who currently resides with her parents, Lee and Rui Sato, in Surprise, Arizona. She moved to the United States three years ago from Guadalajara, Mexico. She is just starting her junior year at Sunset High School. Growing up, Akari's parents reported her to be a happy child with many friends. They noted that throughout her academic career, Akari has always been an "A" student and that she has always been actively involved at school from taking part in yearbook club to playing varsity tennis.

Over the past several months, Akari's parents and teacher have noticed a sudden decline in her grades and overall demeanor. Akari's parents noted that this past summer, Akari and her boyfriend broke up, and she was extremely upset. Additionally, Akari's father was recently laid off from his job. As a result of her father being unemployed, Akari has been helping her family pay rent with her part-time job as a cashier at a local supermarket. However, she feels that she is not bringing in enough money to support her family and feels a sense of shame in dishonoring her mother and father.

Due to the family's recent financial struggles, Akari's parents admitted that they have been arguing more than usual. Both at home and in school, Akari has been increasingly feeling sad, crying, and making negative remarks about herself, such as stating "I am a failure." In addition to these negative statements, Akari has been avoiding her friends, frequently missing varsity tennis practice, and is not turning in her homework assignments consistently.

Overall, Akari's mother and teacher noted concerns in the areas of withdrawal, negative self-talk, and episodes of sadness. Withdrawal can be defined as Akari sitting alone during lunch or not talking during group projects or activities. Negative self-talk can be defined as Akari making self-deprecating statements about herself, such as "nobody likes me," or "I am a failure. Finally, episodes of sadness can be defined as any incident in which Akari is found crying or sobbing by her teachers or other school staff.

Tier 1

Tier 1 of suicide prevention and intervention is an intervention service delivery model that builds off of the universal supports that already in place through SWPBS and social-emotional RTI (Miller, 2014). At Akari's high school, Tier 1 of suicide prevention and intervention involved all staff attending an in-service training regarding the risk factors and warning signs of suicidal behavior. In addition to staff taking part in the in-service training, all students at Akari's high school were taught about mental illness and the importance of maintaining mental wellness through Mindwise's Sings of Suicide program.

To further support all educators, school administrators, psychologists, and counselors developed a suicide manual which defined the range of suicidal behaviors as indicated by the Columbia Classification Algorithm of Suicide Assessment. Moreover, within the suicide manual, explicit protocol were developed for working with children who were thinking about suicide or who have engaged in suicidal behavior. Finally, students at Akari's high school were universally screened for social-emotional concerns using the DESSA-HSE mini.

After being screened using the DESSA-HSE mini, Akari was identified at-risk for displaying social-emotional concerns. A follow-up phone call with Akari's parents revealed that they were concerned about their daughter's mental well-being. In speaking with Akari about her emotional state, she revealed to the school psychologist, Mr. Brown, that she "does not belong on this planet" and was experiencing suicidal thoughts. Subsequently, Mr. Brown decided to complete a C-SSRS to determine her level of suicidal risk.

Tier 2

After interviewing Akari using the C-SSRS, Mr. Brown noted that she only recently began having suicidal thoughts and noted that no plan was in place to commit suicide. Therefore, Mr. Brown determined that Akari was at low risk for committing suicide and not an imminent danger to herself. Following the C-SSRS interview, Mr. Brown asked Akari if it was okay that the school counselor, Mrs. Wilson, come into the office and join the conversation. After Akari indicated that it was okay for Mrs. Wilson to join the meeting, follow-up clarifying questions were asked in regards to Akari's social-emotional well-being. Additionally, the school psychologist and school counselor worked together to identify school staff and peers who are close with Akari in an effort to build a social support system for her. Subsequently, Mr. Brown left Akari with the school counselor to inform the school principal of the ongoing concerns and contact Akar's parents.

While talking to Akari's parents, Mr. Brown and the school principal informed them of Akari's thoughts and feelings and steps the school would be taking to best support her social-emotional needs. Moreover, the school psychologist provided Akari's parents a list of outside mental health clinicians that she could seek additional support from. Additionally Mr. Brown informed Akari's parents that as a safety precaution they might want to ensure that any fire arms or medications in the home are securely stored and properly locked up.

The following school day, an emergency CST meeting was held, and it was determined that Akari would join four other students in Mr. Brown's POD-TEAMS Depression Prevention Program. In addition to Mr. Brown's POD-TEAMS Depression Prevention Program, Akari's school counselor worked with her in developing a safety plan and showed her a cell phone application that she could use to keep her safety plan on her at all times. Akari's parents also received a copy of her safety plan and were shown how Akari can use it. While taking part in Tier 2 interventions and supports, Akari's progress was monitored on a bi-weekly basis using the DESSA-HSE mini. Additionally, every two weeks Mr. Brown would also use the C-SSRS to determine whether Akari's risk for suicide increased.

After seven weeks into Tier 2, Akari's progress monitoring data revealed that she continued to be in the at-risk range. Additionally, she told her French teacher that she wanted to kill herself this weekend and detailed how she planned to do so. Consequently, Akari's French teacher called Mr. Brown and informed him of the difficulties Akari was experiencing. Before entering Mr. Brown's office, he completed a room sweep and removed any items and objects that Akari may take or use to harm herself, such as pens, pencils, paperclips, stables, and hand sanitizer. Upon interviewing Akari using the C-SSRS, Mr. Brown noted that she continued to have suicidal thoughts. Additionally, Akari informed the school psychologist that she planned to kill herself by ingesting bleach at home over the weekend when her parents went on vacation. Subsequently, Mr. Brown decided that Akari was in need of Tier 3 interventions and supports.

Tier 3

Immediately after confirming that Akari was still experiencing suicidal thoughts and had outlined a concrete plan for how to kill herself, Mr. Brown contacted the school counselor. He then reminded Akari of the terms in which he would have to notify her parents in case of emergency, one of which being desire to hurt oneself. While the school counselor contacted the school principal, Mr. Brown remained with Akari to ensure her safety and security. He then reviewed her safety plan with her. When Akari's parents came into the school, they were provided additional information on her mental health and risk for suicide. Additionally, it was decided that Akari be taken to the local hospital for further evaluation. Both Mr. Brown and the school principal accompanied Akari and her family to the local hospital to minimize distress and provide support.

Later in the day, Akari's parents notified the school that she was going to be held by the hospital for 24 hours. Therefore, the next day, an emergency CST was held to develop a school reentry plan for Akari and notify her parents again of outside practitioners in the area who could provide additional mental health support. Moreover, the school worked with Akari's parents to help them identify and plan for the removal of materials and items in their home that Akari may use to commit suicide. Aside from developing a reentry plan and removing access to lethal means within Akari's home, it was determined that she would receive individualized cognitive behavior therapy with Mr. Brown two times per week. Additionally, with Akari's parent's permission, the school counselor kept into regular contact with the hospital she was staying at to receive updates on her progress.

Upon returning to school the following week, Akari began receiving individualized counseling with Mr. Brown two times per week. Her progress was monitored on a weekly basis using the DESSA-HSE mini, and she was screened for suicidal risk using the C-SSRS. In addition to receiving counseling from Mr. Brown, Akari's parents located an outside mental health counselor and a psychiatrist to work with Akari. After eight weeks, Akari's weekly progress monitoring data revealed that she was no longer fell in the at-risk range. Additionally, her grades began to improve, and her teachers noted that she was no longer displaying episodes of sadness. Over the upcoming weeks, Akari's progress will continue to be monitored. If Akari continues to show improvement, she will no longer be in need of Tier 3 interventions and supports. However, if Akari regresses in treatment, the team may want to consider completing a psycho-educational evaluation to determine if she qualifies for special education services as a student with an emotional disability.

Discussion Questions

1. Do educators have a legal responsibility to prevent youth suicide whenever possible? Why or why not?
2. What are the differences between attempted suicide, completed suicide, and non-suicidal self-injurious behavior?
3. What does the interpersonal psychological theory of suicide propose?
4. What are some of the warning signs of suicidal behavior displayed by youth?
5. What are some of the risk and protective factors for youth suicide?
6. What is a safety plan and why might it be useful in supporting a student who may be deemed at-risk for suicide?
7. Why is it important for educators to consider a child's culture when engaging in suicide prevention and intervention efforts?

Overcoming Challenges to MTSS Implementation

Learning Objectives

After reading this chapter, you should be able to:

- Identify key challenges to implementing Multi-Tiered Systems of Support (MTSS).
- Discuss how to overcome barriers to implementing MTSS.
- Define implementation science.
- Summarize the stages of implementation science.
- Recite the three major implementation drivers that may streamline efforts in implementing MTSS.
- Discuss the role of using implementation drivers to successfully employ MTSS and evidence-based supports within MTSS.

Challenges to MTSS Implementation

Although Multi-Tiered Systems of Support (MTSS) has offered educators much promise in preventing and addressing deficits in children early on, it is not without its challenges. For schools and districts seeking to adopt MTSS, several reemerging barriers have been cited and can be generally be categorized into the following five areas: misperceptions over MTSS, insufficient training regarding MTSS, educator support for MTSS, fidelity of MTSS implementation, and school resources. Each of these areas can hinder the adoption of MTSS and preventative practices into schools and ultimately hurt a child's right to a sound education. Therefore, it is important for educators to understand these challenges and outline a plan of action to overcome them.

Misperceptions Regarding MTSS

The first challenge in implementing MTSS revolves around educators' misperceptions regarding what the model is and is not. First, and as mentioned throughout this book, MTSS is not RTI or SWPBS but rather "houses" these intervention service delivery models. Additionally, despite growing recognition that academic, behavioral, and social-emotional deficits often do not exist independently of one another, schools often implement service delivery models under MTSS in an autonomous or fragmented fashion (Eagle, Dowd-Eagle, Snyder, & Holtzman, 2015). Recall that the four "pillars" that create the framework of MTSS also link all intervention service delivery models together under it. Therefore, all intervention service delivery models under MTSS are connected by the four common features of varying levels of interventions and supports, universal screening, progress monitoring, and data-based decision-making (Eagle et al., 2015; Harn, Basaraba, Chard, & Fritz, 2015). In understanding that intervention service delivery models under MTSS are not competing initiatives but rather complement one another, educators will be better prepared to implement MTSS.

Even with the understanding that intervention service delivery models are not competing initiatives, educators may often overlook the time frame that it may take to implement MTSS. Educators should keep in mind that developing and implementing MTSS is an ongoing process and is one that does not happen over a short time frame. Research indicates that bridging the research to practice gap to implement systemic change in a school may extend over a period of two to four years (Eagle et al., 2015). MTSS is a large undertaking that calls for great systemic change. Therefore, the time period of two to four years may be much longer in implementing a cohesive MTSS framework (Eagle et al., 2015). This longer time frame is due to schools first having to properly outline and implement the intervention service delivery models that comprise MTSS and subsequently integrating such models under the framework of MTSS. Consequently, viewing service delivery models, such as RTI and SWPBS, as two separate competing initiatives is counterproductive and may further complicate an already intricate process and extend the timeline for proper implementation under MTSS (Eagle et al., 2015; Harn et al., 2015).

An additional misperception regarding MTSS is that it serves as a general framework to usher students into special education. MTSS is not an outline for admitting children into special education (Heward, 2017; Schaffer, 2017). It is a premise for preventing students from experiencing difficulty and prescribing additional interventions and supports should a child show significant deficits (Heward, 2017). As a result, MTSS provides teachers and administrators set procedures and guidelines to follow in order to assist children with learning, behavioral, or social-emotional deficits before being considered for special education (Averill & Reinaldi, 2011; Wexler, 2017). The overreaching goal of MTSS is to prevent difficulties before they lead to special education placement and additional difficulties throughout the child's life, such as not graduating from school or significant and social-emotional concerns.

A final misperception regarding MTSS is that district administrators and teachers may perceive that universal screening will lead to the over-identification of students in need of additional services, and schools do not possess the time, staff, or funds necessary to support at-risk children (Eklund, Meyer, Way, & Mclean, 2017; Kilgus & Eklund, 2016). Consequently, many schools continue to rely on methods of determining students at-risk in a reactionary fashion using existing data (office discipline referrals, school suspensions, and teacher-designed tests). These methods oppose preventative measures for identifying at-risk youth through universal screening and providing at-risk youth varying levels of interventions and supports. Such reactionary measures are likely to identify fewer students as needing interventions and in turn may prevent students in need of remedial supports from receiving it, possibly leading to a referral to special education later on (Kilgus & Eklund, 2016).

Obtaining Educator Buy-In

Due to the complexity of implementing MTSS, garnering administrative and teacher support is vital. Oftentimes such reticence results from insufficient training in more progressive intervention service delivery models and the MTSS framework in general (Dulaney, Hallam, & Wall, 2013; Eagle et al., 2015). A study by Dulaney et al. (2013) found that although most superintendents perceived that they were improving schools and increasing student achievement, they were unable to articulate a systemic plan under an MTSS framework to support such improvement. Additionally, Dulaney et al. (2013) found that some superintendents were unable to define MTSS and how MTSS could unite a district's improvement efforts through common language and purpose. Similarly, a study by Reinke, Stormont, Herman, Puri, and Goel (2011) found that although 75% of teachers reported working or referring students with behavioral or emotional deficits over the past year, over 60% believed these students did not receive adequate services due to a lack of adequate prevention programs, followed by 51% indicating a lack of adequate training in addressing behavioral and social-emotional concerns. Results from Dulaney et al. (2013) and Reinke et al. (2011) highlight the importance of teachers and administrators receiving adequate training in MTSS in order to understand the model and implement it correctly in their schools. Without adequate training and an understanding of MTSS, there is little momentum or rationale for adopting the model.

Arguably, the most critical individuals needed to support efforts in regards to MTSS and preventative practices are district and school administrators. Previous research has continuously found that administrative support is vital for sustaining staff buy-in to adopting MTSS and intervention service delivery models (Little, Marrs, & Bogue, 2017; Pinkelman, McIntosh, Rasplica, Berg, & Strick, 2015; Vekaria, 2017). Administrators can play a key role in helping to dispel misperceptions regarding MTSS. It is important for administrators to garner staff support for MTSS early on as schools are at greatest risk for abandoning such an initiative within the first two years of implementation (Pinkelman et al., 2015).

In order for MTSS to be implemented correctly, all school staff need to commit to the notion that all children have the best opportunity to learn, grow, and succeed under such a framework. Additionally, educators need reassurance and sound rationale that adopting preventative practices under MTSS is not just another passing educational trend but one that has real-life implications for bettering the lives of children socially, emotionally, behaviorally, and academically. Therefore, educators need an understanding of the history of MTSS and research that supports delivery of interventions and supports under such a model. Being equipped with such an understanding is really powerful motivator in why systemic change needs to move away from reactionary practices and toward preventative ones.

Unfortunately, staff may have difficulty moving past reactionary practices and buying into MTSS due to lack of knowledge about the model and a desire to hang onto practices that they know (Pinkelman et al., 2015). In any field, overcoming past ineffective practices is challenging and scary. Additionally, it is largely steeped in tradition that may have been misguided or perhaps a more effective method or model took its place. For example, earlier in this book, it was discussed how the traditional medical model fell out of favor as the public health approach gained popularity and showed effectiveness in preventing widespread physical illness. Furthermore, a thorough overview was provided on how the laws and regulations guided ill-advised educational practices in identifying children with specific learning disabilities through the discrepancy model rather than through best evidence-based practices. Just as physicians needed to learn how to focus their efforts on effectively treating physical illness as opposed to simply diagnosing it, educators need to focus on how to effectively teach all learners rather placing efforts into categorizing struggling students.

Students with difficulties are not necessarily children that need special education services. However, given education's history with children who may need more repetition and practice, this idea is still very new to the field and hard to accept. Recall that the impetus and perception supplied to educators by advocates and policymakers alike was that in special education was needed to help struggling students (Vanderheyden, 2018). Additionally, in order to stem the growth of the specific learning disability category, the severe discrepancy model was introduced, and school psychologists were mandated to provide testing to students in need. All these questionable practices emerged out of advocacy and policy as opposed to sound evidence-based research. Sadly, scholars who expressed significant concerns over the direction education was moving to assist struggling learners were never completely heard. However, these scholars continually questioned the validity, reliability, and utility of practices and decisions made in placing children into special education (Vanderheyden, 2018). Their concerns centered on the idea that by simply testing and placing struggling learners into special education, these children were unlikely receiving effective interventions and supports to remediate their deficits (Vanderheyden, 2018). Still, today teachers and administrators call for overuse of testing and special education despite all evidence pointing to preventative practice first. Consequently, students under such a refer-test-place model likely receive little to no evidence-based supports in general or special education (Vanderheyden, 2018).

The continued overuse of psycho-educational testing and special education is troubling, but it is one the field was taught to embrace since the introduction with Education for all Handicapped Children Act. Educators, like physicians and mental health practitioners, are a helping-based profession. Each of these professions has been taught to ask "What shall we do?" as opposed to "Should we do something?" or even "Can we do something different that is evidence-based?" (Vanderheyden, 2018, p. 4). It is this very logic that suggests that something being done for struggling learners is better than nothing and that something for the field of education remains psycho-educational testing and special education placement. However, well-trained educators in MTSS understand that there are other factors to consider when a child is having difficulty other than a disability. These factors may include ineffective general education instruction or poorly outlined classroom expectations. By providing struggling students evidence-based interventions and supports, educators are helping children with learning and behavioral difficulties avoid further delay that may result in special education.

Maintaining Fidelity

Aside from educator "buy-in," in order for MTSS to improve student outcomes, it has to be implemented with fidelity. **Fidelity** or integrity refers to the degree to which a practice, such as MTSS or intervention, is implemented as intended (McKenna & Parenti, 2017). When practices or interventions are delivered as they are intended, they have the best chance of succeeding. A simple example of fidelity can be applied to the process of making Jell-O. When making Jell-O, the last step requires the gelation to be placed in the refrigerator to reach a solidified state. If the maker of the Jell-O does not follow this last step, the gelation will never reach the semi-solid state that it is known for, and as a result, the directions were not followed with fidelity. Consequently, the Jell-O was not made properly and is less likely to reach its ideal state.

Fidelity does not just involve correctly following the steps to implementing a practice or intervention. It also entails how well the steps are carried out (McKenna & Parenti, 2017). In going back to the Jell-O example, the maker may follow all the steps in numerical order but put too much sugar in. Consequently, just because all the steps were followed does not mean the Jell-O will taste good. As such, fidelity is not just about adherence to steps but also concerns the quality of how the steps are carried out (King-Sears, Walker, & Barry, 2018). Other factors that may influence whether a practice or intervention is delivered with integrity include inadequate access to materials, insufficient teacher skill, inappropriate training, lack of "buy-in", or desire to deliver the intervention, and complexity of the model or support. For example, a teacher who is well-trained, motivated, and with a sound understanding of a multi-step reading intervention is more likely to implement the support with fidelity. On the contrary, a teacher who has received little training, is unmotivated, and lacks an understanding of the complex intervention to be delivered to students is less likely to implement the support as intended. Even if a teacher is motivated and well-trained on the intervention or practice to be delivered, lack of proper materials may greatly impact whether interventions are carried out with integrity and in turn impact how well MTSS is implemented overall.

Like any recipe, MTSS contains many moving parts and requires both adhering to the steps of implementation and the quality of how such steps are implemented. Within MTSS, there are multiple models of intervention service delivery, such as social-emotional RTI and suicide prevention and intervention, and each of these models contains varying levels of support, universal screening, progress monitoring, and data-based decision-making. Ultimately, the fidelity of MTSS is really based on how well intervention service delivery models and the interventions themselves are being delivered. For instance, a commonality across all intervention service delivery models that link them under MTSS is that students are universally screened to determine areas of deficit. If a school's MTSS model fails to universally screen students under the intervention service delivery model of school-wide positive behavior support but does so under response to intervention, the MTSS model, as a whole, is not being implemented with fidelity. This is because MTSS requires universal screening across all intervention service delivery models. Likewise, SWPBS is also not being delivered with fidelity as the intervention service delivery model calls for students to be screened for the presence or absence of behavioral deficits.

In delving further into MTSS and within an intervention service delivery model itself, if interventions, supports, or programs are not delivered with integrity, students are less likely to succeed and their performance declines (King-Sears et al., 2018). On the contrary, when evidence-based interventions are implemented as intended, student performance increases. Therefore, maintaining a high degree of fidelity during teaching practice or intervention implementation is essential to maximizing student benefit. Taken altogether, understanding how fidelity impacts MTSS and ultimately affects student learning and growth is highly important in ensuring all elements of MTSS are implemented effectively. In the next section, a discussion will be held on how educators can overcome the pitfalls of poor fidelity management.

Addressing Concerns Over School Resources

A final barrier to effectively implementing MTSS involves possessing adequate school resources (Bambara, Nonnemacher, & Kern, 2009; Mars & Little, 2014; Pinkelman, McIntosh, Rasplica, Berg, & Strickland-Cohen, 2015). For purposes of this discussion, school resources are defined as time and funding. Often staff may find time constraints for effectively planning and implementing MTSS due to their primary job responsibilities, differing schedules between team members, school holidays, weather-related days off, and summer break. A study by Bambara et al. (2009) revealed that 88% of participants cited time-related barriers to implementing SWPBS with the leading time barrier being school schedules providing few opportunities for school personnel to collaborate and plan. Additionally, school staff reported difficulties with taking on additional job responsibilities in regards to implementing intervention service delivery models on top of their current duties (Bambara et al., 2009; Mars & Little, 2014; Pinkelman et al., 2015). A similar difficulty is likely to arise in districts trying to organize and employ MTSS.

Aside from time, many educators cited funding as a challenge to MTSS and intervention service delivery model implementation (Bambara et al., 2009; Mars & Little, 2014; Pinkelman et al., 2015). Staff needing consistent and ongoing professional development and materials such as books, videos, and computer programs all may be cost-prohibitive to districts that receive little financial support from their respective states. One educator indicated that their state-provided them less than $200 a year to help implement SWPBS (Pinkelman et al., 2015). In order for districts to initiate MTSS, adequate funding needs to be secured and allocated. Without adequate school resources, it will be very difficult for educators to establish buy-in and learn about MTSS.

Overcoming Barriers to MTSS Implementation

MTSS is a large endeavor for schools and educators who are always under pressure by parents and policymakers to improve learning and behavioral outcomes for children. In order to effectively overcome barriers associated with implementing MTSS, educators will have to be both vigilant and creative. Luckily for educators, their vigilance and creativity are two traits that have never been short in the field. Therefore, it is important for educators to form a positive understanding of MTSS and one which offers them a great opportunity to improve student learning and behavior. After all, beliefs and attitudes among educators are often viewed to be a prerequisite to considerable change within school districts and the adoption of evidence-based practices (Cook, Lyon, Kubergovic, Wright, & Zhang, 2015). As suggested earlier, if educators do not see significant reason why a change in practices is needed, they are unlikely to adopt new initiatives like MTSS. Fortunately, there are several ways in which educators can overcome barriers to MTSS implementation, including completing a needs assessment, garnering "buy-in," improving fidelity procedures regarding MTSS, and addressing concerns over time and resources.

Creating a Needs Assessment

To better provide an understanding of the misperceptions, apprehensions, and knowledge of MTSS, a needs assessment may prove useful (Pinkelman et al., 2015). A **needs assessment** is a systemic process for identifying and prioritizing needs or "gaps" between current and desired conditions (Altschuld & Watkins, 2014; Morrison & Harms, 2018). Through a needs assessment, a better understanding of current conditions and what staff want to accomplish through MTSS can be obtained. Subsequently, staff needs can be put into prioritized order to guide decisions about how to proceed with implementing MTSS to establish "buy-in" (Altschuld & Watkins, 2014). Additionally, a needs assessment may prove useful in identifying which staff may be most unlikely to adopt MTSS practices. Previous research has suggested that new teachers may be less likely to offer their support and implement new practices due to learning the responsibilities of their job (Pinkelman et al., 2015).

Step 1: Identification of Key Stakeholders

The first step to developing a needs assessment entails the identification of key stakeholders with specialized areas of expertise and influence that align with the district and school's priorities and goals (Skalski et al., 2015). During this step, school administrators and mental health practitioners may review the school or district improvement plan and subsequently work together in forming a needs assessment team comprised of teachers, paraprofessionals, and counselors to assist in developing a comprehensive needs assessment. A school or district improvement plan outlines changes the school or district needs to make in order to improve teaching and ultimately lead to increased student achievement (Bernhardt, 2017).

Step 2: Identification of Goals, Objectives, and Parameters

After identifying key stakeholders, the second step in developing a needs assessment entails the identification of goals, objectives, and parameters of the needs assessment (McGoldrick & Tobey, 2016; Skalski et al., 2015). During this step, it is important for educators developing the needs assessment to have a shared vision in order to prevent competing initiatives from emerging. For example, through an administrative lens, the main purpose of completing a needs assessment for MTSS is to improve overall teaching practice and raise student performance. However, for a school psychologist or school counselor, the overall purpose of completing a needs assessment might be to evaluate teacher and administrator understanding of MTSS. In order to best prevent differing initiatives from undermining the purpose of the needs assessment, it is advised that administrators and school-based mental health practitioners work together to come up with a shared vision as to why the needs assessment is being completed. Additionally, the needs assessment team may want to generate two or three overarching goals as to why a needs assessment is being developed and what is to be accomplished by completing a needs assessment (McGoldrick & Tobey, 2016). With many schools and districts adopting MTSS into their improvement plans, needs assessment teams may want to formulate and set goals, objectives, and parameters around MTSS and evaluate what staff want to accomplish through MTSS.

Step 3: Identification of Perceived Strengths and Weaknesses

The third step of a needs assessment involves the development of questions or statements revolving around MTSS in regards to areas of perceived strength, areas of perceived weakness, and availability of time and resources to properly implement MTSS (McGoldrick & Tobey, 2016; Skalski et al., 2015). For example, a question may ask school staff to indicate their knowledge of MTSS on a scale of one to five, with one indicating little knowledge of MTSS and five indicating great knowledge of MTSS. Another question might ask staff to identify the greatest obstacle they see to implementing universal screening and list common barriers to implementation such as lack of educator support, lack of school resources, insufficient training, lack of personnel, lack of funding, and time constraints.

To ensure that information is collected accurately, needs assessment questions should be developed in a clear, concise, and easily understandable manner (McGoldrick & Tobey, 2016). School psychologists' background in research may particularly come in handy here as a simple tweak in language can lead to different people interpreting the same question in contrasting ways. One of the most common mistakes in creating a needs assessment is presenting respondents with double-barreled questions. For example, a double-barreled question might ask, "How would you rate your knowledge of universal screening and progress monitoring?" In this example, the question is double-barreled because it is asking respondents about two separate constructs under one question. To correct this, the needs assessment should ask two separate questions "How would you rate your knowledge of universal screening?" and "How would you rate your understanding of progress monitoring?" By avoiding double-barreled questions and keeping them clear and concise, designers of a needs assessment can ensure data being provided is accurate.

Step 4: Collection of Existing Data and Analysis

The fourth step of a needs assessment entails the collection and analysis of existing data (McGoldrick & Tobey, 2016; Skalski et al., 2015). Data can assist in informing the needs assessment team as to whether the district or school is on target for meeting improvement plan objectives and readiness for adopting areas: demographics (enrollment, attendance, retention, ethnicity, gender), school climate (discipline referrals, classroom management, perceived safety), student learning and achievement (grades, universal screening measures, formative assessments, state testing), family and community engagement (attendance from families and the community in school functions and decisions, existing community partnerships), and staff quality and retention (staff attendance, staff turnover rate, professional development) (Skalski et al., 2015). Through analysis of such data, educators can present to administrators and key stakeholders data trends over time, identify at-risk populations, note needed areas of professional development, and indicate whether the district and school are currently meeting or exceeding goals outlined in the school improvement plan. For instance, perhaps the school's goal was to have 30% of parents attend a school forum on social-emotional learning but data from the event revealed only 15% attendance.

Step 5: Pilot Testing the Needs Assessment

After collecting and analyzing existing data, the team may want to pilot the needs assessment with multiple stakeholders to increase the tools' reliability and validity (McGoldrick & Tobey, 2016). For example, piloting the needs assessment should not only be completed by a team of third-grade reading teachers but also should encompass all teachers, teacher aides, administrators, and school mental health staff to provide an accurate overview of strengths and weaknesses. By collecting a variety of information from multiple sources, administrators and school-based mental health practitioners can gain a full understanding of the circumstances, needs, and school climate in adopting MTSS. Additionally, by piloting the questionnaire with various school staff, the needs assessment team can ensure that questions are clear, concise, and easily understood by educators in various roles.

Step 6: Outlining a Timeline and Data Collection

The final step to developing a needs assessment involves outlining a timeline and means for collecting data (McGoldrick & Tobey, 2016; Skalski et al., 2015). In order to complete this task, developers of the needs assessment should consider how data will be collected, when it will be collected by, and which professionals will be involved in data analysis. In data collection and analysis, tools like Google Forms, SurveyMonkey, or QuestionPro may greatly ease data collection and interpretation by allowing the needs assessment to be posted and easily accessed online. To ensure data are collected in a timely and organized manner, a professional should be allocated to lead efforts. Preferably, the professional should be a school psychologist, math teacher, or both given their extensive training statistics and statistical analysis. Both professions working together may provide a unique and ideal relationship in effectively tabulating, interpreting, and utilizing needs assessment data. For example, a math teacher proficient in statistical analysis might find a means to best tabulate and calculate the data, and the school psychologist could then interpret the meaning of the data.

Resource Mapping

Once the results of a needs assessment have been analyzed, the needs assessment team can begin the process of resource mapping. **Resource mapping** consists of evaluating programs, personnel, and services that are available to students and identifying how such resources are currently being used (Skalski et al., 2015). From there, a determination can be made as to whether such resources can be integrated and utilized more efficiently and effectively (Skalski et al., 2015). An important feature of resource mapping is the optimization and enhancement of available interventions and programs made available to students.

One of the most significant areas of resource mapping includes improving the overall infrastructure of service delivery to children through identifying areas of service overlap and discrepancies in service delivery (Skalski et al., 2015). By analyzing the results of a needs assessment and engaging in resource mapping, a school psychologist may uncover that a school initiative for developing a strong MTSS framework includes providing intensive levels of social-emotional support to at-risk youth. However, it may be noted that the school currently lacks a full-time mental and behavioral health professional to provide such services due to time constraints. Consequently, the school psychologist or school counselor may work with an administrator to adjust existing school-based mental health professional's schedules to provide intensive social-emotional supports to youth. Overall through completing a needs assessment and resource mapping for MTSS, opportunities are created for the district or school to identify areas of deficiency, overcome complacency, and build appropriate infrastructure to meet initiatives. Results from a needs assessment will assist in establishing "buy-in" from educators by placing their needs into a prioritized order to guide decisions about how to proceed in implementing major reform efforts under an MTSS framework (Altschuld & Watkins, 2014) (Table 7.1).

TABLE 7.1 • Example of a Staff Availability Resource Map

Position	Name	What Days and Times Are They Available?	Contact Information	Grades or Populations Served?
General Education Teacher			Phone: ________ Email: ________	
Special Education Teacher			Phone: ________ Email: ________	
School Counselor			Phone: ________ Email: ________	

(Continued)

TABLE 7.1 ● Example of a Staff Availability Resource Map *(Continued)*

Position	Name	What Days and Times Are They Available?	Contact Information	Grades or Populations Served?
School Psychologist			Phone: ________ Email: ________	
School Administrator			Phone: ________ Email: ________	
Community Partner(s) (If needed)			Phone: ________ Email: ________	

Enhancing Educator Buy-In

After completing a needs assessment and engaging in resource mapping, areas of professional development can be identified. **Professional development** can be defined as "the primary vehicle through which implementers learn the rationale for an intervention, its core components, the mechanisms through which components impact student outcomes, and the skills necessary to implement the components with high intensity" (Owens et al., 2014, pp. 101–102). Through professional development, misperceptions and apprehensions toward MTSS can be addressed and educators can be provided critical information on why adopting MTSS will best assist children in the learning environment. A good outline for professional development on MTSS may mirror that of this book and include: the background and history of MTSS, faulty past practices, statistics that lead to moving toward preventative practice models, an overview of the four "pillars" of MTSS, and an outline of the four intervention service delivery models housed under MTSS.

In addition to completing a needs assessment and receiving professional development, educators may be more likely to adopt MTSS if they are reinforced for their efforts (Pinkelman et al., 2015). Therefore, educators may be more likely to adhere to best practices within an MTSS framework if they receive public acknowledgment for their hard work in implementing MTSS or are provided rewards such as gift cards or class coverage (Pinkelman et al., 2015). Perhaps even more rewarding than tangible rewards, educators may be more likely to support efforts in implementing MTSS if they see their efforts paying off through improved student outcomes or if their ideas regarding improving MTSS are put into place (Bambara et al., 2009; Pinkelman et al., 2015). Through district newsletters and staff meetings, positive examples can be provided in which schools within the district have experienced a 20% decrease in behavioral referrals since implementing SWPBS and have seen a 30% increase in students achieving grade-level benchmarks through RTI (Fan, Denner, Bocanegra, & Ding, 2016). By receiving training, seeing results, and being rewarded for their efforts in implementing MTSS, educator's knowledge and acceptance of the framework is likely to grow.

As mentioned earlier, in order to advance MTSS efforts, administrative support is vital. Administrators can assist districts and schools in implementing MTSS by providing staff clear guidelines to follow and outlining roles for staff within a MTSS. Without clear guidelines from administrators, faculty often operate from different frameworks and become confused over responsibilities when undertaking new district and school initiatives (Mars & Little, 2014). Consequently, a lack of leadership can undermine the success of MTSS if staff do not have a clear direction over the steps in MTSS implementation or their responsibilities within an MTSS framework.

Additionally, administrators can show their support for MTSS efforts by becoming involved with staff and collaborating in the process of MTSS implementation. Administrators can collaborate with staff through attending trainings on MTSS, participating in professional learning committees, and taking part in child study teams (Bambara et al., 2009; Dulaney et al., 2013; Mars & Little, 2014). In interviewing school administrators, principals reported that their presence at data reviews and intervention discussion was important in moving MTSS initiatives forward and obtaining staff buy-in (Vekaria, 2017). Through collaborating with staff, administrators can actively change or strengthen their own views on MTSS and how to best assist faculty and students within an MTSS framework (Bambara et al., 2009). Often a positive attitude exhibited by a school administrator greatly sets the tone for the entire school building. Therefore, it is paramount that district administrators lead efforts in developing a positive and supportive school culture in welcoming MTSS (Bambara et al., 2009; Dulaney et al., 2013; Mars & Little, 2014). Other ways in which school administrators can further their understanding toward MTSS and increase staff buy-in include observing other schools implementing MTSS, attending state or national conferences on preventative practices, inviting speakers into their buildings to train staff and themselves on MTSS, and providing staff specialized roles and responsibilities under MTSS.

Maintaining Fidelity

Even with an exemplary needs assessment, resource mapping, and educator "buy-in," a great challenge to implementing MTSS centers on being able to execute the model with fidelity (King-Spears, Walker, & Barry, 2018; McKenna & Parenti, 2017). In order to best ensure that MTSS is being carried out as an effective framework for preventative practice, educators should break it down into its component parts. In other words, educators must ensure that all parts that comprise MTSS are being implemented with integrity. Therefore, before building the MTSS "house," educators must first ensure intervention service delivery models, supports, and screeners that comprise it are being employed effectively. Arguably, the easiest way for educators to tackle the task of implementing MTSS with fidelity is to start small. Schools looking to implement several intervention service delivery models all at once to form MTSS are likely to fail. Therefore, educators should first seek to master the implementation of one intervention service delivery model at a time instead of approaching all of them at once. To ensure that intervention service delivery models are being executed accordingly and with integrity, schools may wish to develop a team of educators who can work on setting up models, such as social-emotional RTI or suicide prevention and intervention. These teams should consist of educators from various disciplines across grade levels and include an administrator and school psychologist (Vekaria, 2017).

Once a team has been properly established, the components of the intervention service delivery model can be outlined and prioritized. Additionally, a fidelity checklist can be formulated on key areas of intervention service delivery model implementation and subsequently scored to determine the integrity of execution. Fortunately for team members, there are some great fidelity checklists already in existence for the more popular intervention service delivery models. For example, the **SWPBS Tiered Fidelity Inventory (TFI)** is a fidelity checklist that was developed to assist school personnel in determining whether they are applying the core features of school-wide positive behavioral interventions and supports effectively (Lewis, McIntosh, Simmonsen, Mitchell, & Hatton, 2017). The TFI is a free resource available to educators and was developed as part of the US Department of Education's Office of Special Education Programs National Technical Assistance Center on Positive Behavioral Interventions and Supports. For intervention service delivery models who do not have a fidelity matrix developed yet, such as social-emotional RTI, educators may want to review the TFI and model their integrity matrixes after it. Either way, in developing fidelity checklists for intervention service delivery models that fall under MTSS, educators merely need to consider what makes up each model.

For example, in reviewing the social-emotional RTI flowchart in Appendix D, each bullet point at Tier 1, Tier 2, and Tier 3 can be broken down and turned into a fidelity-based question. Therefore, in turning bullet 1 of the social-emotional RTI diagram into a fidelity check question, it might read, "Are social expectations being taught through character development sessions?" Subsequently, the next fidelity check question might read "Is a positive school motto in place?" Another question might read, "Are students being taught skills to maintain mental wellness through evidence-based strategies?" Table 7.2 provides a brief example of a fidelity checklist for social-emotional RTI. By ensuring that intervention service delivery models are being implemented accordingly, MTSS has a greater likelihood of being executed with fidelity.

TABLE 7.2 ● Example Fidelity Checklist for Social-Emotional RTI

Question	Answer	
Are social expectations being taught through evidence-based character development sessions?	Yes	No
Is a positive school motto in place?	Yes	No
Are students being taught skills to maintain mental wellness through evidence-based interventions?	Yes	No
Are staff trained on the warning signs of social-emotional concerns?	Yes	No
Are students being universally screened for social-emotional concerns using an evidence-based screening tool?	Yes	No

After developing a fidelity checklist, the team may want to first pilot an intervention service delivery model on a smaller scale and then evaluate areas of weakness. Subsequently, educators can develop a plan to overcome areas of deficit in implementing the model and then seek to implement it on a larger scale at the school or district level. For example, a school may first start by piloting social-emotional RTI in kindergarten and first grade. Once perfecting social-emotional RTI in kindergarten and first grade, the school may implement the intervention service delivery model in the remaining grades. From there, educators may want to look into how they are going to implement a three-tiered intervention service delivery model for suicide prevention and intervention the following year and link the two models under an MTSS framework.

Just as intervention service delivery models need to be carried out with fidelity so do the programs and interventions that comprise them. Therefore, teachers need clear parameters about what the intervention is, what is should look like, how to use it, and how to ensure that it is being executed as intended (King-Spears et al., 2018). Like intervention service delivery models, a fidelity checklist can be utilized to break down the intervention or program into its component parts and determine whether it is being used correctly. In addition to a fidelity checklist, three other steps can be used to help educators implement interventions with fidelity and include modeling the intervention or program, coaching the practitioner prior to implementation, and observing for fidelity during implementation (King-Spears et al., 2018).

One of the best ways to familiarize teachers with an intervention or program is through the use of modeling. **Modeling** entails an expert teacher demonstrating how to effectively use an intervention to a novice instructor. Modeling can assist teachers in having a clear idea over what the intervention or program looks like, sounds like (e.g., tone of voice), and why it is important to use all the steps (King-Spears et al., 2018). In addition to modeling, coaching may be utilized in which the teacher is first provided a copy of a blank fidelity checklist and subsequently practices the intervention in front of the expert teacher. The expert teacher then observes and fills out the fidelity checklist to provide the instructor with feedback as to how well the intervention or program was implemented. From there, a discussion can be held as to areas of strength and areas of improvement.

Finally, in conducting observations on teachers, intervention experts, administrators, and school psychologists can ease stress on educators by informing them that observations are for the purpose of improving services to students rather than a teacher evaluation (McKenna & Parenti, 2017). To further reduce teacher anxiety over being observed, it may greatly assist educators to be involved in the development of fidelity assessment measures as it may provide them a sense of ownership and inside knowledge on how they will be assessed (McKenna & Parenti, 2017). Additionally, teachers may become more comfortable with the observation process if they are provided opportunities to observe one another implementing interventions and providing feedback on fidelity to one another.

Addressing Concerns Over Time and Resources

The final barriers to implementing MTSS includes time and resources (Bambara et al., 2009; Pinkelman et al., 2015). In thinking about the time and effort it will take to implement the MTSS, the concept may become extremely daunting for educators. With most schools in the United States operating only nine months of a year instead of twelve months, time in adopting MTSS practices is limited. In order to overcome time restrictions, educators in previous studies have suggested that aligning, combining, and adapting new endeavors with already existing school protocols and teams may prove as a useful solution (Bambara et al., 2009; Pinkelman et al., 2015). For instance, ongoing evaluation of Tier 1 data across the academic, behavioral, and social-emotional domains may be incorporated into monthly instructional support team meetings. Additionally, districts may wish to consider having core team members meet over the summer months to establish sound MTSS procedures and protocols for staff to follow. Finally, having one or more school staff members highly trained in MTSS to readily provide consultation to educators and answer questions may assist in streamlining MTSS implementation (Bambara et al., 2009).

Persistent budgetary deficits at the district, local, state, and federal levels may greatly impact how effectively MTSS can be implemented. However, sound plans to overcome budgetary deficits and savings associated with implementing preventative practices may assist in successfully employing MTSS. Arguably, the first step in obtaining resources and training for MTSS involves districts identifying funding streams. Luckily, the Every Student Succeeds Act has funding streams built into it. For example, Title IV of ESSA provides the most relevant and direct funding stream for social-emotional learning authorizing more than 7.3 billion dollars over four years to support programs aimed at improving educational opportunities for students (Grant et al., 2017). Therefore, it is important for districts to become aware and have knowledge of how to tap into available grants and funding streams to best fund efforts under MTSS.

One way districts can identify areas in which funding is needed is to complete an assessment of available funding streams (Cammack, Brandt, Slade, Lever, & Stephan,

2014). Through completing a comprehensive assessment of existing funding opportunities at the national, state, and local levels, districts can identify grants, fee-for-service payments, contracts, and interagency agreements that may provide finances for MTSS resources and training (Cammack et al., 2014). For example, in completing a funding streams assessment, a district might note that Title 1 of ESSA authorizes $62.5 billion dollars in education spending in the form of grants to states (Grant et al., 2017).

In addition to analyzing existing funding opportunities, districts may benefit from completing a **cost-benefit analysis** to calculate which resources and training on MTSS will best benefit the district and staff (Cammack et al., 2014). A resource or training is thought to be a benefit, rather than a cost to a district when the value of the resources gained exceeds the monetary value of the resources used (Cammack et al., 2014). Still, districts may need to spend less on MTSS resources and training than expected. Many components of MTSS can be implemented with little to no money after initial training and resources have been obtained (Pinkelman et al., 2015). Additionally, many resources for MTSS and intervention service delivery models within MTSS are available for free through websites such as What Works Clearinghouse, RTI Action Network, and Intervention Central. Furthermore, states often offer free online resources for districts ready to undertake MTSS (Fan et al., 2016).

Although, the start-up costs to obtain resources and training for MTSS may appear daunting, districts who fail to adopt an MTSS framework pose the risk of facing significant increased expenditures. Failure to identify and service students at-risk for academic, behavioral, or social-emotional deficits may lead to special education placement. While little information exists on how much school districts in the United States are expending on students with disabilities, the Special Education Expenditure Project (SEEP) revealed that in the 1999–2000 school year, the cost to educate a general education student was $6556 compared to $12,474 for students with disabilities (Chambers, Perez, Harr, & Shkolnik, 2005). A more recent report by the New York State Association of School Business Officials (2015) revealed that NYS schools spend two and a half times more on special education students than they do on general education students. The report also noted that while spending for general education rose 15% over 6 years, spending on special education grew 26% (New York State Association of School Business Officials, 2015). Higher costs associated with special education include psycho-educational assessments, smaller class sizes, and the need for special education aides and specialists.

MTSS is a large undertaking for districts and contains many moving parts. In order to overcome barriers to implementing MTSS, educators must first have a sound understanding of the construct, why it came about, and how such a model placing students in the best place to succeed. Schools implementing MTSS or intervention service delivery models under the model should take comfort in knowing that there are many free resources and funding streams available to assist them in overcoming challenges to implementation. Additionally, since there are commonalities across all intervention service delivery models, educators will become familiarized with general aspects of implementation through repetition. For example, educators will become familiarized that each intervention service delivery model from RTI to suicide prevention and intervention has tiered systems of supports. Through familiarity, appropriate resources, and proper funding, MTSS is likely to be less of a daunting task for educators to tackle.

Optimizing MTSS Through Implementation Science

Central to effectively organizing and overcoming barriers to employing MTSS involves understanding implementation science as an outline for systems-level change and utilizing implementation teams to act as a catalyst for such change. **Implementation science** is defined as the scientific study of methods utilized to promote the systematic uptake of evidence-based practices into routine, everyday practice (Owens et al., 2014). Therefore, implementation science is concerned with the ongoing process of integrating evidence-based interventions or research findings into the school day (Ownes et al., 2014). The overall goal of implementation science is to achieve improved and effective outcomes that lead to a higher level of school performance in academics, behavior, social-emotional functioning, and even teaching practices.

Like MTSS and intervention service delivery models, implementation science has historical roots in public health and medical science (Forman et al., 2013). However, implementation components and outcomes differ and exist independently from MTSS and intervention service delivery models. For example, a poorly planned intervention service delivery model can still be implemented well (Fixsen, Naoom, Blase, Friedman, & Wallace, 2005). On the contrary, a well-planned intervention service delivery model can still be implemented poorly (Fixsen et al., 2005). Therefore, in the context of MTSS, implementation science is concerned with reaching desirable outcomes through adopting effective intervention service models into everyday practice under an MTSS framework. At its core, using effective implementation practices builds the capacity of district and school teams to enhance systems that support all teachers and their students (Anderson, Freeman, & O'Habib, 2018).

Through implementation science, implementation is viewed as a process with the following distinguishable stages: exploration, installation, initial implementation, and full implementation (Fixsen et al., 2005). The **exploration stage** occurs when a district has not started training and is still in the assessment phase of determining the readiness of schools to move forward with an implementation effort (Freeman, Miller, & Newcomer, 2015). For instance, the school district may be evaluating whether schools are prepared to integrate Response to Intervention, SWPBS, and Social-Emotional-RTI under the umbrella of an MTSS framework.

The **installation stage** reflects the adoption of a new program and development of performance assessment processes, initial training efforts, and the securing of resources (Freeman et al., 2015). During the installation stage, district teams help secure needed resources to complete the work ahead and prepare staff for new practices. The installation stage involves administrators selecting appropriate staff to implement MTSS, identifying resources to provide training in MTSS, and assuring access to equipment and materials (Fixsen et al., 2005).

The **initial implementation stage** entails staff attempting to utilize newly learned skills and is highlighted by the learning curve staff experience as the district adjusts and integrates new changes into daily work (Fixsen et al., 2005; Freeman et al., 2015). For example, staff may be learning how service delivery models integrate under an MTSS framework through the use of universal screening across the academic, behavioral, and social-emotional domains. Staff may have been familiar with completing universal screening to assess the risk for reading deficits but may still be learning that universal screeners exist to assess for social-emotional deficits in children.

Finally, the **full implementation stage** is reached when over half of school personnel change their practices under MTSS with a high level of fidelity (Freeman et al., 2005). During the full implementation stage, the "new" ways of providing services under an MTSS framework have become accepted, standard, and routine practices by over 50% of district staff. During the full implementation stage, MTSS continues to be improved upon by the district as an accepted, sound, and everyday practice (Fixsen et al., 2005; Freeman et al., 2015).

Implementation Drivers

Although districts will advance through each of the implementation stages at different rates, it is widely reported that most districts will take a "letting it happen" approach to employing evidence-based interventions and programs as opposed to a "making it happen" approach (Forman et al., 2013). Through taking a "letting it happen" approach, districts may adopt a program and, with minimal supports, educators are expected to use the information provided in their everyday practices and are held accountable for intended program outcomes (Forman et al., 2013). On the contrary, by embracing a "making it happen," approach a district may adopt a program and educators are provided supports to learn how to use the program and resolve organizational and systematic issues that may arise. As a consequence of taking a "letting it happen" approach, it takes an average of 17 years for best evidence-based practices, such as MTSS, to reach clinical practice and only 14% of implementations actually result in substantive changes due to evidence-based practices being poorly managed (Balas & Boren, 2000; Bauer, Damschroder, Hagedorn, Smith, & Kilbourne, 2015). However, districts may be able to significantly reduce the time it takes for evidence-based practices, such as MTSS, to reach clinical practice and increase the fidelity in which evidence-based practices are employed through the use of implementation teams and implementation drivers. Through utilizing implementation teams, drivers and adopting "making it happen" approach, researchers have found that it only takes approximately three years for best evidence-based practices to reach clinical practice and that 80% of implementations result in substantive changes (Balas & Boren, 2000; Fixsen, Blase, Timbers, & Wolf, 2001; Green & Seifert, 2005).

In terms of education, implementation teams consist of a group of members who are charged with designing and leading the implementation of district-wide change (Higgins, Weiner, & Young, 2012). Members of implementation teams have extensive knowledge in evidence-based programming, systems-level change, fidelity management, data-based decision-making, and district and school-wide reform efforts (Eagle et al., 2015; Freeman et al., 2015; Higgins et al., 2012). Implementation drivers are core components that are associated with successful employment of evidence-based practices (Freeman et al., 2015). Three major implementation drivers that may outline and streamline efforts in implementing MTSS include competency, organization, and leadership (Eagle et al., 2015; Freeman et al., 2015). **Competency drivers** seek to build the knowledge of educators in understanding and implementing MTSS through activities, in-service trainings, and district-wide resources (videos on MTSS, MTSS books, etc.). A key to examining the competence of educators' knowledge of MTSS involves designing a self-assessment tool to determine what educators know about MTSS and what they would like to learn about MTSS.

Organizational drivers involve building an infrastructure to facilitate the implementation of MTSS through developing internal and external partnerships, locating funding, allocating resources, and using data for decision making (Freeman et al., 2015). Needs assessments and resources for organizational drivers to be utilized effectively are often developed and employed through administrators who have a sound understanding of the evidence-based program to be implemented (Eagle et al., 2015). Program administrators may work independently or collaborate with other practitioners to effectively implement evidence-based programs, such as MTSS. For instance, a school psychologist and principal may work together to build a sound infrastructure for building MTSS.

Finally, **leadership drivers** focus on management strategies that may arise when implementing MTSS and involve decision-making and providing guidance in the process of employing evidence-based programs (Eagle et al., 2015; Freeman et al., 2015; Owens et al., 2014). Within implantation science, two types of leadership styles are identified: technical leadership and adaptive leadership (Eagle et al., 2015; Freeman et al., 2015). **Technical leadership** utilizes an established protocol to respond to concerns that are often defined without ambiguity and a clear solution is evident (Eagle et al., 2015; Freeman et al., 2015). Within MTSS, an action plan may be utilized to provide clarification to educators on the differences between universal screening and progress monitoring and when each is utilized. **Adaptive leadership** refers to guiding others through complex and more difficult to recognize challenges that are typically not resolved through traditional approaches (Eagle et al., 2015; Freeman et al., 2015). Freeman et al. (2015) provide an example that adaptive leadership may be needed when districts encounter resistance to implementing MTSS from educators within the school.

In order for districts to streamline the incorporation of MTSS, the use of implementation science and implementation teams may significantly advance the utilization of best evidence-based practices and the fidelity in which they are used. A study conducted by Bohanon and Wu (2014) showed that schools that utilized components of implementation science in their employment of SWPBS had improved behavioral outcomes and SWPBS was completed with greater fidelity. Overall, through using implementation science as an outline, districts will better understand what they will need to implement MTSS, educator's competence on MTSS will be built, organizational supports will be put into place, and appropriate management of MTSS procedures will be provided through both technical and adaptive leadership.

Conclusion

MTSS has offered educators much hope in preventing and addressing deficits in children. Despite MTSS offering promise in helping students, several reemerging barriers to implementation have been cited. Common barriers to implementing MTSS include misperceptions over what MTSS is, insufficient training regarding MTSS, educator "buy-in" over MTSS, difficulty implementing MTSS with fidelity, and access to school resources (Bambara et al., 2009; Dulaney et al., 2013; Mars & Little, 2014; Pinkelman et al., 2015). Each of these areas can impede the adoption of MTSS into schools and slow the implementation of preventative practices. In order to overcome barriers to implementing MTSS, administrative support is vital and school staff need to be committed to the notion MTSS offers children the best to learn and grow. To ensure that administration and staff are committed to MTSS, they must understand what MTSS is and how it came to be in regards to its history and legislative upbringing. To better provide an understanding of staff's knowledge and apprehensions regarding MTSS, a needs assessment may prove useful. From the needs assessment, an understanding of current conditions and what staff what to accomplish through MTSS can be obtained. Subsequently, staff needs can be put into prioritized order and addressed to increase "buy-in" and guide decisions over how to proceed with MTSS implementation.

After administrative and teacher "buy-in" are obtained, MTSS must be implemented with fidelity. In order to implement MTSS with fidelity, educators must recognize that multi-tiered systems of support is comprised of intervention service delivery models and those intervention service delivery models are made up of supports, data collection measures, and data-based decision-making. Each of the aforementioned components must be implemented with integrity in order for MTSS to be executed with fidelity. To best employ these components with fidelity, educators will need to overcome the barriers of time and resources. To overcome time constraints, educators should look into what school initiatives can be combined and aligned under MTSS and consider how to effectively utilize the summer months for better planning MTSS initiatives. Finally, to overcome barriers to resources, educators should be aware that there are many funding streams built into ESSA to assist in the adoption of MTSS and a cost-benefit analysis may assist districts in better prioritizing their funds. Despite MTSS implementation having many challenges, the reward of seeing students learn, grow, and meet their true potential is well worth the undertaking.

Discussion Questions

1. What are some common misperceptions regarding MTSS?
2. Why is it important that all school staff to buy into MTSS in order for all students to succeed?
3. Why do you think it is so difficult for educators to move past faulty past practices and accept new school initiatives like MTSS?
4. What factors may interfere with MTSS being implemented with fidelity?
5. How can completing a needs assessment help in setting up MTSS?
6. Why do you think it is important for educators to be aware of implementation science when employing MTSS?

Roles and Responsibilities Under MTSS

Learning Objectives

After reading this chapter, you should be able to:

- Identify key roles and responsibilities that school psychologists play within Multi-Tiered Systems of Support (MTSS).
- Summarize the roles school psychologists play in program evaluation.
- Compare the similarities and differences between general and special education teacher's roles and responsibilities within MTSS.
- Explain how a school counselor may work with teachers in appraising their classroom.
- Indicate how school counselors may link students and families to outside clinicians and providers.
- Discuss how school administrators seek to empower school teams to welcome system change in educational initiatives.

Introduction

Throughout this book, an ongoing discussion has revolved around not only Multi-Tiered Systems of Support (MTSS) but also that of implementing intervention service delivery models that are housed under MTSS. To best implement MTSS, educators and future educators need to know the critical roles and responsibilities that they and their professional colleagues have in implementing the framework. Therefore, in this chapter an overview will be provided as to the roles and responsibilities key educational stakeholders have in implementing MTSS.

Evolution of School Psychology

To say that the field of school psychology and its history is intertwined with that of MTSS and teaching is an understatement. As readers may recall before founding the field of school psychology, Witmer was a teacher who discovered that with additional educational services and supports that students may overcome their learning and behavioral deficits (Witmer, 1996). Therefore, an argument could be made that school psychology and teaching not only had great influence over the founding principles of MTSS but even that of the public health model used by the medical field today (D'Amato et al., 2011; Routh, 2019; Witmer, 1996).

Although the field of school psychology might have greatly impacted educational and medical practices currently in place, the field arguably has remained one of the most unchanged and underdeveloped fields in any occupation (McKevitt, 2012; Reschly, 2000; Stoiber & Vanderwood, 2008). Whereas the medical field moved beyond lobotomy to treat mental illness in the 1960s, businesses transitioned from the typewriter to computers in the 1970s and 1980s, and the internet transformed the way scholars and students access everyday information in the 1990s, the field of school psychology continued on the path of completing endless psycho-educational assessment from the early 1900s (McKevitt, 2012; Reschly, 2000; Stoiber & Vanderwood, 2008).

Sadly, the profession who had so much vested in preventative practice and whose advocacy efforts always centered on recognizing the field's true potential lost out to poor decisions by policymakers to restrict the occupation's true abilities. As a result, teachers and administrators became habituated to the practice of school psychology being synonymous with testing for special education and having limited knowledge beyond psycho-educational assessment (Reiser, Cowan, Skalski, & Klotz, 2010). Still, school psychologists across the nation and through national associations, such as NASP and Division 16 of the American Psychological Association (APA), continued to advocate for change toward preventative measures. By 2015, advocacy efforts and a desire to improve outcomes for all learners led to the passage of the Every Student Succeeds Act (ESSA).

Beyond any other bill before it, the passage of the ESSA marked a period in educational history in which preventative practices were fully endorsed over reactionary ones through the inclusion of MTSS. With provisions from ESSA going into effect during the 2017–2018 school year, an increased focus was placed on evidence-based instructional practices and data-based decision-making to augment educational outcomes for all students (Every Student Succeeds Act, 2015). School psychologists are uniquely trained in both of these areas and consequently have offered the field an opportunity to finally expand its professional duties beyond psycho-educational testing. As a result, school psychologists are now beginning to increase their professional duties in other areas they have expertise in, such as counseling, consultation, and leadership practices. With school psychology practices shifting away from completing psycho-educational assessments, an increased emphasis is being placed on where the field will head next and what will propel school psychology into a new era (National Association of School Psychologists, 2016). Increasingly, a focus has been placed on implementation science (Eagle, Dowd-Eagle, Snyder, & Holtzman, 2015; Forman et al., 2013; Freeman, Miller, & Newcomer, 2015).

The idea of implementation science having a profound impact on the future of school psychology began to gain momentum at the 2012 School Psychology Futures Conference (Forman et al., 2013; Hicks, Shahidullah, Carlson, & Palejwala, 2014). During the conference, national and international school psychology organizations met to outline and determine future directions for the field of school psychology. At the conference, implementation science was listed as one of three major themes influencing the future role of school psychologists (Forman et al., 2013; Hicks et al., 2014). Implementation science and its incorporation into school psychology practices gained further momentum when the APA Division 16 cited implementation science as being "essential to the process of translating evidence-based interventions (EBIs) into the unique context of schools" (Forman et al., 2013, p. 77). Most recently, the utilization of implementation science to streamline MTSS was discussed at the 2018 National Association of School Psychologists conference in Chicago, Illinois (Anderson, Freeman, & O'Habib, 2018).

Although implementation science has been cited as being significantly important to the future role of school psychologists, until recently there was little regulatory and statutory platform for the field to exercise and expand upon their areas of expertise. However, with the Reauthorization of the Individual Education Act of 2004 and The ESSA of 2015, school psychologists have been provided an ideal platform to exercise and expand their practices. On legislative and evidence-based fronts, ESSA, MTSS, and implementation science not only lend themselves to the practice of school psychology but enhance it. Ultimately, school psychologists are a natural fit to both support and lead efforts in executing MTSS using implementation science for systemic school and district-wide change (Forman et al., 2013).

School Psychologist Roles and Responsibilities

School Psychologists may be best positioned to lead efforts in linking common components of ESSA, MTSS, and implementation science as they have expertise in best evidence-based practices, research and program evaluation, intervention integrity, data collection, data-based decision-making, and systemic change (National Association of School Psychologists, 2020; National Association of School Psychologists, 2014). Each of these components are stressed in ESSA, MTSS, and implementation science. Additionally, school psychologists have extensive training in curricular and instructional methodology, systemic problem-solving procedures, and mental and behavioral health supports (Eagle et al., 2015; National Association of School Psychologists, 2020; Splett, Fowler, Weist, McDaniel, & Dvorsky, 2013). Therefore, school psychologists are uniquely trained to provide leadership on the adoption, execution, and sustainability of MTSS using key components of implementation science (Eagle et al., 2015; Fan, Denner, Bocanegra, & Ding, 2016; Forman et al., 2013; Hicks et al., 2014). When used as a "leader" and "change agent," school psychologists may act as a catalyst for systematic district-wide change through effectively understanding, utilizing, and connecting the critical components of implementation science with that of MTSS and the ESSA.

As mentioned, several components that link ESSA, MTSS, implementation science, and school psychologist training are in the areas of best evidence-based practices, research and program evaluation, intervention integrity, data collection, data-based decision-making, and systemic change (National Association of School Psychologists, 2020; National Association of School Psychologists, 2016). Although implementation science and ESSA both call for the aforementioned components, each emphasizes them for different reasons. To review, implementation science views components, such as data-based decision-making and program evaluation, as essential to enhance the likelihood that a program or framework is adopted into everyday practice (Fixsen, Naoom, Blase, Friedman, & Wallace, 2005). Conversely, ESSA promotes components, such as data-based decision-making and program evaluation, as a means to bring schools and students to proficiency and to meet statutory regulations (Every Student Succeeds Act, 2015). Finally, under ESSA, MTSS has been designated as a preventative practice framework that "houses" three-tiered intervention service delivery models. These intervention service delivery models contained in MTSS are designed to bring all students and schools to proficiency using evidence-based practices, ongoing assessment, data collection, and data-based decision-making. Therefore, although the same components are stressed across

ESSA, MTSS, and implementation science, each of these features are being utilized for different reasons. School psychologists can streamline systemic change by linking ESSA, MTSS, and implementation science as the field has extensive training in common components to each of the aforementioned frameworks (see Table 8.1).

TABLE 8.1 ● Key Features and Commonalities Across ESSA, MTSS, Implementation Science, and School Psychology Training

Every Student Succeeds Act: (ESSA, 2015)	MTSS (Freeman et al., 2015)	Implementation Science (Fixsen et al., 2005; Freeman et al., 2015)	School Psychologist Training (NASP, 2014, 2016, 2020)
ESSA Calls For: • Implementation of MTSS • Evidence-based learning supports • Use of screening assessments • Monitoring of student progress • Data collection • Data analysis • Data-based instructional decision-making • States to develop plans implementing ESSA components with fidelity • Positive systemic change	***Features of MTSS:*** • Varying levels of evidence-based supports and programs • Universal screening • Progress Monitoring • Data-based decision-making • Supports, programs, and data collection implemented with fidelity • Implementation of supports, programs, and collection of data for systemic school-wide change ***Foundations in Public Health Model**	***Implementation Team Members Possess Knowledge In:*** • Evidence-based programming • Data collection • Data analysis • Data-based decision making • Fidelity management • Systems-level change ***Influenced by public health and medical science**	***School Psychologists Trained In:*** • Varying levels of evidence-based interventions and programs • MTSS • Universal screening • Progress monitoring • Data collection • Data analysis • Data-based decision-making • Research and program evaluation • Program and intervention integrity • Systemic problem-solving procedures ***Practices highly influenced by Public Health Model and medical science**

Program Evaluation

One way in which school psychology lends itself to ESSA, MTSS, and implementation science is through the evaluation of evidence-based practices. The term **"evidence-based"** refers to the "quality of the scientific evidence that is presented to demonstrate an intervention produces intended effects" (McKevitt, 2012, p. 34). Since the turn of the millennium, training and use of evidence-based programs and interventions have continued to gain momentum in school psychology graduate programs and in everyday practice (Shernoff, Bearman, & Kratochwill, 2017). ESSA, MTSS, and implementation science are linked to school psychology training in that each calls for the employment of evidence-based practices. In fact, ESSA is the first federal education law to outline and define the term "evidence-based," placing a strong emphasis on using empirically supported practices to best support learners. ESSA goes as far as to require the use of EBIs in order for districts to access a number of funding streams by distinguishing between "strong," "moderate," and "promising" evidence. More specifically under Section 8002 (21) (A), ESSA defines the term "evidence-based" stating:

> *The term "evidence-based," when used with respect to a State, local educational agency, or school activity, means an activity, strategy, or intervention that—(i) demonstrates a statistically significant effect on improving student outcomes or other relevant outcomes based on—(I) strong evidence from at least 1 well-designed and well-implemented experimental study; (II) moderate evidence from at least 1 well-designed and well-implemented quasi-experimental study; or (III) promising evidence from at least 1 well-designed and well-implemented correlational study with statistical controls for selection bias. (p. 393)*

While ESSA provides brief statutory guidance in defining what the term "evidence-based" means, implementation science seeks to promote the adoption of evidence-based procedures into everyday practice and is concerned with the process of how smoothly these practices are adopted. Therefore, implementation science calls for educators to have extensive knowledge of evidence-based programming in order to effectively guide systemic change (Freeman et al., 2015). Moreover, within implementation science, implementation drivers serve as critical components needed to successfully employ evidence-based practices.

School psychologists may play a pivotal role in leading intervention teams to adopt best evidence-based practices within an MTSS framework due to their training and standards set by the National Association of School Psychologists (2020). NASP (2020) indicates that when providing direct and indirect services to children and their families, school psychologists should apply current "evidence-based" methods and strategies to promote student learning. Additionally, NASP (2020) suggests that school psychologists include evidence-based strategies when developing and delivering intervention programs. Therefore, both MTSS and implementation science are ripe with opportunities for school psychologists to evaluate and assimilate best evidence-based practices into schools on a daily basis.

One way in which school psychologists can foster evidence-based practices into schools is by acting as a program evaluator for implementation teams. **Program evaluation** involves the systemic evaluation of whether a program or intervention that has been introduced directly led to a significant improvement in the performance of students (Conoley, Powers, & Gutkin, 2016). School psychologists are uniquely trained to take on the role of program evaluator as they possess knowledge in data collection, survey design, statistical analysis, evaluation management, and database use. Therefore, school psychologists can lead efforts in program evaluation by completing an analysis of whether the introduction of a program leads to desired gains in student performance.

For instance, through universal screening, a school psychologist might obtain a baseline measurement that indicates 40% of first-grade students are below proficiency in reading fluency. The school psychologist may then work with the school administrators and reading teachers in selecting a new core reading program that shows a strong evidence-base for improving reading fluency. After the new reading program has been introduced for several months, the school psychologist might again universally screen the first-grade students to determine whether the program was effective at improving reading fluency scores. If the new reading program is not showing desired results, the school psychologist may conduct interviews or complete observations of the program being executed to determine what areas are interfering in the process of adopting an EBI into everyday practice. In assessing areas that may prevent an intervention from being easily employed, the school psychologist should consider whether teachers are effectively trained in the intervention, whether the intervention is being implemented with fidelity, whether enough materials are available, and the complexity of the intervention.

School psychologists may further their role in program evaluation by completing an analysis of whether a proposed program contains a strong evidence-base. For example, school psychologists may assist implementation teams in examining the scholarly literature behind a proposed Tier II reading program or evaluate whether a social-emotional universal screener is psychometrically sound (National Association of School Psychologists, 2016). School psychologists can help schools in selecting programs by providing an overview of what the scholarly literature says on such programs by using empirical search engines like Google Scholar or Microsoft Academic. Additionally, many school psychologists have access to scholarly literature through their professional organizations. For instance, the National Association of School Psychologists provides members' access to their scholarly journal entitled, *School Psychology Review*. By reviewing literature, school psychologists can remain attuned to best evidence-based practices and interventions and help ensure they are adopted into the everyday practices of school systems.

Fidelity Management

School psychologists' expertise is not only needed to evaluate whether a program possesses strong evidence to be effective but to implement evidence-based interventions and programs as they are intended. In order to be successful at improving student outcomes, EBIs and programs need to be delivered with fidelity. If interventions and programs are not delivered with fidelity, they will not produce desired results for students and educators. As mentioned earlier, fidelity is defined as the degree to which interventions and programs are implemented as intended (McKenna & Parenti, 2017). If interventions and supports are not employed according to the procedures outlined, it is difficult for educators to determine whether or not poor student outcomes are the result of an effective intervention being implemented poorly or whether the intervention itself is ineffective (Sanetti, Kratochwill, & Long, 2013). Consequently, if educators do not find that an EBI is benefiting students, they are less likely to adopt the support into everyday practices. Often educators may be quick to determine that the intervention being implemented is ineffective in helping students but fail to consider whether it was delivered as intended. Fortunately, school psychologists are trained in understanding the importance of fidelity and how to deliver interventions with integrity.

One of the major roles of school psychologists is to address intervention acceptability and fidelity during the development, implementation, and evaluation of instructional services. Therefore, school psychologists play a central role in working with teachers, school counselors, and administrators in evaluating whether an intervention is shown to be effective through the literature and implementing interventions and programs with fidelity. School psychologists can assist educators in implementing interventions and supports with fidelity and ease the process of adopting them to everyday practice by developing a fidelity checklist. Through developing a fidelity checklist, school psychologists can help educators understand critical components to an intervention, support, or lesson and how to implement them correctly.

School psychologists looking to develop a fidelity checklist for an intervention or program should first familiarize themselves with the support being implemented by either reviewing literature on the support or, if available, familiarizing themselves with the program's manual. After becoming familiar with the intervention or program, school psychologists should note materials needed to implement the support, organization of materials, key steps to implementation, recommended time(s) spent on each step, ease of intervention implementation, and if/when student participation is required. In developing fidelity checklists, school psychologists' expertise in research and survey design may greatly assist them in constructing surveys that avoid double-barreled questions and are easy to understand. Figure 8.1 provides a brief example of a general fidelity checklist to be used for an intervention or program.

FIGURE 8.1 ● Fidelity Checklist

Name of intervention/program __________ Name of observer__________

Point Code:

- 2 points = High level of implementation integrity
- 1 point = Inconsistent level of implementation integrity
- 0 points = Instructional element not implemented
- N/O = Not observed

Area being Evaluated	Rating				Comments
Preparation					
Teacher materials are ready	2	1	0	N/O	
Student materials are ready	2	1	0	N/O	
Student materials are presented in an organized fashion	2	1	0	N/O	
Teacher is familiar with the lesson	2	1	0	N/O	
Teacher briefly reviews previous lesson	2	1	0	N/O	
Teacher introduces purpose for today's lesson	2	1	0	N/O	
Instructional Presentation					
Area being Evaluated	Rating				Comments
Follows steps in lesson	2	1	0	N/O	
Follows standardized/prescribed wording in lesson (if provided)	2	1	0	N/O	
Appropriate time spent on each component of lesson	2	1	0	N/O	
Models skills/strategies appropriately	2	1	0	N/O	
Models skills/strategies with ease	2	1	0	N/O	
Transitions between steps/activities were smooth	2	1	0	N/O	
Scaffolds student learning	2	1	0	N/O	
Lesson was easy to follow	2	1	0	N/O	
Student Engagement					
Encourages student participation	2	1	0	N/O	
Checks students understanding of content presented	2	1	0	N/O	
Allows students time to respond to questions	2	1	0	N/O	
Allows students to ask questions regarding content presented	2	1	0	N/O	
Takes time after class to answer any student questions	2	1	0	N/O	

Source: Adapted from the Center on Instruction (2008).

Aside from ensuring that interventions and programs are implemented with fidelity, school psychologists can lead a team of educators in developing or using an integrity checklist to ensure that basic components of MTSS or intervention service delivery models are being implemented accordingly. If MTSS or intervention service delivery models are not being implemented with fidelity, their proper adoption into everyday practice is unlikely. Therefore, school psychologists can play a central role in researching and developing fidelity checklists for both MTSS and intervention service delivery models. After developing fidelity checklists for MTSS, intervention service delivery models, or interventions themselves, school psychologists can greatly enhance fidelity by conducting observations (Eagle et al., 2015; Gresham, MacMillan, Beebe-Frankenberger, & Bocian, 2000). Through developing fidelity checklists and completing observations, school psychologists can best ensure that supports under MTSS are in the best position to improve school and student performance. Additionally, through such practices, school psychologists can best promote the process of systematically adopting EBIs and supports into everyday practice.

Data Collection and Interpretation

As noted throughout this book, proper data collection and interpretation is paramount in determining whether interventions and supports in place are producing desired results. Although the utilization of data to inform instructional practice appears to be one that most educators would welcome for the benefit of their schools and students, both teachers and administrators often become overwhelmed by data. Previous research indicates that educators often struggle to understand why data are important, what data are useful, and how to interpret data (Huguet, Marsh, & Farrell, 2014; Skalski & Romero, 2011). Adding to these pressures is that policymakers and parents are both calling for higher accountability in helping students succeed academically, behaviorally, and social-emotionally. Consequently, many educators have learned to be defensive, dismissive, wary, or even scared over data collection and interpretation. However, the collection and analysis of data are vital to ESSA, MTSS, and implementation science. Luckily, school psychologist's training in data collection and interpretation can be a great asset in helping educators view data as less daunting.

ESSA (2015) outlines the importance of using data across a number of areas including student academic achievement, student growth, school climate, and nonacademic skills, such as social awareness, self-management, and self-efficacy. Collecting and interpreting data in each of these areas are important for schools looking to access one of the many funding streams under ESSA and to qualify for federal grants (Cammack, Brandt, Slade, Lever, & Stephan, 2014). To assist school districts in qualifying for funds under ESSA, school psychologists may compile office discipline referral and behavioral screening data to show how the school climate has changed since implementing School-Wide Positive Behavior Supports (SWPBS). Subsequently, school psychologists may analyze such data and present it to school administrators or the school board in order to help administrators formulate a plan to qualify for grants or funds under ESSA.

While ESSA is concerned with how data can be utilized on a broader level, such as what is the overall climate of a school, MTSS utilizes data to inform decisions on student progress and whether the interventions and supports in place are producing desired results (Eagle et al., 2015). For example, after analyzing a student's data in responding to an intervention, the school psychologist may determine that adequate progress has not been made in remediating the child's deficit. Therefore, the school psychologist may recommend to the child study team that the child is in need of more intensive supports or that an alternative intervention should be tried.

Finally, implementation science seeks to make data collection and interpretation a practice that is adopted into the everyday routine of the school. Moreover, implementation science uses data to determine how successful the adoption of a best evidence-based practice has been. Through implementation science, data may be utilized to determine whether implementing MTSS has been successful in schools and if so how successful. For instance, a school psychologist may analyze data before, during, and after implementation of MTSS and determine whether it has been effective and how it can be made more effective if desired results are not met. The school psychologist may then present their findings to administrators or key stakeholders involved in implementing MTSS. After presenting such findings, administrators and school psychologists may determine that further data collection is needed to evaluate how the process of adopting MTSS can be improved.

For example, as part of the process of implementing MTSS, a school may have introduced a fidelity checklist to better assess how well the construct is being employed on a daily basis. Subsequently, the school may compare baseline data from when the fidelity checklist was first introduced to determine how well MTSS was being implemented to completed fidelity checklist data several months later. In analyzing the data, the school psychologist may determine that since the introduction of the checklist, the fidelity of MTSS implementation has increased. To further assess whether the checklist assisted in clarifying the process and components of MTSS for educators, school psychologists may want to develop a brief survey. The brief survey may inquire about whether the fidelity checklist made the process of implementing MTSS easier for educators and improved their understanding of it. Again the focus on implementation science is on whether a best evidence-based practice or construct has been adopted into everyday practice and whether the process of implementing a best evidence-based practice or construct is seamless.

In working with data, both ESSA and implementation science suggest that a wide variety of sources may be utilized to determine whether desired outcomes have been met and adequate progress has been made. Data sources outlined by ESSA and implementation science include qualitative and quantitative measures such as formative assessments, summative assessments, grades, state test results, absenteeism rates, suspension rates, expulsion rates, office discipline referrals, universal screening, and progress monitoring data (Bauer, Damschroder, Hagedorn, Smith, & Kilbourne, 2015; ESSA, 2015; Freeman et al., 2015). Given that the data collected under ESSA and implementation science vary widely, school psychologists can greatly help teachers and administrators in sorting out the most important data to collect. Additionally, school psychologists' training in statistical analysis, report writing, and dissemination of results can assist educators in easily understanding data and drawing conclusions from such data. Through ESSA, MTSS, and implementation science, the field of school psychology has the greatest opportunity it ever has to break away from traditional reactionary practices and move forward in establishing itself as a profession that can greatly benefit students and educators. By capturing this opportunity, school psychologist's versatility and in-depth knowledge of preventative practices can finally be utilized.

Current Limitations in School Psychology Practice

Although School Psychologists possess a wealth of knowledge and training in the core components of building an effective MTSS framework, their expertise often goes unrecognized and underutilized. Historically, studies have shown that despite school psychologists being specially trained in preventative practices and service delivery models, over 50% of their work is consumed by heavy psycho-educational assessment caseloads (Brown, Holcombe, Bolen, & Thomson, 2006; Hosp & Reschly, 2002; McKevitt, 2012; Reschly, 2000; Stoiber & Vanderwood, 2008). In order to successfully embrace and sustain MTSS, school psychologists must be utilized in ways that exploit their training in preventative practices in lieu of reenacting their former more restrictive testing-based role. With MTSS gaining momentum in schools, it appears as if a broadening of roles for school psychologists may be underway. Sullivan and Long (2010) found that 87.5% of school psychologists reported being directly involved in Response to Intervention efforts. A more recent study by Avant and Swerdlik (2016) found that 51% of school psychologists and school social workers reported expanded roles under MTSS in having increased opportunities to serve on leadership teams. Additionally, 70% of respondents perceived increased responsibilities for managing and collecting data (Avant & Swerdlik, 2016).

Despite school psychologists' roles expanding, many professionals in the field continue to engage in the "traditionalistic" practices of conducting psycho-educational evaluations and writing reports in addition to their responsibilities under MTSS (Sullivan & Long, 2010). Although psycho-educational assessment and special education procedures are necessary responsibilities for school psychologists, each has prevented the field of school psychology from taking on a broader role in integrating service delivery models under an MTSS framework (Splett et al., 2013). The continued overuse of school psychologists in the domains of psycho-educational assessment and report writing is largely a result of schools failing to adopt an MTSS framework. As mentioned earlier, commonly held concerns among educators for not fully embracing an MTSS revolve around time, financial constraints, and lack of personnel to support students at risk from developing future academic, behavioral, or social-emotional delays. However, lack of preventative efforts under an MTSS model and failure to provide school psychologists an outlet to alter their roles can be more time-consuming and costly to districts.

Cheney, Flower, and Templeton (2008) point out that although students with the most severe emotional or behavioral problems comprise between one and five percent of the school's population, these students tend to consume more than 50% of teachers' and administrators' time, leading to other students losing out on critical learning time and teachers leaving the profession. Despite students with severe emotional and behavioral deficits consuming time, distracting from the learning environment, and contributing to teacher turnover rates, recent estimate suggest that only one in eight schools screen students for behavioral and emotional risk (Bruhn, Woods-Groves, & Huddle, 2014). Additionally, a recent study by Eklund, Meyer, Way, and Mclean (2017) found that just over half of school psychologists provided school-based mental health services and of those school psychologists who provide mental health services only 10% of their time each week is spent engaged in individual counseling, group counseling or crisis intervention efforts. Ultimately, the delay in identifying and servicing students at risk for academic, behavioral, or social-emotional deficits early may lead to special education placement later on in their academic career (Lane, Oakes, & Menzies, 2010). Additionally, through screening and servicing academic, behavioral, and social-emotional deficits through early intervention, school personnel will have more time to dedicate to the integration of service delivery models under an MTSS framework.

Administrative Support for School Psychologist Role Reallocation

In order to effectively implement MTSS, school psychologists and administrators must work together. Administrators can assist school psychologists by working with them to outline the barriers and organizational climate in their schools in welcoming MTSS (Eagle et al., 2015). For instance, school psychologists and administrators may work together in developing a needs assessment to understand staff's current understanding of MTSS, what they want to accomplish through MTSS, and what barriers may exist in effectively implementing MTSS (Eagle et al., 2015). Additionally, school psychologists can conduct comprehensive needs assessments to address deficits in the areas of attendance, school climate, school crisis, and ongoing social-emotional concerns. From completing such assessments, school psychologists and school administrators can work together to coordinate efforts with other school personnel and community providers to form partnerships and obtain training and materials in needed areas (Eagle et al., 2015; Miller, 2014; National Association of School Psychologists, 2016). For example, the school psychologist might complete a needs assessment in which educators identify a need for a social skills training program.

In addition to working on completing needs assessments, school psychologists and school administrators can work together in monitoring intervention implementation. Previous studies suggest that school principals play a critical role in improving intervention outcomes through encouraging that interventions be administered with fidelity (Kam, Greenberg, & Walls, 2003; Rohrbach, Graham, & Hansen, 1993). School psychologists can assist in ensuring that interventions are delivered with integrity through offering training on the importance of fidelity, providing observations during intervention implementation, and offering ongoing coaching to educators implementing interventions (Eagle et al., 2015; Gresham et al., 2000). Eagle et al. (2015) suggest that school psychologists may play a key role in supporting the delivery of interventions with integrity by acting in the role of "intervention coordinator." In such a role, the school psychologist can work with the MTSS team in setting concrete goals, training mentors to oversee the monitoring of interventions, offering ongoing feedback to mentors, and assessing data to determine whether adequate progress is being made toward meeting goals.

To fully embrace change under MTSS, administrators must support school psychologists' alteration in roles with more of their time being dedicated to preventative efforts, such as counseling and consultation, as opposed to the special education determination process. Additionally, to address the expanding role of school psychologists and promote childhood mental health and wellness, the National Association of School Psychologists (2021) recommends a ratio of one school psychologist per 500 students. Caseloads exceeding 500 students place school psychologists at significant risk for burnout. Studies suggest that approximately 30% of school psychologists experience burnout due to managing large caseloads, insufficient time, and lack of resources (Boccio, Weisz, & Lefkowitz, 2016a; Huebner & Mills, 1994; Mills & Huebner, 1998). Additionally, studies suggest that school psychologists may be at greater risk for developing burnout than other psychological service providers (Boccio, Weisz, & Lefkowitz, 2016b; Huebner, 1993).

One source of burnout school psychologists may experience is administrators pressuring them to behave unethically. A recent study revealed that approximately one-third of school psychologists were pressured to behave unethically by their administrators through avoiding recommending certain support services due to costs, making to do with inadequate assessment and/or intervention materials, and making students eligible for special education who did not meet eligibility requirements (Boccio et al., 2016a). In regards to MTSS, administrators can support school psychologists' efforts by consulting with them on interventions, assessments, and progress monitoring materials needed to best assist students. Moreover, administrators can support school psychologists by reinforcing that the proper number of progress monitoring data points have been collected before altering interventions and reinforcing their decisions to allow ample time for an intervention to work before moving the child into a higher tier or referring the child to special education.

Through administrators supporting school psychologists in their role reallocation and providing them manageable caseloads, they will be able to work collaboratively across disciplines to design and deliver quality academic, behavioral, and social–emotional support (Splett et al., 2013). Moreover, school psychologists will be able to work with educators in the areas of evidence-based interventions and programs, data collection, data analysis, and systemic problem-solving to ensure MTSS is implemented successfully (Kamphaus, 2012; National Association of School Psychologists, 2016). By working collaboratively with other educators, school psychologists will become a greater asset to schools and districts in supporting the implementation of MTSS.

General Education Teacher Roles and Responsibilities

Aside from school psychologists, one of the educational professionals that plays a vital role in implementing MTSS and the intervention service delivery models that comprise it is the general education teacher. Due to their significant role in instructing all learners, general education teachers are often regarded as being on the "front lines" of MTSS implementation and are largely considered "first responders" to assisting children academically, behaviorally, and social–emotionally (Sink, 2016; Wixson & Valencia, 2011). Therefore, general education teachers are responsible for the delivery of the core curriculum and to implement classroom-level interventions and supports (Bjorn, Aro, Koponen, Fuchs, & Fuchs, 2015; Shanklin, 2008). For example, within RTI, the general education teacher's role may be to provide instruction in the core reading curriculum, such as Fountas and Pinnell's Leveled Literacy intervention. Moreover, within SWPBS, the general education teacher's role may be to implement the Good Behavior Game.

Through MTSS, general education teachers are expected to ensure the instruction and supports being provided are appropriate for the developmental and maturity levels of the students being taught (Werts & Carpenter, 2013). Therefore, general education teachers may collaborate with special education teachers, school administrators, school counselors, or even school psychologists to assess and determine what programs and materials are needed (Werts & Carpenter, 2013). Moreover, general education teachers provide critical insight in determining the effectiveness of a core program or support being implemented and any barriers to implementation (Pinkelman, McIntosh, Rasplica, Berg, & Strickland-Cohen, 2015; Werts & Carpenter, 2013). Consequently, general education teachers can provide vital insight as to whether a program or support is a good fit in meeting the needs of students and are in an ideal position to identify which students may be in need of more assistance through use of universal screening and student observation (Werts & Carpenter, 2013).

For students who may be initially struggling with the core curriculum, behavioral expectations, or social-emotional regulation, the general education teacher can differentiate their instruction and provide scaffolding (Werts & Carpenter, 2013). **Scaffolding** involves teachers breaking down new concepts so that they can be learned more easily by students with the hope that children eventually gain a better understanding of the concepts being taught (Meyer & Behar-Horenstein, 2015). Through using techniques such as differentiated instruction and scaffolding, general education teachers can assist students in transferring the skills that they are learning in the classroom to real life (Shanklin, 2008). Overall, general education teachers within MTSS are expected to identify target goals, assess individual student needs, monitor data on students' progress, and use this data to inform instructional decisions (Meyer & Behar-Horenstein, 2015; Werts & Carpenter, 2013). In the event that a student is struggling or is in need of Tier 2 or Tier 3 interventions or supports, general education teachers tend to collaborate and seek out assistance from school counselors, school psychologists, or special education teachers (Werts & Carpenter, 2013). Lastly, general education teachers attend grade level and child study team meetings to collaborate and monitor students who are struggling academically, behaviorally, or social-emotionally (Meyer & Behar-Horenstein, 2015; Werts & Carpenter, 2013).

Evolution of Special Education Teacher Practice

Although MTSS and the intervention service delivery models are considered general education initiatives, special education teachers play a critical role as both an interventionist and collaborative partner for general educators (Simonsen et al., 2010). Since the mid-1880s, the role of the special education teacher has went through many changes with both special education teachers and school psychologists initially training and working in residential facilities for children with disabilities (Brownell, Sindelar, Kiely, & Danielson, 2010). However, by the 1960s a series of public laws led to special education teacher's roles evolving to teaching students with special needs in self-contained classrooms (Brownell et al., 2010; Hoover & Patton, 2008).

The role of the special education teacher further developed with the passage of Education for All Handicapped Children Act of 1975 (Brownell et al., 2010; Hoover & Patton, 2008). Through the Education for All Handicapped Children Act, students with disabilities were required to be provided equal access to public education (Brownell et al., 2010; Hoover & Patton, 2008). Consequently, both special education teachers and school psychologists became an integral part of providing supports and services to children within the public school system instead of operating in residential placements or in self-contained classrooms (Brownell et al., 2010; Hoover & Patton, 2008). The push to incorporate students with disabilities into least restrictive and general education settings continued into the 1990s, and as a result, special education teachers began increasingly teaching alongside general education instructors (Brownell et al., 2010; Hoover & Patton, 2008). As can be seen, with each major change in the role of the special education teacher came an increased role and responsibility for them to provide support not only to general education instructors but to students with and without disabilities (Brownell et al., 2010; Hoover & Patton, 2008). In sum, the role of special educators evolved from educating the same learners all day in one classroom to that of providing remediation and instructional supports in various classrooms to many different learners (Hoover & Patton, 2008).

Current Special Education Teacher Roles and Responsibilities

Within MTSS, special education teacher's roles have continued to evolve, and they have increasingly been called on to collaborate with general educators. More specifically, the special educator's role within MTSS has evolved into that of an interventionist with specific training and knowledge in (1) content and how to teach it, (2) specific problems that students with difficulties and disabilities may experience in a particular content area, (3) the role of technology in supporting learning, and (4) the role of specific assessments and interventions in providing more intensive, explicit instruction within a curricular context (Brownell et al., 2010; Hoover & Patton, 2008). Therefore, special education teachers within MTSS may be able to collaborate with general education instructors in helping them to differentiate their instruction for children at-risk for learning, behavioral, or social-emotional deficits (Bjorn et al., 2015). Through collaborating with general educators, special education teachers are helping to ensure that interventions being provided are not endorsing a "one-size-fits-all" model but one that acknowledges the need to adapt the intervention-fit diverse learners (Simonsen et al., 2010). By assisting general educators in differentiating their instruction for struggling students, special education teachers are helping to ensure that these children do not develop chronic academic, behavioral, or social-emotional deficits (Bjorn et al., 2015; Simonsen et al., 2010).

One of the ways that special education teachers may assist general educators in adapting their instruction to further support their instruction to assist all learners is through helping them utilize explicit instruction. In brief, **explicit instruction** is a method to teach skills or concepts to children using direct and structured teaching (Hughes, Morris, Therrien, & Benson, 2017). Explicit instruction helps make lessons or concepts clear to students through modeling for them how to start and successfully complete a task (Hughes et al., 2017). Additionally, explicit instruction provides students ample time to practice the concepts that have been taught to them (Hughes et al., 2017). Another way special education teachers can support general educators in meeting the needs of all learners is to provide peer coaching and performance feedback (Simonsen et al., 2010). Through providing peer coaching and performance feedback, special education teachers can help general educators increase the fidelity with which interventions are implemented (Simonsen et al., 2010). Aside from providing peer coaching and performance feedback, special education teachers can assist in universally screening and in monitoring student academic, behavioral, and social-emotional progress. Finally, special educators can participate in child study team meetings for students and assist in monitoring the fidelity of intervention implementation (Bjorn et al., 2015; Simonsen et al., 2010). Ultimately, special education teachers tend to become increasingly involved in supporting students as they move from Tier 1 to Tier 3 ((Bjorn et al., 2015; Simonsen et al., 2010).

School Counselor Roles and Responsibilities

Like all educational professionals, MTSS has required school counselors to further refine and advance their skill set. Consequently, rather than school counselors engaging in their historical roles of working with a small group of students on their vocational, educational, collegiate, and personal goals, the profession is now further involved in the everyday lives of children than it ever has been (Sink, 2016). According to the American School Counselor Association (ASCA), school counselors collaborate with families, teachers, administrators, school psychologists, and community providers to maximize student success (2019). Within MTSS, school counselors may work with administrators and school psychologists to identify a standards-based counseling curriculum to address the social-emotional development of all learners (ASCA, 2019). After identifying the counseling program, school counselors may push into the classroom to deliver it (Belser, Shillingford, & Joe, 2016; Sink, 2016). In addition to selecting and potentially delivering Tier 1 interventions, school counselors may help to appraise a student's learning environment and inform teachers and administrators of potential hindrances (Sink, 2016). For example, a school counselor may appraise a teacher's classroom and note that no behavioral rules or expectations are clearly posted or that the room may be in need of a "cool-down corner" to assist students who are struggling emotionally. Therefore, the school counselor may provide vital feedback to the teacher on how to appropriately word school rules and suggest where these rules should be posted in the classroom environment. Moreover, the school counselor may assist the teacher in selecting materials for the "cool-down corner."

At Tier 2, school counselors may assist teachers in identifying common supports that may assist struggling students. For example, the school counselor may use a behavior contract to assist a student who has accumulated several discipline referrals or a social-emotional check-in/check-out with a student who is experiencing mild difficulty coping with everyday stress or anxiety (Belser et al., 2016). If these interventions and supports prove ineffective, the school counselor may consult with the teacher to revise the interventions and supports being provided (Belser et al., 2016). Additionally, the school counselor may assist students academically by running a study skills workgroup or providing further social-emotional support through Skillstreaming (Belser et al., 2016; Sink, 2016). Finally, at Tier 2, the school counselor may work with the school psychologist in interpreting progress monitoring data and determining whether additional Tier 3 supports are needed.

At Tier 3 of MTSS, school counselors may work to develop more individualized supports for students with fellow educators, such providing critical information on Functional Behavior Assessment/Behavior Intervention Plan (FBA/BIP) development or providing one-on-one mentoring (Belser et al., 2016). Although school counselors may provide some brief short-term individual counseling for students at Tier 3, ASCA has identified providing long-term intensive counseling as an inappropriate role for school counselors (ASCA, 2019; Belser et al., 2016). Consequently, for students experiencing significant and chronic emotional and behavioral problems, school counselors may refer or consult with the school psychologist or outside clinicians, such as a mental health counselor (ASCA, 2019; Belser et al., 2016). It is important to note that through each intervention service delivery model comprising MTSS, school counselors provide vital advocacy and support for students and their families. Moreover, school counselors are a critical resource in linking children and parents to school and community services (ASCA, 2019). For example, a school counselor may assist a family in locating an outside clinician to assist a child suffering from significant episodes of sadness or a local tutor to help a child who is struggling academically. As such, within MTSS, school counselors are one of the ultimate collaborative professionals that schools have on hand and are a highly useful resource for educators and families.

School Administrator Roles and Responsibilities

Although the role of the administrator was discussed earlier in relation to supporting school psychologists, effective school leadership plays a huge part in properly implementing MTSS and effectively using all educators. Therefore, school administrators are responsible for installing a system to support diverse student needs by (1) creating a shared vision over MTSS, (2) building a collaborative and caring work environment to facilitate MTSS, (3) enabling need-based educator supports in regards to MTSS (e.g., in-service training), (4) using data to make decisions, and (5) reviewing and participating in policy changes regarding MTSS with local educational agencies (Choi, McCart, Hicks, & Sailor, 2019). Through engaging in these responsibilities, school administrators seek to empower school teams to welcome systemic change in educational initiatives, such as MTSS and efficiently and adequately put such an initiative into place (Choi et al., 2019; Meyers & Behar-Horenstein, 2015).

One of the major ways in which school administrators may support MTSS implementation is through establishing organizational support to embark on such a large initiative (Eagle et al., 2015). Therefore, in establishing MTSS and the intervention service delivery models that comprise it, school leaders are responsible for allotting and dedicating time, resources, finances, and staff to the initiative (Eagle et al., 2015). Moreover, school administrators may work with school counselors and school psychologists to help identify the needs of staff and barriers to implementation as discussed earlier (Choi et al., 2019; Eagle et al., 2015). Once resources and a common vision over MTSS has been established, school administrators may allocate blocks of time within the school day for staff to work together in establishing and maintaining MTSS and the intervention service delivery models that comprise it (Eagle et al., 2015). Moreover, school administrators may locate in-service trainings and provide opportunities for educational professionals to embrace and work outside of their traditional roles (Eagle et al., 2015). For example, a school administrator may provide an opportunity for school counselors to work with teachers on implementing a Tier 1 social-emotional program as opposed to engaging in their traditional role of scheduling classes. Overall, school administrators support the implementation of MTSS by working with staff to establish a clear vision, action plans, and decisions regarding the effectiveness of MTSS (Choi et al., 2019). Table 8.2 summarizes the roles and responsibilities of educators within an MTSS framework.

TABLE 8.2 ● Roles and Responsibilities of Educators Within MTSS

Position	Roles Within MTSS
School administrator	• Develop a needs assessment to evaluate barriers to implementing MTSS by working with the school psychologist, school counselor, and a small team of educators. • Facilitate and provide support for MTSS to ensure educator "buy-in" and empowerment. • Create a shared vision regarding MTSS by working with educational staff. • Secure financing for MTSS initiatives. • Establish continuous educator supports and resources for MTSS in regards to in-service trainings, books, or videos. • Facilitate ongoing monitoring of overall MTSS effectiveness using data. • Set up regular MTSS meetings to analyze data and make data-based decisions in regards to school progress. • Review and participate in policy changes regarding MTSS with local education agencies. • Provide opportunities for school psychologists, school counselors, and special education teachers to work outside of their traditional roles.
School psychologist	• Assist teachers and school teams in the evaluation and selection of evidence-based interventions and programs at Tier 1, Tier 2, and Tier 3. • Lead teams in selecting and implementing school-wide universal screening systems in the academic, behavioral, and social-emotional domains. • Lead teams in selecting and implementing progress monitoring efforts in the academic, behavioral, and social-emotional domains. • Consult with teachers, administrators, and other school staff to determine whether students are making adequate progress or whether intervention changes are needed. • Support teachers and administrators in implementing interventions and programs with fidelity. • Conduct small-group or individual interventions and counseling services to support students' social, emotional, and behavioral well-being.

Position	Roles Within MTSS
	• Engage in crisis prevention and intervention efforts. • Participate in meetings regarding a student's functional behavior and the development of behavior intervention plan to remediate maladaptive student conduct.
General education teacher	• Utilize evidence-based core curricula and instruction in all areas of instruction. • Deliver core instruction with fidelity. • Differentiate and scaffold core instruction to accelerate student learning. • Collaborate with special education teachers, school counselors, school administrators, and school psychologists to assess and determine universal programs and supports. • Assist in the universal screening of students. • Provide insight into the barriers of implementing a universal curriculum or program. • Attend grade level and child study team meetings to collaborate and monitor students who are struggling.
Special education teacher	• Assist general education teachers in further differentiating and scaffolding core instruction and curricula to meet the needs of all learners. • Support general educators in utilizing explicit instruction to help make lessons or concepts clear to students. • Provide peer coaching and performance feedback to general education teachers. • Monitor the fidelity of intervention and program implementation. • Participate in child study team meetings. • Increasingly become involved in supporting the needs of students at Tier 2 and Tier 3.
School counselor	• Partner with administrators, school psychologists, and teachers to assist in the selection of evidence-based programs. • Provide direct services to students through small group and individualized interventions for students displaying minor behavior or social-emotional problems. • Refer and consult with in-school and out-of-school clinicians for students display significant academic, behavioral, or social-emotional concerns (i.e., consulting with the school psychologist or a mental health counselor). • Maximize access to school-based and community-based resources and link children and families to these supports. • Provide consultation to teachers and administrators to assist in addressing student academic, behavioral, or social-emotional concerns. • Appraise learning environments for hindrances to student progress. • Assist in data collection and analysis and revise interventions and programs where appropriate.

Source: ASCA (2019), Bjorn et al. (2015), Brownell et al. (2010), Choi et al. (2019), Huguet et al. (2014), McKevitt (2012), Sink (2016), and Wixson and Valencia (2011).

Conclusion

To properly implement MTSS, educators and future educators need to be aware of the roles and responsibilities of their colleagues. By being aware of their colleagues' roles, responsibilities, and areas of expertise, educators can utilize them effectively in implementing MTSS and in best providing support to students. One of the most versatile and critical professions in adequately implementing MTSS is that of school psychology. School psychologists' unique training in evidence-based practices, research and program evaluation, intervention integrity, data collection, data-based decision-making, and systemic change makes them an ideal professional in facilitating efforts under MTSS. Additionally, school psychologists' expertise in each of the aforementioned domains assists them in linking commonalities across ESSA, implementation science, and MTSS. By recognizing and understanding these commonalities, school psychologists can best assist schools in meeting their goals and reaching their true potential in assisting students.

Other than school psychologists, both general and special education teachers play vital roles in delivering EBIs, supports, and curriculums to students. While general education teachers are typically viewed as "front line" responders, special education teachers may greatly assist them in differentiating their instruction to meet the needs of diverse learners. Additionally, general and special education teachers can provide important feedback on whether a Tier 1 program or intervention is working, barriers to implementation, and data on how students are responding to the supports being provided.

To further assist general and special education teachers, school counselors may appraise the classroom environment that children learn in and providing critical feedback. Moreover, school counselors may assist children and their families by linking them to resources both inside and outside the school system, such as a school psychologist or mental health counselor, for more advanced mental and behavioral health support. For students displaying some difficulties, school counselors may offer one-to-one mentoring or group counseling to assist children in overcoming their areas of concern. Finally, school counselors may provide important feedback in the development of an FBA/BIP for students who are experiencing significant behavioral concerns.

Arguably, much of whether MTSS and the intervention service delivery models that comprise it are successful comes down to the school administrator. The success of implementing MTSS largely comes down to a school administrator's ability to lead due to the profession having to account for the time, resources, finances, and staff needed to undertake such a large initiative. Once these factors are accounted for, the school administrator may work with educators to establish buy-in and develop a common vision over how to best implement MTSS. Through all educators being respectful and knowledgeable about each of their roles and responsibilities under MTSS, the take of employing the model and the intervention service delivery models that comprise it will be less daunting.

Discussion Questions

1. Why is it important for school psychologists to act as a program evaluator for implementation teams?
2. How is the development of a fidelity checklist important to delivering evidence-based interventions and supports with integrity?
3. Why do you think educators may become overwhelmed and struggle with data collection and interpretation?
4. How can general education and special education teachers work together to support children's academic, behavioral, and social-emotional development?
5. Why is it important for school counselors to assist teachers in appraising their classroom environment?
6. In what way can school administrators help educators to develop a shared vision over MTSS?

9 Implementation of MTSS in Alternative Settings

Learning Objectives

After reading this chapter, you should be able to:

- Define alternative practice settings.
- Discuss why alternative practice settings may be slow to explore implementation of Multi-Tiered Systems of Support (MTSS) and intervention service delivery models that comprise MTSS.
- Identify the characteristics of individuals living in or attending alternative practice settings.
- Describe the considerations for implementing MTSS in alternative practice settings.
- Predict barriers to implementing MTSS in alternative practice in alternative practice settings.

An Introduction to Alternative Practice Settings

The promise and success of Multi-Tiered Systems of Support (MTSS) in public schools have led to an increasing interest in it being implemented in alternative settings. **Alternative practice settings** are designed to provide specialized instruction and assistance to children and adults who require more intensive support than can be offered in traditional school and community placements (Swoszowski, McDaniel, Jovilette, & Melius, 2013). These settings are generally closed environments with specific organizational rules and routines and vary from large institutional care facilities to small group homes (Mazzone, Nocentini, & Menesini, 2018). Alternative settings include self-contained and juvenile justice schools, correctional facilities, day habilitation treatment programs, and residential placements (Griffiths et al., 2019; Swoszowski et al., 2013). Children and adults living or attending alternative settings have often been transferred to them for a wide variety of reasons including physical and verbal aggression, drug use, academic failure, possession of weapons, significant social-emotional concerns, and considerable difficulty completing activities of daily living, like dressing and bathing oneself (Griffiths et al., 2019; Swoszowski et al., 2013).

The Need for MTSS in Alternative Practice Settings

Despite growing interest in the implementation of MTSS in these settings, little scholarly literature exists and exploration of how to implement the framework remains in its infancy stages. However, scholars, policymakers, and advocates have long voiced concerns that individuals living in residential and correctional settings have been subject to outdated reactionary practices involving the undue use of force, cruel, and demeaning disciplinary practices, restrictions on basic human rights, inappropriate use of behavior intervention plans, and segregation from both the school environment and surrounding community (Gagnon, Barber, & Soyturk, 2018). Climates created by these reactionary and ongoing practices in alternative settings fail to teach individuals appropriate behavior and compensatory strategies for overcoming emotional difficulties (Gagnon et al., 2018; Gelbar, Jaffrey, Stein, & Cymbala, 2015). Additionally, these reactionary practices increase the likelihood of individuals being the recipient of negative consequences and punitive sanctions and may actually lead to increased recidivism and decreased safety (Gagnon et al., 2018; Gelbar et al., 2015). Still for many alternative settings, lack of awareness, understanding, and comfort in implementing preventative practices under a three-tier framework exists.

Ironically, despite the medical and educational fields increasingly moving away from reactionary practices, alternative settings have been slow to explore the implementation of three-tiered intervention service delivery models until recently (Scheuermann, Nelson, Wang, & Bruntymyer, 2015). Often alternative placements may be the slowest to adopt updated models of practice due to the bureaucracies that monitor and evaluate these settings requiring a great deal of information before moving forward (Scheuermann et al., 2015). In addition to needing a great deal of information, many of these settings are underfunded, have outdated or inconsistent methods of data collection and analysis, or are simply not collecting the right information (Gagnon et al., 2018; Scheuermann et al., 2015). Consequently, gathering the data needed to make informed decisions on altering past practices in such settings is unnecessarily arduous or even nonexistent. As has been implied throughout this book, school systems often fell victim to these very same difficulties but have been relatively quick to learn from faulty past practices. However, alternative settings may not feel the same pressure as schools to adopt preventive practices quickly, in part, because these settings might operate outside of well-defined and implemented oversight mechanisms (Gagnon et al., 2018). Moreover, many of these settings have not received the same amount of widespread scrutiny by the public, policymakers, and media.

To put this into perspective, almost everyone can recall a recent news story in which a school or teacher was not following proper protocol in the past year but much rarer are these stories at the agency and correctional facility level. This is not to say such stories do not exist or happen just as frequently as they do throughout the school systems. It is to say that alternative settings may not receive as much pressure to change faulty past practices, in part, because these placements often care for and oversee extreme subsets of the general populace.

Characteristics of Individuals in Alternative Practice Settings

The individuals attending and residing in residential placements represent an extremely small population of people who violated the law or who are so disabled or mentally decompensated that they require intensive programs, supports, and living facilities to meet their needs. For instance, the prevalence of intellectual and developmental disabilities in the general population is between one and three percent (Munir, 2016). From that percentage, only a fraction of individuals with intellectual or developmental disabilities end up in alternative settings run by a state or community agency. To further illustrate why alternative settings may not receive the same amount of attention to alter past practices, consider that in the United States there are only 301 juvenile justice schools compared to 132,853 K-12 public schools (Gagnon et al., 2018). Therefore, it is much more likely that the community and media are aware of poorly outline procedures and protocols in typical school settings as opposed to those in juvenile facilities.

As can be inferred, individuals attending and living in alternative placement settings represent some of the most demanding populations in society and are often influenced by combinations of abuse, neglect, disabilities, trauma, mental health conditions, and substance abuse (Jolivette, 2016). Consequently, many of these individuals enter alternative placements nonvoluntarily or because they have experienced a history of nonsuccess within traditional educational systems or in the surrounding community (Jolivette, 2016). Despite presenting with considerable difficulties, all individuals attending alternative placement facilities should be afforded developmentally, culturally, and age-appropriate evidence-based supports to place them in the best position to succeed. For this reason, federal and state agencies have been increasingly emphasizing the use of evidence-based practices and preventative measures to best assist individuals in alternative settings. For example, the recent *Guiding Principles for Providing High-Quality Education in Juvenile Justice Secure Care Settings* (2014) advocates for a MTSS to improve youth behavior.

As a result of this federal guidance, much of the research regarding preventative practices in alternative settings has focused on the intervention service delivery model of positive behavior support (PBS) being implemented in juvenile justice facilitates. Nevertheless, from the few scholarly articles that explore the utilization of PBS in juvenile settings, some broader principles can be drawn in consideration of employing MTSS in other alternative placements. After all, individuals living or attending alternative settings often display with both behavior and emotional deficits but likely have not received adequate evidence-based support throughout their life.

Interestingly, the top three reasons children are removed from public districts and placed in alternative schools include physical aggression, chronic truancy, and verbally disruptive behavior (Griffiths et al., 2019). However, like in public schools, the frequency of these behaviors and the use of physical restraints have significantly been reduced in alternative placement settings by using intervention service delivery models, like PBS. In particular, a study by Gelbar et al. (2015) revealed that after implementing PBS the total number of physical restraints decreased by 25% and the total duration of time students spent in physical restraints decreased by 46% in one clinical day treatment school. Other studies completed in residential and alternative settings have shown that implementation of PBS and evidence-based interventions under the model increase on-task behavior and school attendance, decrease problem behavior, and reduce variability in staff's response to challenging conduct (Griffiths et al., 2019; Johnson et al., 2013; Swoszowski et al., 2013).

Arguably the reason why MTSS poses so much promise in alternative settings is that many of the very same difficulties that plague school systems exist within the confines of these placements. Just as in schools, individuals residing in residential and correctional facilities may engage in both externalizing and internalizing behaviors such as physical aggression, verbal aggression, teasing, self-injurious behavior, emotional dysregulation, withdrawal, and negative self-talk (Gagnon et al., 2018; Mazzone et al., 2018; Zubritsky, Wald, Jaquette, & Balestra, 2018). Additionally, just as in schools, individuals within the walls of these settings may encounter either a positive, welcoming, and comforting climate that promotes well-being or a negative, cold, and uncaring environment that fosters failure, isolation, and little empathy. In fact, over half the children living in residential care settings report being victimized or bullied by their peers (Mazzone et al., 2018). Therefore, MTSS offers alternative settings an opportunity to systematically promote behavioral and social-emotional well-being through the intervention service delivery models of positive behavior support, social-emotional RTI, and suicide prevention and intervention. Of course, in any of these alternative settings, modifications and special considerations will have to be made in implementing MTSS.

Considerations for Implementing MTSS in Alternative Settings

Consideration 1: Individuals in Alternative Settings Have Significant Concerns

As touched upon earlier, the first consideration that must be made in implementing MTSS in alternative settings is that children and adults living in or attending these placements often present with significant mental health and co-occurring learning problems (Scott & Cooper, 2013; Styelinger, Gavigan, & Albright, 2017). Estimates indicate that approximately 50%–80% of children in alternative, residential, correctional school settings have learning disabilities and approximately 85% of teenagers in the juvenile justice system are functionally illiterate (Scott & Cooper, 2013; Styelinger et al., 2017). Additionally, the National Alliance on Mental Illness (2017) reports that approximately 15% of men and 30% of women in jail have a serious mental illness and that at least 83% of inmates with mental illness do not have access to needed treatment.

Like children and adults in correctional facilities, individuals with intellectual and developmental disabilities are at increased risk for having mental health problems (Munir, 2016). Studies have generally found that individuals living with intellectual and developmental disabilities are three to four times more likely to have a mental illness than in the general population (Munir, 2016). Although these deficits are prevalent across populations in residential and correctional settings, it is likely that individuals residing in such facilities never received appropriate evidence-based interventions and supports. To elaborate, even though many schools are beginning to implement interventions that promote mental and behavioral wellness, it remains unlikely that such supports have been adequately supplied to children or adults living in or attending residential or juvenile justice facilities before they arrived in such settings. Recall that many of the intervention service delivery models that are currently being implemented in schools were not into place until the early 2000s. Even today MTSS and intervention service delivery models, such as social-emotional RTI and suicide prevention and intervention, remain new concepts to districts.

Therefore, many children and adults residing or attending residential, correctional, or day habilitation settings were likely not taught effective evidence-based strategies to manage their behavioral or emotional deficits.

Practitioners in these settings should seek to tailor evidence-based interventions and supports to the populations they are working with. For example, in an alternative school that serves students with severe developmental disabilities, Tier 1 school expectations may be taught and prompted using modeling, picture cues, posters, and basic sign language (Simonsen, Britton, & Young, 2010). For students not responding to Tier 1 interventions and supports, Tier 2 may consist of utilization of video modeling and re-teaching of behavioral expectations in small groups. Video modeling has been shown to be an evidence-based intervention for teaching prosocial behavior to students with autism and has shown great promise in remediating behavioral deficits in children with social-emotional concerns (Haydon et al., 2017). Finally, for children with the most intensive needs, Tier 3 would entail the development of a functional behavior assessment and behavior intervention plan.

Consideration 2: Personnel Working in Alternative Settings

The second consideration in implementing MTSS in alternative settings involves taking into consideration the background and training of the personnel who work for such facilities (Scott & Cooper, 2013). Due to the complexity of difficulties that individuals living in residential and correctional facilities present with, the professionals working in these placements are much more diverse than those in school settings. Consequently, agencies that oversee residential settings, day programs, and correctional facilities are often staffed with personnel from a wide range of disciplines with conflicting views on appropriate interventions and treatment (Scott & Cooper, 2013). Some of the professionals found in these settings include medical directors, psychiatrists, nurses, mental health counselors, social workers, occupational therapists, direct support professionals, physical therapists, speech pathologists, recreation therapists, corrections officers, police officers, teachers, treatment team leaders, and clinical, counseling, and school psychologists.

With the exception of school psychologists and to some extent teachers, most of these professionals working in these settings are either unaware of preventive practices under MTSS or have a vague understanding of it. Moreover, each of these professionals may have conflicting views on appropriate interventions and treatment for those residing in these settings. Therefore, like the schools, alternative settings looking to implement MTSS have to create an open dialogue among all professionals about why movement away from reactionary past practices is needed. In order to have this conversation, appropriate data and reasoning need to be presented to staff. Additionally, just as in the school system, a needs assessment should be completed to address gaps between current conditions and desired outcomes and to create "buy-in." Suggested questions to assess the alternative setting's readiness to adopt MTSS and intervention service delivery models under it include: (1) What practices are currently being implemented to address behavioral and social-emotional concerns? (2) Are these practices preventative or reactionary in nature? (3) Are these practices evidence-based? (4) What understanding do staff and the agency have of MTSS? and (5) What outcomes are expected from employing MTSS? (Gelbar et al., 2015). Through answering these questions and creating an open dialogue, professionals employed in alternative settings can work together to provide evidence-based supports for individuals attending and living there.

Consideration 3: Overcoming Faulty Past Practices

A third consideration in moving toward MTSS in alternative settings involves overcoming faulty past practices. Possibly even more than in the schools, residential and correctional settings have been and often remain engrained in faulty past practices that are punitive, involve negative consequences, or lack an evidence base (Gelbar et al., 2015). Even though the medical field moved toward a preventative practice model in the 1970s, many of these facilities continue to operate under a reactionary model where diagnosis leads to individual treatment. As such, rather than addressing behavioral or emotional concerns through three-tiered preventative frameworks and on an agency-wide level, individuals residing in these settings tend to be treated on a case-by-case basis. Due to treating individuals on a case-by-case basis, best evidence-based care is often delayed, confusing for staff to implement, and inadequate.

For example, in a state residential setting where eight individuals live with developmental disabilities, there may be as many as eight behavior intervention plans in place. In each of these behavior intervention plans, three to five target behaviors may be defined for each individual, and multiple strategies may be used to address each behavior. Therefore, direct support staff are required to undertake the daunting task of knowing eight different behavior plans and tracking approximately 24–40 behaviors throughout the day. Obviously, this task is not probable for staff, and the individuals residing in such facilities are likely not receiving evidence-based interventions that are implemented with fidelity due to having too many interventions to remember. Moreover, the data being collected on each individual are likely inaccurate and often does not provide the state agency correct information to make informed decisions on widespread treatment protocol.

As discussed throughout this book, an easier way to address and prevent common behavior and social-emotional concerns is through creating a caring, welcoming, and comforting environment through Tier 1 supports. By developing a culture that welcomes and calls for respect, empathy, and kindness, an environment is created in which individuals feel cared about and safe (NASP School Safety and Crisis Response Committee, 2015). Through using a standard protocol approach in preventing and addressing behavioral and social-emotional concerns, general interventions and supports can be utilized and are more likely to be implemented with fidelity. This is opposed to a reactionary approach of attempting to address behaviors and social-emotional concerns on a case-by-case basis when they arise.

For instance, just as in a classroom setting, a residential, day habilitation, or correctional facility may post clear expectations, have a positive motto, reward positive behavior, and actively supervise common areas where conflicts can arise. These general standard protocol supports are much easier for staff to remember and implement on a daily basis as opposed to eight individual behavior plans that consist of different interventions for each individual. Of course, for individuals not responding to the Tier 1 behavior interventions in place, they would receive increased supports and evidence-based interventions at Tier 2. Only when individuals are not responsive to Tier 1 and Tier 2 supports should they receive interventions that address their individualized needs in the form of a behavior intervention plan or individual counseling.

Consideration 4: Data Collection and Analysis

As mentioned, a fourth consideration in implementing MTSS in alternative practice settings revolves around the proper data collection and analysis. Often alternative practice settings collect a lot of data, but these data are aggregated ineffectively, misplaced or lost, or comes from a wider variety of sources. For example, both at a day habilitation and residential placements, data may come in the form of daily reports, data tracking sheets, minor incident logs, major incident logs, community outing checklists, family outing checklists, or "as needed" **PRN medication** forms. One of the reasons that data collection remains a hurdle for many alternative settings is that these placements lack a reliable and confidential system to collect, summarize, and use data effectively.

As mentioned, many correctional, state, or community agencies are underfunded and continue to rely strictly on paper-based forms to collect data as opposed to an electronic application, like the School-Wide Information System. Therefore, in alternative placements, there may be no way of telling which locations in a day habilitation setting behaviors are most likely occurring so that staff can appropriately monitor and increase support in these areas. Additionally, many staff working for alternative settings remain ineffectively trained in defining behavior in observable and measurable terms, tracking data, and even analyzing data from such a wide variety of sources. In drawing from a wide variety of data, staff and teams may have difficulty sorting through and knowing what information is most important in the implementation of MTSS. Inaccurate reporting of data and lack of proper data can lead to significant problems in interpreting whether MTSS is effective and whether the interventions being implemented under MTSS are working. Furthermore, the lack of a centralized database to store and evaluate such data makes it difficult to determine what group homes or day habilitation treatment centers are underperforming.

Aside from drawing from a wide variety of existing data sources, staff in alternative settings may not have access to measures of universal screening or progress monitoring, such as the BIMAS-2 or DESSA-mini. Although there is a growing number of universal screening and progress monitoring measures for children, these assessments may not be useful or applicable for children with significant developmental disabilities or adults in alternative settings. Therefore, school psychologists in such settings may need to research and develop their own universal and progress monitoring measures to best adapt to the population they are working with. In order to do this, school psychologists and administrators in alternative settings should look to establish local norms either on existing measures or on measures that are created (Kubiszyn & Borich, 2016). Local norms are useful in working with populations with unique needs and who are not accommodated by existing norms. Local norms allow for within-group comparisons, and therefore individuals are compared against others who share similar characteristics such as grade, school attended, race or intellectual ability rather than against the general population as a whole (Kubiszyn & Borich, 2016). This is opposed to national norms, which compare individuals to their same-age peers across a nation. Overall, the development of local norms and utilization of universal screening and progress monitoring measures may greatly assist alternative settings in obtaining better insight as to their populations' behavioral and social-emotional needs. Additionally, it may help these placements in making data-based decisions to meet their agency and facility-wide goals.

Consideration 5: 24-Hour MTSS Implementation

A fifth consideration in implementing MTSS is the time that individuals spend in alternative settings. To elaborate, for individuals who spend all day in their group residential home or are confined to correctional settings, MTSS will have to be implemented 24 hours a day, 7 days per week, and 12 months per year. This is unlike the schools in which MTSS and the intervention service delivery models that comprise it only having to be implemented 8 hours per day, 5 days per week, and 10 months per year. Due to residential and correctional facilities operating 24 hours per day, multiple shift changes occur. These shift changes can greatly disrupt the implementation of

MTSS and the intervention service delivery models that comprise it if all staff are not trained well. For example, perhaps the morning and afternoon staff at a correctional facility are trained well in implementing both PBS and social-emotional RTI, but the night shift remains ineffective at delivering the prescribed interventions and supports. Consequently, both intervention service delivery models under MTSS are not being delivered with fidelity across all shifts and can greatly hinder their effectiveness. Therefore, staff across all shifts will require ongoing training to implement each intervention service delivery model under MTSS with integrity.

For 24-hour group residential homes whose individuals attend day programs, coordinated efforts may be needed to ensure that MTSS is being carried out across all settings (Jolivette, 2016). For instance, residents in a state group home for the developmentally disabled may also attend a state-operated day habilitation facility. To best assist individuals in generalizing the strategies they learn in both environments and to encourage appropriate prosocial behavior, consistency is needed. Therefore, the day habilitation setting should coordinate efforts with residential group homes in coming up with consistent behavior expectations, motto, and reward systems to best promote appropriate behavior at Tier 1. Likewise, a school within a juvenile detention center should coordinate efforts with corrections officers and the jail itself in consistently implementing PBS, social-emotional RTI, and suicide prevention and intervention efforts across both environments.

In other words, the implementation of MTSS across environments needs to be seamless and delivered accordingly in order for it to have the best chance at succeeding. If Tier 1 of PBS is being implemented in the day habilitation environment but not in the residential setting, inconsistencies exist and generalization of expectations under the model may not occur. Alternative settings should look to establish a liaison across day habilitation and residential settings to ensure that supports and interventions are carried out the same across environments accordingly. For example, perhaps a state-run group home and a state-operated day habilitation facility share the same expectations for individuals living in and attending both settings. The liaison can assist in educating staff on how to best teach individuals about these shared expectations across both settings. Additionally, the liaison can complete a fidelity checklist across both settings to ensure these behaviors are being taught the same way in both placements.

Consideration 6: Acquisition of School Psychologists

A final consideration and modification in implementing MTSS across alternative settings involves the acquisition and utilization of school psychologists. Although the profession of school psychology has become simultaneous with public schools, the profession did not ultimately get its start there. Recall that the profession of school psychology was founded in Witmer's laboratory, and the very first placements for school psychologists involved residential schools and community-based centers. With alternative settings looking to implement preventative practices under MTSS, these placements need practitioners proficient in the model. School psychologists' unique training in preventative practice, evidence-based interventions, learning and development, consultation, data-based decision-making, and behavior management makes the profession enticing for alternative settings looking to implement MTSS.

However, many of these placements may overlook the profession of school psychology because they often view the practice as one that is exclusive to school districts. Not surprisingly, the most recent National Association of School Psychologists Membership survey estimated that approximately 17% of school psychologists practice outside the school setting (Walcott & Hyson, 2018). Moreover, although it is estimated that 17% of school psychologists practice outside the school setting, it remains unknown how many in the professional practice in residential, day habilitation, or correctional facilities. Still, school psychologists practicing in these alternative settings exist and can offer great knowledge in evidence-based practice and data-based decision-making to these placements.

For example, in the Greater Buffalo, NY area, one of the biggest employers of school psychologists outside the public schools is the state Office for People with Developmental Disabilities (OPWDD, 2020). At present, the agency employs 12 school psychologists in their group home and day habilitation settings across Western, NY, making up the majority of practicing psychologists in the department (OPWDD, 2020). In their capacity at the OPWDD, these school psychologists work alongside clinical and counseling psychologists in developing group counseling programs, researching evidence-based interventions, collecting and analyzing data, and advocating for people with developmental disabilities. In this manner, each practitioner of psychology at OPWDD utilizes their distinctive training to meet the needs of a population that presents with significant learning, behavioral, and social-emotional challenges.

To further advance the field of school psychology and draw awareness to practitioners beyond the school setting, national and state associations of school psychology should look to advertise and obtain information on practitioners and these placements. Additionally, state and national associations of school psychology should focus on how the field can best implement MTSS in alternative placements. Alternative settings offer school psychologists great opportunities to lead in the execution of MTSS and intervention service delivery models under it. School psychologists employed in these settings can create a strong team by collaborating with clinical and counseling psychologists and each field seeking one another's insights. This collaboration is needed in addressing the unique needs of individuals attending and living in these alternative settings and to promote their social, emotional, and behavioral well-being.

Conclusion

MTSS is a term used by schools to describe the integration or triangular, multi-tiered intervention service delivery models that seek to remediate maladaptive learning, behavioral, or social-emotional deficits. Although MTSS is broad in nature, intervention service delivery models that fall under MTSS exhibit commonalities in the areas of evidence-based supports and instructional practices, universal screening, progress monitoring, and data-based decision-making (Freeman et al., 2015; Harn et al., 2015; National Association of School Psychologists, 2016). Integrating and aligning of each of these elements forms the framework for MTSS. School psychologists' expertise in the areas of data-based decision-making, evidence-based interventions, implementation fidelity, systematic problem-solving, and program evaluation ideally positions them to play an integral role in implementation teams and in MTSS execution in both school and alternative settings.

Although MTSS is in its infancy stages in being implemented in alternative placements outside the school system, it appears to be a promising approach to providing evidence-based interventions and supports for individuals attending and living in these facilities. Future research and literature are sorely needed to fully explore the utility and versatility of implementing MTSS in day habilitation, residential, and correctional settings and how school psychologists can best be utilized in such settings. Appendix A provides a chart of each intervention service delivery model under MTSS discussed in this book.

CASE EXAMPLE

MTSS WITHIN AN ALTERNATIVE PRACTICE SETTING

Li Chen is a 24-year-old Asian American male with moderate intellectual disability who attends a state operated day habilitation facility in San Jose, California. While at the day habilitation facility, Li takes part in scheduled activities, formulized, training, and receives staff supports to continue to promote his skill development. Additionally, day habilitation staff work with Li and his peers to help them retain their self-help, socialization, and adaptive skills. Along with Li Chen, 100 other individuals with mild to moderate developmental disabilities attend the day habilitation facility and are placed in classrooms consisting of seven to ten people with up to three direct support staff.

Despite staff efforts to curb problem behaviors and social-emotional concerns from arising in individual's attending the day habilitation facility, an increasing number of attendees are being sent home early or are not earning their rewards for meeting behavioral and social-emotional expectations. Consequently, day habilitation staff are reporting that individuals attending the facility appear to be struggling with the behaviors of teasing one another and engaging in verbal and physical aggression. Day habilitation staff also report that individuals attending the facility appear to struggle with identifying, understanding, and reporting their feelings. Li Chen's day habilitation staff note that he has been sent home early for the past week becoming a danger to himself and others.

In response to growing concerns at the day habilitation facility, the school psychologist suggests utilization of MTSS to prevent and curb problem behaviors and social-emotional concerns from arising. More specifically, the school psychologist suggests using PBS and social-emotional RTI to create a warm and caring day habilitation environment, teach behavioral expectations, and better support the mental well-being and social-emotional development of the individuals attending the facility. Being aware that one of the day habilitation staff, Mrs. Dandon, is a former high school special education teacher of 15 years, the school psychologist enlists her help in adopting and adapting PBS and subsequently social-emotional RTI for the day habilitation setting. Taking into account the cognitive ability and cultural makeup of the individuals attending the day habilitation center, the school psychologist leads efforts in introducing and training staff on the central tenants of MTSS, PBS, and social-emotional RTI. Once staff have been trained, the day habilitation center begins to implement both PBS and social-emotional RTI under MTSS.

At Tier 1, the day habilitation facility creates a mascot and adopts a simple but catchy motto to encourage teamwork and teach prosocial behavior. Since the day habilitation facility is on Cadet Street, their new mascot is the Cadet Street Caterpillar, and their motto for all caterpillars attending the day habilitation facility is to "Be safe. Be nice. Be cool." Key expected behaviors outlined under "be safe" are for day habilitation attendees to keep their hands and feet to themselves at all times and walk in the hallways and on the sidewalks. Key expected behaviors under "be nice" are for attendees to use an indoor voice, use kind words, and say or use sign language to say please and thank you. Key expected behaviors under "be cool" are to help others out and listen to directions.

In addition to the day habilitation motto, a slogan has also been adopted to remind all attendees to be "as cool as a caterpillar" when they are upset and ask for help through using their words or signing "help please." Day habilitation staff have posted these behavior expectations both in the halls and classrooms at the facility using both words and pictures. Additionally, there are posters of other adults with developmental disabilities exemplifying the behavior expectations. Aside from the motto, the day habilitation staff have adopted, adapted, and simplified the Good Behavior Game to be used in classrooms. Throughout the day, frequent verbal praise is given, and "caterpillar coupons" are given when a staff member observes an attendee being safe, nice, or cool. Moreover, on a weekly basis, the school psychologist pushes into the day habilitation classrooms to provide explicit instruction on a "feeling of the week" to help day habilitation attendees learn about their feelings, how to identify feelings in others, and how to manage their emotions better (Figure 9.1).

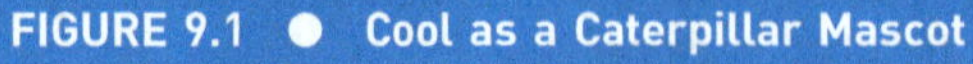

FIGURE 9.1 ● Cool as a Caterpillar Mascot

At Tier 2, attendees who are continuing to struggle behaviorally or social-emotionally receive additional support. For attendees who are still struggling behaviorally despite Tier 1 efforts, like Li Chen, a check-in/check-out is used. Additionally, components of the First Step to Success program have been adapted and modified to assist Li Chen and his fellow peers who have been struggling behaviorally. For attendees who have been struggling socially-emotionally, coping cards with both words and pictures are used along with a modified and adapted version of the Skillstreaming curriculum.

Since Li Chen did not respond to Tier 2 PBS efforts at the day habilitation facility, it was determined that he may need more intensive services. At Tier 3, a functional behavior assessment was conducted, and it was determined that Li Chen's behaviors appear to be in response to wanting to receive attention from peers or staff and wanting to escape/avoid nonpreferred activities and tasks, such as filling the vending machines or folding clothes. As a result of findings from the functional behavior assessment, the school psychologist worked with day habilitation team members to create a behavior intervention plan for Li Chen. Additionally, Li Chen received one-on-one cognitive behavior therapy with the school psychologist. For Li Chen's peers who continued to struggle socially-emotionally in spite of Tier 2 efforts, they received additional mental health support through one-on-one counseling using the C.A.T project, an extension of Coping Cat, or the POD-TEAMS Depression Prevention Program. In the months that followed, Li Chen's behavioral outbursts decreased considerably, and it was deemed he was no longer in need of a behavior support plan. Subsequently, Li Chen is now only receiving Tier 1 supports. Aside from Li Chen, day habilitation staff and data show that both behavioral and social-emotional concerns among attendees have been significantly reduced.

Discussion Questions

1. Why do you think it is important for educators to be aware of alternative practice settings and the populations served in these settings?
2. What are some of the characteristics of individuals attending and living in alternative practice settings?
3. As an educator, would you ever consider implementing MTSS and working in an alternative practice setting (i.e., being employed by school housed in a juvenile detention center or a teacher in a psychiatric institution)? Why or why not?
4. What are some of the similarities and differences in implementing MTSS in school settings vs. those in alternative placements?
5. What are some of the barriers of implementing MTSS and the intervention service delivery models that comprise MTSS in alternative practice settings?

Appendix A

Response to Intervention Flowchart

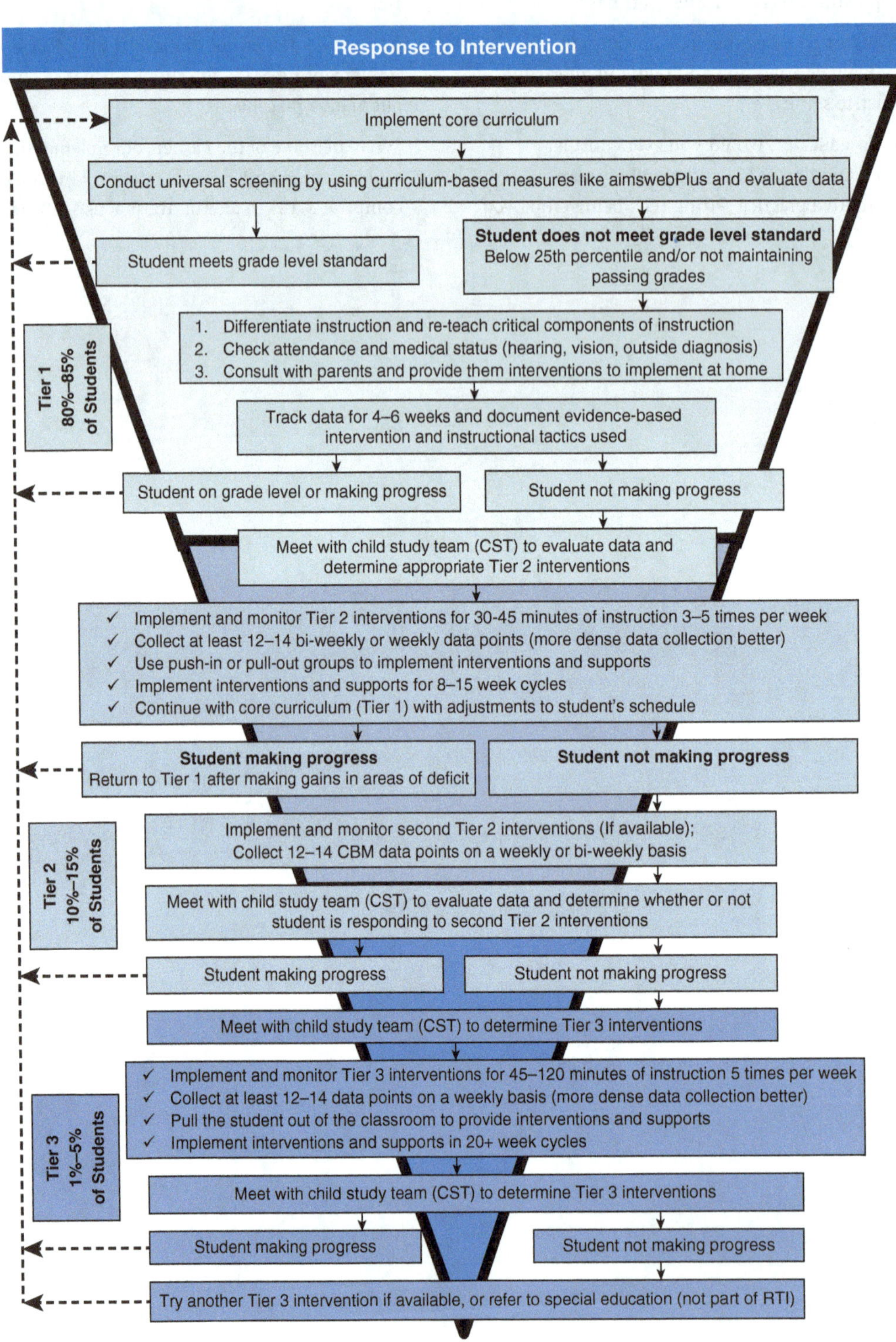

Appendix B

School-Wide Positive Behavior Support Flowchart

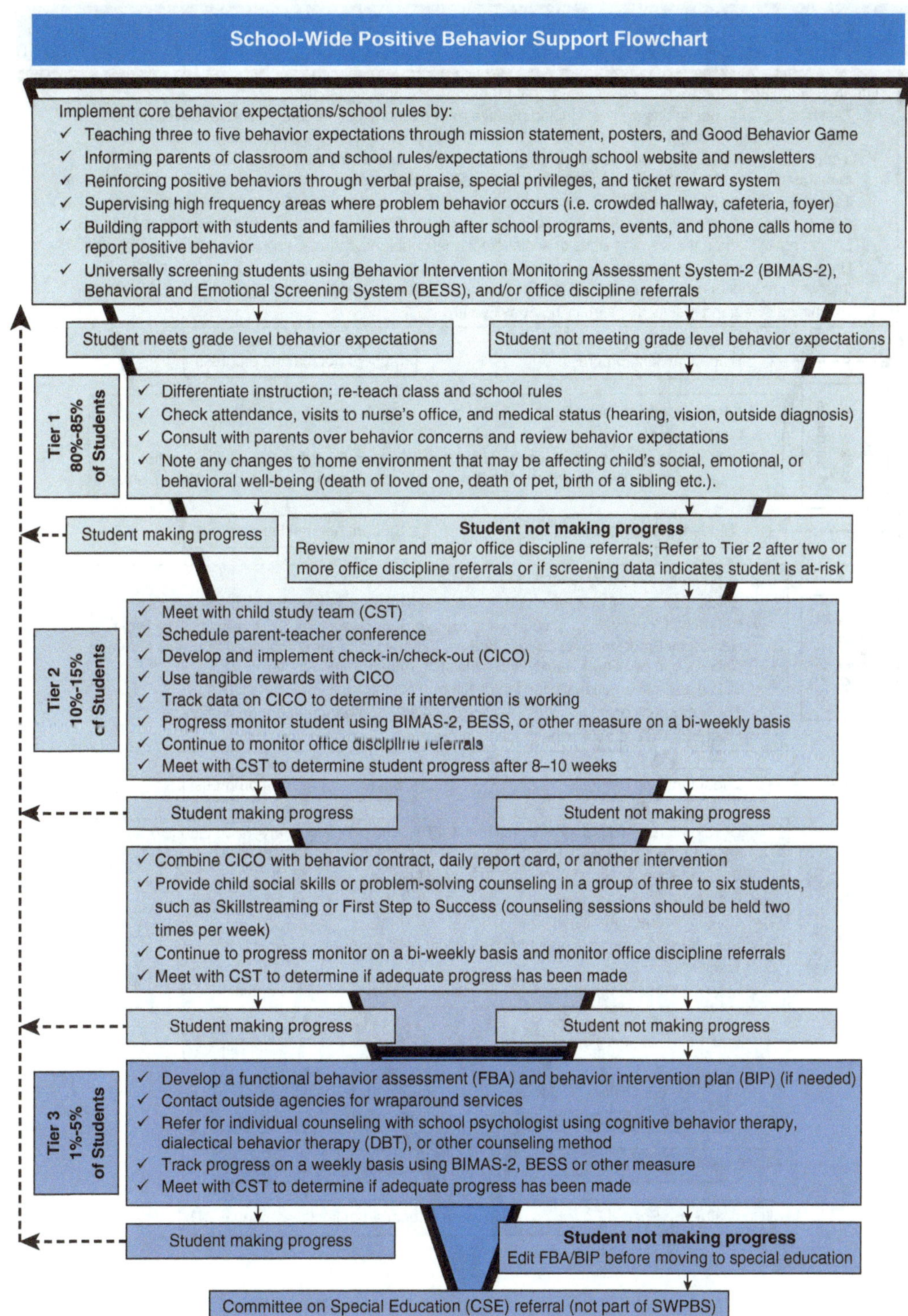

Appendix C

Social-Emotional RTI Flowchart

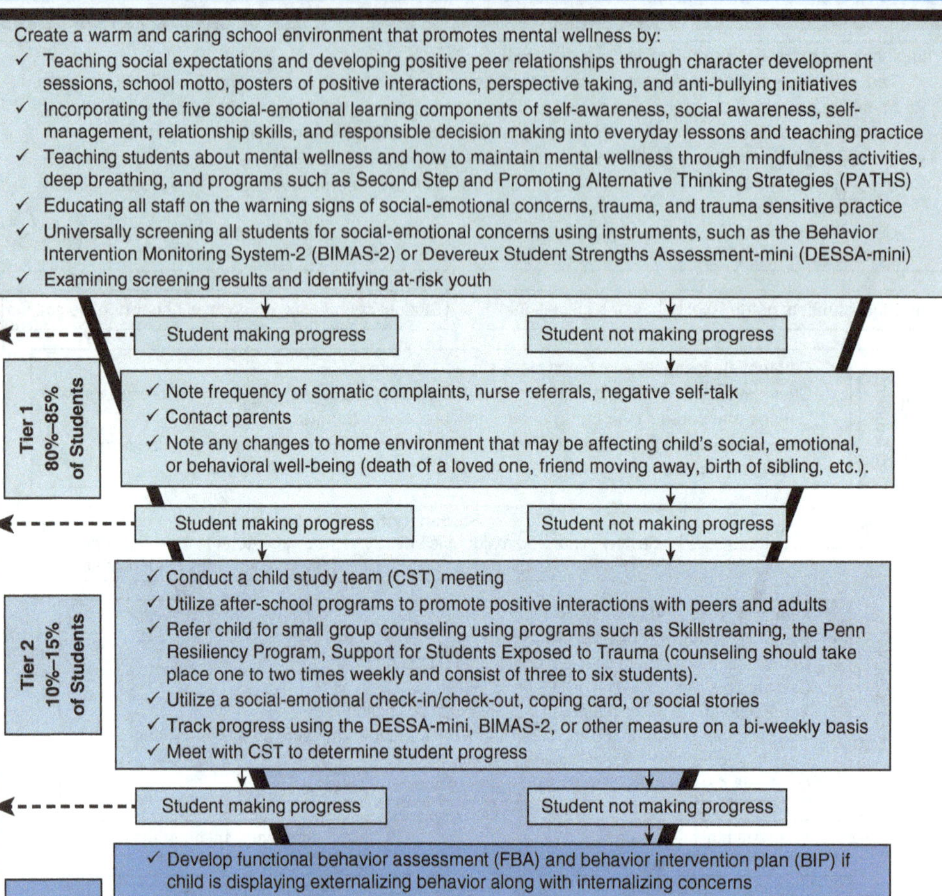

Appendix D

Suicide Prevention and Intervention Flowchart

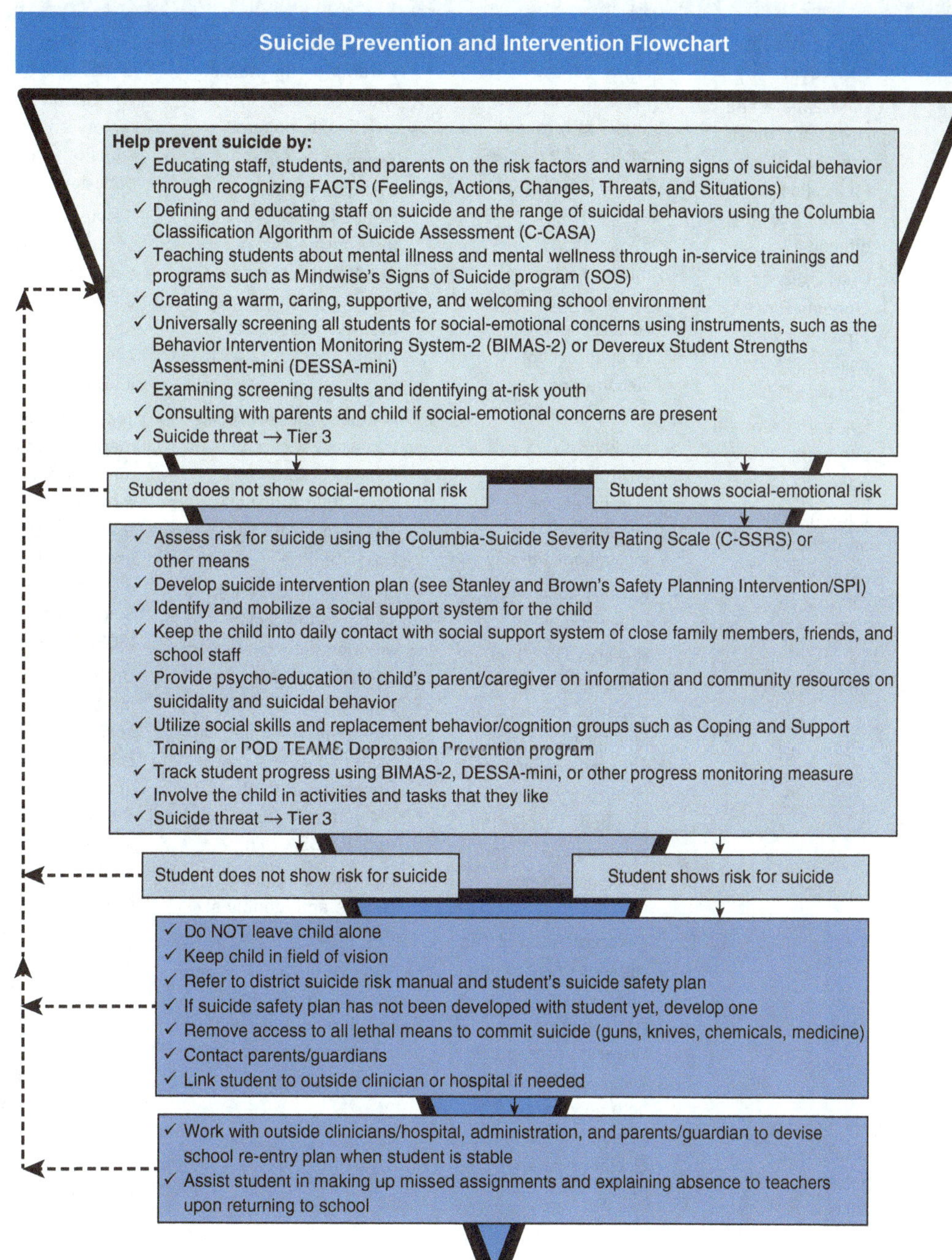

Appendix E

All Intervention Service Delivery Models

Tier	Academics/RTI	Behavior/SWPBS	Social-Emotional RTI	Suicide Prevention
Tier 1 80%–85% of Students	• Implement core curriculum • Differentiate and re-teach critical components of instruction for students having difficult • Universally screen students three times per year using CBM (i.e., aimswebPLUS) • Evaluate universal screening data • Refer students in bottom 25 percent on universal screening to Tier 2	• Define and teach three to five behavior expectations to all students through posters of expectations, school motto, Good Behavior Game etc. • Inform parents of classroom and school rules/expectations through school website and newsletters • Modify the environment and provide active supervision throughout the day • Reward positive behavior • Universally screen students using Behavior Intervention Monitoring Assessment System-2 (BIMAS-2), Behavioral, Emotional Screening System (BESS), and/or office discipline referrals • Recommend students with two or more office referrals or who in at-risk range on universal screener to Tier 2 (preferably use both universal screening and office discipline referral data)	• Educate all staff and parents on the warning signs of social-emotional concerns • Teach students skills to maintain mental wellness and incorporate social-emotional learning components into everyday lessons • Utilize programs that promote mental wellness and prosocial behavior, such as Second Step and Promoting Alternative Thinking Strategies (PATHS) • Universally screen all students for social-emotional concerns using instruments, such as the Behavior Intervention Monitoring System-2 (BIMAS-2) or Devereux Student Strengths Assessment-mini (DESSA-mini) • Examine screening results and identify at-risk youth • Meet with CST to develop interventions for at-risk youth and monitor progress	• Educate staff, students, and parents on the risk factors and warning signs of suicidal behavior • Define range of suicidal behaviors using the Columbia Classification Algorithm of Suicide Assessment (C-CASA) • Teach students about mental illness and mental wellness through in-service trainings and program's like Mindwise's Signs of Suicide program (SOS) • Universally screening all students for social-emotional concerns using instruments, such as the Behavior Intervention Monitoring System-2 (BIMAS-2) or Devereux Student Strengths Assessment-mini (DESSA-mini) • Examine screening results and identifying at-risk youth • Consult with parents and child if social-emotional concerns are present • Suicide threat → Tier 3

(Continued)

Tier	Academics/RTI	Behavior/SWPBS	Social-Emotional RTI	Suicide Prevention
Tier 2 **10%–15% of Students**	• Provide 30–45 minutes of instruction, 3–5 times per week • Track 12–14 data points on bi-weekly or weekly basis • Use push-in or pull-out groups to implement interventions and supports • Implement interventions and supports in 8–15 week cycles • Attempt alternative Tier 2 interventions, if available	• Meet with child study team (CST) • Schedule parent-teacher conference • Develop and implement check-in/check-out (CICO) • Use tangible rewards with CICO • Track CICO data to determine if intervention is working • Progress monitor at-risk students using BIMAS-2, BESS, or other measure on a bi-weekly basis • Continue to monitor office discipline referrals • Provide group counseling to student if needed • Attempt alternative interventions if available • Meet with CST and refer for a functional behavior assessment (FBA) if at-risk students fails to respond to Tier 2 interventions	• Utilize after-school programs to promote positive interactions with peers and adults • Refer at-risk students for small group counseling using programs such as Skillstreaming or the Penn Resiliency Program (counseling should take place 1–2 times weekly and consist of three to six students) • Utilize a social-emotional check-in/check-out, coping card, or social stories • Track progress using the DESSA-mini, BIMAS-2, or other progress monitoring measure on a bi-weekly basis	• Assess risk for suicide using the Columbia-Suicide Severity Rating Scale (C-SSRS) • Develop suicide intervention plan (see Stanley and Brown's Safety Planning Intervention/SPI) • Provide resources to student's parent/caregiver on suicidality and suicidal behavior • Utilize social skills and replacement behavior/cognition groups such as Coping and Support Training or POD-TEAMS Depression Prevention program • Involve child in activities and tasks that they like • Track student progress using DESSA-mini or BIMAS-2 • Suicide threat → Tier 3

(Continued)

(Continued)

Tier	Academics/RTI	Behavior/SWPBS	Social-Emotional RTI	Suicide Prevention
Tier 3 1%–5% of Students	• Provide 60 minutes of instruction, five times per week • Track 12–14 weekly data points • Utilize pull-out groups of students with interventionist • Implement interventions and supports in 20+ week cycles • Attempt alternative Tier 3 intervention, if available	• Develop a functional behavior assessment (FBA) and behavior intervention plan (BIP) (if needed) • Contact outside agencies for wraparound services • Refer for intensive counseling with school psychologist (if needed) • Track progress on a weekly basis using BIMAS-2, BESS or other measure • Meet with CST to determine if adequate progress has been made • Revise and edit BSP as needed	• Develop functional behavior assessment (FBA) and behavior intervention plan (BIP) if at-risk student is displaying externalizing behavior along with internalizing concerns • Develop school-based counseling treatment plan and provide intensive counseling • Provide 1:1 counseling with school psychologist • Contact wraparound services • Seek outside support if student poses risk to self or others • Track student progress using DESSA-mini or BIMAS-2 on a weekly basis	• Do NOT leave child alone • Refer to district suicide risk manual and student's suicide intervention plan • If suicide intervention plan has not been developed with student yet, develop one • Remove access to all lethal means to commit suicide (guns, knives, keys, medicine) • Contact parents/ guardians • Link student to outside clinician, hospital, or agency if needed • Work with outside clinicians/hospital, administration, and parents/guardian to devise school re-entry plan when student is stable

• Glossary •

Aborted or Self-Interrupted Attempt. Entails an individual taking steps to self-injure but stopping themselves before any injury occurs.

Acculturation. The process by which an individual adopts, acquires, and adjusts to a new cultural environment.

Acculturative Stress. Stress or the psychological impact of adapting to a new culture.

Adaptive Leadership. Refers to guiding others through complex and difficult to recognize challenges that are typically not resolved through traditional approaches.

Adverse Childhood Experiences. Potentially traumatic events that occur in childhood between 0 and 17 years of age.

Alternative Settings. Settings that are designed to provide specialized instruction and assistance to children and adults who require more intensive support than can be offered in traditional school and community placements. These settings are generally closed environments with specific organizational rules and routines and vary from large institutional care facilities to small group homes.

Attempted Suicide. A potentially self-injurious behavior that is associated with some intent to die as a result of the behavior.

Behavior and Emotional Screening System (BESS). An abbreviated, standardized, and norm referenced universal screener that consists of 25–30 items and derives scores from the following four areas: externalizing problems, internalizing problems, school problems, and adaptive skills.

Behavior Contract. A formal written agreement between a child and school staff member to outline the expectations of the student, teacher, and occasionally parents to help the student succeed behaviorally in school.

Behavior Intervention Monitoring Assessment System (BIMAS-2). A universal screener, progress monitoring, and intervention planning measure of behavioral, social, and emotional functioning in children and adolescents ages 5–18 years.

Behavior Intervention Plan. A plan that provides educators specific interventions and supports to utilize when a child is engaging in maladaptive behaviors.

Bounce Back Program. An extension of the Cognitive Behavioral Intervention for Trauma in Schools (CBITS) program designed to be implemented with children five to eleven years of age.

C.A.T. Project. An extension of the Coping Cat program ranging in age from 14 to 17.

Check-In/Check-Out. A multicomponent behavior intervention that typically consists of a children and teachers setting goals at the start of the day and checking out at the end of the day to review whether the child met behavioral goals.

Cognitive Behavioral Intervention for Trauma in Schools (CBITS). A Tier 3 cognitive behavior therapy program for children ages 10–15 that is designed to be implemented by school-based mental health practitioners on a weekly basis over the course of ten weeks.

Cognitive Behavior Therapy. An evidence-based treatment that brings together two systems of therapy: cognitive therapy and behavior therapy.

Cognitive Profile Analysis. An analysis of a child's performance on an intelligence test to help determine the presence or absence of a learning disability.

Columbia Classification Algorithm of Suicide Assessment. A classification systems used to provide educators and mental health practitioners suggested set terms and definitions to utilize in understanding and clearly relaying information regarding suicide.

Columbia Suicide Severity Rating Scale (C-SSRS). A suicide screener that measures risk for suicide across four constructs: severity of ideation, intensity of ideation, behavior, and lethality.

Competency Drivers. Drivers that seek to build the knowledge of educators in understanding and implementing MTSS through activities, in-service trainings, and district-wide resources.

Completed Suicide. A self-injurious behavior resulting in fatality and is associated with some intent to die as a result of engaging in the behavior.

Coping Cards. Small index-sized cards that children can carry with them in their pocket to remind them of particular triggers that may cause them to feel upset and provide them coping strategies learned for overcoming internalizing distress, such as using deep breathing.

Coping Cat. A 16-session manualized counseling curriculum designed for children ages seven to thirteen who are exhibiting signs and symptoms of anxiety disorders.

Coping and Support Training (CAST). A school-based small group counseling program for children 14–19 years of age that is designed to assist youth in overcoming suicidal risk factors, such as depressive symptoms and hopelessness.

Cost-Benefit Analysis. The process of calculating which resources and training on MTSS will best benefit the district and staff.

Cultural Adaptations. The modification of an existing intervention, such as changing the materials, cultural references, or language, in order to make the intervention more compatible with a specific population.

Cultural Humility. The ability to self-reflect on one's own values and beliefs.

Culturally Responsive Practices and Instruction. A pedagogy that both empowers and recognizes that students are both similar to, but also uniquely different from, one another in regards to their intellectual ability, social-emotional development, ethnic background, religious beliefs, language, customs, and beliefs.

Culture. The customary beliefs, material traits, and social forms held by racial, religious, or social groups.

Curriculum-Based Measures (CBM). A brief normative assessment used by educators to quickly determine the level and rate of performance in acquiring necessary skills or content knowledge.

Cut Point Score. A score that is used to determine whether a student is at risk for poor academic and behavioral outcomes.

Data-Based Decision-Making. The continual process of collecting and interpreting data to alter and improve instructional and behavioral practices to best benefit learners.

Devereux Student Strengths Assessment-Mini (DESSA-mini). A norm-referenced, strengths-based social-emotional scale that can be utilized as a universal screener or progress monitoring measure for children in kindergarten through eighth grade.

Differentiated Instruction. Refers to teachers tailoring the classroom environment, instructional practices, and teaching environments to create appropriately different learning experiences for students with different interests, needs, readiness, and learning profiles.

Education for All Handicapped Children Act (EHCA). An act that required that all public schools accepting federal funds to provide children with disabilities equal access to education and to educate them in the least restrictive educational environment possible.

Every Students Succeeds Act (ESSA). The main federal education law in the United States that governs K-12 public education policy. In 2015, the law replaced its predecessor the No Child Left Behind Act.

Evidence-Based. Refers to the quality of the scholarly evidence that is presented to demonstrate an intervention produces intended effects (McKevitt, 2012, p. 34).

Evidence-Based Interventions. Treatments or supports that have been scholarly reviewed and demonstrate empirical support for effectiveness.

Evidence-Based Programs. Empirically based supports and protocols that are often sold by companies in a standardized and manualized format.

Exploration Stage. A stage in implementation science that consists of the adoption of a new program and development of performance assessment processes, initial training efforts, and the securing of resources.

Externalizing Behaviors. Negative conduct, such as verbal or physical aggression, that is directed outwardly toward others and is considered undercontrolled.

Fidelity. The degree to which a practice or intervention is implemented as intended.

First Step to Success. An early intervention program for children in grades kindergarten through three that is designed to assist children who are at risk for developing aggressive and antisocial patterns of behavior.

Full Implementation Stage. A stage in implementation science that consists of over half of school personnel changing their practices under MTSS with a high level of fidelity.

Functional Behavior Assessment. A systemic process for gathering information to determine why a student may be engaging in challenging behavior.

Gatekeeper Training. Training that involves the dissemination of information on youth suicide in regards to demographic information, statistics, risk factors, protective factors, warning signs, misunderstandings, vulnerable populations, and minorities.

Historical Oppression. The pervasive, chronic, and intergenerational experiences of oppression that may be normalized, imposed, and internalized into the daily lives of a marginalized group of people.

Idioms of Distress. Cultural variations in an individual's likelihood to express suicidality and the way in which suicide is expressed and methods or means of attempting suicide.

Implementation Science. The scientific study of methods utilized to promote the systemic uptake of evidence-based practices into routine, everyday practice.

Initial Implementation Stage. A stage in implementation science that entails staff attempting to utilize newly learned skills and is highlighted by the learning curve staff experience as the school district adjusts and integrates new changes into daily work.

Internalizing Concerns. Negative concerns that are direct inward toward the individual and are considered overcontrolled, such as episodes of sadness or fearfulness.

Interrupted Attempt. A behavior in which an individual takes steps toward suicide but the act is stopped by others before the potential for harm has begun.

Intervention Service Delivery Models. Triangular three-tiered frameworks that are utilized to provide evidence-based interventions and programs to children in general education. These evidence-based supports increase in intensity and duration as children do not respond to the interventions and programs provided.

Leadership Drivers. Drivers that focus on management strategies that may arise when implementing MTSS and involve decision-making and providing guidance in the process of employing evidence-based programs.

Local Norms. Norms that compare a student's performance on a measure to their peers within their school districts.

Major Infractions. Infractions that lead to office discipline referrals and result in administrative action. They are also known as major office discipline referrals.

Medical Model. The traditional model of medical practice that focuses on the health of a single individual patient and entails the person waiting to be diagnosed with an illness to receive treatment.

Mindfulness. A therapeutic technique that assists individuals in becoming aware of the present moment by acknowledging one's feelings, thoughts, and bodily sensations.

Minor Infractions. Violations of school conduct that are documented but do not lead to an office discipline referral or result in administrative action.

Minority Stress. The stressors and hardships cultural minorities experience because of their social identity or position.

Modeling. Entails an expert teacher demonstrating how to effectively use an intervention to a novice instructor.

Multitiered Systems of Support (MTSS). A problem-solving framework that houses and integrates intervention service delivery models and is used to improve learning, behavior, and social-emotional outcomes in children.

National Norms. Norms that compare a student's performance on a measure to their peers across the nation to determine whether they are meeting academic and behavioral expectations.

Needs Assessment. A systemic process for identifying and prioritizing needs or "gaps" between current and desired conditions.

No Child Left Behind Act (NCLB). The main federal education law in the United States until the ESSA was signed into law in December 2015.

Nonsuicidal Self-Injurious Behavior. An individual engaging in self-harm that deliberately results in injury or the potential for injury to oneself.

Office Discipline Referrals. Written records of behavioral problems that violate school discipline codes.

Organizational Drivers. Drivers that involve building an infrastructure to facilitate the implementation of MTSS through developing internal and external partnerships, locating funding, allocating resources, and using data for decision-making.

Penn Resiliency Program. A 12-week curriculum designed to teach cognitive, behavioral, and social skills to children ages 10–14 prevent symptoms of depression in children or to remediate risk for depression.

POD-TEAMS Depression Prevention Program. A manualized counseling curriculum designed to assist children ages 13–17 who are at risk for depression.

Preparatory Acts. Incidents in which an individual takes steps toward making a suicide attempt, such as either assembling a method to kill oneself or preparing for one's death by suicide.

Professional Development. The primary vehicle through which implementers learn the rationale for an intervention, its core components, the mechanics through which components impact student outcomes, and the skills to implement the components with high intensity.

Program Evaluation. The systemic evaluation of whether a program or intervention that has been introduced directly led to a significant improvement in the performance of students (Shaw, 2016).

Progress Monitoring. The repeated brief assessment of skills and strategies learned to determine whether a child is responding to the interventions and services being provided.

Promoting Alternative Thinking Strategies. A Tier 1 school-based program for children in grades kindergarten through six that is designed to improve children's ability to discuss and understand emotions, promote social competencies, and manage behavior.

Problem-Solving Process. The process that Lightner Witmer proposed which called for the assessment of a suspected disorder or deficit, developing a hypothesis concerning the appropriate intervention, and the provision and evaluation of the intervention.

Psycho-Education. Providing the child and their caregiver's information and resources on suicidality and teaching them about how to utilize a safety plan at home.

Psycho-Educational Testing. A comprehensive assessment of how a child learns or how a child's social, emotional, or behavioral functioning is impacting their academic performance in school.

Public Health Model. A medical model of practice that emphasizes the overall health of the public through epidemiologic methodology and the prevention of health problems.

Push-In Group Intervention. Instruction that involves either the teacher or content specialist delivering interventions within the classroom to help a small group of students remediate their deficits in reading, writing, or mathematics.

Push-Out Group Intervention. Instruction that involves students leaving the general education classroom to receive supplemental instruction through a specialist or teacher. For instance, three kindergarten students may relocate to the reading specialist's room to receive supplemental instruction in letter–word identification.

Rate of Improvement. The average weekly increases or growth which indicates whether a child is making enough progress to close the gap between current and expected performance.

Relationship Skills. An individual's ability to establish and maintain healthy and rewarding relationships with diverse groups and individuals.

Resource Mapping. The process of evaluating programs, personnel, and services that are available to students and identifying how such resources are currently being used.

Response to Intervention. A triangular three-tiered intervention service delivery model that is focused on providing high quality instruction in reading, writing, and mathematics.

Responsible Decision-Making. Requires the ability to make constructive choices about social interactions and personal behavior based on social norms, ethical standards, and safety concerns.

Safety Plan. A prioritized written list of coping strategies and sources of support children can use if they have been deemed at-risk for suicide.

School-Wide Information System (SWIS). A web-based system developed to collect, summarize, and utilize student behavior data for decision-making.

School-Wide Positive Behavior Support (SWPBS). A triangular three-tiered intervention service delivery model focused on improving school culture and the individual behavior of all students.

Second Step. A Tier 1 SEL program designed to promote interpersonal and intrapersonal competencies and reduce the development of behavioral, social, and emotional problems in children in preschool through eighth grade.

Self-Awareness. The ability to recognize one's own emotions, values, and thoughts and how each may influence behavior.

Self-Management. The ability to successfully regulate emotions, thoughts, and behaviors in different situations and across different contexts.

Severe Discrepancy. See severe discrepancy model.

Severe Discrepancy Model. The traditional model used to determine whether a child has a specific learning disability that has largely been unproven. It was thought that a large point disparity between a child's performance on an intelligence test in comparison to their performance on an achievement test suggested that the child possessed a disability that prevented them from working up to their true potential.

Skillstreaming. A prosocial and emotional program based on social learning theory for children 4–18 years of age that focuses on anger control, conflict management, life skills, character development, and social-emotional learning.

Social, Academic, and Emotional Behavior Risk Screening (SAEBRS). A brief norm referenced nineteen item universal screener for children in grades kindergarten through twelve that is divided into three subscales: social behavior, academic behavior, and emotional behavior.

Social Academic Instructional Group (SAIG). A group intervention used to build a sense of belongingness and restorative practices.

Social-Emotional Check-In/Check-Out. A modified check in/check out designed for children with internalizing deficits in which a student checks in with the CICO coordinator in the morning, afternoon, and at the end of the school day to briefly discuss how they are doing emotionally and provide them healthy coping strategies.

Social-Emotional Learning. The processes through which children and adults acquire and effectively apply the knowledge, attitudes, and skills necessary to understand and manage emotions, set and achieve positive goals, feel and show empathy for others, establish and maintain positive relationships, and make responsible decisions.

Social-Emotional RTI. A triangular three-tiered intervention service delivery model focused on promoting mental wellness and preventing mental illness from developing in children.

Social Discord. The suicide risk factors of alienation, conflict, or lack of integration with one's community, friends, or family.

Strengths and Difficulties Questionnaire. A brief, norm referenced universal screener for social, emotional, and behavioral concerns in children ages 2–17.

Student Risk Screening Scale-Internalizing and Externalizing (SRSS-IE). A 12-item social-emotional and behavior screener and progress monitoring measure that assists in identifying children who are at risk for internalizing and externalizing behavior problems.

Students Exposed to Trauma (SSET). A Tier 2 manualized curriculum that seeks to help children between 10 and 14 years of age who have been exposed to traumatic events learn how to manage their distress.

Suicidal Ideation. Passive or fleeting thoughts about wanting to be dead or active thoughts about killing oneself.

Suicide. Death that results from deliberate self-injurious behavior with any intent to die as a result of the behavior.

SWPBS Tiered Fidelity Inventory (TFI). A fidelity checklist that was developed to assist school personnel in determining whether they are applying the core features of school-wide positive behavior interventions and supports effectively.

Technical Drivers. Drivers that utilize an established protocol to respond to concerns that are often defined without ambiguity and a clear solution is evident.

Tier 1. Refers to universal supports that are delivered to all students. Approximately, 80%–85% of students are expected to respond at the Tier 1 level.

Tier 2. Refers to targeted supports that are delivered to approximately 10%–15% of students with deficits that are beyond the capacity of Tier 1.

Tier 3. Refers to tertiary supports that are designed for one to five present of students with chronic or long-standing deficits that are beyond the capacity of Tier 1 or Tier 2.

Toxic Stress. Exposure to severe and prolonged stress in the absence of protective factors, such as safety, security, social support, or appropriate coping techniques.

Trauma. A real or perceived experience that is significantly distressing and causes feelings of fear, terror, or hopelessness.

Trauma-Informed Approaches and Supports. Preventing adverse events and experiences from occurring by building individual capacity for self-regulation, supporting the individuals experiencing adverse effects from trauma, and avoiding retraumatizing affected individuals.

Treatment Plans. Documents that utilize a child's strengths to deal with presenting concerns and assist the child in reaching or achieving identifiable goals.

Universal Screening. A tool used for the brief systemic assessment of the school population to determine children who are not responding to Tier 1 interventions. These brief assessments are used as the first step in identifying children at risk for academic, behavioral, or social-emotional deficits.

Wait-to-Fail. The practice of children with learning deficits having to wait to academically fall substantially behind their peers in order to receive assistance or be classified as a child with a disability.

• References •

Abramowitz, E. A. (1981). School psychology: A historical perspective. *The Spring Hill Symposium*, 10(2), 121–126.

Al Otaiba, S., Baker K., Lan, P., Allor, J., Rivas, B., Yovanoff, P., & Kamata, A. (2019). Elementary teacher's knowledge of response to intervention implementation: A preliminary factor analysis. *Annals of Dyslexia*, 69(1), 34–53. doi 10.1007/s11881-018-00171-5

Al Otaiba, S., Wagner, R. K., & Miller, B. (2014). "Waiting to fail" redux: Understanding inadequate response to intervention. *Learning Disabilities Quarterly*, 37(3), 129–133. doi 10.1177/0731948714525622

Alegria, M., Chatter, P., Wells, K., Cao, Z., Chen, C., Takeuchi, D., ... Meng, X. (2008). Disparity in depression treatment among racial and ethnic minority populations in the United States. *Psychiatry*, 59(11), 1264–1272. doi: 10.1176/appi.ps.59.11.1264

Alfonso, V. C., & Flanagan, D. P. (2018). *Essentials of specific learning disability identification* (2nd ed.). Hoboken, NJ: Wiley.

Ali, A., & Katz, D. L. (2016). Disease prevention and health promotion: How integrative medicine fits. *American Journal of Preventive Medicine*, 49(5), S230–S240. doi 10.1016/j.amepre.2015.07.019

Allison, A. C., & Ferreira, R. J. (2017). Implementing cognitive behavioral intervention for trauma in schools (CBITS) with Latino youth. *Child & Adolescent Social Work Journal*, 34(2), 181–189. doi:10.1007/s10560-016-0486-9

Altschuld, J. W., & Watkins, R. (2014). A primer on needs assessment: More than 40 years of research and practice. *New Directions for Evaluation*, 144(1), 5–18. doi: 10.1002/ev.20099

American Foundation for Suicide Prevention. (2020, October 12). *State laws: Suicide prevention in schools (K-12)*. Retrieved from https://www.dato-cms-assets.com/12810/1602535612-k-12-schools-issue-brief-10-12-20.pdf

American Psychological Association. (2016). *County-level analysis of U.S. licensed psychologists and health indicators*. Washington, DC: Author.

American Public Health Association. (2021). *What is public health?* Retrieved from https://www.apha.org/what-is-public-health#:~:text=Public%20health%20promotes%20and%20protects,injured%20in%20the%20first%20place

American School Counselor Association. (2019). *ASCA national model: A framework for school counseling programs* (4th ed.). Alexandria, VA: Author.

American School Counselor Association. (2020). *Member demographics*. Retrieved from https://www.schoolcounselor.org/getmedia/9c1d81ab-2484-4615-9dd7-d788a241beaf/member-demographics.pdf

Anderson, G., Freeman, E., & O'Habib, E. (2018, February). How to move a mountain: MTSS and system change. In PowerPoint presentation at the National Association of school Psychologists 2018 Conference, Chicago, IL.

Arby, T., Bryce, C. I., Swanson, J., Bradley, R. H., Fabes, R. A., & Corwyn, R. F. (2017). Classroom-level adversity: Associations with children's internalizing and externalizing behaviors across elementary school. *Developmental Psychology*, 53(3), 497–510. doi: 10.1037/dev0000268

Arden, S., & Pentimonti, J. M. (2017). Data-based decision making in multi-tiered systems of support: Principles, practices, tips, & tools. *Perspectives on Language and Literacy*, 43(4), 19–23. Retrieved from https://mydigitalpublication.com/publication/?i=445106&article_id=2908444&view=articleBrowser&ver=html5#{%22issue_id%22:445106,%22page%22:18}

Ardoin, S. P., & Christ, T. J. (2009). Curriculum-based measurement of oral reading: Standard errors associated with progress monitoring outcomes from DIBELS, AIMSweb, and an experimental passage set. *School Psychology Review*, 38(2), 266–283. Retrieved from https://pdfs.semanticscholar.org/b33b/436fb395d005b562cd643abfd7104b1da0f4.pdf

Artiles, A. J., Bal, Aydin, & King-Thorius, K. (2010). Back to the future: A critique of response to intervention's social justice views. *Theory Into Practice*, 49(4), 250–256. doi: 10.1080/00405841.2010.510447

Au, K. (2009). Isn't culturally responsive instruction just good teaching? *Social Education*, 73(4), 179–183. Retrieved from https://www.socialstudies.org/system/files/publications/articles/se_7304179.pdf

Avant, D. W., & Swerdlik, M. E. (2016). A collaborative endeavor: The roles and functions of school social workers and school psychologists in implementing multi-tiered systems of supports/response to intervention. *School Social Work Journal*, 41(1), 56–72.

Averill, O. H., & Rinaldi, C. (2011). Multi-tier system of supports. *District Administration*, 47(8), 91–95. Retrieved from https://www.researchgate.net/profile/Claudia_Rinaldi/publication/257943817_Multitier_System_of_Supports_A_Description_of_RTI_and_PBIS_Models_for_District_Administrators/links/0046352669d913a09d000000.pdf

Bailey, J. S., Wolf, M. M., & Phillips, E. L. (1970). Home-based reinforcement and the modification of pre-delinquent's classroom behavior. *Journal of Applied Behavior Analysis*, 3(3), 223–233.

Balas, E. A., & Boren, S. A. (2000). Managing clinical knowledge for health care improvement. *Yearbook of Medical Informatics*, 1(1), 65–70. Retrieved from https://autusta.aws.openrepository.com/augusta/bitstream/10675.2/617990/1/Balas_Boren_2000.pdf

Ball, C. R., & Christ, T. J. (2012). Supporting valid decision making: Uses and misuses of assessment data within the context of RTI. *Psychology in the Schools*, 49(3), 231–243. doi: 10.1002/pits.21592

Bambara, L. M., Nonnemacher, S., & Kern, L. (2009). Sustaining school-based individualized positive behavior support. *Journal of Positive Behavior Interventions*, 11(3), 161–176. doi: 10.1177/1098300708330878

Bardach, N. S., Coker, T. R., Zima, B. T., Murphy, J. M., Knapp, P., Richardson, L. P., ... Mangione-Smith, R. (2014). Common and costly hospitalizations for pediatric mental health disorders. *Pediatrics*, 133(4), 602–609. DOI: 10.1542/peds.2013-3165

Bartholomew, M., & De Jong, D. (2017). Barriers to implementing the response to intervention framework in secondary schools: Interviews with secondary principals. *NASSP Bulletin*, 101(4), 261–277. doi 10.1177/0192636517743788

Bastounis, A., Callaghan, P., Banerjee, A., & Michail, M. (2016). The effectiveness of the Penn Resiliency Programme (PRP) and its adapted versions in reducing depression and anxiety and improving explanatory style: A systematic review and meta-analysis. *Journal of Adolescence*, 52, 37–48. doi: 10.1016/j.adolescence.2016.07.004

Bauer, M. S., Damschroder, L., Hagedorn, H., Smith, J., & Kilbourne, A. M. (2015). An introduction to implementation science for the non-specialist. *BMC Psychology*, 3(32), 1–12. doi: 10.1186/s40359-015-0089-9

Beaujean, A., Benson, N. F., McGill, R. J., & Dombrowski, S. (2018). A misuse of IQ scores: Using the dual discrepancy/consistency model for identifying specific learning disabilities. *Journal of Intelligence*, 6(3), 1–25. Retrieved from https://www.mdpi.com/2079-3200/6/3/36

Begeny, J. C., Laugle, K. M., Krouse, H. E., Lynn, A. E., Tayrose, M. P., & Stage, S. A. (2010). A control-group comparison of two reading fluency programs: The Helping Early Literacy with Practice Strategies (HELPS) program and the Great Leaps K-2 reading program. *School Psychology Review*, 39(1), 137–155. doi: 10.1080/02796015.2010.12087795

Behavior Intervention Monitoring System 2. (n.d.). Retrieved from http://www.edumetrisis.com/products/282-bimas-2

Belfied, C., Bowden, B., Klapp, A., & Levin, H. M. (2015). *The economic value of social and emotional learning*. Retrieved from https://www.researchgate.net/publication/272748098_The_Economic_Value_of_Social_and_Emotional_Learning

Bellis, M. A., Hughes, K., Sharples, O., Hennell, T., & Hardcastle, K. A. (2012). Dying to be famous: Retrospective cohort study of rock and pop star mortality and its association with adverse childhood experiences. *BMJ Open*, 2(6), 1–8. doi: 10.1136/bmjopen-2012-002089

Belser, C. T., Shillingford, A. M., & Joe, J. R. (2016). The ASCA model and a multi-tiered system of supports: A framework to support students of color with problem behavior. *The Professional Counselor*, 6(3), 251–262. doi: 10.15241/cb.6.3.251

Benson, N. F., Floyd, R. G., Kranzler, J. H., Eckert, T. L., & Fefer, S. (2018, February). Contemporary assessment practices in school psychology: National survey results. Paper presented at the meeting of the National Association of school Psychologists, Chicago, IL.

Berg, E. (2019). Multi-tiered approaches to trauma-informed care in schools: A systemic review. *School Mental Health*, 11(4), 650–664. doi: 10.1007/s12310-019-09326-0

Berg, J. K., & Cornell, D. (2016). Authoritative school climate, aggression toward teachers, and teacher distress in middle school. *School Psychology Quarterly*, 31(1), 122–139. doi: 10.1037/spq0000132

Bernhardt, V. L. (2017). *Data analysis for continuous school improvement* (5th ed.). New York, NY: Routledge.

Bjorn, P. M., Aro, M. T., Koponen, T. K., Fuchs, L. S., & Fuchs, D. H. (2015). The many faces of special education within RTI frameworks in the United States and Finland. *Learning Disability Quarterly*, 39(1), 1–9. doi: 10.1177/0731948715594787

Boccio, D. E., Weisz, G., & Lefkowitz, R. (2016a). Administrative pressure to practice unethically and burnout within the profession of school psychology. *Psychology in the Schools*, 53(6), 659–672. doi: 10.1002/pits.21931

Boccio, D. E., Weisz, G., & Lefkowitz, R. (2016b). School psychologists' management of administrative pressure to practice unethically. *Journal of Applied School Psychology*, 32(4), 313–328. doi: 10.1080/15377903.2016.1207737

Bock, R. (1998). *Why children succeed or fail at reading: Research from NICHD's program in learning disabilities.* Retrieved from https://archive.org/details/ERIC_ED427293

Bohanon, H., Gilman, C., Parker, B., Arnell, C., & Sortino, G. (2016). Using school improvement and implementation science to integrate multi-tiered systems of support in secondary schools. *Australian Journal of Special Education*, 40(2), 99–116. doi: 10.1017/jse.2016.8

Bohanon, H., & Wu, M. J. (2014). Developing buy-in for positive behavior support in secondary settings. *Preventing School Failure*, 58(4), 223–229. doi:10.1080/1045988X.2013.798774

Borghans, L., Golsteyn, B. H., Heckman, J. J., & Humphries, J. E. (2016). What grades and achievement tests measure. *Proceedings of the National Academy of Sciences*, 113(47), 13354–13359. doi: 10.1073/pnas.1601135113

Bowman-Perrott, L., Burke, M. D., de Marin, Zhang, N., & Davis, H. (2015). A meta-analysis of single-case research on behavior contracts: Effects on behavioral and academic outcomes among children and youth. *Behavior Modification*, 39(2), 247–269. doi: 10.1177/0145445514551383

Bowman-Perrott, L., Burke, M. D., Zaini, S., Zhang, N., & Vannest, K. (2016). Promoting positive behavior using the good behavior game: A meta-analysis of single-case research. *Journal of Positive Behavior Interventions*, 18(3), 180–190. doi: 10.1177/1098300715592355

Breux P., & Boccio D. E. (2019). Improving schools' readiness for involvement in suicide prevention: An evaluation of the creating suicide safety in schools (CSSS) workshop. *International Journal of Environmental Research and Public Health*, 16(12), 1–15. doi: 10.3390/ijerph16122165

Breux, P., & Samet, M. (2019). *A guide for suicide prevention in New York schools.* Retrieved from https://www.preventsuicideny.org/wpcontent/uploads/2019/08/SchoolsSuicidePreventionGuide.pdf

Breux, P., Samet, M., Nickerson, A., & Schaffer, G. E. (2018). *Helping students at risk for suicide: Assessment, intervention, and follow-up for school-based practitioners training curriculum.* Albany, NY: Suicide Prevention Center of New York State and New York Association of School Psychologists.

Bridge, J. A., Asti, L., Horowitz, L. M., Greenhouse, J. B., Fontanella, C. A., Sheftall, A. H., ... Campo, J. V. (2015). Suicide trends among elementary school-aged children in the United States from 1993 to 2012. *JAMA Pediatrics*, 169(7), 673–677. doi: 10.1001/jamapediatrics.2015.0465

Bridgeland, J., Bruce, M., & Hariharan, A. (2013). *The missing piece: A national survey on how social and emotional learning can empower children and transform schools.* Washington, DC: Civic Enterprises/Hart Research Associates. Retrieved from https://casel.org/wp-content/uploads/2016/01/the-missing-piece.pdf

Brown, M. B., Holcombe, D. C., Bolen, L. M., & Thomson, W. S. (2006). Role function and job satisfaction of school psychologists practicing in an expanded role model. *Psychological Reports*, 98(2), 486–496. doi: 10.2466/pr0.98.2

Brown, R. C., & Plener, P. L. (2017). Non-suicidal self-injury in adolescence. *Current Psychiatry Reports*, 19(20), 1–8. doi: 10.1007/s11920-017-0767-9

Brownell, M. T., Sindelar, P. T., & Danielson, L. C. (2010). Special education teacher quality and preparation: Exposing foundations, constructing a new model. *Council for Exceptional Children*, 76(3), 357–377. doi: 10.1177/001440291007600307

Bruhn, A. L., Woods-Groves, S., & Huddle, S. (2014) A preliminary investigation of emotional and behavioral screening practices in K–12 schools. *Education and Treatment of Children* 37(4), 611–634. doi: 10.1353/etc.2014.0039

Bruns, E. J., Duong, M. T., Lyon, A. R., Pullmann, M. D., Cook, C. R., Cheney, D., & McCauley, E. (2016). Fostering SMART partnerships to develop an effective continuum of behavioral health and supports in schools. *American Journal of Orthopsychiatry*, 86(2), 156–170. doi: 10.1037/ort0000083

Brunwasser, S. M., Gillham, J. E., & Kim, E. S. (2009). A meta-analytic review of the Penn Resiliency Program's effect on depressive symptoms. *Journal of Consulting and Clinical Psychology*, 77(6), 1042–1054. doi: 10.1037/a0017671

Burke, T. A., Hamilton, J. L., Ammerman, B. A., Stange, J. P., & Alloy, L. B. (2017). Suicide risk characteristics among aborted, interrupted, and actual suicide attempters. *Psychiatry Research*, 242, 357–364. doi: 10.1016/j.psychres.2016.05.051

Burstein, B., Agostino, H., & Greenfield, B. (2019). Suicidal attempts and ideation among children and adolescents in US emergency departments, 2007–2015. *JAMA Pediatrics*, 173(6), 598–600. doi: 10.1001/jamapediatrics.2019.0464

Butler, H. A., Pentoney, C., & Bong, M. P. (2017). Predicting real-world outcomes: Critical thinking ability is a better predictor of life decisions than intelligence. *Thinking Skills and Creativity*, 25, 38–46. doi: 10.1016/j.tsc.2017.06.005

Cammack N. L., Brandt N. E., Slade E., Lever, N. A., & Stephan S. (2014). Funding expanded school mental health programs. In M. Weist, N. Lever, C. Bradshaw, & J. Owens (Eds.), *Handbook of school mental health: Research, training, practice, and policy* (pp. 17–30). New York, NY: Springer.

Cardemil, E. V., Reivich, K. J., & Seligman, M. E. P. (2002). The prevention of depressive symptoms in low-income minority middle school students. *Prevention & Treatment*, 5(1), Article 8. doi: 10.1037/1522-3736.5.1.58a

Carey, R. L., Yee, L. S., & DeMatthews, D. (2018). Power, penalty, & critical praxis: Employing intersectionality in educator practices to achieve school equity. *The Educational Forum*, 82(1), 111–130. doi: 10.1080/00131725.2018.1381793

Castro-Olivo, S. M. (2017). Introduction to special issue: Culturally responsive school-based mental health interventions. *Contemporary School Psychology*, 21(3), 177–180. doi: 10.1007/s40688-017-0137-y

Castro-Olivo, S., Preciado, J., Le, L., Marciante, M., & Garcia, M. (2018). The effects of culturally adapted version of First Steps to Success for Latino English language learners: Preliminary pilot study. *Psychology in the Schools*, 55(1), 36–49. doi: 10.1002/pits.22092

Cavanaugh, B. (2016). A preliminary investigation examining the use of minor discipline referral data to identify students at risk for behavioral difficulties: Observations within systems of schoolwide positive behavior interventions and supports. *Journal of Applied School Psychology*, 32(4), 354–366. doi: 10.1080/15377903.2016.1207739

Center for Deployment Psychology. (n.d.). *Columbia suicide severity rating scale (C-SSRS)*. Retrieved from https://deploymentpsych.org/system/files/member_resource/C-SSRS%20Factsheet.pdf

Centers for Disease Control and Prevention. (2020). *Introduction to public health model*. Retrieved from https://www.cdc.gov/violenceprevention/about/publichealthapproach.html

Center for Mental Health Services, Substance Abuse and Mental Health Services Administration (SAMHSA) (2012). *Preventing suicide: A toolkit for high schools* (HHS Publication No. 02-2650). Retrieved from http://store.samhsa.gov/product/Preventing-Suicide-A-Toolkit-for-High-Schools/SMA12-4669

Centers for Disease Control and Prevention. (2017). *Ten leading causes of death by age group, United States—2017*. Retrieved from https://www.cdc.gov/injury/images/lc-charts/leading_causes_of_death_by_age_group_2017_1100w850h.jpg

Centers for Disease Control and Prevention. (2018). *Introduction to epidemiology*. Retrieved from https://www.cdc.gov/training/publichealth101/epidemiology.html

Center on Instruction. (2008). *Fidelity checklist*. Retrieved from http://www.rtictrl.org/files/Fidelity%20Checklist%20A.pdf

Centers for Disease Control and Prevention. (2019). *What are childhood mental health disorders*. Retrieved from https://www.cdc.gov/childrensmentalhealth/basics.html

Chambers, J. G., Perez, M., Harr, J. J., & Shkolnik, J. (2005). Special education spending estimates from 1969–2000. *Journal of Special Education Leadership*, 18(1), 5–13. Retrieved from http://www.casecec.org/documents/JSEL/JSEL_18.1_Apr2005.pdf

Cheney, D., Flower, A., & Templeton, T. (2008). Applying response to intervention metrics in the social domain for students at risk of developing emotional or behavioral disorders. *Journal of Special Education*, 42(2), 108–126. doi: 10.1177/0022466907313349

Choi, J. H., McCart, A. B., Hicks, T. A., & Sailor, W. (2019). An analysis of mediating effects of school leadership on MTSS implementation. *Journal of Special Education*, 53(1), 15–27. doi: 10.1177/0022466918804815

Christ, T. J., Zopluoglu, C., Monaghen, B. D., & Van Norman, E. R. (2013). Curriculum-based measurement of oral reading: Multi-study evaluation of schedule, duration, and dataset quality on progress monitoring outcomes. *Journal of School Psychology*, 51(1), 19–57. doi: 10.1016/j.jsp.2012.11.001

Chu, J., Chi, K., Chen, K., & Leino, A. (2014). Ethnic variations in suicidal ideation and behaviors: A prominent subtype marked by nonpsychiatric factors among Asian Americans. *Journal of Clinical Psychology*, 70(12), 1211–1226. doi: 10.1002/jclp.22082

Chu, J., Floyd, R., Diep, H., Pardo, S., Goldblum, P., & Bongar, B. (2013). A tool for the culturally competent assessment of suicide: The Cultural Assessment of Risk for Suicide (CARS) Measure. *Psychological Assessment*, 25(2), 424–434. doi: 10.1037/a0031264

Chu, J., Khoury, O., Ma, J., Bahn, F., Bongar, B., & Goldblum, P. (2017). An empirical model and ethnic differences in cultural meanings via motives for suicide. *Journal of Clinical Psychology*, 73(10), 1343–1359. doi: 10.1002/jclp.22425

Chu, J. P., Goldblum, P., Floyd, R., & Bongar, B. (2010). The cultural theory and model of suicide. *Applied and Preventative Psychology*, 14(1–4), 25–40. doi: 10.1016/j.appsy.2011.11.001

Chung, D. T., Ryan, C. J., Hadzi-Pavlovic, D., Singh, S. P., Stanton, C., & Large, M. M. (2017). Suicide rates after discharge from psychiatric facilities: A systematic review and meta-analysis. *JAMA Psychiatry*, 74(7), 694–702. doi: 10.1001/jamapsychiatry.2017.10

Cicero, K. (n.d.). *44 children's books about mental health*. Retrieved from childmind.org/article/best-childrens-books-about-mental-health/

Clarke, G., McGlinchey, E. L., Hein, K., Gullion, C. M., Dickerson, J. F., Leo, M. C., & Harvey, A. G. (2015). Cognitive-behavioral treatment of insomnia and depression in adolescents: A pilot randomized trial. *Behaviour Research and Therapy*, 69, 111–118. doi: 10.1016/j.brat.2015.04.009

Clay, R. R. (2018). The cultural distinctions in whether, when and how people engage in suicidal behavior. *American Psychological Association CE Corner*, 49(6), 28–35. Retrieved from https://www.apa.org/monitor/2018/06/ce-corner

Cognitive Behavioral Intervention for Trauma in Schools [CBITS]. (n.d.). Retrieved from https://cbitsprogram.org/

Collaborative for Academic, Social, and Emotional Learning [CASEL]. (2019). *Overview of SEL*. Retrieved from https://casel.org/overview-sel/

Collins, L. W., & Zirkel, P. A. (2017). Functional behavior assessments and behavior intervention plans legal requirements and professional recommendations. *Journal of Positive Behavior Interventions*, 19(3), 180–190. doi: 10.1177/1098300716682201

Columbia University. (2022). *The Columbia lighthouse project/ Columbia suicide severity rating scale*. Retrieved from https://childadolescentpsych.cumc.columbia.edu/professionals/research-programs/columbia-suicide-severity-rating-scale-c-ssrs

Conoley, J. C., Powers, K., & Gutkin, T. B. (2020). How is school psychology doing: Why hasn't school psychology realized its promise? *School Psychology*, 35(6), 367–374. doi: 10.1037/spq0000404

Cook, C. R., Lyon, A. R., Kubergovic, D., Wright, & Zhang (2015). A supportive beliefs intervention to facilitate the implementation of evidence-based practices within a multi-tiered systems of supports. *School Mental Health*, 7(1), 49–60. doi: 10.1007/s12310-014-9139-3

Copeland, W. E., Keeler, G., Angold, A., & Costello, E. J. (2007). Traumatic events and posttraumatic stress in childhood. *Archives of General Psychiatry*, 64(5), 577–584. doi: 10.1001/archpyshc.64.5.577

Cortiella, C., & Horowitz, S. H. (2014). *The state of learning disabilities: Facts, trends, and emerging issues*. New York, NY: National Center for Learning Disabilities.

Crean, H. F., & Johnson, D. B. (2013). Promoting alternative thinking strategies (PATHS) and elementary school aged children's aggression: Results from a cluster randomized trial. *American Journal of Community Psychology*, 52(1–2), 56–72. doi: 10.1007/s10464-013-9576-4

Cross, C. (2001). *Heavier than heaven: A biography of Kurt Cobain*. Hyperion: New York, NY.

Cuellar, A. (2015). Preventing and treating child mental health problems. *Future of Children*, 25(1), 111–134. Retrieved from https://files.eric.ed.gov/fulltext/EJ1062954.pdf

D'Amato, R. C., Zafiris, C., McConnell, E., & Dean, R. S. (2011). The history of school psychology: Understanding the past to not repeat it. In M. Bray & T. Kehle (Eds.), *The Oxford handbook of school psychology* (pp. 9–46). New York, NY: Oxford University Press Inc.

Dart, E. H., Furlow, C. M., Brewer, E., Collings, T. A., Gresham, F. M., & Chenier, K. H. (2015). Peer-mediated check-in/check-out for students at-risk for internalizing disorders. *School Psychology Quarterly*, 30(2), 229–243. doi: 10.1037/spq0000092

David-Ferdon, C., Crosby, A. E., Caine, E. D., Hindman, J., Reed, J., & Iskander, J. (2016). Grand rounds: Preventing suicide through a comprehensive public health approach. *Centers for Disease Control and Prevention Morbidity and Mortality Weekly Report*, 65(34), 894–897. Retrieved from: https://www.cdc.gov/mmwr/volumes/65/wr/mm6534a2.htm?s_cid=mm6534a2_w#suggestedcitation

Dazzi, T., Gribble, R., Wessely, S., & Fear, N. T. (2014). Does asking about suicide and related behaviours induce suicidal ideation? What is the evidence? *Psychological Medicine*, 44(16), 3361–3363. doi: 10.1017/S0033291714001299

Dean, H. (2012, July). *Introduction to public health, epidemiology, and surveillance*. PowerPoint presentation at the U.S. Department of Health and Human Services, CDC Science Ambassador Program, Atlanta, GA.

DeRigne, L., Porterfield, S., & Metz, S. (2009). The influence of health insurance on parent's reports of children's unmet mental health needs. *Maternal and Child Health Journal*, 13(2), 176–186. doi:10.1007/s10995-008-0346-0

Deutz, M. H. F., Shi, Q., Vossenm H. G. M., Huijding, J., Prinzie, P., Dekovic, M., ... Woltering, S. (2018). Evaluation of the strengths and differences questionnaire-dysregulation profile (SDQ-DP). *Psychological Assessment*, 30(9), 1174–1185. doi: 10.1037/pas0000564

Drevon, D. D., Hixson, M. D., Wyse, R. D., & Rigney, A. M. (2018). A meta-analytic review of the evidence for check-in check-out. *Psychology in the Schools*, 56(3), 393–412. doi: 10.1002/pits.22195

Drummond, R. (1994). *The student risk screening scale (SRSS)*. Grants Pass, OR: Josephine County Mental Health Program.

Dulaney, S. K., Hallman, P. R., & Wall, G. (2013). Superintendent perceptions of multi-tiered systems of support (MTSS): Obstacles and opportunities for school system reform. *AASA Journal of Scholarship and Practice*, 10(2), 30–45. Retrieved from http://aasa.org/uploadedFiles/Publica-tions/Journals/AASA_Journal_of_Scholarship_and_Practice/JSP_Summer2013.FINAL.pdf#page=30

Durand, V. M., & Crimmins, D. B. (1988). Motivational assessment scale. In M. Hersen & A. Bellack (Eds.), *Dictionary of behavioral assessment techniques* (pp. 309–310). Elmsford, NY: Pergamon.

Durlak, J. A., Weissberg, R. P., Dymnicki, A. B., Taylor, R. D., & Schellinger, K. B. (2011). The impact of enhancing students' social and emotional learning: A meta-analysis of school-based universal interventions. *Child Development*, 82(1), 405–432. doi: 10.1111/j.1467-8624.2010.01564.x

Dusenbury, L., & Weissberg, R. P. (2018). *Emerging insights from states' efforts to strengthen social and emotional learning* (CASEL Report). Retrieved from https://casel.org/wp-content/uploads/2018/06/CSI-Insights.pdf

Eagle, J. W., Dowd-Eagle, S. E., Snyder, A., & Holtzman, E. G. (2015). Implementing a multi-tiered system of support (MTSS): Collaboration between school psychologists and administrators to promote systems-level change. *Journal of Educational and Psychological Consultation*, 25(2–3), 160–177. doi: 10.1080/10474412.2014.929960

Edmunds, D. (2015). *Toolbox coping cards (version 1)* [Mobile application software]. Retrieved from https://apps.apple.com/us/app/toolbox-coping-cards/id985109073

Eklund, K., Kilgus, S. P., Izumi, J., DeMarchena, S. L., & McCollom, E. M. (2021). The resilience education program: Examining the efficacy of a Tier 2 internalizing intervention. *Psychology in the Schools*, 58(11), 2114–2129. doi: 10.1002/pits.22580

Eklund, K., Kilpatrick, K. D., Kilgus, S. P., & Haider, A. (2018). A systemic review of state-level social-emotional learning standards: Implications for practice and research. *School Psychology Review*, 47(3), 316–326. doi: 10.17105/SPR-2017.0116.V47-3

Eklund, K., Meyer L., Way, S., & Mclean, D. (2017). School psychologists as mental health providers: The impact of staffing ratios and Medicaid on service provisions. *Psychology in the Schools*, 54(3), 279–293. doi: 10.1002/pits.21996

Elias, M. J., Zins, J. E., Weissberg, R. P., Frey, K. S., Greenberg, M. T., Haynes, N. M., … Shriver, T. P. (1997). *Promoting social and emotional learning: Guidelines for educators*. Alexandria, VA: Association for Supervision and Curriculum Development.

Ervin, R. A., Schaughency, E., Matthews, A., Goodman, S. D., & McGlinchey, M. T. (2007). Primary and secondary prevention of behavior difficulties: Developing a data-informed problem solving model to guide decision making at a school-wide level. *Psychology in the Schools*, 44(1), 7–18. doi: 10.1002/pits.20201

Espelage, D. L., Low, S., Polanin, J. R., & Brown, E. C. (2015). Clinical trial of Second Step© middle-school program: Impact on aggression & victimization. *Journal of Applied Developmental Psychology*, 37, 52–63. doi: 10.1016/j.appdev.2014.11.007

Espin, C. A., Wayman, M. M., Deno, S. L., & McMaster, K. L. (2017). Data-based decision making: Developing a method for capturing teachers' understanding of CBM graphs. *Learning Disabilities Research & Practice*, 32(1), 8–21. doi: 10.1111/ldrp.12123

Every Student Succeeds Act, 114 U.S.C. § 1177. (2015).

Fagan, T. K. (1996). Witmer's contributions to school psychological services. *American Psychologist*, 51(3), 241–243.

Fagan, T. K., & Wise, P. S. (2007). *School psychology past, present, and future* (3rd ed.). Bethesda, MD: National Association of School Psychologists.

Fallon, L. M., McCarthy, S. R., & Sanetti, L. M. (2014). School-wide positive behavior support (SWPBS) in the classroom assessing perceived challenges to consistent implementation in Connecticut schools. *Education and Treatment of Children*, 37(1), 1–24. doi: 10.1353/etc.2014.0001

Fan, C., Denner, P. R., Bocanegra, J. O., & Ding, Y. (2016) School psychologists' willingness to implement RtI: The role of philosophical and practical readiness. *Contemporary School Psychology*, 20(4), 383–391. doi: 10.1007/s40688-016-0096-8

Farmer, E. M., Burns, B. J., Phillips, S. D., Angold, A., & Costello, E. J. (2003). Pathways into and through mental health services for children and adolescents. *Psychiatric Services*, 54(1), 60–66. doi: 10.1002/pits.20203

Farmer, R. F., & Chapman, A. L. (2016). *Behavioral interventions in cognitive behavior therapy: Guidance for putting theory into action* (2nd ed.). Washington, DC: American Psychological Association.

Farrell, P. (2010). School psychology: Learning lessons from history and moving forward. *School Psychology International*, 31(6), 581–598. doi: 10.1177/0143034310386533

Federal Register. (2006). Part II Department of Education. 34 CFR Parts 300 and 301. Assistance to States for the education of children with disabilities and preschool grants for children with disabilities *Final Rule*, 71(256), 46540–46845.

Felitti, V. J., Anda, R. F., Nordenberg, D., Williamson, D. F., Spitz, A. M., Edwards, V., … Marks, J. S. (1998). Relationship of childhood abuse and household dysfunction to many of the leading causes of death in adults. The Adverse Childhood Experiences (ACE) Study. *American Journal of Preventive Medicine*, 14(4), 245–258. doi: 10.1016/s0749-3797(98)00017-8

Fetterman, H., Ritter, C., Morrison, J. Q., & Newman, D. S. (2020). Implementation fidelity of culturally responsive school-wide positive behavior interventions and supports in a Spanish-language magnet school: A case study emphasizing content. *Journal of Applied Psychology*, 36(1), 89–106. doi: 10.1080/15377903.2019.1665607

Fixsen, D. L., Blasé, K. A., Timbers, G. D., & Wolf, M. M. (2001). In search of program implementation: 792 replications of the teaching-family model. In G. A. Bernfeld, D. P. Farrington, & A. W. Leschied (Eds.), *Offender rehabilitation in practice: Implementing and evaluating effective programs* (pp. 149–166). London: Wiley.

Fixsen, D. L., Naoom, S. F., Blase, K. A., Friedman, R. M., & Wallace, F. (2005). *Implementation research: A synthesis of the literature*. Tampa, FL: University of South Florida. Retrieved from http://nirn.fpg.unc.edu/sites/nirn.fpg.unc.edu/files/resources/NIRN-MonographFull-01-2005.pdf

Flannery, K. B., Fenning, P., Kato, M. M., & Bohanon, H. (2011). A descriptive study of office disciplinary referrals in high schools. *Journal of Emotional and Behavioral Disorders*, 21(2), 138–149. doi: 10.1177/1063426611419512

Fletcher, J. M., Lyon, G. R., Barnes, M., Stuebing, K. K., Francis, D. J., Olson, R. K., ... Shaywitz, B. A. (2002). Classification of learning disabilities: An evidence-based evaluation. In R. Bradley, L. Danielson, & D. Hallahan (Eds.), *Identification of learning disabilities: Research to Practice* (pp. 185–285). Mahwah, NJ: Lawrence Erlbaum Associates.

Fletcher, J. M., Lyon, G. R., Fuchs, L. S., & Barnes, M. A. (2019). *Learning disabilities: From identification to intervention* (2nd ed.). New York, NY: The Guildford Press.

Fletcher, J. M., & Miciak, J. (2017). Comprehensive cognitive assessments are not necessary for the identification and treatment of learning disabilities. *Clinical Neuropsychology*, 31(1), 2–7. doi: 10.1093/arclin/acw103

Floyd R. G. (2010). Assessment of cognitive abilities and cognitive processes: Issues, applications, and fit within a problem-solving model. In G. Peacock, R. Ervin, E. Daly, & K. Merrell (Eds.), *Practical handbook of school psychology: Effective practices for the 21st century* (pp. 48–66). New York, NY: The Guilford Press.

Foley, E. A., Dozier, C. L., & Lessor, A. L. (2019). Comparison of components of the good behavior game in a preschool classroom. *Journal of Applied Behavior Analysis*, 52(1), 84–104. doi: 10.1002/jaba.506

Ford, D. Y., & Kea, C. D. (2009). Creating culturally responsive intervention: For students' and teachers' sakes. *Focus on Exceptional Children*, 41(9), 1–16. Retrieved from https://pdfs.semanticscholar.org/4084/5155a0afe7be67867c264402996981cf9443.pdf

Forman, S. G., Codding, R. S., Reddy, L. A., Sanetti, L. M., Shapiro, E. S., Gonzales, J. E., ... Stoiber, K. C. (2013). Implementation science and school psychology. *School Psychology Quarterly*, 28(2), 77–100. doi: 10.1037/spq0000019

Forman, S. G., & Selman, J. S. (2011). Systems-based service delivery in school psychology. In M. A. Bray., & T. J. Kehle (Eds.), *The Oxford handbook of school psychology* (pp. 628–646). New York, NY: Oxford University Press.

Franco, D. (2018). Trauma without borders: The necessity for school-based interventions in treating unaccompanied refugee minors. *Child and Adolescent Social Work Journal*, 35(6), 551–565. doi: 10.1007/s10560-018-0552-6

Freeman, R., Miller, D., & Newcomer, L. (2015). Integration of academic and behavioral MTSS at the district level using implementation science. *Learning Disabilities: A Contemporary Journal*, 13(1), 59–72. Retrieved from http://www.morningsideacademy.org/wp-content/uploads/2015/10/LDCJ-3-15-web.pdf#page=10

Friedman, I. A. (1995). Student behavior patterns contributing to teacher burnout. *Journal of Educational Research*, 88(5), 281–289. Retrieved from https://www.researchgate.net/publication/241739612_Student_Behavior_Patterns_Contributing_to_Teacher_Burnout/link/5a4f3c7d0f7e9bbfacfcf5ee/download

Fuchs, L. S., Fuchs, D., Compton, D. L., Wehby, J., Schumacher, R. F., Gersten, R., & Jordan, N. C. (2015). Inclusion verses specialized intervention for very-low-performing students: What does access mean in an era of academic challenge? *Exceptional Children*, 81(2), 134–157. doi: 10.1177/0014402914551743

Gage, N. A. (2015). *Evidence-based practices for classroom and behavior management: Tier 2 and Tier 3 strategies* (Document No. IC-15). Retrieved from University of Florida, Collaboration for Effective Educator, Development, Accountability, and Reform Center website: http://ceedar.education.ufl.edu/tools/innovation-configurations/

Gage, N. A., Lee, A., Grasley-Boy, N., & George, H. P. (2018). The impact of school-wide positive behavior interventions and supports on school suspensions: A statewide quasi-experimental analysis. *Journal of Positive Behavior Interventions*, 20(4), 217–226. doi: 10.1177/1098300718768204

Gagnon, J. C., Barber, B. R., & I. Soyturk. (2018). Positive behavior interventions and supports implementation in secure care juvenile justice schools: Results of a national survey of school administrators. *Behavioral Disorders*, 44(1), 3–19. doi: 10.1177/0198742918763946

Garvik, M., Idsoe, T., & Bru, E. (2014). Effectiveness study of a CBT-based adolescent coping with depression course. *Emotional and Behavioural Difficulties*, 19(2), 195–209: doi: 10.1080/13632752.2013.840959

Gelbar, N. W., Jaffery, R., Stein, R., & Cybala, H. (2015). Case study on the implementation of school-wide positive behavioral interventions and supports in an alternative educational setting. *Journal of Educational and Psychological Consultation*, 25(4), 287–313. doi: 10.1080?10474412.2014.929958

Gladstone, T. R., Beardslee, W. R., & Diehl, A. (2015). The impact of parental depression on children. In A. Reupert, D. Maybery, J. Nicholson, M. Göpfert, & M. V. Seeman (Eds.),

Parental psychiatric disorder: Distressed parents and their families (3rd ed.). Cambridge: Cambridge University Press.

Glenn, C. R., Lanzillo, E. C., Esposito, E. C., Santee, A. C., Nock, M. K., & Auerbach, R. P. (2017). Examining the course of suicidal and nonsuicidal self-injurious thoughts and behaviors in outpatient and inpatient adolescents. *Journal of Abnormal Child Psychology*, 45(5), 971–983. doi: 10.1007/s10802-016-0214-0

Goforth, A. N., Farmer, R. L., Kim, S. Y., Naser, S. C., Lockwood, A. B., & Affrunti, N. (2021). Status of school psychology in 2020: Part 1, demographics of the NASP membership survey. *NASP Research Reports*, 5(2), 1–17. Retrieved from https://www.nasponline.org/Documents/Research%20and%20PolicyResearch%20Center/NRR_2020-Membership-Survey-P1.pdf

Goforth, A. N., Nicholas, L. M., Stanick, C. F., Shindorf, Z. R., & Holter, O. (2017). School-based considerations for supporting Arab American youths' mental health. *Contemporary School Psychology*, 21(3), 191–200. doi: 10.1007/s40688-016-0117-7

Goldston, D. B., Molock, S. D., Whitbeck, L. B., Murakami, J. L., Zayas, L. H., & Hall, G. C. (2008). Cultural considerations in adolescent suicide prevention and psychosocial treatment. *The American Psychologist*, 63(1), 14–31. doi: 10.1037/0003-066X.63.1.14

Gopalan, G., Horen, M. J., Bruns, E., Corey, M., Meteyer, S., Pardue, M., ... Matarese, M. (2017). Caregiver perceptions of parent peer support services within the wraparound service delivery. *Journal of Family Studies*, 26(7), 1923–1935. doi: 10.1007/s10826-017-017-0704-x

Gotay, S. (2013) Enhancing emotional awareness of at-risk youth through game play. *Journal of Creativity in Mental Health*, 8(2), 151–161. doi: 10.1080/15401383.2013.792221

Grant, S., Hamilton, L. S., Wrabel, S. L., Gomez, C. J., Whitaker, A., Tamargo, J., ... Ramos, A. (2017). *Social and emotional learning interventions under the every student succeeds act: Evidence review*. Santa Monica, CA: RAND Corporation. Retrieved from https://www.rand.org/content/dam/rand/pubs/research_reports/RR2100/RR2133/RAND_ RR2133.pdf

Green, A. (2011). *Don't feed the worry bug*. Jersey City, NJ: Monsters in My Head.

Green, C., Moshe, J., Shattuck, M., Azerrad, M., & Khoshbin, N. (Producers), & Schnack, A. J. (Director). (2006). *About a son* [Video documentary]. Los Angeles, CA: Shout Factory.

Green, L. A., & Seifert, C. M. (2005). Translation of research into practice: Why we can't "just do it". *The Journal of the American Board of Family Practice*, 18(6), 541–545. doi: 10.3122/jabfm.18.6.541

Greenberg, M. T., Domitrovich, C. E., Weissberg, R. P., & Durlak, J. A. (2017). Social and emotional learning as a public health approach to education. *Future of Children*, 27(1), 13–32. doi: 10.1353/foc.2017.0001

Gresham, F. M. (1991). Conceptualizing behavior disorders in terms of resistance to intervention. *School Psychology Review*, 20(1), 23–36.

Gresham, F. M. (2005). Response to intervention: An alternative means of identifying students as emotionally disturbed. *Education and Treatment of Children*, 28(4), 328–344. Retrieved from http://www.pent.ca.gov/pos/rti/rtialternativemeans_gresham.pdf

Gresham, F. M. (2007). Response to intervention and emotional and behavioral disorders: Best practices in assessment for intervention. *Assessment for Effective Intervention*, 32(4), 214–222. doi: 10.1177/15345084070320040301

Gresham, F. M., MacMillan, D., Beebe-Frankenberger, M. E. & Bocian, K. M. (2000). Treatment integrity in learning disabilities intervention research: Do we really know how treatments are implemented? *Learning Disabilities Research & Practice*, 15(4), 198–205.

Gresham, F. M., Reschly, D., & Shinn, M. R. (2010). RTI as a driving force in educational improvement: Historical legal, research, and practice perspectives. In M. R. Shinn & H. M. Walker (Eds.), *Interventions for achievement and behavior problems in a three-tier model, including RTI* (pp. 47–78). Bethesda, MD: National Association of School Psychologists.

Griffiths, A., Diamond, E. L., Alsip, J., Furlong, M., Morrison, G., & Do, B. (2019). School-wide implementation of positive behavioral interventions and supports in an alternative school setting: A case study. *Journal of Community Psychology*, 47(6), 1493–1513. doi: 10.1002/jcop.22203

Hale, J. B. (2008). *Response to intervention: Guidelines for parents and practitioners*. Retrieved from http://www.wrightslaw.com/idea/art/rti.hale.htm

Hale, J. B., Fiorello, C. A., Miller, J. A., Wenrich, K., Teodori, A., & Henzel, J. N. (2008). WISC-IV interpretation for specific learning disabilities identification and intervention: A cognitive hypothesis testing approach. In A. Prifitera, D. Saklofske, & L. Weiss (Eds.), *WISC-IV clinical assessment and intervention* (2nd ed.). (pp. 109–172). San Diego, CA: Academic Press.

Hallahan, D. P., & Mock, D. R. (2003). A brief history of the field of learning disabilities. In H. Swanson, K. Harris, & S. Graham (Eds.), *Handbook of learning disabilities* (pp. 16–29). New York, NY: The Guilford Press.

Hamilton, L., Halverson, R., Jackson, S., Mandinach, E., Supovitz, J., & Wayman, J. (2009). *Using student achievement data to support instructional decision making* (NCEE 2009-4067). Washington, DC: National Center for Education

Evaluation and Regional Assistance, Institute of Education Sciences, U.S. Department of Education. Retrieved from http://ies.ed.gov/ncee/wwc/publications/practiceguides/

Harlacher, J. E., Sanford, A., & Nelson Walker, N. (2014). *Distinguishing between Tier 2 and Tier 3 instruction in order to support implementation of RTI.* RTI Action Network Monthly Newsletter. Retrieved from http://www.rtinetwork.org/essential/tieredinstruction/tier3/distinguishing-between-tier-2-and-tier-3-instruction-in-order-to-support-implementation-of-rti

Harn, B., Basaraba, D., Chard, D., & Fritz, R. (2015). The impact of schoolwide prevention efforts: Lessons learned from implementing independent academic and behavior support systems. *Learning Disabilities: A Contemporary Journal*, 13(1), 3–20. Retrieved from http://www.morningsideacademy.org/wp-content/uploads/2015/10/

Hasbro. (2017). *Jenga* [Board game]. Pawtucket, RI: Author.

Hawken, L. S., Bundock, K., Kladis, K., O'Keeffe, & Barrett, C. A. (2014). Systemic review of the check-in check-out intervention for students at risk for emotional and behavioral disorders. *Education and Treatment of Children*, 37(4), 635–658. doi: 10.1353/etc/2014.0030

Haydon, T., Musti-Rao, S., McCune, A., Clouse, D. E., McCoy, D., Karla, H. D., & Hawkins, R. O. (2017). Using video modeling and mobile technology to teach social skills. *Intervention in School and Clinic*, 52(3), 154–162. doi: 10.1177/053451216644828

Hazelden Betty Ford Foundation. (2019). *Preventing teen suicide.* Retrieved from https://www.hazelden.org/web/public/prevent_teen_suicide.page

Hedegaard, H., Curtin, S. C., & Warner, M. (2018). *Suicide rates in the United States continue to increase* (Issue Brief No. 309). Hyattsville, MD: National Center for Health Statistics. Retrieved from https://www.cdc.gov/nchs/products/databriefs/db309.htm

Heiser, P., Garruto, J., & Faustino, P. (2018). *Of sound mind: Do schools have enough mental health support staff to meet student need?* Retrieved from New York School Boards Association website: https://www.nyssba.org/clientuploads/nyssba_pdf/report-of-sound-mind-120318.pdf

Herrenkohl, T. L., Hong, S., & Verbrugge, B. (2019). Trauma-informed programs based in schools: Linking concepts to practices and assessing the evidence. *American Journal of Community Psychology*, 64(3–4), 373–388. doi: 10.1002/ajcp.12362

Heward, W. L., Alber-Morgan, S. R., & Konrad, M. (2017). *Exceptional children: An introduction to special education* (11th ed.). Upper Saddle River, NJ: Pearson.

Hicks, T. B., Shahidullah, J. D., Carlson, J. S., & Palejwala, M. H. (2014). Nationally certified school psychologists' use and reported barriers to using evidence-based interventions in schools: The influence of graduate program training and education. *School Psychology Quarterly*, 29(4), 1–19. doi: 10.1037/spq0000059

Hieneman, M. (2015). Positive behavior support for individuals with behavior challenges. *Behavior Analysis in Practice*, 8(1), 101–108. doi: 10.1007/s40617-015-0051-6

Higgins, M. C., Weiner, J., & Young, L. (2012). Implementation teams: A new lever for organization change. *Journal of Organizational Behavior*, 33(3), 366–388. doi: 10.1002/job.1773

Hoover, J. J., & Patton, J. R. (2008). The role of special educators in a multitiered instructional system. *Intervention in School and Clinic*, 43(4), 195–202. doi: 10.1177/1053451207310345

Horner, R. H., & Sugai, G. (2015). School-wide PBIS: An example of applied behavior analysis implemented at a scale of importance. *Behavior Analysis in Practice*, 8(1), 80–85. doi: 10.1007/s40617-015-0045-4

Horowitz, L. M., Bridge, J. A., Pao, M., Bourdreaux, E. D. (2014). Screening youth for suicide risk in medical settings: Time to ask questions. *American Journal of Preventive Medicine*, 47(3S2), S170–S175. doi: 10.1016/j.amepre.2014.06.002

Hosp, J. L., & Reschly, D. J. (2002). Regional differences in school psychology practice. *School Psychology Review*, 31(1), 11–29. doi: 10.1080/02796015.2002.12086139

Huebner, S. E. (1993). Burnout among school psychologists in the USA: Further data related to its prevalence and correlates. *School Psychology International*, 14(2), 99–109. doi: 10:1177/0143034393142001

Huebner, S. E., & Mills, L. B. (1994). Burnout in school psychology: The contribution of personality characteristics and role expectations. *Special Services in the Schools*, 8(2), 53–67. doi: 10.1300/J008v08n02_04

Hughes, C. A., Morris, J. R., Therrien, W. J., & Benson, S. K. (2017). Explicit instruction: Historical and contemporary contexts. *Learning Disabilities Research & Practice*, 32(3), 140–148. doi: 10.1111/ldrp.12142

Huguet, A., Marsh, J. A., & Farrell, C. (2014). Building teachers' data-use capacity: Insights from strong and developing coaches. *Education Policy Analysis Archives*, 22(52), 1–27. doi: 10.14507/epaa.v22n52.2014

Humphrey, N., Barlow, A., Wigelsworth, M., Lendrum, A., Pert, K., Joyce, C., … Turner, A. (2016). A cluster randomized controlled trial of the promoting alternative thinking strategies (PATHS) curriculum. *Journal of School Psychology*, 58, 73–89. doi: 10.1016/j.jsp.2016.07.002

Hunter, K. K., Chenier, J. S., & Gresham, F. M. (2014). Evaluation of check in/check out for students with internalizing problems. *Journal of Emotional and Behavioral Disorders*, 22(3), 135–148. doi: 10.1177/1063426613476091

Individuals With Disabilities Education Act, 20 U.S.C. § 1400. (2004).

Interian, A., Chesin, M., Kline, A., Miller, R., St. Hill, L., Latorre, M., … Stanley, B. (2017). Use of the Columbia-Suicide Severity Rating Scale (C-SSRS) to classify suicidal behaviors. *Archives of Suicide Research*, 22(2), 278–294. doi: 10.1080/13811118.2017.1334610

Jenkins, L. N., Demaray, M. K., Wren, N. S., Secord, S. M., Lyell, K. M., Magers, A. M., … Tennant, J. (2014). A critical review of five commonly used social-emotional and behavioral screeners for elementary or secondary schools. *Contemporary School Psychology*, 18(4), 241–254. doi: 10.1007/s40688-014-0026-6

Jenkins, J. R., Hudson, R. F., & Johnson, E. (2007). Screening for at-risk readers in a response to intervention framework. *School Psychology Review*, 36(4), 582–600. doi: 10.1080/02796015.2007.12087919

Johnson, L. E., Wang, E. W., He, Z., Carpenter, C., Nelson, C. M., & Scheuermann, B. K. (2013). Youth outcomes following implementation of universal SW-PBIS strategies in a Texas secure juvenile facility. *Education and Treatment of Children*, 36(3), 135–145. doi: 10.1353/etc.2013.0019

Johnston, J. M., Foxx, R., Jacobson, J. W., Green, G., & Mulick, J. A. (2006). Positive behavior support and applied behavior analysis. (2006). *The Behavior Analysist*, 29(1), 51–74. Retrieved from https://www.ncbi.nlm.nih.gov/pmc2223172/

Jolivette, K. (2016). *Multi-tiered systems of support in residential juvenile facilities* (Issue Brief). Washington, DC: The National Technical Assistance Center for the Education of Neglected or Delinquent Children and Youth (NDTAC). Retrieved from https://neglected-delinquent.ed.gov/sites/default/files/NDTAC-IssueBrief-508.pdf

Jones, J. M. (2009). Counseling with multicultural intentionality: The process of counseling and integrating client cultural variables. In J. M. Jones (Ed.), *The psychology of multiculturalism in the schools: A primer for practice, training, and research* (pp. 191–114). Bethesda, MD: National Association of School Psychologists.

Jones, J. M. (2014). Best practices in providing culturally responsive interventions. In A. Thomas & P. Harrison (Eds.), *Best practices in school psychology* (6th ed.). Bethesda, MD: National Association of School Psychologists.

Jones-Smith, E. (2019). *Culturally diverse counseling: Theory and practice*. Thousand Oaks, CA. SAGE Publications.

Joyce-Beaulieu, D., & Sulkowski, M. L. (2020) *Cognitive behavior therapy in k-12 school settings: A practitioner's workbook* (2nd ed.). New York, NY: Springer.

Juszczak, L., Melinkovich, P., & Kaplan, D. (2003). Use of health and mental health services by adolescents across multiple delivery sites. *Journal of Adolescent Health*, 32(6 Suppl.), 108–118. doi:10.1016/S1054139X(03)00073-9

Kam, C.-M., Greenberg, M. T., & Walls, C. T. (2003). Examining the role of implementation quality in school-based prevention using the PATHS curriculum. *Prevention Science*, 4(1), 55–63. Retrieved from https://link.springer.com/article/10.1023/A:1021786811186

Kamphaus, R. W. (2012). Screening for behavioral and emotional risk: Constructs and Practicalities. *School Psychology Forum*, 6(4), 88–97. Retrieved from https://www.nasponline.org/publications/periodicals/spf/volume-6/volume-6-issue-4-(winter-2012)/screening-for-behavioral-and-emotional-risk-constructs-and-practicalities

Kansas Technical Assistance Network. (2012). Kansas MTSS Project. In National Association of State Directors of Special Education Annual Conference, Sacramento, CA.

Katsiyannis, A., Yell, M. L., & Bradley, R. (2001). Reflections on the 25th anniversary of the individuals with disabilities education act. *Remedial Special Education*, 22(6), 324–334. doi: 10.1177/074193250102200602

Kearns, D. M., & Fuchs, D. (2013). Does cognitively focused instruction improve the academic performance of low-achieving students, *Exceptional Children*, 79(3), 263–290. Retrieved from https://gseuphsdlibrary.files.wordpress.com/2013/03/does-cognitively-focused-instruction-improve-the-academic-performance-of-low-achieving-students.pdf

Kendall, P. C., Crawford, E. A., Kagan, E. R., Furr, J. M., & Podell, J. L. (2018). Child-focused treatment for anxiety. In J. R. Weisz & A. E. Kazdin (Eds.), *Evidence-based psychotherapies for children and adolescents* (pp. 17–34). New York, NY. The Guilford Press.

Kerker, B. D., Zhang, J., Nadeem, E., Stein, R. E., Hurlburt, M. S., Heneghan, A., … McCue Horwitz, S. (2015). Adverse childhood experiences and mental health, chronic medical conditions, and development in young children. *Academic Pediatrics*, 15(5), 510–517. doi 10.1016/j.acap.2015.05.005

Kieran, L., & Anderson, C. (2019). Connecting universal design for learning with culturally responsive teaching. *Education and Urban Society*, 51(9), 1202–1216. doi: 10.1177/0013124518785012

Kilanowski, L. (2010). *Response to intervention: Essentials of implementation*. Unpublished manuscript. Department of School Psychology, Niagara University, Niagara University, United States of America.

Kilapatrick, D. A. (2015). *Essentials of assessing, preventing, and overcoming reading difficulties*. Hoboken, NJ: Wiley.

Kilapatrick, K. D., Maras, M. A., Brann, K. L., & Kilgus, S. P. (2018). Universal screening for social, emotional, and behavioral risk in students: DESSA-mini risk stability over time and its implications for screening. *School Psychology Review*, 47(3), 244–257. doi: 10.17105/SPR-2017-0069.V47-3

Kilgus, S. P., & Eklund, K. R. (2016). Consideration of base rates within universal screening for behavioral and emotional risk: A novel procedural framework. *School Psychology Forum*, 10(1), 120–130. Retrieved from https://www.researchgate.net/publication/299437499_Consideration_of_Base_Rates_Within_Universal_Screening_for_Behavioral_and_Emotional_Risk_A_Novel_Procedural_Framework

Kilgus, S. P., Taylor, C. N., & von der Embse, N. P. (2018). Screening for behavioral risk: Identification of high risk cut scores within the social, academic, and emotional behavior risk screener. *School Psychology Quarterly*, 33(1), 155–159. doi: 10.1037/spq0000230

King, D., & Coughlin. (2016). Looking beyond rti standard treatment approach: It's not too late to embrace the problem-solving approach. *Preventing School Failure*, 60(3), 244–251. doi: 10.1080/1045988X.2015.1110110

King-Spears, M. E., Walker, J. D., & Barry, C. (2018). Measuring teachers' intervention fidelity. *Intervention in School and Clinic*, 54(2), 89–96. doi: 10.1177/1053451218765229

Kochanek, K. D., Murphy, S. L., Xu, & Arias, E. (2019). Deaths final data for 2017. *National Vital Statistics Reports*, 68(9), 1–77. Retrieved from https://www.cdc.gov/nchs/data/nvsr/nvsr68/nvsr68_09-508.pdf

Kremer, K. P., Flower, A., Huang, J., & Vaughn. (2017). Behavior problems and children's academic achievement: A test of growth-curve models with gender and racial differences. *Children and Youth Services Review*, 67(1), 95–104. doi: 10.1016/j.childyouth.2016.06.003

Kubiszyn, T., & Borich, G. (2016). *Educational testing and measurement: Classroom application and practice* (11th ed.). Hoboken, NJ: Wiley.

Kudo, M. F., Lussier, C. M., & Swanson, H. L. (2015). Reading disabilities in children: A selective meta-analysis of the cognitive literature. *Research in Developmental Disabilities*, 40, 51–62. doi: 10.1016/j.rdd.2015.01.002

Kuypers, L. M. (2011). *The zones of regulation: A curriculum designed to foster self-regulation and emotional control*. Santa Clara, CA: Social Thinking Incorporated.

LaFromboise, T. D., & Malik, S. S. (2016). A culturally informed approach to American Indian/Alaska Native youth suicide prevention. In N. Zane, G. Bernal, & F. T. L. Leong (Eds.), *Evidence-based psychological practice with ethnic minorities: Culturally informed research and clinical strategies* (pp. 223–245). Washington, DC: American Psychological Association. doi: 10.1037/14940-011

Lai, M., & Schildkamp, K. (2013). Data-based decision making: An overview. In K. Schildkamp, M. Lai, & L. Earl (Eds.), *Data-based decision making in education: Challenges and opportunities* (17th ed., pp. 9–21). Dordrecht: Springer.

Lane, K. L., Oakes, W. P., Ennis, R. P., & Hirsch, S. E. (2014). Identifying students for secondary and tertiary prevention efforts: How do we determine which students have Tier 2 and Tier 3 needs? *Preventing School Failure: Alternative Education for Children and Youth*, 58(3), 171–182. doi: 10.1080/1045988X.2014.895573

Lane, K. L., Oakes, W., & Menzies, H. (2010). Systematic screenings to prevent the development of learning and behavior problems: Considerations for practitioners, researchers, and policy makers. *Journal of Disability Policy Studies*, 21(3), 160–172. doi: 10.1177/1044207310379123

Langer, D. A., Wood, J. J., Wood, P. A., Garland, A. F., Landsverk, J., & Hough, R. L. (2015). Mental health service use in schools and non-school-based outpatient settings: Comparing predictors of service use. *School Mental Health*, 7(3), 161–173. doi: 10.1007/s12310-015-9146-z

Lauricella, M., Valdez, J. K., Okamoto, S. K., Helm, S., & Zaremba, C. (2016). Culturally grounded prevention for minority youth populations: A systematic review of the literature. *The Journal of Primary Prevention*, 37(1), 11–32. doi: 10.1007/s10935-015-0414-3

LaVome Robinson, W., Droege, J. R., Hipwell, A. E., Stepp, S. D., & Keenan, K. (2016). Brief report: Suicidal ideation in adolescent girls: Impact of race. *Journal of Adolescence*, 53, 16–20. doi: 10.1016/j.adolescence.2016.08.013

Leavell, H., & Clark, A. (1965). *Preventive medicine for doctors in the community*. New York, NY: McGraw-Hill.

Lenz, A. S. (2015). Meta-analysis of the coping cat program for decreasing severity of anxiety symptoms among children and adolescents. *Journal of Child and Adolescent Counseling*, 1(2), 51–65. doi: 10.1080/23727810.2015.1079116

Lester, L., & Cross, D. (2015). The relationship between school climate and mental and emotional wellbeing over the transition from primary to secondary school. *Psychology of Well-Being* 5(1), 1–15. doi: 10.1186/s13612-015-0037-8

Leverson, M., Smith, K., McIntosh, K., Rose, J., & Pinkelman, S. (2019). *PBIS cultural responsiveness field guide: Resources for trainers and coaches*. OSEP Technical Assistance Center on Positive Behavioral Interventions and Supports. Retrieved from https://www.pbis.org/resource/pbis-cultural-responsiveness-field-guide-resources-for-trainers-and-coaches

Lewis, T. J., McIntosh, K., Simmonsen, B., Mitchell, B. S., & Hatton, H. L. (2017). Schoolwide systems of positive behavior support: Implications for students at risk and with emotional/behavioral disorders. *American Educational Research Association Open*, 3(2), 1–11. doi: 10.1177/2332858417711428

Little, S., Marrs, H., & Bogue, H. (2017). Elementary school psychologists and response to intervention (RTI). *Contemporary School Psychology*, 21(2), 103–114. doi: 10.1007/s40688-016-0104-z

Lo, C. B., Bridge, J. A., Shi, J., Ludwig, L., & Stanley, R. M. (2020). Children's mental health emergency department visits: 2007–2016. *Pediatrics*, 145(6), e20191536. doi: 10.1542/peds.2019-1536

Low, S., Cook, C. R., Smolkowski, K., & Buntain-Ricklefs, J. (2015). Promoting social–emotional competence: An evaluation of the elementary version of Second Step. *Journal of School Psychology*, 53(6), 463–477. doi: 10.1016/j.jsp.2015.09.002

Macklem, G. L. (2011). *Evidence-based school mental health services: Affect education, emotion regulation training, and cognitive behavior therapy*. New York, NY: Springer.

Madigan, K., Cross, R. W., Smolkowski, K., & Strycker, L. A. (2016). Association between schoolwide positive behavioural interventions and supports and academic achievement: A 9-year evaluation. *Educational Research and Evaluation*, 22(7–8), 402–421. Retrieved from https://www.tandfonline.com/doi/pdf/10.1080/13803611.2016.1256783?needAccess=true

Maki, K. E., Floyd, R. G., & Roberson, T. (2015). State learning disability eligibility criteria: A comprehensive review. *School Psychology Quarterly*, 30(4), 457–469. doi: 10.1037/sqp0000109

Maliphant, R., Frederickson, N., & Cline, T. (2013). Educational psychology practice and training: The legacy of Burt's appointment with the London county council. *Educational and Child Psychology*, 30(3). 46–59. Retrieved from https://www.ucl.ac.uk/educational-psychology/resources/EP_Practice_and_Training_-_The_Legacy_of_Burt_(2013).pdf

Maras, M. A., Thompson, A. M., Lewis, C., Thornburg, K., & Hawks, J. (2015). Developing a tiered response model for social-emotional learning through interdisciplinary collaboration. *Journal of Educational and Psychological Consultation*, 25(2–3), 198–223. doi: 10.1080/10474412.2014.929954

Mars, H., & Little, S. (2014). Perceptions of school psychologists regarding barriers to response to intervention (RTI) implementation. *Contemporary School Psychology*, 18(1), 24–34. doi: 10.1007/s40688-013-0001-7

Mazzone, A., Nocentini, A., & Menesini, E. (2018). Bullying and peer violence among children and adolescents in residential care settings: A review of the literature. *Aggression and Violent Behavior*, 38, 101–112. doi 10.1016/j.avb.2017.12.004

McCurdy, M., Skinner, C. H., & Ervin, R. A. (2017). Functional behavior assessment of nonverbal behavior. In S. Miller (Ed.), *Handbook of nonverbal assessment* (2nd ed. pp. 269–286). New York, NY. Springer International Publishing.

McDonough, E. M., Flanagan, D. P., Sy, M., & Alfonso, V. C. (2017). Specific learning disorder. In S. Goldstein & M. DeVries (Eds.), *Handbook of DSM-5 disorders in children and adolescents* (pp. 77–104). Cham: Springer.

McDougal, J. L., Bardos, A. N., & Meier, S. T. (2016). *Behavior intervention monitoring system 2* [Measurement instrument]. Retrieved from http://www.edumetrisis.com/products/282-bimas-2

McGill, R. J., Dombrowski, S. C., & Canivez, G. L. (2018). Cognitive profile analysis in school psychology: History, issues, and continued concerns. *Journal of School Psychology*, 71, 108–121. doi: 10.1016/j.jsp.2018.10.007

McGoldrick, B., & Tobey, D. (2016). *Needs assessment basics* (2nd ed.). Alexandria, VA: ATD Press.

McIntosh, K., Barnes, A., Eliason, B., & Morris, K. (2014). *Using discipline data within SWPBIS to identify and address disproportionality: A guide for school teams*. OSEP Technical Assistance Center on Positive Behavioral Interventions and Supports. Retrieved from https://www.pbis.org/resource/using-discipline-data-within-swpbis-to-identify-and-address-disproportionality-a-guide-for-school-teams

McIntosh, K., Campbell, A. L., Carter, D. R., & Zumbo, B. D. (2009). Concurrent validity of office discipline referrals and cut points used in schoolwide positive behavior support. *Behavioral Disorders*, 34(2), 100–113. Retrieved from https://www.researchgate.net/publication/41651841_Concurrent_Validity_of_Office_Discipline_Referrals_and_Cut_Points_Used_in_Schoolwide_Positive_Behavior_Support

McIntosh, K., & Goodman, S. (2016). *Integrated multi-tiered systems of support: Blending RTI and PBIS*. New York, NY. Guildford Press.

McKenna, J. & Parenti, M. (2017). Fidelity Assessment to improve teacher instruction and school decision-making. *Journal of Applied School Psychology*, 33(2), 331–346. doi: 10.1080/15377903.2017.1316334

McKevitt, B. C. (2012). School psychologists' knowledge and use of evidence-based, social-emotional learning interventions. *Contemporary School Psychology*, 16(1), 33–45. doi: 10.1007/BF03340974

Merikangas, K. R., He, J., Burstein, M., Swanson, S. A., Avenevoli, S., Cui, L., ... Swendsen, J. (2010). Lifetime prevalence of mental disorders in US adolescents: Results from the national comorbidity study-adolescent supplement (NCS-A). *Journal of American Academy of Child and Adolescent Psychiatry*, 49(10), 980–989. doi: 10.1016/j.jaac.2010.05.017

Merrill, R. M. (2017). *Introduction to epidemiology* (7th ed.). Burlington, MA: Jones & Bartlett Learning.

Meyer, M. M., & Behar-Horenstein, L. S. (2015). When leadership matters: Perceptions from a teacher team implementing response to intervention. *Education and Treatment of Children*, 38(3), 383–402. doi: 10.1353/etc.2015.0022

Miller, D. N. (2014). Levels of responsibility in school-based suicide prevention: Legal requirements, ethical duties, and best practices. *International Journal of Behavioral Consultation and Therapy*, 9(3), 15–18. doi: 10.1037/h0101635

Miller, D. N., Eckert, T. L., & Mazza, J. J. (2009). Suicide prevention programs in the schools: A review and public health perspective. *School Psychology Review*, 38(2), doi: 10.1080/02796015.2009.12087830

Mills, L. B., & Huebner, E. S. (1998). A prospective study of personality characteristics, occupational stressors, and burnout among school psychology practitioners. *Journal of School Psychology*, 36(1), 103–120. doi: 10.1016/S0022-4405(97)00053-8

Miron, O., Yu, K., & Wilf-Miron, R. (2019). Suicide rates among adolescents and young adults in the United States, 2000–2017. *Journal of the American Medical Association*, 321(23), 2362–2364. doi: 10.1001/jama.2019.5054

Mitchell, R. R., Tingstrom, D. H., Dufrene, B. A., Ford, W. B., & Sterling, H. E. (2015). The effects of the good behavior game with general-education high school students. *School Psychology Review*, 44(2), 191–207. doi: 10.17105/spr-14-0063.1

Mordock, J. B. (1988). The school psychologist working in residential and day treatment centers. *School Psychology Review*, 17(3), 421–428. Retrieved from http://www.nasponline.org/publications/periodicals/spr/volume-17/volume-17-issue-3

Morrison, J. Q., & Harms, A. L. (2018). *Advancing evidence-based practice through program evaluation: A practical guide for school-based professionals*. New York, NY: Oxford University Press.

Morsette, A., Swaney, G., Stolle, D., Schuldberg, D., van den Pol, R., & Young, M. (2009). Cognitive behavioral intervention for trauma in schools (CBITS): School-based treatment on a rural American Indian reservation. *Journal of Behavior Therapy and Experimental Psychiatry*, 40(1), 169–178. doi: 10.1016/j.jbtep.2008.07.006

Moy, G. E., & Hazen, A. (2018). A systematic review of the second step program. *Journal of School Psychology*, 71, 18–41. doi: 10.1016/j.jsp.2018.10.006

Munir, K. M. (2016). The co-occurrence of mental disorders in children and adolescents with intellectual disability/intellectual developmental disorder. *Current Opinion in Psychiatry*, 29(2), 95–102. doi: 10.1097/YCO.0000000000000236

Murray, L. K., Cohen, J. A., Ellis, B. H. & Mannarino, A. (2008). Cognitive behavioral therapy for symptoms of trauma and traumatic grief in refugee youth. *Child and Adolescent Psychiatric Clinics of North America*, 17(3), 585–604. doi: 10.1016/j.chc.2008.02.003

NASP School Safety and Crisis Response Committee. (2015). *Preventing childhood trauma: Guidelines for administrators and crisis teams*. Bethesda, MD: National Association of School Psychologists.

National Alliance on Mental Health. (2017). *Mental illness fact sheet*. Retrieved from https://1oihv73ijapnbgi4y1whci11-wpengine.netdnassl.com/wpcontent/uploads/sites/139/2016/08/NAMI-advocacy-fact-sheets-7.11.17.pdf

National Alliance on Mental Health. (2019). *Mental health facts: Children and teens*. Retrieved from https://www.nami.org/learn-more/mental-health-by-the-numbers

National Alliance on Mental Health. (2022). *Mental health by the numbers*. Retrieved from https://www.nami.org/learn-more/mental-health-by-the-numbers

National Association of School Psychologists. (2014). *Who are school psychologists?* Retrieved from https://www.nasponline.org/about-school-psychology/who-are-school-psychologists

National Association of School Psychologists. (2015). *School psychologists: Qualified health professionals providing child and adolescent mental and behavioral health services* [White paper]. Bethesda, MD: Author.

National Association of School Psychologists. (2016). *Leveraging essential school practices, ESSA, MTSS, and the NASP practice model: A crosswalk to help every school and student succeed*. Retrieved from http://www.nasponline.org/research-and-policy/current-law-and-policy-priorities/policy-priorities/the-every-student-succeeds-act/essa-crosswalk

National Association of School Psychologists. (2020). *NASP 2020 domains of practice*. Retrieved from https://www.nasponline.org/standards-and-certification/nasp-2020-professional-standards-adopted/nasp-2020-domains-of-practice

National Association of School Psychologists. (2021). *Shortages in school psychology: Challenges to meeting the growing needs of U.S. students and schools*. https://www.nasponline.org/x43315.xml

National Center for Education Statistics. (2016). *The condition of education*. Retrieved from https://nces.ed.gov/programs/coe/

National Center for Education Statistics. (2018). *International comparisons of achievement*. Retrieved from https://nces.ed.gov/fastfacts/display.asp?id=1

National Center for Education Statistics. (2019). *Fast facts*. Retrieved from https://nces.ed.gov/fastfacts/display.asp?id=372

New York State Association of School Business Officials. (2015). *The educational dollar: A look at spending and funding trends*. Retrieved from https://www.nysasbo.org/uploads/files/1442244064_Spending%202015%20(5).pdf

New York State Office of Professions (2021). *License statistics*. Albany, NY: Author. Retrieved from www.op.nysed.gov/prof/psych/psychcounts.htm

Nickerson, A. B., Breux, P., Schaffer, G. E., & Samet, M. (2021). An initial evaluation of the helping students at risk for suicide professional development workshop. *School Psychology Review*. doi: 10.1080/2372966X.2021.1919494

No Child Left Behind Act of 2001, P.L. 107-110, 20 U.S.C. § 6319 (2002).

Nolan, J. D., Jenson, W., & Houlihan, D. (2013). The good behavior game: A classroom-behavior intervention effective across cultures. *School Psychology International*, 35(2), 191–205. doi: 10.1177/0143034312471473

Noltemeyer, A., Palmer, K., James, A. G., & Wiechman, S. (2019). School-wide positive behavioral interventions and supports (SWPBIS): A synthesis of existing research. *International Journal of School & Educational Psychology*, 7(4), 253–262. doi: 10.1080/21683603.2018.1425169

Novak, M., Mihić, J., Bašić, J., & Nix, R. L. (2017). PATHS in Croatia: A school-based randomised-controlled trial of a social and emotional learning curriculum. *International Journal of Psychology*, 52(2), 87–95. doi: 10.1002/ijop.12262

Oakes, W. P., Lane, K. L., & Ennis, R. P. (2016). Systematic screening at the elementary level: Considerations for exploring and installing universal behavior screening. *Journal of Applied School Psychology*, 32(3), 214–233. doi: 10.1080/15377903.2016.1165325

Oakland, T. (2000). International school psychology. In T. Fagan & T. Wise (Eds.), *School psychology: Past, present, and future* (2nd ed.) (pp. 355–382). Washington, DC: National Association of School Psychologists.

Office for People with Developmental Disabilities. (2020). *Psychologists*. Retrieved from https://opwdd.ny.gov/

Oral, R., Ramirez, M., Coohey, C., Nakada, S., Waltz, A., Kuntz, A., … Peek-Asa, C. (2016). Adverse childhood experiences and trauma informed care: The future of health care. *Pediatric Research*, 79(1), 227–233. doi: 10.1038/pr.2015.197

Ormiston, H. E., Nygaard, M. A., & Heck, O. C. (2020). The role of school psychologists in the implementation of trauma-informed multi-tiered systems of support in schools. *Journal of Applied School Psychology*. 37(4), 319–351. doi: 10.1080/15377903.2020.1848955

Owens, J. S., Lyon, A. R., Brandt, N. E., Warner, C. M., Nadeem, E., Spiel, C., & Wagner, M. (2014). Implementation science in school mental health: Key constructs in a developing research agenda. *School Mental Health*, 6(2), 99–111. doi: 10.1007/s12310-013-9115-3

Peng, P., Wang, C., & Namkung, J. (2018). Understanding the cognition related to mathematics difficulties: A meta-analysis on the cognitive deficit profiles and the bottleneck theory. *Review of Educational Research*, 88(3), 434–476. doi: 10.3102/0034654317753350

Pennington, B., Simacek, J., McComas, J., McMaster, K., & Elmquist, M. (2019). Maintenance and generalization in functional behavior assessment/behavior intervention plan literature. *Journal of Behavioral Education*, 28(1), 27–53. doi: 10.1007/s10864-018-9299-6

Pentimonti, J. M., Walker, M. A., & Edmonds, R. Z. (2017). The selection and use of screening and progress monitoring tools in data-based decision making within an MTSS framework. *Perspectives on Language and Literacy*, 43(3), 34–40. Retrieved from www.onlinedigeditions.com/publication/?i=425075&article_id=2836414&view=articleBrowser&ver=html5#{"issue_id":425075,"view":"articleBrowser","article_id":"2836414"}

Perfect, M. M., Turley, M. R., Carlson, J. S., Yohanna, J., & Saint Gilles, M. P. (2016). School-related outcomes of traumatic event exposure and traumatic stress symptoms in students: A systematic review of research from 1990 to 2015. *School Mental Health*, 8(1), 7–43. doi: 10.1007/s12310-01609175-2

Pinkelman, S. E., McIntosh, K., Rasplica, C. K., Berg, T., & Strickland-Cohen, M. K. (2015). Perceived enablers and barriers related to sustainability of school-wide positive behavioral intervention and supports. *Behavioral Disorders*, 40(3), 171–183. Retrieved from http://files.eric.ed.gov/fulltext/ED562832.pdf

Posner, K., Brodsky, B., Yershova, K., Buchanan, J., & Mann, J. (2014). The classification of suicidal behavior. In M. K. Nock (Ed.), *Oxford library of psychology. The Oxford handbook of suicide and self-injury* (pp. 7–22). New York, NY: Oxford University Press.

Posner, K., Brown, G. K., Stanley, B., Brent, D. A., Yershova, K. V., Oquendo, M. A., … Mann, J. J. (2011). The Columbia-Suicide Severity Rating Scale: Initial validity and internal consistency findings from three multisite studies with adolescents and adults. *American Journal of Psychiatry*, 168(12), 1266–1277. doi: 10.1176/appi.ajp.2011.10111704

Posner, K., Oquendo, M. A., Gould, M., Stanley, B., & Davies, M. (2007). Columbia classification algorithm of suicide assessment (C-CASA): Classification of suicidal events in the FDA's pediatric suicidal risk analysis of antidepressants. *American Journal of Psychiatry*, 164(7). 1035–1043. doi: 10.1176/appi.ajp.164.7/1035

Prenger, R., & Schildkamp. (2018). Data-based decision making for teacher and student learning: A psychological perspective on the role of the teacher. *Educational Psychology*, 38(6), 734–752. doi: 10.1080/01443410.2018.1426834

Preston, A. L., Wood, C. L., & Stecker, P. M. (2016). Response to intervention: Where it came from and where it's going. *Preventing School Failure*, 60(3), 173–182. doi: 10.1080/1045988X.2015.1065399

Pullen, P. C., van Dijk, W., Gonsalves, V. E., Lane, H. B., & Ashworth, K. E. (2018). Response to intervention and multi-tiered systems of support: How do they differ and how are they the same, if at all? In P. Pullen & M. Kennedy (Eds.), *Handbook of response to intervention and multi-tiered systems of support* (pp. 5–10). New York, NY: Routledge.

Raffaele Mendez, L. M. (2016). *Cognitive behavioral therapy in schools: A tiered approach to youth mental health*. New York, NY: Routledge Publishing.

Ranjbar, N., & Erb, M. (2019). Adverse childhood experiences and trauma-informed care in rehabilitation clinical practice. *Archives of Rehabilitation Research and Clinical Translation*, 1(1–2), 1–8. doi: 10.1016/j.arrct.2019.100003

Ratts, M. J., Singh, A. A., Nassar-McMillan, S., Butler, S. K., & McCullough, J. R. (2016). Multicultural and social justice counseling competencies: Guidelines for the counseling profession. *Journal of Multicultural Counseling and Development*, 44(1), 28–48. doi: 10.1002/jmcd.12035

Reinke, W. M., Stormount, K. C., Herman, R. P., & Goel, N. (2011). Supporting children's mental health in schools: Teacher perceptions of needs, roles, and barriers. *School Psychology Quarterly*, 26(1), 1–13. doi: 10.1037/a0022714

Reiser, D., Cowan, K., Skalski, S., & Klotz, M. (2010). A more valuable resource. *Principle Leadership*, 12–16. Retrieved from https://www.nasponline.org/Documents/Resources%20and%20Publications/Handouts/Families%20and%20Educators/School_Psychologists_Nov10_NASSP.PDF

Remley, T. P., Jr & Herlihy, B. (2016). *Ethical, legal, and professional issues in counseling* (5th ed.). Boston, MA: Pearson

Reschly, D. J. (2000). The present and future status of school psychology in the United States. *School Psychology Review*, 29(4), 507–522. Retrieved from https://www.homeworkforyou.com/static/uploadedfiles/User_783810112015ContentServer.pdf

Reschly, D. J. (2008). School psychology paradigm shift and beyond. In A. Thomas & J. Grimes (Eds.), *Best practices in school psychology V* (pp. 3–15). Bethesda, MD: National Association of School Psychologists.

Restori, A. F., Katz, G. S., & Lee, H. B. (2009). A critique of the IQ/achievement discrepancy model for identifying specific learning disabilities. *Europe's Journal of Psychology*, 4(5), 128–145. doi: 10.5964/ejop.v5i4.244

Rohrbach, L. A., Graham, J. W., & Hansen, W. B. (1993). Diffusion of a school-based substance abuse prevention program: Predictors of program implementation. *Preventive Medicine*, 22(2), 237–260. doi: 10.1006/pmed.1993.1020

Routh, D. K. (2019). A history of clinical child and adolescent psychology. In T. Ollendick, S. White, & B. White (Eds.), *The Oxford handbook of clinical child and adolescent psychology* (pp. 3–16). New York, NY: Oxford University Press.

Rutter, M., & Yule, W. (1975). The concept of specific reading retardation. *Journal of Clinical Psychology*, 16, 181–196. doi: 10.1111/j.1469-7610.1975.tb01269.x

Sanetti, L. M. H., Kratochwill, T. R., & Long, A. C. J. (2013). Applying adult behavior change theory to support mediator-based intervention implementation. *School Psychology Quarterly*, 28(1), 47–62. doi: 10.1037/spq0000007

Sanford, A. K., Pinkney, C. J., Brown, J. E., Elliott, C. G., Rotert, E. N., & Sennott, S. C. (2020). Culturally and linguistically responsive mathematics instruction for English learners in multitiered support systems: PLUSS enhancements. *Learning Disability Quarterly*, 43(2), 101–114. doi: 10.1177/0731948719836173

Sapthiang, S., Van Gordon, W., & Shonin, E. (2019). Mindfulness in schools: A health promotion approach to improving adolescent mental health. *International Journal of Mental Health*, 17(1), 112–119. doi: 10.1007/s11469-018-0001-y

Savage, J. (1993, July 22). *Interview for The Observer with Kurt Cobain* [Tape recording]. New York, NY: Live Nirvana Interview Archives.

Schaffer, G. E. (2017). *Nuts & bolts: Multi-tiered systems of support: A basic guide to implementing preventative practice in our schools and community*. Pennsauken, NJ: Bookbaby.

Scheuermann, B., Nelson, C. M., Wang, E. W., & Bruntmyer, T. (2015). Monitoring process and outcomes for positive behavior interventions and supports in residential settings: Better uses of data. *Residential Treatment for Children and Youth*, 32(4), 266–279. doi: 10.1080/0886571X.2015.1113455

Schildkamp, K., Poortman, C., Luyten, H., & Ebbeler, J. (2017). Factors promoting and hindering data-based decision making in schools. *School Effectiveness and School Improvement*, 28(2), 242–258. doi: 10.1080/09243453.2016.1256901

Schoon, P. M., Porta, C. M., & Schaffer, M. A. (2019). *Population-based public health clinical manual: The henry street model for nurses* (3rd ed.). Indianapolis, IN: Sigma.

Schultz, D., Barnes-Proby, D., Chandra, A., Jaycox, L. H., Maher, E., & Pecora, P. (2012). Toolkit for adapting cognitive behavioral intervention for trauma in schools (CBITS) or supporting students exposed to trauma (SSET) for implementation with youth in foster care. *Rand Health Quarterly*, 2(1), doi: 10.7249/TR772

Scott, T. M., & Cooper, J. (2013). Tertiary-tier PBIS in alternative, residential, and correctional school settings: Considering intensity in the delivery of evidence-based practice. *Education and Treatment of Children*, 36(3), 101 - 119. doi: 10.1353/etc.2013.0029

Seligman, L., & Reichenberg, L. W. (2014). *Theories of counseling and psychotherapy: Systems, strategies, and skills* (4th ed.). Boston, MA: Pearson.

Seroczynski, A. D., & Jobst, A. D. (2016). Latino youth and the school-to-prison pipeline: Addressing issues and achieving solutions. *Hispanic Journal of Behavioral Science*, 38(4), 423–445. doi: 10.1177/0739986316663926

Shanklin, N. (2008). At the crossroads: A classroom teacher's key role in RTI. *Voices from the Middle*, 16(2), 62–63.

Shapiro, E. S. (2008). Best practices in setting progress-monitoring monitoring goals for academic skill improvement. In A. Thomas & J. Grimes (Eds.), *Best practices in school psychology V* (pp. 141–157). Bethesda, MD: National Association of School Psychologists.

Shapiro, E. S. (2013). Commentary on progress monitoring with CBM-R and decision making: Problems found and looking for solutions. *Journal of School Psychology* 51(1), 59–66. doi: 10.1016/j.jsp.2012.11.003

Sharma, S. A., & Christ, T. (2017). Five steps toward successful culturally relevant text selection and integration. *The Reading Teacher*, 71(3), 295–307. doi: 10.1002/trtr.1623

Sheridan, D. C., Spiro, D. M., Fu, R., Johnson, K. P., Sheridan, J. S., Oue, A. A., ... Hansen, M. L. (2015). Mental health utilization in a pediatric emergency department. *Pediatric Emergency Care*, 31(8), 555–559. doi: 10.1097/pec.00000 00000000343

Shernoff, E. S., Bearman, S. K., & Kratochwill, T. R. (2017). Training the next generation of school psychologists to deliver evidence-based mental health practices: Current challenges and future directions. *School Psychology Review*, 46(2), 219–232. doi: 10.17105/SPR-2015-0118.V46.2

Shinn, M. R. (2007). Identifying students at risk, monitoring performance, and determining eligibility within RTI; Research on educational need and benefit from academic intervention. *School Psychology Review*, 36(4), 601–617.

Shinn, M. R., & Walker, H. M. (2010). *Interventions for achievement and behavior problems in a three-tier model including RTI*. Bethesda, MD: National Association of School Psychologists.

Shollenberger, T. L. (2015). Racial disparities in school suspension and subsequent outcomes: Evidence from the National Longitudinal Study of Youth, In D. J. Losen (Ed.), *Closing the school discipline gap: Equitable remedies for excessive exclusion* (pp. 31–43), New York, NY: Teachers College Press

Shrestha, M., Lautenschleger, J., & Soares, N. (2020). Non-pharmacologic management of attention-deficit/hyperactivity disorder in children and adolescents: A review. *Translational Pediatrics*, 9(Suppl. 1), S114–S124. doi: 10.21037/tp.2019.10.01

Silva, C., & Van Orden, K. A. (2018). Suicide among Hispanics in the United States. *Current Opinion in Psychology*, 22, 44–49. doi: 10.1016/j.copsyc.2017.07.013

Simonsen, B., Britton, L., & Young, D. (2010). School-wide positive behavior support in an alternative school setting. *Journal of Positive Behavior Interventions*, 12(3), 180–191. doi: 10.1177/1098300708330495

Simonsen, B., Shaw, S. F., Faggella-Luby, Sugai, G., Coyne, M. D., Rhein, B., ... Alfano, M. (2010). A schoolwide model for service delivery: Redefining special educators as interventionists. *Remedial and Special Education*, 31(1), 17–23. doi: 10.1177/0741932508324396

Singer, J. B., Erbacher, T. A., & Rosen, P. (2018). School-based suicide prevention: A framework for evidence-based practice. *School Mental Health*, 11(1), 54–71. doi: 10.1007/s12310-018-9245-8

Sink, C. A. (2016). Incorporating a multi-tiered system of supports into school counselor preparation. *The Professional Counselor*, 6(3), 203–219. doi: 10.15241/cs.6.3.203

Skalski, A. K., Minke, K., Rossen, E., Cowan, K. C., Kelly, J., Armistead, R., & Smith, A. (2015). *NASP practice model implementation guide*. Bethesda, MD: National Association of School Psychologists.

Skalski, K., & Romero, M. (2011). Data-based decision making. *Principal Leadership*, 11(5), 12–16. Retrieved from http://citeseerx.ist.psu.edu/viewdoc/download?doi=10.1.1.307.3906&rep=rep1&type=pdf

Smith-Millman, M. K., & Flaspohler, P. D. (2019). School-based suicide prevention laws in action: A nationwide investigation of principals' knowledge of and adherence to state school-based suicide prevention laws. *School Mental Health*, 11(2), 321–334. doi: 10.1007/s12310-018-9287-u

Smolkowski, K., Girvan, E. J., McIntosh, K., Nese, N. T., & Horner, R. H. (2016). Vulnerable decision points for disproportionate office discipline referrals: Comparisons of discipline for African American and white elementary school students. *Behavioral Disorders*, 41(4), 178–195. doi: 10.17938/bedi-41-04-178-195.1

Spaulding, L. S., & Pratt, S. M. (2015). A review and analysis of the history of special education and disability advocacy in the United States. *American History Journal*, 42(1), 91–109.

Splett, J. W., Fowler, J., Weist, M. D., McDaniel, H., & Dvorsky, M. (2013). The critical role of school psychology in the school mental health movement. *Psychology in the Schools*, 50(3), 245–258. doi: 10.1002/pits.21677

Sprick, R., & Borgmeier, C. (2010). Behavior prevention and management in three tiers in secondary schools. In H. Walker & M. Shinn (Eds.), *Interventions for achievement and behavior problems in a three-tier model including RTI* (pp. 435–468). Bethesda, MD: National Association of School Psychologists.

Stanley, B., & Brown, G. K. (2012). Safety planning intervention: A brief intervention to mitigate suicide risk. *Cognitive and Behavioral Practice*, 19(2), 256–264. doi: 10.1016/j.cbpra.2011.01.001

Starecheski, L. (2015). *Take the ACE quiz–and learn what it does and doesn't mean.* Retrieved from https://www.npr.org/sections/health-shots/2015/03/02/387007941/take-the-ace-quiz-and-learn-what-it-does-and-doesnt-mean

Stewart, R. M., Benner, G. J., Martella, R. C., & Marchand-Martella, N. E. (2007). Three-tier models of reading and behavior: A research review. *Journal of Positive Behavior Interventions*, 9(4), 239–252. doi: 10.1177/10983007070090040601

Stoiber, K. C., & Vanderwood, M. L. (2008). Traditional assessment, consultation, and intervention practices: Urban school psychologists' use, importance, and competence ratings. *Journal of Educational and Psychological Consultation*, 18(3), 264–292. doi: 10.1080/10474410802269164

Stone, D. M., Holland, K. M., Bartholow, B., Crosby, A. E., Davis, S., & Wilkins, N. (2017). *Preventing suicide: A technical package of policies, programs, and practices.* Atlanta, GA: National Center for Injury Prevention and Control, Centers for Disease Control and Prevention.

Stout, E., Hindman, J., & Heinan, M. (2016, June). Applying the public health approach to suicide prevention: Presented by ASTHO and the CDC, Washington, DC.

Stuebing, K. K., Fletcher, J. M., LeDoux, J. M., Lyon, G. R., Shaywitz, S. E., & Shaywitz, B. A. (2002). Validity of IQ-discrepancy classification of reading disabilities: A meta-analysis. *American Educational Research Journal*, 39(2), 469–518. doi: 10.3102/00028312039002469

Styelinger, M. E., Gavigan, K., & Albright, K. (2017). *Literacy behind bars: Successful reading and writing strategies for use with incarcerated youth and adults.* Lanham, MD: Rowman and Littlefield.

Sugai, G., & Horner, R. H. (2008). What we know and need to know about preventing problem behavior in schools. *Exceptionality*, 16(2), 67–77. doi: 10.1080/09362830801981138

Sugai, G., & Horner R. H. (2009). Response-to-intervention and school-wide positive behavior supports: Integration of multi-tiered system approaches. *Exceptionality*, 17(4), 223–237. doi: 10.1080/09362830903235375

Sullivan, A. L., & Long, L. (2010). Examining the changing landscape of school psychology practice: A survey of school-based practitioners regarding response to intervention. *Psychology in the Schools*, 47(10), 1059–1070. doi: 10.1002/pits.20524

Support for Students Exposed to Trauma [SSET]. (n.d.). Retrieved from https://ssetprogram.org/

Swick, D., & Powers, J. D. (2018). Increasing access to care by delivering mental health services in schools: The school-based support program. *School Community Journal*, 28(1), 129–144. Retrieved from http://www.schoolcommunitynetwork.org/SCJ.aspx

Swoszowski, N. C., McDaniel, S. C., Jolivette, K., & Melius, P. (2013). The effects of tier II check-in/check-out including adaptation for non-responders on the off-task behavior of elementary students in a residential setting. *Education and Treatment of Children*, 36(3), 63–79. doi: 10.1353/etc.2013.0024

Taylor, C. N., Kilgus, S. P., & Huang, F. (2018). Treatment utility of universal screening for behavioral risk: A manipulated assessment study. *Journal of Applied School Psychology*, 34(3), 242–258. doi: 10.1080/15377903.2017.1394949

TEAMS/POD Intervention Team. (2003). *The adolescent coping with stress course leader manual: An eight-session curriculum developed for the prevention of unipolar depression in adolescents with an increased future risk.* Portland, OR: Kaiser Permanente Center for Health Research. Retrieved from https://research.kpchr.org/Research/Research-Areas/Mental-Health/Youth-Depression-Programs

The Trevor Project. (2019). *Program and services.* Retrieved from https://www.thetrevorproject.org/about/programs-services/

Thomas, H. (2009). Discovering Lightner Witmer: A forgotten hero of psychology. *Journal of Scientific Psychology*, 3–13. Retrieved from http://www.psyencelab.com/uploads/5/4/6/5/54658091/discovering_lightner_witmer.pdf

Tibbets, T. J. (2013). *Identifying and assessing students with emotional disturbance.* Baltimore, MD: Brookes Publishing.

Toms, O. M., Campbell-Whatley, G., Stuart, S., & Schultz, T. (2018). The effects of check-in check-out on the academic planning and behavior of African American males. *Journal for Multicultural Education*, 12(3), 278–293. doi: 10.1108/JME-03-2017-0016

United States Department of Education. (2016). *The state of racial diversity in the educator workforce.* Retrieved from https://

www2.ed.gov/rschstat/eval/highered/racial-diversity/state-racial-diversity-workforce.pdf

United States Department of Education Office of Civil Rights. (2014). *Civil rights data collection data snapshot: School Discipline*. Retrieved from https://ocrdata.ed.gov/assets/downloads/CRDC-School-Discipline-Snapshot.pdf

United States Government Accountability Office. (2018). *K-12 Education: Discipline disparities for black students, boys, and students with disabilities*. Retrieved from https://www.gao.gov/assets/gao-18-258.pdf

U. S. Office of Education. (1977). Assistance to states for education for handicapped children: Procedures for evaluating specific learning disabilities. *Federal Register*, 42, G1082–G1085.

Vanderheyden, A. M. (2018). Why do school psychologists cling to ineffective practices? Let's do what works. *School Psychology Forum*, 12(1), 1–9. Retrieved from https://www.researchgate.net/profile/Amanda_Vanderheyden/publication/324065605_Why_Do_School_Psychologists_Cling_to_Ineffective_Practices_Let's_Do_What_Works/links/5abbb91c0f7e9bfc04558d01/Why-Do-School-Psychologists-Cling-to-Ineffective-Practices-Lets-Do-What-Works.pdf

van Geel, M., Keuning, T., Visscher, A. J., & Fox, J. (2016). Assessing the effects of a school-wide data-based decision-making intervention on student achievement growth in primary schools. *American Educational Research Journal*, 53(2), 360–394. doi: 10.3102/0002831216637346

Van Norman, E. R., & Christ, T. J. (2016). Curriculum-based measurement of reading: Accuracy of recommendations from three-point decision rules. *School Psychology Review*, 45(3), 296–309. Retrieved from https://www.researchgate.net/publication/311640043_Curriculum-based_measurement_of_reading_Accuracy_of_recommendations_from_three-point_decision_rules

Vaughn, S., & Fuchs, L. S. (2003). Redefining learning-disabilities and inadequate response to instruction: The promise and potential problems. *Learning Disabilities Research and Practice*, 18(3), 137–146. doi: 10.1111/1540-5826.00070

von der Embse, N., Rutherford, L., Mankin, A., & Jenkins, A. (2019). Demonstration of a trauma-informed assessment to intervention model in a large urban school district. *School Mental Health: A Multidisciplinary Research and Practice Journal*, 11(2), 276–289. doi: 10.1007/10.1007/s12310-018-9294-z

Vekaria, H. (2017). Ask the administrators: Interviews provide guidance for MTSS implementation. *Perspectives on Language and Literacy*, 43(4), 37–39. Retrieved from https://mydigitalpublication.com/publication/?i=445106&article_id=2908449&view=articleBrowser&ver=html5#{%22issue_id%22:445106,%22view%22:%22articleBrowser%22,%22article_id%22:%222908449%22}

Vellutino, F. R., Scanlon, D. M., & Lyon, G. R. (2000). Differentiating between difficult-to-remediate and readily remediated poor readers: More evidence against the IQ-achievement discrepancy definition for reading disability. *Journal of Learning Disabilities*, 33(3), 223–238. doi: 10.1177/002221940003300302

Viner, R. M., Russell, S. J., Croker, H., Packer, J., Ward, J., Stansfield, C., ... Booy, R. (2020). School closure and management practices during coronavirus outbreaks including COVID-19: A rapid systematic review. *Lancet Child Adolescent Health*, 4(5), 397–403. doi: 10.1016/S2352-4642(20)30095-X

Walcott, C. M., & Hyson, D. (2018). *Results from the NASP 2015 membership survey, part one: Demographics and employment conditions* [Research report]. Bethesda, MD: National Association of School Psychologists.

Walker, H. M., Seeley, J. R., Small, J., Severson, H. H., Graham, B. A., Feil, E. G., ... Forness, S. R. (2009). A randomized controlled trial of the First Step to Success early intervention: Demonstration of program efficacy outcomes in a diverse, urban school district. *Journal of Emotional and Behavioral Disorders*, 17(4), 197–212. doi:10.1177/1063426609341645

Weersing, R. V., Jeffreys, M., Do, M. T., Swartz, K. T. G., & Bolano, C. (2017). Evidence-based update of psychological treatments for children and adolescent depression. *Journal of Clinical Child & Adolescent Psychology*, 46(1), 11–43. doi: 10.1080/15374416.2

Wenzel, A. (2018). Cognitive reappraisal. In S. Hayes & S. Hofmann (Eds.), *Process-based CBT: Science and core clinical competencies of cognitive behavioral therapy* (325–338). Oakland, CA: Context Press.

Werts, M. G., & Carpenter, E. S. (2013). Implementation of tasks in RTI: Perceptions of special education teachers. *Teacher Education and Special Education*, 36(3), 247–257. doi: 10.1177/08884064413495420

Wexler, D. (2017). School-based multi-tiered systems of support (MTSS): An introduction to MTSS for neuropsychologists. *Applied Neuropsychology: Child*, 7(4), 306–316. doi: 10.1080/21622965.2017.1331848

Wexler, L. M., & Gone, J. P. (2012). Culturally responsive suicide prevention in indigenous communities: Unexamined assumptions and new possibilities. *American Journal of Public Health*, 102(5), 800–806. doi: 10.2105/AJPH.2011.300432

Whalen, D. J., Dixon-Gordon, K., Belden, A. C., Barch, D., & Luby, J. L. (2015). Correlates and consequences of suicidal cognitions and behaviors in children ages 3 to 7 years. *Journal of the American Academy of Child and Adolescent Psychiatry*, 54(11), 926–937. doi: 10.1016/j.jaac.2015.08.009

What Works Clearinghouse. (2010). *Read well* [pdf.]. Retrieved from https://ies.ed.gov/ncee/wwc/Docs/InterventionReports/wwc_readwell_060810.pdf

What Works Clearinghouse. (2012). *First step to success* [pdf.]. Retrieved from https://files.eric.ed.gov/fulltext/ED530141.pdf

What Works Clearinghouse. (2014). *Open court reading* [pdf]. Retrieved from https://ies.ed.gov/ncee/wwc/Docs/InterventionReports/wwc_opencourt_102114.pdf

White, H., LaFleur, J., Houle, K., Hyry-Dermith, P., & Blake, S. M. (2017). Evaluation of a school-based transition program designed to facilitate school reentry following a mental health crisis or psychiatric hospitalization. *Psychology in the Schools*, 54(8), 868–882. doi: 10.1002/pits.22036

Wienen, A. W., Reijnders, I., van Aggelen, M. H., Bos, E. H., Batstra, L., & de Jonge, P. (2018). The relative impact of school-wide positive behavior support on teachers' perceptions of student behavior across schools, teachers, and students. *Psychology in the Schools*, 56(2), 232–241. doi: 10.1002/pits.22209

Witek, J. (2014). *In my heart: A book of feelings*. New York, NY: Abrams Appleseed.

Witmer, L. (1922, June 4). Mental tests, The New York Times, p. 97.

Witmer, L. (1996). Clinical psychology: Reprint of Witmer's 1907 article. *American Psychologist*, 51(3), 248–251. (Reprinted from The Psychological Clinic, 1, 1–9, (1907).

Wixson, K. K., & Valencia, S. W. (2011). Assessment in RTI: What teachers and specialists need to know. *The Reading Teacher*, 64(4), 466–469. doi: 10.2307/41203435

World Health Organization. (2012). *Public health action for the prevention of suicide*. Retrieved from https://apps.who.int/iris/bitstream/handle/10665/75166/9789241503570_eng.pdf;jsessionid=ECD6523D4483F9526FBB7EF578EC78BF?sequence=1

Xie, J., Tong, Z., Guan, X., Du, B., Qiu, H., & Slutsky, A. S. (2020). Critical care crisis and some recommendations during the COVID-19 epidemic in China. *Intensive Care Medicine*, 1–4. doi: 10.1007/s00134-020-05979-7

Yu, D. L., & Seligman, M. E. P. (2002). Preventing depressive symptoms in Chinese children. *Prevention & Treatment*, 5(1), Article 9. doi: 10.1037/1522-3736.5.1.59a

Zakszeski, B. N., Ventresco, N. E., & Jaffe, A. R. (2017). Promoting resilience through trauma-focused practices: A critical review of school-based implementation. *School Mental Health*, 9(4), 310–321. doi: 10.1007/s12310-017-9228-1

Zigarelli, J. C., Jones, J. M., Palomino, C. I., & Kawamura, R. (2016). Culturally responsive cognitive behavioral therapy: Making the case for integrating cultural factors in evidence-based treatment. *Clinical Case Studies*, 15(6), 427–442. doi: 10.1177/1534650116664984

Ziomek-Daigle, J., & Bernadette, H. D. (2019). Integrating behavioral and social/emotional supports within the response to intervention (RtI) model. *Journal of Professional Counseling: Practice, Theory & Research*, 46(1–2), 27–38. doi: 10.1080/15566832.2019.1671741

Zones of Regulation. (2019). *The zones of regulation: A framework to foster self-regulation and emotional control*. Retrieved from http://www.zonesofregulation.com/index.html

Zubritsky, C., Wald, H., Jaquette, N., & Balestra, A. (2018). Breaking the cycle of recidivism: From in-jail behavioral health services to community support. *Journal of Criminology and Forensic Studies*, 1(2), 1–6. Retrieved from http://www.bc-systemofcare.org/test/wordpress/wp-content/uploads/2019/03/ChancesR-JOCFS180010.pdf

Index

T

U